PAKISTAN
The Ground Zero of Terrorism

UNCORRECTED PAGE PROOFS

PAKISTAN

The Ground Zero of Terrorism

Rohan Gunaratna and Khuram Iqbal

REAKTION BOOKS

Published by
Reaktion Books Ltd
33 Great Sutton Street
London EC1V 0DX

www.reaktionbooks.co.uk

First published 2011

Printed and bound in/by

British Library Cataloguing in Publication Data

ISBN:

Contents

Abbreviations

AI	Ansar-ul-Islam
ANP	Awami National Party
BLA	Baloch Liberation Army
BRA	Baloch Republican Army
CID	Criminal Investigations Department
FATA	Federally Administered Tribal Areas
FC	Frontier Corps
FCR	Frontier Crimes Regulations
FR	Frontier Region
HUJI	Harkat-ul-Jihad-e-Islami
HUM	Harkat-ul-Mujahideen
ISAF	International Security Assistance Force
ISI	Inter-Services Intelligence
JEM	Jaish-e-Muhammad
JUI-F	Jamiat Ulema-i-Islam Fazl
LI	Lashkar-e-Islam
LEJ	Lashkar-e-Jhangvi
LET	Lashkar-e-Tayyeba
LEAS	Law Enforcement Agencies
MQM	Muttahida Qaumi Movement
NATO	North Atlantic Treaty Organization
NWA	North Waziristan
NWFP	North West Frontier Province
PA	Political Agent
PML-N	Pakistan Muslim League-Nawaz
PPP	Pakistan People's Party
RAW	Research and Analysis Wing
ROZS	Reconstruction Opportunity Zones
SMP	Sipah-e-Muhammad Pakistan
SSP	Sipah-e-Sahaba Pakistan
ST	Sunni Tehrik
SWA	South Waziristan
TJP	Tehrik-e-Jafria Pakistan
TNSM	Tehrik-e-Nifaz-e-Shariat-e-Muhammadi
TTP	Tehrik-e-Taliban Pakistan
TILM	Tehrik-e-Islami Lashkar-e-Muhammadi

Introduction

If Pakistan – the Taliban's closest international supporter – throws its weight behind Saudi Arabia on the bin Laden issue, the pressure on the Taliban may become unbearable. As of this time, Pakistan has not yet made its position clear.[1]

. . . while Pakistani support for the Taliban has been long-standing, the magnitude of recent support is unprecedented.[2]

Either you are with us, or you are with the terrorists.[3]

The Beginning

Since its turbulent formation in 1947, Pakistan – politically unstable, economically weak and militarily confronted – has grappled with a range of internal and external threats. None of these, however, can match the gravity of what the country now faces.

Pakistan is suffering from a grave, unprecedented crisis likely to last for years. Located at the strategic crossroads of Asia and the Middle East, Pakistan borders three great powers: Iran, China and India. Pakistan also shares a border with Afghanistan, the most pivotal state in the fight against terrorism. The complexity of the problem is compounded by geopolitical rivalry, the threats of its neighbours and decades of internal instability. The failure of the Pakistani leadership to mitigate the violence within the country is contributing to regional instability and global insecurity. Given that the country is the only nuclear power in the Muslim world, it is both a domestic and international imperative to restore stability and security in Pakistan. Without steadfast international goodwill and support, Pakistan cannot achieve this feat.

Ideological extremism, along with its vicious byproduct, terrorism, is the tier one national security threat facing most countries, including Pakistan. Both the conceptual and operational structures of terrorist and extremist groups located in Pakistan have affected similar groups within and beyond the region. There have been reports about the presence of terrorists of Chinese origin in the Federally Administered Tribal Areas (FATA), especially the Uighur militants whom the Chinese government has long considered a security threat. FATA is also base for a handful of members of the East Turkestan Islamic Movement (ETIM), an organization with members located in Afghanistan, the United Arab Emirates (UAE) and some Central Asian republics. In some circles it is believed that CIA operatives are in league with the leadership of ETIM. Similarly, Jundullah, which conducted its first suicide attack in Iran on 29 December 2008, is also operating from Pakistani soil.[4] The rising tide of militancy in tribal Pakistan and Islamism in mainland Pakistan has affected all of its neighbours: Afghanistan, India, China and Iran. It is often asserted that terrorist conspiracies targeting the USA, UK and mainland Europe typically involve a Pakistan link, but the international community tends to forget that Pakistan also suffers. This last point and the efforts of the Pakistani government in combating the problem should not be ignored whenever the Pakistan link is mentioned.

Governments advance their narrow foreign policy interests by providing covert support to groups that engage in guerilla and terrorist operation. One glaring example was the support given to the anti-Soviet international fighters, known as the Mujahideen, by the CIA, ISI and Saudi Arabia during the Soviet-Afghan War (1979–89). India has also armed, trained, financed and directed threat groups. After a while such groups develop their own momentum and it then becomes difficult for the sponsor state to control them.

The Context

Often misunderstood, Pakistan's geography and history has been featured significantly whenever the contemporary wave of violence is being discussed. The consequences of Cold War events precipitated the region's steadfast rise of politico-religious extremism and terrorism. Other cataclysmic events – the revolution in Iran and the Soviet invasion of Afghanistan – have also profoundly shaped and affected Pakistan. Located along the fault lines of the Cold War, the events of 9/11 plunged Pakistan into the frontline in the fight against terrorism. It is thus crucial that the international community works with Pakistan to win the fight against ideological extremism and operational terrorism.

The Pak-Afghan region was very volatile during the Soviet invasion of Afghanistan, and the current surge of violence in Pakistan as a direct consequence of the unintended spill-over effect from the US-led intervention in Afghanistan, which began on 7 October 2001, is no different. The insurgent and terrorist infrastructure that flourished in Afghanistan for a decade migrated across the Afghan-Pakistan border. Facing prolonged political upheaval and economic turmoil, Pakistan lacks the capital to restore peace and security. While Pakistan is often blamed for supporting militancy, the nation itself is more a victim than a villain. Most Pakistanis today feel betrayed by the US because, having assisted the West to defeat the Soviets in Afghanistan, Pakistan did not receive support to rehabilitate and reintegrate the mujahideen they had mobilized against the Soviets.

In its efforts to root out terrorism, Pakistan itself has become a victim of terrorism. Particularly after the Lal Masjid operation in Islamabad, Pakistan lost more than 1,000 troops in operations against extremists/miscreants, while thousands of civilians and personnel from law enforcement agencies were killed in suicide bombings across the country. Between 2004 and 7 February 2009, 4,712 people were killed and 6,856 injured in 5,074 incidents of terrorism in the regions of FATA and NWFP alone.[5] Contrary to common belief, Pakistan has demonstrated a determination beyond its capacity to eradicate the menace of terrorism. For the first time in the known history of FATA, armed forces made inroads in the region and challenged the militants. Furthermore, state institutions and all other mainstream political partners have come together to present an unprecedented unified stance against militancy and extremism.

In recognition of Pakistan's pivotal role in fighting Al Qaeda, the US declared Pakistan a non-NATO ally on 18 March 2004.[6] Nonetheless, the West has focused on Afghanistan and Iraq as their international priorities. While the US spends US$6 billion per month to maintain its 146,000 troops in Iraq and US$1 billion per month for 40,000 troops in Afghanistan, it provides less than US$1 billion per annum to Islamabad to maintain its 100,000 troops in tribal Pakistan.[7] The West continued to regard Afghanistan as central even after Al Qaeda retreated across the border into Pakistan in late 2001. A significant number of Al Qaeda members, especially those belonging to Saudi Arabia, Kuwait, Jordan and Egypt crossed over to Iran. Iranian security forces arrested dozens of these Arabs, handing some of them over to their respective countries through diplomatic channels, but it is suspected that the rest are still residing in Iranian territories. Al Qaeda's core leadership has been operating in tribal Pakistan, and its operational leadership in mainland Pakistan, since 2002. Cross-border attacks in Afghanistan, and many others made by Al Qaeda since then, were either inspired or directed by groups based in tribal Pakistan.

To exacerbate the situation, the 2003 Iraq invasion created a new front against insurgency and terrorism. The diversion of resources to Iraq was not only a monumental waste of treasure and blood, but also a significant distraction away from confronting the priority threat. By 1 January 2009 US expenditure in Iraq had amounted to about US$600 billion.[8] Nearly 100,000 Iraqis[9] and 4,000 US personnel had lost their lives and a further 30,000 were wounded.[10] Although the US invasion removed Saddam Hussein, America lost international goodwill and its reputation as a bastion of freedom and democracy suffered. While the US constantly portrayed the invasion of Iraq as 'liberation' from Saddam's tyrannical rule, the Iraqis and the Muslim world did not perceive it in the same light. The depth of suffering, resentment and anger experienced by the Iraqis was reflected when Muntazer al-Zaidi, a journalist for Cairo-based Al Baghdadia Television, shouted 'It is the farewell kiss, you dog' and threw his shoes at President Bush during his farewell visit to Iraq on 14 December 2008.[11] The invasion of Iraq by the Bush Administration unwittingly created the much-needed Muslim support and sympathy to revive a declining extremist threat globally.

This in no way suggests, however, that FATA should have been militarily targeted instead of Iraq. The complex problem in FATA can only be managed by the Pakistani government. An outside force without sufficient knowledge of the people, culture, militant groups and the terrain would only worsen the situation.

The Background

The contemporary wave of violence evolved over three generations. In the 1920s the Ikwanul Muslimeen (Muslim Brotherhood [MB]) produced the first generation of ideologues and activists. Originating in Egypt, the MB spread their ideology throughout the Middle East. Maulana Abu A`la Maududi, their founder, was born in India but moved to Pakistan at the time of partition in 1947. In response to the threat, Arab governments incarcerated the leaders and members of the Brotherhood, but the use of torture in prisons only produced a more violent and committed leadership. In the 1970s splinters of the brotherhood produced the second generation of ideologues, notably the Islamic Group of Egypt and the Egyptian Islamic Jihad. Members of the second generation fought against the Soviets in Afghanistan and joined different factions of jihadi groups inspired by Maududi. Deobandism, the school of thought articulated by the Madrasa Deobandi in India, spawned the third generation of recruits in Pakistan. This appeared in the 1990s and fought the Northern Alliance in Afghanistan, the Indian forces in Kashmir, and in other conflict zones where Muslims suffered. The third generation was inspired by the ideological reference provided by Al Qaeda, a product of the anti-Soviet multinational campaign. When Al Qaeda later came under threat it survived under the protection of the Pakistani groups inspired by the Madrasa Deobandi. The conflict in Afghanistan was pivotal in the formation of the third generation of militants.

Ideology alone was insufficient to produce a generation of fighters. While Afghanistan formed the central battlefield, the ideology, indoctrination and training to fight the superpowers originated in Pakistan, whose role as the frontline state in the fight against the Soviets in Afghanistan began immediately after the invasion on 27 December 1979. To fight the estimated 118,000 Soviet troops who served in Afghanistan,[12] tens of thousands of Muslim fighters travelled to Pakistan and gathered in the tribal regions before operating in Afghanistan, some even with their families. Their homes were referred to as guesthouses and camps, and their weapon dumps were located in Pakistan, along the Afghan border. Engaged on what the Muslim world described as a 'jihad' (holy war), the mujahideen (fighters of god) were armed with state-of-the-art weaponry and steadfastly supported by Pakistan, the US, UK and Saudi Arabia. The mujahideen, as even the Western governments called them, fought the Soviets for a decade. Working with the Afghan factions, the foreign fighters checkmated the Soviet military, the largest land army in the world, and helped lead to the decline of the Soviet threat in the late 1980s. The ten-year campaign drained the Soviet superpower of its resources and spirit.

A New Class of Warrior

The fight in the name of Allah, conceived by ideologues, orchestrated by politicians, financed by the Saudis and armed by the US, culminated in the collapse of the Soviet Empire. One of the unintended consequences of the Soviet collapse, however, was the emergence of a new force of zealots that would confront the post-Cold War world. Defeating the Soviet military made the zealots motivated, experienced and capable. The success gave birth to multiple terrorist and extremist groups including Al Qaeda, a small group that harnessed the eagerness and the passion of the most dedicated anti-Soviet fighters. The international community had no visionary programme to reintegrate and rehabilitate the tens of thousands of mujahideen, the six million refugees, or to rebuild the destroyed nation of Afghanistan. According to the United Nations High Commissioner for Refugees (UNHCR), Pakistan hosted the single largest refugee population in the world for more than two decades. It was estimated that by the end of 2001 there were approximately five million Afghan refugees in Pakistan.[13] The instability spread to its then protector and defender Pakistan.

After a protracted battle with Afghan, Pakistani and other foreign fighters, notably Arab, the Soviet military withdrew from Afghanistan in February 1989. The defeat and humiliation of the Soviets in Afghanistan heralded the demise of the Soviet Empire and the end of the Cold War. As some anticipated, the West abandoned Afghanistan after the withdrawal of the Soviets. In the early 1990s regional forces,,in particular Pakistan, took the lead in trying to achieve a settlement to Afghanistan's civil war. The international neglect paved the way for the grave deterioration of security in Afghanistan. Pakistan became the most important sanctuary for both local and foreign fighters. After the US abandoned Pakistan, its one-time ally Islamabad lacked the capacity to integrate even the local fighters into mainstream Pakistani society. While most of the foreign fighters returned home, a few thousand remained in tribal Pakistan, settling in Peshawar and adjacent areas, and many were said to have married local women.[14] Others went to lands of jihad from the Balkans to the Horn of Africa and to Southeast Asia. The flow of foreign fighters also fuelled the insurgency in Kashmir in 1989.[15] A few hundred fighters also relocated to Sudan with Osama bin Laden in 1991. After the Taliban came to power in 1995, Osama and his battle-hardened Arab fighters returned to Afghanistan in May 1996.

Centrality of Afghanistan and Pakistan

The fighting in Afghanistan did not stop after the Soviets withdrew. The Pakistani government was the principal force behind the Taliban Islamic movement. Its leaders and many of its members had studied in Pakistani madaris (Islamic seminaries) during the Soviet occupation of their country. Of the many groups willing to fight the Northern Alliance, Pakistan chose to back the Taliban. Contrary to public perception, this was not for ideological reasons, but to restore stability in Afghanistan. Since the threat from India to Pakistan was significant, Pakistan needed a friendly regime in Kabul to provide the much-needed strategic depth against India, so ensuring that the western flank of Pakistan was free of enemies and that the Hindu Kush mountains continued to provide depth to Pakistan's strategic objective. By supporting and building the Taliban into a credible force, Islambad believed that Pakistan would have the strategic depth it needed.

With leaders that were ruthless, arrogant and destructive, the Taliban regime was brutal. Mullah Omar, the supremo, had studied in an Islamic seminary but never completed his Islamic education. The regime brutally destroyed Afghanistan's historical and cultural heritage. The giant Buddhas in Bamiyan are just one example of the many priceless cultural and historical artefacts and monuments that were destroyed. The Taliban took Afghanistan backwards by denying education to women, banning television and restricting religious freedoms. It was proposed, for example, that Hindus and Jews should wear a colour code to distinguish them from Muslims, but this was not implemented. Thousands of Shias were tortured and massacred,[16] notably in the northern region of Mazar and among the Hazara ethnic group in Hazarajat. Once in power the Taliban became an intolerant Muslim regime.

The Pakistan government had brought the Taliban to power, but Islamabad failed to guide and control it. The true mentors of the Taliban leadership lived in madaris (Islamic seminaries) located in tribal and mainland Pakistan, and it was evident that the Taliban preferred the guidance it received from the elders in the madaris rather than from the government. The madaris continued to produce both the finance and recruits for the Taliban. After it became evident that the Taliban was hosting Al Qaeda and some two dozen terrorist groups in its backyard, it was a mistake for Pakistan to continue to support the Taliban. This policy has, in turn, damaged Pakistan gravely.

The Terrorist Disneyland

Throughout the 1990s Afghanistan developed into the most important sanctuary for training terrorists and guerrillas. Several groups fighting local campaigns in the Middle East, Asia, Africa, the Balkans and the Caucasus established a presence in Afghanistan. Muslim youth from all over the world travelled there to receive training, weapons, finance and ideology. Pakistan and Iran were the gateways to landlocked Afghanistan and most recruits entered Afghanistan through Pakistan after a period of study there, gaining their ideological indoctrination at the madaris.

Both Shiite and Sunni Muslims were among those who fought against the Soviets and the Northern Alliance. The Arab Sunni fighters were a small component of the multiple groups that fought the Soviets, but were the most active. Arabs make up about 10 per cent of the whole Muslim population, but play a very important role in determining the Islamic practices of non-Arab Muslims. The Taliban, then the ruling party of the Islamic Emirate of Afghanistan, depended on Al Qaeda for support and entrusted its closest ally with responsibility for supervising all the foreign training camps and supporting the diverse Islamic movements. These movements portrayed themselves as fighting for the faith and the faithful. They also projected themselves as the ones who delivered victory in Afghanistan. While this was far from the truth, those who trained in Afghanistan earned the epitaph 'muj' or mujahideen. Today, they are still respected for defending Islam and Muslims in Afghanistan, Chechnya, Kashmir, Xingjiang, Mindanao, Bosnia, Algeria, Eritrea and other theatres where fellow Muslims have suffered.

While the threat remained the same, the target began to shift in the early 1990s. The Islamic movements, spearheaded by an Arab vanguard, turned their sights on the US, the remaining superpower. The tip of the spear was the Islamic Army or Al Qaeda (The Base), a small group of Arabs led by Osama bin Laden. The US, an active player in the Arab world, emerged as the principal target owing to its support for many Middle Eastern regimes and for Israel. A decade after fighting the Soviets, Al Qaeda attacked US embassies in East Africa in 1998 and the USS *Cole* at Aden in 2000. After the attacks on the most iconic landmarks on the US mainland in 2001, the US received an international mandate to lead a coalition to dismantle the robust insurgent and terrorist infrastructure in Afghanistan.

The US and Saudi Arabia believed that Pakistan had leverage over the Taliban, but it did not. The Taliban had developed its own momentum and dynamic. In a meeting with the Director General of Pakistan's Inter-Services Intelligence (ISI) immediately after the 9/11 attacks, the Deputy Secretary of State Richard Armitage threatened: 'We will bomb you to the Stone Age.'[17] The US intervention unleashed a wave of terror beyond Afghanistan, affecting Pakistan most severely. It only temporarily weakened the terrorist movement and dispersed the terrorist threat globally. As the US dominated the fight, the approaches to managing the threat were lethal and kinetic. As such, the enduring ideological source of the threat was not neutralized.

The principal operational and ideological source of the threat shifted from Afghanistan to Pakistan. Together with other foreign groups with base camps in Afghanistan, Al Qaeda and the Afghan Taliban relocated and linked up with like-minded groups in tribal as well as mainland Pakistan. After uniting under the banner of Tehrik-e-Taliban Pakistan, the tribal and other groups along the Afghanistan-Pakistan border emerged as the dominant threat to the two countries. While the international community dispatched troops and allocated resources to Afghanistan, the Pakistani military, law enforcement and intelligence services remained gravely challenged. Al Qaeda, Afghan Taliban and its associated groups were poised to wage a ruthless insurgency in Afghanistan and terrorist and propaganda campaigns globally. As the Pakistani security forces came into contact with Al Qaeda, the militant groups in tribal Pakistan that were protecting Al Qaeda turned against the state of Pakistan. Furthermore, foreign fighters and Pakistani groups operating against Afghan and coalition forces started to attack the Pakistani government and Western targets inside Pakistan. Gradually the attacks in Pakistan mirrored those in Afghanistan. In 2008 the number of fatalities and casualties in Pakistan caused by suicide and non-suicide attacks exceeded the toll in Afghanistan.[18]

The Future

The twenty-first century dawned with the creation of a well-organized terrorist and extremist infrastructure in landlocked Afghanistan. Al Qaeda, Afghan Taliban and its associated groups exploited Pakistan, the gateway to Afghanistan. While many governments tried to understand the source of the terrorist threat, terrorism rapidly evolved from a nuisance to the pre-eminent threat to international security today. Those who failed to understand terorrism and dismissed its potent nature were surprised on 11 September 2001. An aircraft laden with 10,000 gallons of fuel had the lethality of a tactical nuclear weapon. If the terrorists had access to a nuclear weapon, they would have used it. With the us-led coalition intervention in Afghanistan, the CIA and ISI teamed up to hunt down the perpetrators in Pakistan. The epicentre of the conflict shifted from Afghanistan to Pakistan.

While the Al Qaeda operational leadership moved to mainland Pakistan, most notably to urban areas in Sindh and Punjab, the core leadership and membership received sanctuary and support in tribal Pakistan. The mountainous and rugged terrain separating Pakistan and Afghanistan provided many opportunities for Al Qaeda and other foreign terrorist groups to hide and subsist. Al Qaeda and the other groups started to reconstitute themselves along the tribal belt. The Pashtunwali code ensured that the tribes protected and supported these 'guests' who had come to their aid a decade before against the Soviet 'occupiers'. The tribal Pakistanis perceived the us intervention in Afghanistan as an 'occupation'. Furthermore, the tribal Pakistanis continued to perceive the foreign and Pakistani groups training in Afghanistan as 'warriors'. They do not see them as terrorists killing innocent men, women and children, but as defending Islam and Muslims, their faith and the faithful.

After abandoning Afghanistan and retreating to Pakistan, Al Qaeda had to depend on other groups. Operational and ideological contact with Al Qaeda influenced Pakistani tribal and mainland groups to different degrees, inspiring many groups to follow in their footsteps. As such, the shift to Pakistan strategically strengthened the global network of terror led by Al Qaeda. Consisting of Al Qaeda, its operationally connected associated groups and ideologically inspired cells, the movement's new headquarters is Pakistan's Federally Administered Tribal Areas (FATA). Inhabitants of the FATA had fought against the Soviet invader. When the us intervened in Afghanistan, those living in the Pashtun areas of Afghanistan and Pakistan saw no difference between the Soviet and American invasions. The West made a distinction between those who fought the Soviets and those who fought the us-led coalition forces. Many Muslims in Pakistan, however, see the fight in Afghanistan as a struggle against foreign occupation and the coalition forces are their next enemy.

Some of the mujahideen who had defeated the Soviet military, the land army of a superpower, came to be organized under Al Qaeda, which decided to take on the remaining superpower. The conflicts against the armies of the two superpowers have hardened the fighters and a sense of invincibility permeates the psyche and informs the persona of these groups. Driven by the belief that they are fighting for God, these pious and fierce men live secret lives. The ideologues of Al Qaeda, the Taliban and their associated entities convince them to seek martyrdom. In exchange for eternal life, they actively seek death on earth. Convinced of entry to paradise and an audience with God, they are determined to fight to the end. There is no room in their doctrine for negotiation or compromise but only selflessness and sacrifice for the sake of God. At the turn of the century, Pakistan has become an unwitting host to the world's most determined, experienced and deadly class of threat groups.

This book is divided into seven chapters. Chapter One explains tribal Pakistan. Chapter Two discusses the Pakistani Taliban. Chapter Three analyses terrorism in Karachi, and Four covers the mainland terrorist groups. Chapter Five discusses the threat to the region, notably to India and Iran. Chapter Six discusses the suicide threat to Pakistan, and chapter Seven shows why Pakistan is presently the ground zero of terrorism, the epicentre from where the globat threat of ideological extremism emanates.[19]

1
Tribal Pakistan: The Epicentre of Global Terrorism

Pakistani public as a whole is now more favorable toward the Taliban than it was before the attacks of September 11 and recognizes no compelling reasons to cut Pakistan's traditionally strong links with the Taliban government.[1]

Pakistan has not been responsive to [American] requests that it use its full influence on the Taliban surrender of Bin Ladin.[2]

There are terrorists holed up in those mountains who murdered 3,000 Americans. They are plotting to strike again. If we have actionable intelligence about high-value terrorist targets and President Musharraf will not act, we will.[3]

Threat Landscape

Terrorism, guerrilla warfare and insurgency have emerged as the pre-eminent national security threat to most countries in the early twenty-first century. The threat is spreading from conflict zones to neighbouring regions and countries far away. Iraq, Afghanistan and Pakistan are among the best-known case studies. The spectrum of threat groups includes both Muslim and non-Muslim groups, but Al Qaeda presents the most formidable threat.

Afghanistan, a conflict zone stemming from international neglect after the Soviet withdrawal, emerged as the epicentre of terrorism until the us-led intervention. Since then, the ground zero of international terrorism has shifted from Afghanistan to Pakistan's tribal region. Many of the major terrorist attacks attempted or conducted in the West after 9/11 have been organized or inspired by Al Qaeda's senior leadership located in this rugged and inaccessible mountainous region. Three profound developments characterize the post-9/11 global threat.

First, after the us-led intervention in Afghanistan, the ground zero of terrorism moved from Afghanistan to the FATA, which is now the single most important base of operations, a place where leaders, trainers and planners are all located.

Second, after the us invasion and occupation of Iraq, Al Qaeda relocated to FATA, thereby gaining a foothold in the Middle East and establishing a forward operational base closer to the West. From FATA, Al Qaeda could direct the battle globally, including the ongoing one in Iraq.

Third, by investing in sustained communication and propaganda from FATA, Al Qaeda co-opted several like-minded groups in Asia and the Middle East. In place of one single Al Qaeda, there are several Al-Qaedas: Tawhid Wal Jihad became Al Qaeda in Iraq, the Salafist Group for Call and Combat became Al Qaeda Organization of the Islamic Maghreb, and Al-Jemmah Al-Islamiyah's Noordin Mohammad Top Faction became Al Qaeda Organization of the Malay Archipelago.[4]

The long-term strategic significance of Al Qaeda successfully carving out a semi-safe haven in FATA is yet to be realized. In addition to the inaccessible Afghan-Pakistan border emerging as the new headquarters of the global jihad movement, Al Qaeda and its associates are seeking to change the geopolitics of the region. Together with self-radicalized, home-grown cells, they have recruited globally and struck at Al Qaeda's enemies both through its operational network and through cells it has inspired. Groups trained in FATA are mounting attacks in western China (Xinjiang), Iraq, Algeria, Somalia and other conflict zones. As the assassination attempts on leaders in both Pakistan and Afghanistan show, Al Qaeda and its associated groups aim to eliminate leaders who are hostile to the ter-rorists and extremists. The subject of Al Qaeda dominates the inter-national media, but until the London bombings in July 2005 its active presence in FATA was not a subject of intense international debate.

Tribal Pakistan

The variables that should be explored to understand this myriad of prob-lems include colonial administrative/political and judicial structures of governance, Pashtun cultural code (*Pashtunwali*), the nature of the Paki-stan-Afghan border, the socio-economic profile, the Pakistan military's approach to counter militancy and the resultant rise of militant Islam.

Background

The tribal areas of Pakistan known as Federally Administered Tribal Areas (FATA) in the constitution of Pakistan[5] comprise seven tribal agencies (Bajur, Orakzai, Mohmand, Khyber, Kurram, North Waziristan, South Waziristan) and six frontier regions: Frontier Region (FR) Peshawar, Frontier Region (FR) Kohat, Frontier Region (FR) Bannu, Frontier Region (FR) Laki Marwat, Frontier Region (FR) Dera Ismail Khan and Frontier Region (FR) Tank. The name FATA is a misnomer.[6] Islamabad has never maintained jurisdiction over more than 100m either side of the few government-built roads in the tribal areas. FATA functions as a semi-autonomous region. In theory, tribal areas come under the federal government's jurisdiction, but in practice they are autonomous.

FATA covers an area of 27,220 square kilometres and is located on the porous north-western border known as the Durand Line, 1,200km long, between Pakistan and Afghanistan. To the north is the Lower Dir district in the NWFP, and to the east are the NWFP districts of Bannu, Charsadda, Dera Ismail Khan, Karak, Kohat, Lakki Marwat, Malakand, Nowshera and Peshawar. The district of Dera Ghazi Khan in the Punjab province lies to the south-east, while the Musa Khel and Zhob districts of Baluchistan are situated to the south. Afghanistan lies to the west of FATA.[7]

The population of FATA stood at 3.2 million according to the 1998 national census (the current estimate is 3.5 million) and most belong to Pashtun tribes. The latest weaponry abounds because of the Afghan jihad and it is customary to carry arms. Basic amenities are scarce and religious conservatism holds sway. Afghan jihad, and the state's deliberate attempt

to promote pro-jihadist elements, has resulted in the local clergy's monopoly over these areas.

Historically the British colonial administrators of India used FATA as a buffer against Russian expansionism in Central Asia. The colonial government did not exercise absolute control over FATA:

> Colonial administrators oversaw but never fully controlled the region through a combination of British-appointed agents and local tribal elders. The people were free to govern internal affairs according to tribal codes, while the colonial administration held authority in what were known as 'protected' and 'administered' areas over all matters related to the security of British India.

Although various tribes cooperated with the British on and off in return for financial incentives . . ., this quid pro quo arrangement was never completely successful. Throughout the latter half of the 19th century, British troops were embroiled in repeated battles with various tribes in the area. Between 1871 and 1876, the colonial administration imposed a series of laws, the Frontier Crimes Regulations [FCR], prescribing special procedures for the tribal areas, distinct from the criminal and civil laws that were in force elsewhere in British India. These regulations, which were based on the idea of collective territorial responsibility and provided for dispute resolution to take place through a jirga (council of elders), also proved to be inadequate.[8]

After the promulgation of the FCR, FATA remained a constant source of trouble for the British government. The political autonomy to which FATA was entitled through the FCR always benefited non-state actors in one way or another. Since the British era inaccessible areas have existed where the state has had no presence, providing space for criminals and militants.[9] Tribes regulated their own affairs according to their customs and unwritten codes. They never recognized the British-drawn Durand Line, a poorly marked border separating Pakistan and Afghanistan. The people of FATA and southern Afghanistan had, over the centuries, interacted very closely during all the major events in the region. This has been greatly facilitated by the porous border. It is not surprising that smuggling, particularly in narcotics from Afghanistan, has become lucrative.

When Pakistan gained independence from British rule in 1947, the existing administration of the tribal areas was preserved. The seven agencies of FATA came under the control of the President through the governor of NWFP. There was relative peace in the tribal region after the creation of Pakistan, with no major unrest or armed movement. When the Soviets invaded Afghanistan, however, the Afghan Jihad radically changed the social fabric of Pakistani society. The tribal belt of Pakistan became radicalized. Due to its geographic proximity to Afghanistan, FATA was affected the most. The tradition of carrying weapons that is part of tribal culture made possible the systematic militarization of FATA, which was used as the launching pad for the holy warriors coming from all over the world to fight against the 'godless' Soviets. The Central Intelligence Agency (CIA), through the Inter-Services Intelligence Agency (ISI), funnelled in huge sums of money to help create madrasas to train a generation in warfare and militancy.[10] The Jihadi forces, supported by Pakistan, the US, Saudi Arabia and other major western countries, emerged victorious and the

Soviet forces were driven out of Afghanistan in 1989. After the Soviet with-drawal, however, Pakistan was abandoned to face the consequences of an unfinished war. According to some estimates, more than 70,000 warriors from Pakistan and other Arab countries were recruited and trained for Afghan Jihad. For Pakistan, with its limited resources and capabilities, it was an impossible task to rehabilitate thousands of battle-hardened fighters and bring them back into the mainstream. A dominant majority of Afghan-trained fighters turned their guns against Pakistan and few opted to move to the conflict zones of Kashmir, Chechnya, Arakan (Myanmar), Mindanao (Philippines), southern Thailand, Eritrea and Palestine.

Political Economy of FATA

FATA is Pakistan's most impoverished and economically backward area. In the name of preserving traditional tribal culture and the independence of Pashtun tribes, these areas have been deliberately kept backwards over the years. Since independence, because no major development has taken place, we have seen political alienation, economic deprivation and deep-seated resentment against the centre. The political administration in FATA is the main vehicle for economic development and planning. As a result of state manipulation, developmental funds are neither invested in infrastructural development, nor do they reach the masses; instead they reach only the local elite, the state's hand-picked functionaries.[11] This manipulative and selective patronage of the local elite by the state authorities has resulted in a resource gap between those who have access to the administration and those who do not. The political agent's economic tools and instruments of economic control include the allocation of permits for exports and im-ports in each agency.[12]

The colonial era legacy of using this region as a buffer has resulted in the chronic apathy of the central government and kept the region grossly underdeveloped. The socio-economic and demographic indica-tors are abysmally poor. By raising the bogus threat of Pashtun separatism, the central government has denied the people in the tribal areas their eco-nomic and political rights. The lack of a participatory system of gover-nance at the grassroots, the bias in favour of a traditional feudal economic system, and a social hierarchy that creates conditions favourable for the perpetuation of a cycle of underdevelopment have promoted the growth of militancy and religious conservatism.[13]

FATA's per capita income is half that of Pakistan's national average (US$500). More than 60 per cent of the population lives below the poverty

line and per capita development expenditure is one-third of the national
average. Only 2.7 per cent of the population in the Tribal Areas lives in its
towns, and the ratio of roads per square kilometre in FATA (0.017 per cent)
compares to 0.26 per cent nationally. Overall literacy rate is 17.24 per cent,
compared to 56 per cent nationally. While the male literacy rate is 29.5 per
cent, female literacy is 3 per cent (32.6 per cent nationally). There are very
few schools for females, and many have been closed, bombed or burned
down because powerful religious leaders discourage female education. For
the 3.1 million residents of FATA, there are only 41 hospitals, the per doctor
rate is 1:1,762 as compared to 1:1,359 nationally,[14] and the population per
bed in health institutions is 1:2,179, as against a national figure of 1:1,341.
According to a World Health Organization report of 2001, nearly 75 per
cent of the population has no access to clean drinking water. While problems of infant mortality are severe, the population growth rate is 3.9 per
cent, compared to a nationally cited figure of 1.9 per cent.

Natural resources, including minerals and coal, are underexploited.
Most of the locals depend upon subsistence agriculture since there is little industrial development and very few jobs. Employment opportunities
for the tribal people are very few and far between: there are 80,000 males
in the 18 to 25 age bracket seeking employment.[15] The local economy is
chiefly pastoral, but only a few fertile valleys are used for agriculture. Land
use data from 2003–4 shows that only 7 per cent of FATA's total land area
is cultivated, with more than 82 per cent of the land not available for cul-
tivation.[16] The available farmland supports an average of 18 persons per
cultivated hectare and more than 40 persons per irrigated hectare. Some
44 per cent of farmland is under irrigation, with the remaining cultivated
area relying entirely on rainfall. Most households are engaged in primary-
level activities such as subsistence agriculture, livestock rearing or small-
scale businesses conducted locally. Unfortunately the economy of FATA is
largely based on a flourishing trade in arms and drugs. Poor law enforcement across FATA's borders with Afghanistan encourages the lucrative
smuggling of luxury consumer goods.

Governance System of FATA

Although FATA is part of Pakistan, it functions as a semi-autonomous
region. During the days of British India, FATA and Afghanistan acted as a
buffer zone between British India and the Russian empire, and operated
on its own terms. The traditional pattern of governance continued even
after FATA came under Pakistan in 1947. This form of governance is
embedded in the Political Agent (PA) and the Frontier Crimes Regulations

(FCR) system. FATA's governance is a legacy of the colonial era and has contributed to the current situation, which has turned FATA into a hub for global terrorist activities. Its lack of democratic accountability and the failure to observe basic human rights has generated resentment and grievances against the state.[17]

Political-Administrative Set-up

Under article 247(2) of the constitution, the NWFP governor exercises executive authority in FATA as the president's representative (the president is authorized with powers to make policies regarding peace and good governance).[18] The federal government directly administers FATA and a political agent appointed by the governor administers each agency of FATA. The political agent is also the judicial officer against whose decision there is no right of appeal.[19] Although FATA has had elected representatives in the National Assembly (NA) since 1996, national legislation does not apply to FATA. Pakistan's political parties are legally barred from contesting seats in the tribal areas (elections in FATA are not party-based).

Backed by *khasadars*[20] and levies, political agents exercise a mix of executive, judicial and revenue powers, and have responsibility for maintaining law and order and suppressing crimes in the tribal areas. The government relies on the services of paid intermediaries called *maliks*[21] and holders of the *lungi*[22] system to administer FATA. Political agents can also arbitrarily cancel or suspend the status of *malik* and *lungi* if they think the individuals are not serving the interest of the state. *Maliks* receive financial privileges from the administration in return for cooperation with the government.

A political agent is the supreme authority in tribal areas as he enjoys absolute power. He is the administrator, legislator, judge, revenue collector and economic planner. Such unchecked power has generated unbridled corruption, massive mismanagement of development funds and manipulation of this highly flawed system, which has reinforced underdevelopment, suppression, alienation and grievances against the federal government. For many decades the political agents and *maliks* have misappropriated funds and used them for their own privileges and interests instead of spending them judiciously on development projects.

Under the FCR, the state still denies the people of FATA their fundamental rights to political association and assembly. This has alienated the locals and allowed the Taliban to exploit their grievances against the central government. In the absence of moderate political forces, the influence of radical Islam has grown since the 1980s. Taliban rule in Afghanistan cemented the hold of extremists in tribal areas and many foreign mujahideen have married people from local tribes. They wield significant influence and this has led to the erosion of traditional structures.

The electoral system is firmly under the control of the political administration and intelligence agencies, which have manipulated the polls to ensure success for pro-government candidates. Until the introduction of the adult franchise in 1996, an electoral college of 35,500 *maliks* used to elect candidates for national assembly. FATA has eight seats in the Senate and twelve seats in the National Assembly.

In 2002 the Musharraf government drafted a FATA Local Government Regulation modelled on the Local Government Ordinance. Instead of promulgating the Local Government Ordinance of 2002, in December 2004 the NWFP Governor issued orders to establish the Provisional Agency Councils to facilitate local participation in development and other important matters. The implementation of a local bodies system would have brought political agents under an elected *nazim* (mayor), but this opportunity was intentionally denied to already marginalized segments of tribal areas.

Judicial System

The Pakistan Penal Code (PPC) does not apply in tribal areas and these areas are outside the High and Supreme Court's jurisdiction.[23] The colonial era legal framework enshrined in the Frontier Crimes Regulations (FCR), which was drafted by the British in 1872 to control British India's restive frontier belt, defines the judicial system. After some amendments it was promulgated in 1901. Even after independence, Pakistan maintained the FCR. Unlike FATA, which is still under this draconian judicial structure, NWFP and Baluchistan were governed under this system until only 1963 and 1977, respectively. The FCR is a mix of traditional customs, norms and executive discretion.[24] The British created this draconian law to regulate the restive areas and subjugate the locals. It is a parallel judicial system that does not come under the jurisdiction of Pakistan's superior judiciary. The FCR concentrates discretionary police, judicial and executive authority in the political agent. This system has generated an atmosphere of marginalization conducive for the growth of regressive elements, reinforcing the age-old system.

FCR Jirga

Under the FCR, the Pashtun tribal structure of *jirga*[25] (tribal council of elders) has been preserved in accordance with tribal customs. Disputes between tribes, between the state and tribes, and civil and criminal matters can be referred to the *jirga*. The *jirga* system has been retained for dispensing speedy justice in line with the Pashtun tradition. It should be mentioned, however, that the British distorted that system by making the *jirga* subservient to the political agent. Pakistan retained the distorted system that gives the political agent ultimate authority over initiating cases, appointing the *jirga*, presiding over trials and awarding punishments.[26] The *jirga* is convened by the political agent.

Though the *jirga* system is an efficient and speedy way of dispensing justice, the manipulation of *jirga* by the political agent has made it controversial. While many cases are resolved speedily in an impartial and fair manner, when the political agent or government has a stake in a case the *jirga* verdict often tends to favour those with political and economic clout. Because the political agent hand-picks members of the *jirga*, the decisions of the FCR *jirga* mostly favour state interests and lack public credibility. It is a state-manipulated institution used as a tool by political authorities to serve the interest of the state.

A significant number of clauses of the FCR are cruel, inhumane and against fundamental human rights mentioned in article 8 of 1973 Constitution. For instance, the FCR collective punishment clause allows the political agent to punish a whole tribe for crimes committed on its territory by fines, arrest, property seizures and blockades if a member of that tribe is found guilty of a crime.[27] The political agent can order the arrest of any member of the tribe, seize their property, or block their access to settled districts if they act in a hostile or unfriendly manner. Though the FCR is no longer operative in NWFP and Baluchistan, it is the main source of law in FATA. As a result, Islamist radicals are filling the void created by the absence of democratic, participatory institutions, as well as the suppression of moderate voices.

The Pashtunwali, or the Pashtun code, governed the way of life. The code included the *hujra* (the centre of Pashtun society), *jirga* (a council formed to settle conflicts), *malmastia* (a regulator of host/guest relations) and *da khazoo dranaway* (the respect for females). Furthermore, they adhered to *Jaba* (promise), *Nanawatee* (to seek mercy), *Panah* (to give shelter), *Nang* (to honour), *Badal* (revenge) and *Swara* (a female given as an act of compromise).

The steady Islamization of FATA affected these traditions and customs in the 1980s and '90s. The emergence of the Afghan Taliban gave rise to like-minded forces in FATA. There was a resurgence in politico-religious parties and their militant wings, and the number of madaris, including those preaching hatred, grew. Nonetheless, an admirable security situation prevailed in FATA despite decades of conflict in neighbouring Afghanistan and limited economic development.

Threat Displacement

After Al Qaeda was dislodged from Tora Bora in Afghanistan in early 2002, the group retreated to FATA. After relocating to Waziristan, both Al Qaeda and the Afghan Taliban linked up with the Pakistan Taliban and other Pakistani mainland groups. These two entities survived by reaching out to FATA's politico-religious parties. Thereafter Al Qaeda used its historical affiliations to nurture and build a clerical support base.

Ayman al-Zawahiri, Al-Qaeda's deputy leader, moved to Waziristan and stayed there during part of 2002, before moving to Bajaur Agency.[28] As his wife and two children had been killed during US attacks in Afghanistan, al-Zawahiri married a woman from the Mamund tribe in Bajaur Agency.[29] Just as Osama bin Laden had married a woman from Yemen to strengthen his ties to the Yemeni tribes, so al-Zawahiri's marriage enabled him to develop strong tribal ties to the leadership of Tehrik Nifaz Shariat Muhammadi (TNSM) in Bajaur Agency.[30] Maulana Faqir Muhammad, also from the Mamund tribe, represented TNSM in Bajaur Agency.[31] Similarly al-Zawahiri built a relationship with Liaquat Hussein, who ran the Ziaul Uloom Taleemul Qur'an seminary in Chingai in Bajaur until his death in October 2006.[32] Through these contacts al-Zawahiri was able to avoid arrest and reconstitute a scattered Al Qaeda in disarray. As the de facto head of the *majlis shura* (consultative council) of Al Qaeda, al Zawahiri re-established contact with Al Qaeda cells in Pakistan and overseas. He also built alliances with groups in the Arabian Peninsula, the Horn of Africa, Southeast Asia and Iran.

The situation in FATA began to change after the influx of foreign fighters in 2002. Al Qaeda and its associates began to plan attacks against coalition forces in Afghanistan. They were initially supported by the various Pakistani groups that later formed Tehrik-e-Taliban Pakistan (TTP). Hezb-e-Islami of Gulbuddin Hekmatyar and the Haqqani network also joined them. The Pakistani military responded to the increasing strength of the local Pakistani groups, spawning an insurgency. Owing to the difficulties faced by the Pakistani military in mounting land operations to neutralize Al Qaeda and its associates, the US conducted about 60 drone attacks from June 2004 to January 2009.[33] The first drone attack by the US killed Nek Muhammad and two of his associates in Wana, North Waziristan, on 18 June 2004.[34] Nek, a staunch supporter of Al Qaeda and other foreign fighters, had facilitated operations against us-led coalition forces. Despite the actual circumstances, the Pakistani government affirmed that their own security forces had mounted the attack.[35]

Nek Muhammad was replaced as the most significant leader in FATA by Abdullah Mehsud, a former detainee at Guantanamo Bay, but he died in a raid on 24 July 2007. Under the leadership of Baitullah Mehsud both Afghanistan and Pakistan experienced unprecedented levels of violence. Furthermore, Al Qaeda became more assertive, often using the Pakistani Taliban as its strike arm.

Pakistan deployed its regular military in FATA to counter the emergence of local militias and since then Pakistan has faced an insurgency. In many ways, FATA drifted away from the state of Pakistan. Pashtunwali, the system that governed the day-to-day lives of the people in FATA, was shattered to pieces: faith in religion dwindled and, in the name of Islam, foreign fighters carried out un-Islamic acts.

Pakistani Al-Qaeda

The best-known of the terrorist leaders and operatives of Pakistani origin is the mastermind of the 9/11 attacks, Khalid Sheikh Mohamed (KSM), alias Mokhtar, who had graduated as a mechanical engineer from North Carolina Agriculture and Technical State University in 1986. Together with his nephew, Ramzi Ahmed Yousef, he planned the February 1993 attack on the World Trade Center and the foiled plan to bomb a dozen aircraft over the Pacific (Operation Bojinka) in 1995. Having grown up in Kuwait, Ramzi Ahmed Yousef and KSM were comfortable operating with both Asian and Arab terrorists. KSM planned several other attacks, including an assault on the Bank of America building in Los Angeles using Southeast Asian terrorists as part of a second wave of attacks against the US in 2002. KSM partially funded the Bali bombing in 2002, and claims to have personally beheaded Daniel Pearl, the first American to be killed in an act of terrorism after 9/11.

Another Asian terrorist was Muhammad Naeem Noor Khan, alias Abu Talal, a computer specialist serving as the communications coordinator of Al Qaeda. When arrested in Pakistan on 13 July 2004, his laptop contained surveillance profiles of London's Heathrow Airport, the New York Stock Exchange and Citigroup headquarters in New York, the Prudential Building in Newark, New Jersey, and the International Monetary Fund and World Bank buildings in Washington, DC. These targets had been studied by Dhiren Barot (alias Abu Issa al-Brittani), a protégé of KSM and the Al Qaeda leader in the UK. Barot envisioned placing twelve or thirteen explosive cylinders inside limousines and detonating them in underground car parks to collapse the buildings; he called this the 'Gas Limos Project'. He travelled to the US in August 2000 and March 2001 to study the targets in minute detail and briefed the Al Qaeda leadership on the Afghan-Pakistan border. Barot's cell members were mostly young British nationals of Pakistani heritage, none older than 31. Although known to the British intelligence community and New Scotland Yard since December 2001, Barot was identified and arrested only in August 2004. The dominance of Asians in European and North American operations was inevitable. After the 9/11 attacks it was recognized, even within Al Qaeda, that it was difficult for Arabs to operate in the West. As Arabs were increasingly suspected, Al Qaeda relied on its Asian members, including those living in the West, to take charge of its operations. While Europe-based South Asian members who were either trained or inspired by Al Qaeda dominated the threat landscape, there were also Southeast Asians determined to strike at the US and its allies. In Indonesia, for instance, Encep Nurjaman (alias Riduan Isamuddin, alias Hambali), working together with KSM, spearheaded the bombing of churches in December 2000 and the first Bali bombing, and arranged to house the 9/11 hijackers in Malaysia.

Threat Complexion

Almost all the terrorist and extremist groups that existed in Afghanistan under Taliban rule reconstituted themselves and maintained a robust presence in FATA. Al-Qaeda is providing the crucial knowledge and methodology to mobilize not only the foreign, but also the domestic terrorist groups. Traditionally, the tribes in FATA supported the anti-Soviet multinational Afghan mujahideen campaign (December 1979–February 1989).

They then perceived Western intervention in Afghanistan after 2001 as an extension of the past, with non-Muslims occupying Muslim land. This explains why the hardline Pashtu nationalists and the Islamists are supporting the fight against the US and its allies. Like Sudan between 1991 and 1996, and Afghanistan from 1996 to 2001, FATA has emerged as the most important current terrorist sanctuary.

FATA is of unprecedented significance to the international security and intelligence community for three reasons. First, the operational and ideological leadership of Al Qaeda, Afghan Taliban, the Eastern Turkistan Islamic Movement, Islamic Movement of Uzbekistan, Islamic Jihad Group, the Libyan Islamic Fighters Group and a dozen other groups are located in FATA under the protection of the Pakistani Taliban.[36]

Second, FATA has become a sanctuary for research and development in explosives and training, and for the direction of operations globally, including attacks in the Middle East and the West, as well as in Afghanistan and mainland Pakistan. As long as FATA remains a sanctuary, the incessant attacks against coalition forces in Afghanistan will continue, as will those on mainland Pakistan. These have included multiple assassination attempts on Pervez Musharraf and the successful assassination of Benazir Bhutto. Attacks in the UK and several other operations disrupted in the West were planned in FATA. Rashid Rauf, the mastermind of the foiled liquid explosives plot to blow up aircraft over the Atlantic Ocean in August 2006, escaped during his appearance in a Pakistani court but was later killed, along with an Al Qaeda leader, Abu Zubair al-Masri, in a Predator drone strike in the Mir Ali area of the North Waziristan Agency on 22 November 2008.[37]

Third, Al Qaeda has invested in sustained propaganda to radicalize the Muslim masses. Even in migrant communities Al Qaeda has unleashed a homegrown threat. In 2007 and 2008, Al Qaeda produced a video every three or four days.[38] Al Qaeda aims to politicize, radicalize and mobilize Muslims worldwide into supporting and participating in the fight against the West. In the absence of a robust government response to counter Al Qaeda's message, Muslims are susceptible to extremist propaganda. Heightened extremism leads to support and participation in terrorism.

Despite intermittent pressure, Al Qaeda and other foreign and Pakistani militant groups have re-established a smaller and more rudimentary version of their Afghan training infrastructure in the Shakai Valley of South Waziristan.[39] Operating out of FATA and the neighbouring settled areas, the NWFP, Al Qaeda has trained more than 100 Westerners of Pakistani heritage to mount attacks in Europe and North America. The leader of the 7/7 bombers, Mohammad Siddique Khan, for example, and the leader of the failed 7/21 attacks were both trained in NWFP.[40] Dhiren Barot, the Al Qaeda leader in the UK, visited Waziristan to consult the Al Qaeda leadership when planning attacks on multiple targets in the UK and the US.[41]

Al-Qaeda's Pakistan-Iraq Links

The aforementioned threat complexion can be best explained by examining Al Qaeda's role in Iraq and Afghanistan. After the US invasion of Iraq in March 2003, Abdal Hadi al-Iraqi acted as a conduit between Osama bin Laden and Abu Musab al-Zarqawi, the leader of Tawhid Wal Jihad.[42] As an Iraqi Kurdish member of Al Qaeda's Majlis Shura, Abdal Hadi brokered an alliance between Osama bin Laden and al-Zarqawi. The Al Qaeda leadership accepted Abu Musab's proposal to name his group Al Qaeda in Iraq. As Abu Musab swore a *bayat*, an oath of allegiance to Osama, Tawhid Wal Jihad was integrated into Al Qaeda.[43] The Al Qaeda leadership guided Al Zarqawi not only to wage the local jihad, but the global jihad from its base in Iraq. Another Al Qaeda leader, Mustafa Al-Uzayti, alias Abu Faraj al-Libi, who headed Al Qaeda Internal Operations from 2002 until his capture in May 2005, asked Al-Zarqawi 'to target US interests outside of Iraq'.[44] According to testament reported at Guantanamo Bay: "In September 2004 several members of Al Qaeda involved in terrorist operations, including the detainee [Abu Faraj al-Libi], met in Syria to discuss a variety of terrorist operations, including planned operations in the United States, Europe and Australia.'[45] Abdal Hadi was a key figure in the Al Qaeda strategy to use Iraq to strike the West.

Abdal Hadi and Ammar al-Ruqa'I, alias Abu Layth al-Libi, worked mainly from bases in the Shakai Valley in South Waziristan Agency and from Sedgi and the Shawal Valley in North Waziristan Agency.[46] Although Al Qaeda operated in Afghanistan, the highest leadership is still held by the Taliban leader Mullah Muhammad Omar. Abdal Hadi conducted attacks in southeastern Afghanistan, while Abu Layth al-Libi commanded Al Qaeda attacks in southwestern Afghanistan. They personally trained the fighters and led operations from the front. As well as speaking Kurdish, Arabic and Persian, Abdal Hadi spoke Urdu and the Waziri tribal dialect of Pashtu.[47] Like Abu Layth he was able to build a strong relationship with the Pakistani tribes. Both had long-standing ties to the Taliban going back to the 1990s and hence liaised between Al Qaeda and the Afghan Taliban. As a brilliant military commander, Abdal Hadi was respected both by the Pakistani and Afghan Taliban, but his tough personality brought him into conflict with other senior commanders, including the Egyptians in Al Qaeda. In August 2004 Abdal Hadi was removed from his position as leader of Al Qaeda operations in Afghanistan. He was intent on returning to his native country to serve with Abu Musab, but he was aware that the Al Qaeda leadership in Pakistan would not approve of appointment to Iraq. Abu Musab feared that Hadi al-Iraqi was sent to replace him and refused to assist his entry into Iraq. In Abdal Hadi's absence, Osama bin Laden appointed the Egyptian Khalid Habib as Abdal Hadi's replacement. Khalid Habib is a very able commander and a close friend of Hamza Rabia and al-Zawahiri, both of whom are also Egyptians, but as an introvert he is a less inspiring military commander than Abdal Hadi. When Abdal Hadi failed to enter Iraq and returned to North Waziristan, Al Qaeda decided his military skills were too important to leave unused, and they reappointed him as the commander of Al Qaeda operations in southwestern Afghanistan. Khalid Habib remained in overall command of operations in Afghanistan and regionally in command of operations in southeastern Afghanistan. Although cross-border attacks on coalition and Afghan forces in Afghanistan were Abdal Hadi's priority, he worked with Abu Faraj al-Libi in the targeted multiple operations to assassinate Pakistan's President Pervez Musharraf.

After Pakistan arrested Abu Faraj al-Libi in May 2005, the Egyptians Hamza Rabia and Abu Abd-al Rahman al-Muhajir assumed the roles as number three and four in the organization, respectively. After the death of Hamza Rabia in December 2005, however, his post as head of External Operations was assumed by Abdal Hadi, who already had experience of mounting operations with Al Qaeda commanders in FATA and with Al Qaeda cells in the West. As Abdal Hadi's interaction with Iraq grew, he almost relocated to Iraq with a view of creating a second safe haven for Al Qaeda.

Abdal Hadi conducted operations both on and off the battlefield. He understood the value of using the Muslim migrant and diaspora community residing in the West to target the West. Instead of using operatives from Asia and the Middle East to infiltrate the West, Abdal Hadi is thought to have arranged for several hundred British Muslims to travel to Pakistan or Iraq to receive training. It is estimated that 150 British Muslims travelled to Iraq in 2006 alone.[48] The international intelligence community became aware of Abdal Hadi's important role after the British authorities intercepted a phone call between Abdal Hadi and Mohammed Quayyum Khan (alias Q), a British citizen of Pakistani heritage who worked as a part-time taxi driver in Luton, Bedfordshire.[49] Q provided funds and equipment to Al Qaeda and facilitated Omar Khyam's travel to Pakistan. Omar Khyam, another British citizen of Pakistani heritage, had visited Pakistan in January 2000 and trained with Lashkar-e-Toiba before joining Al-Muhajiroun, a pro-Al Qaeda group in the UK. He later built a cell of well-to-do British Muslims, with British-educated university graduates constituting the majority. When Omar Khyam returned to Pakistan in March 2003 with his cell members to fight in Afghanistan, Abdal Hadi sent word that Al Qaeda 'had enough people … if they really wanted to do something they could go back [to the UK] and do something there.'[50] Abdal Hadi's deputy then met Khyam in Kohat, Pakistan, and instructed him to carry out 'multiple bombings', either 'simultaneously' or 'one after the other on the same day'.[51]

Under Abdal Hadi's orders, Khyam's cell exploited their contacts with Kashmiri groups to set up a training camp in Malakand, adjacent to Bajour in FATA. Together with Mohammad Siddique Khan and Sheezad Tanvir, the leader and deputy leader of the cell that carried out the London bombing on 7 July 2005, they were instructed in bomb-making techniques.[52] After returning to the UK in autumn 2003, they purchased 1,300 pounds of fertilizer to bomb the Bluewater shopping centre in Kent, the Ministry of Sound nightclub in London, high-pressure gas pipelines around south-east England, trains and synagogues. Khyam remained in contact with Abdal Hadi's deputy regarding the preparation of the device. Khyam testified at his trial that the 2001 war in Afghanistan against the Taliban turned his group of friends against their home country for the first time and that the war in Iraq was 'just sort of the final [straw]'.[53] Abdal Hadi similarly met with Mohammad Siddique Khan and Sheezad Tanvir and gave them fresh instructions during a visit to Pakistan from November 2004 to February 2005.[54] Al Qaeda claimed the coordinated simultaneous suicide attacks by the cell led by Mohammad Siddique Khan that killed 52 bus and tube commuters in London. A similar bomb attack two weeks later on 21 July, led by Ibrahim Said Mukthar, who also trained in the Malakand camp, was unsuccessful. Abdal Hadi planned to strike at both Europe and the US. Together with Abu Zubaydah, he met with Jose Padilla from the US and other operatives in 2002 to organize training on building remote-controlled detonation devices for explosives. During 2003 Abdal Hadi also had four meetings with Mohomed Junaid Babar, an American Pakistani from Queens, New York, who provided money, night-vision goggles and sleeping bags to Al Qaeda's attacking coalition forces in Afghanistan. Before returning to New York in early 2004, Babar conceptualized an attack on Times Square during New Year's Eve celebrations. Abdal Hadi worked on a range of operations to hit the US from 2005 onwards. He also tasked Rashid Rauf from Birmingham, a key operative between Al Qaeda and Kashmiri groups, with coordinating the operation to blow up transatlantic airliners in mid-flight and on US soil. The UK authorities, working with several foreign security agencies, mounted Operation Overt to disrupt Al Qaeda plans and preparations in August 2006.[55]

After Abu Musab was killed in June 2006, he was at first replaced by Abu Ayyub al-Masri from the Egyptian Islamic Jihad, but Osama bin Laden later dispatched Abdal Hadi to take his place. Al Qaeda was determined to use Iraq as a forward operational base to hit the West, particularly the United States. Before Abdal Hadi could enter Iraq, however, he was covertly captured in Turkey in late 2006. It was not until April 2007 that the US authorities announced that they had detained Abdal Hadi and taken him to the US detention facility at Guantanamo Bay in Cuba. Abdal Hadi was replaced as head of External Operations, by one of the Egyptians, Abu Ubayda al-Masri, the Al Qaeda leader in Kunar Province, with whom he had worked on plans for several operations in the West. Two other contenders for the post were Khalid Habib al-Masri and the Gulf Arab Hamza al-Jawfi.

Impact on FATA and Surrounding Regions

The population of FATA has suffered more than any other region of Pakistan. After Al Qaeda and its erstwhile host Afghan Taliban linked up with like-minded Pakistani groups and leaders, FATA emerged as a zone of sustained violence. The tribal belt has witnessed unprecedented violence that has included suicide bombings, attacks on *jirgas*, killing women, beheadings, attacks on mosques and funeral prayers, mutilating dead bodies, and target killing of individuals seen as rallying points or icons.

Seeking to exercise their control, Pakistani groups influenced by Al Qaeda have killed more than 600 tribal elders, or *maliks*, including Senator Faridullah Khan, Malik Mirzalam Khan and Malik Khandan (all in South Waziristan), Malik Tuti Gul (North Waziristan) and others in the Khyber, Mohmand and Bajur agencies.[56]

Despite an increase in military and law enforcement personnel, the wave of crime continues to increase, spilling over from FATA to Settled Areas, Provincially Administered Tribal Areas, Frontier Regions and to De Facto Tribal Areas. According to figures issued by the Intelligence Bureau Pakistan, reported crimes for 2008 (figures for 2007 in parentheses) totalled 114,089 (109,475). Broken down by category, these included: crimes against the person 8,830 (8,309); kidnappings 810 (669); assaults on police 341 (315); crimes against property 1,959 (1,829); and vehicle theft 484 (445). There is no indication that this trend will decline.

Since the beginning of the insurgency more than 2,000 military personnel have been killed. There has also been a sharp increase in the numbers of law enforcement personnel being killed or injured. In 2006 25 police officers were killed and 31 injured. After the Lal Majid tragedy in July 2007, both violence and support for violence in FATA and the adjacent areas grew significantly.[57] Over the next three years numbers steadily increased, with 108 killed and 234 injured in 2007, 166 killed and 300 injured in 2008, and 200 killed and 445 injured in 2009.

Today, FATA is suffering as both capital and talent drain away to other parts of the country and overseas owing to its abject socio-economic and political situation. The insecurity has brought economic activity almost to a standstill. With utilities and other infrastructure destroyed, development funds are being diverted to law enforcement activities. The educational system has suffered gravely, potentially affecting the future of the region.[58]

2
Understanding the Pakistani Taliban

Following the terrorist attacks on 11 September 2001, a new breed of terrorist groups inspired by Al Qaeda's political philosophy developed in Pakistan. Unquestionably the Pakistani Taliban is at the head of this list. Pakistani Taliban is a generic term used to describe the diverse ethnic Pashtun and other militant groups located within the FATA and in the neighbouring NWFP. These groups mostly operate against the state of Afghanistan, Pakistan and the US-led coalition forces in Afghanistan. Pakistani Taliban groups have formed alliances, such as Tehrik-e-Taliban Pakistan (TTP), formed on 14 December 2007, and Shura Ittihad Al Mujahideen (SIM), formed on 20 February 2009.[1] Initially these groups emerged in both tribal and mainland Pakistan to protect Al Qaeda and other foreign fighters that retreated from Afghanistan in the aftermath of 'Operation Enduring Freedom'. The Pakistani Taliban developed into a lethal army capable of carrying out its own military operations.

By displaying the characteristics of an insurgency, these highly motivated, well-funded and fortified Pakistani Taliban groups took the upper hand over the Pakistani military. Attacks currently take place on both sides of the Durand Line, the border demarcating Pakistan and Afghanistan. The Pakistani Taliban believes that they are an independent entity within the State of Pakistan and have formed a parallel government based on the judicial system used by the Afghan Taliban. Pakistani soldiers have been captured and murdered, and buses carrying recruits, soldiers and officers for the ISI, army, navy and air force have been blown up. Other targets have included military and civilian installations, mosques, Eid congregations, peace *jirga* (committees), funeral processions and crowded markets.

The Pakistani Taliban have consolidated their presence in the Pakistan-Afghan border region and converted it into a 'no-go' area for the Pakistani security forces. In August 2007 the Mehsud Taliban, a force loyal to Baitullah Mehsud, captured 300 Pakistani troops in the South Waziristan agency of FATA and held them hostage for more than a month.[2] It was considered to be the most mortifying incident in the history of Pakistani Army. The tribal belt of Pakistan became a safe haven for Al Qaeda's fugitives and served as a launching pad for warfare against the US, NATO and other foreign forces stationed in Afghanistan. FATA has emerged as the epicentre of global terrorism.

Al Qaeda pursues its global agenda of terrorism from Pakistan's tribal areas. In order to neutralize Al Qaeda, therefore, it is essential to counter its host, the Pakistani Taliban. Today the Taliban poses a major threat to the global community as well as to Pakistan and Afghanistan. The increasing strength of Taliban groups in Pakistan means that Al Qaeda and other foreign groups have also become stronger. Eliminating the Taliban and Al Qaeda in both Afghanistan and Pakistan would help ensure global security. This section presents an overview of the Pakistani Taliban's transformation into a highly organized movement following 9/11. It also highlights their ideologies and objectives, and provides a framework for understanding the driving forces behind the group.

The Origins of the Pakistani Taliban

How did an entity that was unheard of before the terrorist attacks of 11 September 2001 develop into a well-organized movement within a few years? The local and international media first used the term 'Pakistani Taliban' in late 2003 when referring to the armed militias of local tribesmen from FATA who rose to resist Pakistan's drive against foreign militants linked to Al Qaeda. After the fall of the Taliban regime in Afghanistan in 2001, Al Qaeda's leadership and members found sanctuary in the un-demarcated areas near the Durand Line. In addition to existing links in Pakistan, cross-border networks were established with the anti-Soviet mujahideen. Their settlement in the area was also facilitated by shared ethnicity, religious outlook and the desire to liberate Afghanistan from US occupation. The continued presence and support of the Afghan Taliban and Al Qaeda mobilized local Pashtuns, who later referred to themselves as the Pakistani Taliban.[3]

The dramatic rise of the Pakistani Taliban in FATA and the adjacent areas of NWFP can be attributed to various security, political and administrative factors. The Pakistani government's failure to take swift and decisive action was the foremost factor that led to the emergence of the Pakistani Taliban as an organized fighting force. Their initial targets were the US-led coalition forces and the Afghan military and police forces. Since they did not challenge the Pakistani authorities, the latter did not generally interfere in their activities unless they were involved in local feuds and disturbing law and order. Initial military operations against the Pakistani Taliban were more often used to obtain leverage than to defeat them once and for all.[4] Their dedication to removing foreign forces from Afghanistan also provided the Pakistani Taliban with much-needed legitimacy among the locals. Clerics with Taliban sympathies have frequently used the presence of allied forces to rally support for their cause, since belief in the legitimacy of *Jihad* is very strong among tribesmen in the FATA. The Pakistani Taliban also had a strong intelligence system that enabled the Taliban to undertake a multifaceted campaign against a stronger enemy.

The Musharraf government (October 1999–August 2008) pursued a policy of confronting both the Al Qaeda and Taliban elements. Although Musharraf ordered the Pakistani security forces to attack the Pakistani Taliban, the military did not dislodge them completely. Local government and intelligence authorities used enough discretion to give some breathing space to these elements. This helped the Musharraf government to build an alliance with Muttahida Majlis-e-Amal (MMA), a group of extremist politico-religious parties that rose to power in NWFP during the 2002 general elections. Sympathetic local authorities under the MMA government in the NWFP did not try to stop the Taliban spreading from the tribal areas to adjoining settled districts. By the time the MMA government left office in 2007, the Pakistani Taliban had reached several rural and urban centres in the province. The MMA also opposed the federal government's military operations in the tribal areas. The Musharraf government's policy of alternating military campaigns with peace failed to deliver stability. The stop-start military campaigns have had an effect directly opposite to what was expected and exposed the government's weakness: 'Most of the actions came under external pressure and lacked conviction. The policy was run by Musharraf and his generals who were completely alienated from the public. It was not possible for a government which had little public support to effectively fight extremism.'[5]

The Pakistani Taliban had cultural advantages on their side. Pakistani and Afghan fighters who escaped the American bombardment benefited from the deep-rooted local tribal traditions of providing protection to those in need. Many within the Pashtun tribes on the Pakistani side of the border were convinced that protecting their guests was their cultural-cum-religious duty. It was a repetition of the events during the 1980s' Jihad against the Soviet forces. The leadership of these scattered armed groups mainly consisted of mujahideen from the FATA who took part in the anti-Soviet Afghan Jihad. The majority of foot soldiers belonged to a new generation of militants motivated by a booming Jihadi culture in the FATA following the launch of Operation Enduring Freedom. The tribal system of FATA proved to be a strengthening factor for the Pakistani Taliban. In addition to cultural advantages, the Pakistani Taliban was able to acquire religious legitimacy. For many, the Taliban represents a religious movement that is neither hostile to Pakistan, nor an enemy of the people: many of the Taliban groups in FATA began their operations in the name of Islam and were supported and encouraged by the local population.

The Pakistan military had limited capabilities in counter-insurgency warfare, especially in the rugged mountains of the FATA, where they found that their adversaries' superior knowledge of the territory provided tactical advantages especially at night, when they could conduct surveillance, send reinforcements, attack Pakistani forces and safely withdraw. Government forces had to rely on the extensive use of air power, which ultimately resulted in more collateral damage and the loss of popular support. The Taliban group and foreign fighters in FATA took advantage of the heavy civilian casualties to further the spread of their ideology. The offensives were also very unpopular within Pakistan's officer corps, who did not like fighting their own countrymen.[6] The anti-government and anti-security force sentiments in the area laid the foundation for the Pakistani Taliban to recruit, raise funds, gather intelligence, procure supplies and grow from strength to strength.

The Pakistani Taliban's ability to maintain law and order in FATA, where the federal government had failed, has added to their popularity. *Salweshti* (protection) has been provided to the locals in areas that have typically been lawless. The Pakistani Taliban has also provided an expeditious justice system that is perceived as less corrupt and more effective than the Pakistani judicial system. Militants in Miramshah in North Waziristan, for example, who modelled themselves on the legacy of the ousted Taliban regime in Afghanistan, killed some two dozen alleged criminals in December 2005 and left their bodies hanging for days in the centre of the town.[7] The message was simple: the Taliban had the capability to bring order and ensure quick justice in the region, and this garnered public support for the Pakistani Taliban.

In order to extend their strongholds the Pakistani Taliban employ a careful strategy initially based on establishing networks in the region. They recruit locals for their cause before initiating vigilante activities, which are justified by attacking so-called un-Islamic activities.[8] Law enforcement agents are then targeted when they attempt to limit the Taliban's activities until the terrorists' attacks force the law enforcers and the district administration into submission. This leaves the path clear for the Taliban to pursue its strategy of eliminating the last vestiges of resistance from local politicians, elders, rival religious sects and clerics and enables the establishment of parallel governing structures.

Through the exploitation of such loopholes, the Pakistani Taliban emerged as an effective fighting force in approximately three years. Their initial objective was to fight against foreign forces established in Afghanistan, but eventually their attention was diverted towards Pakistan. In association with Al Qaeda and localized Jihadi groups, Pakistani Taliban carries out sporadic terrorist attacks across Pakistan.

Pakistani Taliban has never been a monolithic entity because most Taliban groups in the FATA are fragmented into smaller units that range from 'hard' to 'soft'. These terms have been much debated: while the hard Taliban mounts attacks in both Afghanistan and Pakistan, the soft Taliban focuses on attacking Afghanistan. Both groups compose members with different tribal loyalties and different agendas, and a few units in each category oppose the Pakistani state and the security forces. Further, they consider the group to be a part of a larger *Jihad*. Although mainstream Muslims disagree, the Pakistani Taliban perceives their mission as a *Jihad* or a Holy War.

Nonetheless, there are soft Taliban groups operating in the FATA that, while not necessarily pro-government, have not yet been involved in attacks against Pakistani forces. Several of these have opposed the presence of foreign militants in their respective areas and concentrated mainly on Afghanistan. After US drone attacks using unnamed aerial vehicles, however, even they have turned against the Pakistani government. Al Qaeda exerts more influence on the Pakistani Taliban than on the Afghan Taliban. Some Islamist militias in FATA that have been mistakenly referred to as the Taliban in the media are merely a religious-cum-social organization without political ambition and in no way trying to undermine the government or its local representatives. These militias can be described as 'puritans'. The majority of the Pakistani Taliban has always been pro-Pakistan. The complex situation in FATA and the diversity of the Taliban groups active there need to be thoroughly examined in order for us to understand the emerging threat from FATA.

Tehrik-e-Taliban Pakistan (TTP)

The TTP was established by Baitullah Mehsud in South Waziristan Agency (SWA) in December 2007.[9] Its first headquarters were located in the Ladha area of South Waziristan. Other traditional strongholds of TTP include North Waziristan, Bajaur, Orakzai and Mohmand, where TTP maintains its organizational structure and representatives.[10] TTP has no organization in Khyber and Kurram.[11] Within the settled areas of NWFP, however, TTP maintains a limited presence in the districts of Peshawar, Nowshera, Mardan, Charsadda, Hangu, Bannu, Laki Marwat, Dera Ismail Khan, Kohat, Tank, Swat, and Dir.

The TTP is variously known as the Taliban Movement of Pakistan, Pakistani Taliban, Tribal Militants, Local Taliban and Mehsud Taliban. The group does not maintain any official website. The TTP was formed 'to enforce Sharia and to unite against the NATO forces in Afghanistan and do defensive jihad against the Pakistan army'.[12] While justifying its stance against Pakistani security forces, TTP's spokesman insisted that, 'The main objective of TTP is to fight NATO and US forces in Afghanistan. However, due to the wrong policies of the Pakistani government, we were forced to resort to a defensive jihad in our country.'[13]

Strategically the Pakistani Taliban want to consolidate their territorial control in the tribal areas and extend it to as many parts of the NWFP as possible, so establishing a political and administrative domain with Islamic features similar to those practised by the Taliban regime in Afghanistan between 1996 and 2001. They also have an ideological agenda of making their domain available to other movements that share their 'Islamic' agenda. Thus their approach involves extending influence and control throughout Afghanistan and Pakistan through allied hard-line groups.

According to Hasan Abbas, a Pakistani expert on the Taliban and Al Qaeda, 'the transition from being Taliban supporters and sympathizers to becoming a mainstream Taliban force in the FATA started when many small militant groups operating independently in the area started networking with one another'.[14] This sequence of developments occurred between 2002 and 2004 while Pakistani forces in the area were concentrating on finding 'foreigners' linked to Al Qaeda. Soon many other local extremist groups that were banned in Pakistan started joining the Taliban ranks in the FATA, some as followers and others as partners. These Punjabi and Sindhi groups came to FATA from their own regions in order to have a greater chance of escaping the Pakistani law enforcement forces. During this process, the Pakistani Taliban never really merged into the organizational structure of the Afghan Taliban under Mullah Omar, although all the Pakistani Taliban groups, including the foreign militants, pledged allegiance to Mullah Omar. Thus, many groups that were formed in these areas to help the Afghan Taliban fight the Americans became the core of the Taliban Movement of Pakistan.

Within a few months of its inception the TTP was able to consolidate its foothold in South Waziristan and adjacent areas. The tribal areas of FATA steadily fell to the Taliban groups and 'Waziristan Shura' came into being. Military operations proved ineffective initially because the militants rejected any offers of a ceasefire. In 2007 the agencies of South and North Waziristan were turned into a no-go area for Pakistani state representatives and security forces. The Taliban groups, which later became the TTP, demonstrated their fighting skills by capturing 300 Pakistani soldiers in August 2007.

The TTP started extending its influence to adjacent settled areas of NWFP after consolidating its structure in FATA. At the beginning of 2008 the region around Peshawar, the capital of North-West Frontier Province, including Shabqadar, Charsadda and Mattni, became a battleground between the security forces and the TTP. Initially restricted to the tribal areas of Pakistan, the TTP has proved itself to be expansionist. Although the claim seemed implausible, in August 2008 the TTP spokesman Maulvi Omar stated that the Taliban had the capability to gain control over Karachi, Pakistan's financial hub.[15] While criticizing Altaf Hussain,[16] the head of Karachi's largest political force, Muttahida Qaumi Movement (MQM), Maulvi Omar stated, 'Hussain considers himself as the "king of Karachi" but will soon realise the power of the Taliban in the near future when his illusion would be shattered after the Taliban take Karachi over'.[17]

Although the possibility of the TTP gaining control of Karachi is slim, there are factors that make the TTP confident enough to claim so. For instance, the Taliban maintains a strong ideological and operational support base in a large Pashtun community that comprises about 11.42 per cent of Karachi's total population of 12.4 million. Most of them do not adhere to the Taliban ideology and way of life, as may be seen from the hundreds of Deobandi madrasas that ban terrorist outfits with direct links to the Taliban. Traditionally, however, some Deobandi madrasas in Karachi have provided the key leadership to the Taliban movement in Afghanistan and Pakistan; more precisely, Mullah Omar, Abdullah Mehsud, Qari Zafar and many other top leaders of the Taliban movement are graduates of Darul-Uloom Islamia Binori in Jamshed Quarters. Although Mullah Omar never studied at the Jamia Binori, he was awarded an honorary degree.

The TTP exploits its links with the tribal Pashtuns of Karachi in order to gather influence there. The Taliban movement in the Waziristan agencies mainly consists of Mehsud, Wazir and Dawar tribes, and there is a significant Mehsud and Wazir presence in the Pashtun-dominated areas of Karachi that has been one of the major sources of funding for their Taliban brothers.[18] Additionally, a large number of Internally Displaced Peoples (IDPs) have migrated to Karachi from the areas of FATA affected when the government carries out military operations against TTP and Al Qaeda. These IDPs could be a major source of 'Talibanization' in Karachi.[19] Although the majority of them do not necessarily support or sympathize with the Pakistani Taliban, some disgruntled individuals could be exploited by the TTP affiliates in Karachi for involvement in terrorist activities.

In September 2008, a month after the warning about taking over Karachi, the TTP, Lashkar-e-Jhangvi (LEJ) and other outlawed Jihadi organizations joined forces to pursue terrorist acts in Karachi.[20] According to Pakistani intelligence, Baitullah Mehsud established contact with various groups in Karachi. The newly established group was headed by Raheemullah, alias Naeem, alias Ali Hassan, son of Wilayat Khan. A resident of Street 3, Shehzad Cinema, Qasba Colony, Orangi Town, Raheemullah has been affiliated with the LeJ and Harkat-ul-Mujahideen (HUM).[21] TTP established contact with many Karachi-based activists including Qari Abid Mehsud, Khalid Dare Walla, Mufti Ilyas, Colonel Tufaan, Qari Hussain Mehsud, Abdul Wahad Mehsud of Kunwari Colony in Metroville and Faizullah Mehsud.[22]

The TTP's timely move to forge an operational partnership with LeJ and HUM demonstrated the truth in Maulvi Omar's claim regarding taking over Karachi. One of Asia's most famous metropolises remains under constant threat from TTP and its allies.

By continuously extending its areas of operation, with the intention of eventually reaching Karachi, the TTP proved that its objectives are not limited to waging Jihad against the foreign forces present in Afghanistan, but also to capture Pakistan. While the intention may be there, the capability is seriously lacking and therefore untenable.

The TTP's fighters frequently cross the border to fight against Afghan and foreign security forces. On 14 June 2008, for instance, the TTP claimed responsibility for a suicide attack that was said to have killed fifteen allied troops in Marko Bazaar on the Torkham-Jalalabad highway in the Afghan province of Nangarhar, although the claim could not be verified by credible sources.[23] The suicide bomber responsible for the attack was named as Qari Suleman from Pakistan's Bajaur Agency. TTP's spokesman Maulvi Omar stated that the attack was committed in retaliation for an American drone attack on the village of Damadola in the Bajaur Agency in October 2006, which had resulted in the death of nearly 80 people. During his first TV interview with Al Jazeera, Baitullah Mehsud acknowledged TTP's activities inside Afghanistan, stating, 'Yes, we send and will send our boys into Afghanistan for jihad'.[24]

In view of the TTP's activities on both sides of the Pakistan-Afghan border, it is possible to conclude that the TTP is a threat both to Pakistan and to Afghanistan and the foreign forces present there.

TTP Leadership

At the time of the TTP's formation in December 2007, Baitullah Mehsud of South Waziristan became the first Central Amir (leader), with Maulana Faqir Muhammad of Bajaur Agency as the Naib Amir (deputy leader). Hafiz Gul Bahadur of North Waziristan, who was the Second Naib Amir, strongly opposed Baitullah Mehsud's policies and believed that the TTP should be more focused on Afghanistan instead of attacking Pakistan; he left the TTP in late 2008 and formed his own group in North and South Waziristan. The General Secretary was Maulana Fazlullah of Swat, and Maulvi Omar of Bajaur Agency, a member of the TTP Shura, was the official spokesman.

At the heart of the TTP is the Mehsud tribal militia that originated from South Waziristan, the stronghold of the Mehsud tribe. After Baitullah Mehsud died on 26 August 2009, the TTP's leadership was contested between Hakimullah Mehsud, Waliur Rehman Mehsud and Maulana Faqir Muhammad, the TTP deputy leader and Taliban commander for Bajaur Agency. Others with an interest in the contest included Maulana Fazlullah from Swat, Tariq Afridi from Darra Adamkhel and Abdul Wali, alias Omar Khalid, from Mohmand Agency. Although Maulana Faqir Muhammad deserved the central leadership, Baitullah's fellow Mehsuds in the TTP would not allow the leadership to pass outside the tribe.[25] The speed with which Maulana Faqir Muhammad withdrew his claim revealed his own weak position and underscored the inevitability of someone from South Waziristan replacing Baitullah.

The Central Amir is in overall charge of the TTP. In conducting the affairs of the movement, he is assisted by a Senior Naib Amir (deputy leader), Naib Amir (deputy leader) and a General Secretary. Regional Amirs are responsible for the management of the respective areas assigned to them and are supposed to coordinate with the central leadership over important decisions such as operations against the Pakistani Security Forces.

A consultative body known as the *Shura* makes policy decisions. This comprises 40 members, mostly Taliban clerics claiming to be trained in Islamic jurisprudence, from the seven tribal agencies of Pakistan and the settled districts of NWFP. The decisions of the *Shura* are binding on the Central Amir.

It is believed that the Deobandi school of thought is dominant within the TTP's leadership and cadres. Its adherents seek to spread the strict Deobandi interpretation of Islam and the implementation of Sunni Sharia to all of Pakistan by force. They believe in waging armed struggle against the enemies of Islam to ensure the supremacy of Islam over all the religions of the world. They consider Shiites to be apostates. The TTP's anti-Shiite stance was strengthened by the incorporation into the organization of large numbers of terrorists belonging to Lashkar-e-Jhangvi, an anti-Shi'a mainland terrorist group.

TTP Leaders

Baitullah Mehsud

Baitullah Mehsud, who preferred to be called a Pakistani Talib, was the Central Amir (leader) of TTP. He was born in 1970 and came from a village called Dwatoi in Tehsil Ladda, an area lying on the border of North and South Waziristan agencies. It is commonly stated that Baitullah did not attend schooling or religious madrasa,[26] but another member of the Mehsud tribe from South Waziristan revealed that Baitullah received his early education in Bannu, a southern district of NWFP, where his father had migrated in search of work, and then moved on to Punjab province for further education.[27] During his student life, Baitullah was affiliated with Jamiat Tulaba-e-Islam (JTI), a student wing of Jamiat Ulema-e-Islam, and a religious political party headed by Maulana Fazlur Rahman.

Baitullah belonged to the Mehsud, the largest tribe in South Waziristan. Like most of his militant counterparts, he did not have any place in traditional tribal leadership, but went to Afghanistan to fight with the Taliban against the Northern Alliance in 1996. His mentor there was Jalaluddin Haqqani, a powerful commander in eastern Afghanistan who had been backed by the US in the fight against the Soviets; Haqqani now controls one of the most powerful networks operating in tribal Pakistan against both Afghanistan and Pakistan. The Haqqani network has been responsible for many suicide attacks, including that in 2008 on the Serena Hotel in Kabul.[28] In May 2004, when Nek Muhammad emerged as a popular commander in his Wazir tribe, Baitullah made a move to secure his own position as a militant commander with the rival Mehsud tribe. In the following month, in his first show of strength, Baitullah's men ambushed a Pakistan Army convoy within the Mehsud territory and killed scores of soldiers.

Many details about camera-shy Baitullah's life remain unclear. He changed his hideouts frequently, leaving no clues as to his whereabouts. He always kept his face hidden from the media, and few outsiders even knew what he looked like. In May 2008, however, Baitullah Mehsud invited local journalists for an interview in South Waziristan. A photograph taken on that occasion shows him as short but well-built, with a long beard, although his face is not clear. Baitullah took a second wife in August 2008 because he did not have any children with his first wife.[29] Such polygamous relationships are a common feature of Pakistani tribal society. It is known that he would sometimes fall unconscious owing to uncontrolled diabetes.[30] In October 2008 it was rumoured that he had died from the condition,[31] a claim that was immediately denied by the TTP.[32]

Baitullah's strategic headquarters were in SWA and Miranshah, with a secondary base in NWA.[33] Because his base was situated at the juncture of North and South Waziristan agencies, Baitullah's militia could easily create problems for the government in the adjacent settled areas of Tank, Dera Ismail Khan and Bannu districts. His meteoric rise stemmed from his ability to organize and command large numbers of fighters, fend off the Pakistani military in South Waziristan, take the fight to neighbouring agencies and districts, and organize a nationwide suicide bombing campaign.[34]

On the night of 5 August 2009 Baitullah Mehsud was killed when US drones fired missiles at the house of his father-in-law Ikramuddin in Zangara village, near Ladha town in South Waziristan. His wife, brother-in-law and others were killed in that attack. The TTP was reluctant to confirm Baitullah's death until 26 August 2009, when the revelation came from the newly appointed Central Amir, Hakimullah Mehsud, who admitted that Baitullah had suffered serious injuries in the attack and remained unconscious for several days.[35]

Hakimullah Mehsud
In October 2008 Baitullah Mehsud nominated three of his commanders in the South Waziristan Agency to coordinate with the TTP chapters in the tribal areas and districts of the NWFP.[36] Baitullah's decision was prompted by his poor health and the constant threat to his life. Waliur Rehman Mehsud, Noor Saeed and Jamshed, alias Zulfiqar Mehsud, alias Hakimullah Mehsud (the latter two unnamed at the time) were appointed to pass on Baitullah Mehsud's instructions. After Baitullah's death it was Hakimullah Mehsud who emerged as his successor on 21 August 2009.[37] Hakimullah was considered close to Baitullah and was known to be his driver, an indication of the trust he had in him.

Hakimullah was born in the region of Kotkai near the town of Jandola in South Waziristan. His only schooling took place at a small village madrasa in Hangu district.[38] Hakimullah soon joined his fellow clansman Baitullah in jihad (holy war), starting as a bodyguard and an aide to the older militants. Baitullah's consolidation of most of Pakistan's Taliban groups into a single entity provided growing opportunities for Hakimullah, who was already famous within the Taliban for his skills in battle, with a legendary ability to handle a Kalashnikov and a Toyota pick-up.[39]

After the formation of TTP, Hakimullah was appointed Taliban commander for the regions of Khyber, Kurram and Orakzai. He came to prominence after a series of spectacular raids against the army leading up to 30 August 2007, when his men held 300 soldiers of the Pakistan Army hostage in the Swat Valley.[40] Twenty-five hardcore Taliban militants were released from government custody in return for the captured soldiers.

His belief in the implementation of Taliban-style Sharia was put into practice when it was imposed in Orakzai Agency in December 2008. The Sikh and Hindu communities living in Orakzai and Khyber agencies were also subject to the levy of a *Jizyah* (tax). Above all, he is believed to be extremely sectarian, with a violently anti-Shi'a agenda that he has pursued in the Khyber, Kurram and Orakzai agencies, with the assistance of his first cousin, Commander Qari Hussain Ahmed Mehsud, sometimes referred to in TTP circles as the Ustad-e-Fidayeen ('father of the suicide bombers').[41]

When he was first introduced to the media in Orakzai Agency in November 2008, Hakimullah said, 'If the Pakistan government continues with its policy of following American dictates, [some day] we can try to capture Peshawar, Hangu and even Islamabad.' He also remarked that he found no difference between Bush and Obama, and that the policies of the former president Pervez Musharraf were still being followed in Pakistan.

Regarding Al-Qaeda, Hakimullah said, 'We are Al-Qaeda's friends. Both the Taliban and the Arab fighters have pledged our allegiance to Amir-ul-Momineen Mullah Omar of Afghanistan, but there is no Al Qaeda in South Waziristan. It's only the US and the Pakistani government's propaganda. They do not have any proof.'

Hakimullah was very apprehensive about the nationalist parties in Pakistan, especially the Peshawar-based Pashtun-nationalist Awami National Party (ANP). According to him, 'we can have an agreement with all the political parties but not with ANP'. He ridiculed the ANP ('We do not care two hoots about the Awami National Party's tirade against Taliban') by claiming that, while the ANP used to say that the Taliban were Pashtuns like them, given the way the situation was developing the ANP might soon take back their claim to being representatives of the Pashtuns.

As well as the kidnapping of 300 Pakistani security personnel in August 2008, Hakimullah was involved in the killing of Haji Namdar, head of the Amar Bil Maarouf Wa Nahi Munkar, a religious extremist outfit based in Khyber Agency, and a terrorist attack on the Pearl-Continental Hotel in Peshawar City on 10 June 2009. His actions, however, were strategically naïve. Indiscriminate suicide bombings that targeted civilians were carried out under his leadership and these led to a dramatic change in public opinion regarding Pakistani Taliban: the TTP completely lost its image as an entity fighting against the 'occupying forces' in Afghanistan and waging a 'defensive Jihad' against the Pakistani state.

Hakimullah appeared on an Al-Jazeera video sitting beside Humam Khalil Abu Mulal al-Balawi, the suicide bomber who would target Camp Chapman, a Central Intelligence Agency (CIA) base near Khost, Afghanistan, on 30 December 2009. The attack claimed eight people including three security contractors, four CIA officers and an officer from Jordan's General Intelligence Directorate (GID). The CIA officers killed included the chief of the base and an analyst from headquarters who reportedly was the agency's foremost expert on Al Qaeda.[42] The video was a clear indication that Hakimullah's group played a major role in the second biggest attack on the CIA in its history. Western intelligence agencies vowed to exact revenge and drone strikes were increased in the tribal areas of Pakistan, specifically targeting Hakimullah Mehsud. In one such attack, two missiles were fired at a compound in Pasalkot village in North Waziristan on 14 January 2010. Initial reports suggested that Hakimullah Mehsud was nearby at the time. Although there were reports that he died from injuries sustained,[43] TTP sources claimed that Mehsud was safe and had left minutes before the assault.

Noor Saeed

Despite his youth Noor Saeed was Baitullah's deputy commander. He belongs to the Shabi Khel sub-tribe in South Waziristan agency. He remains an important Taliban commander in the South Waziristan Agency and a member of TTP Shura (Consultation Committee).

Waliur Rehman Mehsud

Waliur Rehman was the deputy of Baitullah Mehsud and a member of the Mehsud Taliban Shura. He also acted as Baitullah's spokesman, although this position was neither formal nor regular,[44] and took part in negotiations with the government on behalf of the Mehsud Taliban and the TTP. Waliur Rehman succeeded Baitullah Mehsud as the head of the Mehsud Taliban.[45]

Waliur Rehman was formerly associated with Maulana Fazlur Rahman's Jamiat Ulema-i-Islam (JUI-F) and pursued peaceful politics. He attended the Deoband conference organized by the JUI-F in 2001 at Taru Jabba near Peshawar. Since joining the Taliban movement, however, Rehman has embraced the Taliban's ideology based on puritanical Islamic values. Music and television are seen as *bid'aa* (religious innovation) and against the teachings of Islam, and he has banned them in the Mehsud territory. He has warned people not to listen to music, as they will face punishment if caught. The local tribesmen have been advised to sport beards and has made the shaving of beards by barbers in the agency punishable.

Drug dealers and criminals have been warned to change their ways or be punished. His harsh pronouncements have led to a considerable fall in crime in the area.

Waliur Rehman Mehsud believes in waging 'jihad' in both Afghanistan and Pakistan. In an interview he stated that Pakistani Taliban fighters are committed to help the fight in Afghanistan and consider Barack Obama their 'No 1 enemy': 'we will sacrifice our bodies, hearts and money to fight them'. While affirming his commitment to the Afghanistan cause and the Afghan Taliban, he did not rule out terrorist attacks in Pakistan.[46]

Waliur Rehman is also instrumental in recruiting youngsters for 'jihad'. He is a qualified religious scholar, having graduated from a madrasa in Faisalabad, and a gifted orator whose sermons have a considerable impact on his audience.

Qari Hussain Ahmed Mehsud

Qari Hussain Ahmed Mehsud, one of most feared TTP leaders and a cousin of Hakimullah Mehsud, was responsible for training Faisal Shahzad, the New York Times Square bomber. An active member of Sipah-e-Sahaba Pakistan (SSP), a banned anti-Shi'a organization, he drifted towards its militant wing, Lashkar-e-Jhangvi (LeJ). He is the commander of the Fidayeen squad (suicide bomber squad). Although Qari Hussain has had disputes with the Taliban leadership, the continuing backing of his influential Ishangi sub-tribe of Bahlolzai has played a vital role in keeping him associated with the larger Taliban body.[47] Differences between Qari Hussain and Baitullah Mehsud led to the beheading of Polish engineer Peter Stanczak in February 2009.[48] Two drivers and a gunman were killed when the Taliban abducted Stanczek from Attock district on 28 September 2008. Baitullah insisted that the engineer should be handed over to him so that he could negotiate with the government for his own captured Taliban militants, but Qari Hussain refused and put up another list of prisoners, including four LeJ members and an Uzbek. The next day Stanczek was beheaded: a spokesperson for TTP's Darra Adamkhel chapter claimed responsibility. A source was reported as saying, 'Our commander made a good decision by beheading the Polish engineer, as it would create fear amongst the non-believers. If we keep on sending such "gifts" to the Europeans and others, they would soon be compelled to flee the region.'[49] As the master-trainer of suicide bombers in Pakistan, Qari Hussain remains a priority target for Pakistan and the US.

Maulvi Faqir

Maulvi Faqir is the deputy leader of TTP and leads the Taliban in Bajaur Agency. He also oversees Pakistani Taliban's activities in Afghanistan's Kunar province. He was born in 1970 in Chopatra, a village 20km from the Afghan border. He is tall and well built, with a long black beard and Taliban-style haircut, and wears a black turban. Even though polygamy is a common feature of tribal society, Faqir has only one wife.[50] Maulvi Faqir belongs to the powerful local Mamond tribe (not to be confused with the Mohmand tribe of the Mohmand Agency) and has 'a large extended family and almost everyone who is associated with him (by blood or otherwise) is in some way connected to his activities'.[51] His close relatives were staunch activists of TNSM or the Movement for the Enforcement of Islamic Laws. His sons Maulvi Mohammad Karim and Maulvi Jaan Mohammad went to wage jihad in Afghanistan with the head of TNSM in late 2001. They were captured as they attempted to make their way home and were imprisoned in Dera Ismail Khan Jail in southern Pakistan.

Maulvi Faqir was educated in the Hanafi Deobandi tradition at various madrasas in the NWFP.[52] This brought him close to the Arabs operating in the area, an affiliation that has been reinforced as a result of the marriage between one of his close relatives and an important Al Qaeda member of Arab origin.[53] These close links brought him to the attention of the Pakistani government and the US. Government forces raided his house in 2005 in search of important Al Qaeda operatives, and in 2006 he escaped from a US missile attack. Intelligence reports suggested that Ayman al-Zawahiri, Al Qaeda's second in command,, was present at the time of attack, but Maulana Faqir strongly denies any Al Qaeda or Taliban leadership presence in the area: 'According to Pashtun tradition we will definitely exact revenge on America. Ayman al-Zawahiri never came here but if he wanted to come, we will welcome him, and it will be a great pleasure for us to be his host.'[54] Former President Pervez Musharraf, however, is insistent that Al-Qaeda fighters were probably killed in this particular CIA air strike and that evidence suggested the presence of Al Qaeda leaders. Maulana Faqir belongs to a rich and influential Bajaur family and moves relatively freely with his personal security team, although in recent years he has rarely ventured beyond Bajaur and the adjoining tribal belt.[55]

In January 2008 Baitullah nominated Maulvi Faqir as the top negotiator of TTP and named him as the 'political face' of the organization. Commenting on Faqir's appointment, security experts stated that 'Baitullah made a wrong choice for the job' as Faqir 'never budges an inch from his position, and, in the given situation, how can he be a successful negotiator?'[56] In view of Maulvi Faqir's long experience of fighting in

Afghanistan, his stature in the tribal region and his personal relations with Al Qaeda, it is considered that he will remain an important link connecting the Afghan and Pakistani Taliban to Al Qaeda.

Umar Khalid

Umar Khalid is the TTP Amir in Mohmand Agency. He belongs to the Safi tribe and is one of the most influential Taliban leaders. Umar Khalid is involved in cross-border attacks, usually engaging US forces in Afghanistan's Kunar province. The strategic importance of Mohmand Agency allowed him to take 'greater control' following a bloody campaign against the Shah Sahib militant group in July 2008.[57]

Umar Khalid is a 'born Jihadi' who has glorified the fight against 'infidels' through his jihadist poetry. He was formerly a freelance journalist working for pro-jihad publications such as *Zarb-e-Momin* and the daily *Islam*, and was even a member of the Ghalanai Press Club, although this was revoked after he became involved in militant activities.[58] He first took part in operational jihad by joining a Kashmiri militant group to fight against the Indian occupation. Umar Khalid was the Harkat-ul-Mujahideen chief in the Mohmand Agency before becoming a Taliban commander. He closely cooperates with Maulvi Faqir, although unlike him he does not host foreign militants in Mohmand Agency.[59] Umar Khalid claims that some 26,000 trained militants operate under his command, but the reliability of these figures have not yet been confirmed.

Hafiz Gul Bahadur

Hafiz Gul Bahadur belongs to the Madda Khel clan of the Utmanzai Wazir.[60] He is a resident of Lwara, a region bordering Afghanistan, and is reported to have received his religious education from a Deobandi madrasa in Multan. Bahadur subscribes to the Deobandi Islamic revivalist ideology and maintains a political affiliation with the Jamiat Ulema-i-Islam Fazl (JUI-F), a Deobandi political party. He is known for hosting foreign militants, mainly Al Qaeda, Central Asian groups and the cross-border Haqqani network. He was appointed as the first Deputy of the TTP, but parted ways with Baitullah Mehsud in October 2008 because he felt that the latter's policies were weakening the cause of the Afghan resistance against foreign forces. Hafiz Gul Bahadur announced plans to create a new parallel organization, the Muqami Tehreek-e-Taliban or local Taliban. In February 2009, however, differences were briefly resolved between Baitullah Mehsud, Hafiz Gul Bahadur and Mullah Nazir when they jointly announced the formation of the Shura Ittehad-ul-Mujahideen (Alliance of Mujahideen), an umbrella group covering various Taliban factions.

Maulvi Omar

Maulvi Omar was born in Badan village of Bajaur Agency and belongs to the Barozai tribe. He received his early religious education from madaris (seminaries) in Mardan and Bajaur, but soon dropped out. Together with Maulana Faqir, he joined the TNSM, a violent movement for the implementation of sharia in Malakand Division founded by Maulana Sufi Muhammad in the 1990s. Maulvi Omar developed close contacts with Arab fighters when large numbers fled to Pakistan after the fall of the Taliban regime of Afghanistan. He did not remain a military commander but became a trusted associate of Baitullah Mehsud, liaising between the various Taliban groups, and was a key figure in the Taliban's propaganda campaigns. He was seriously injured in a US drone attack in Damadola in Bajaur on 13 January 2006 following intelligence reports that Dr Ayman al-Zawahiri had been invited to a dinner. He was nominated as the TTP's first official spokesman in December 2007. Like many other Taliban commanders, Omar has two wives; his two daughters were reportedly married to Arab fighters, one of whom, Sheikh Usman, was killed in a drone attack in Bajaur in October 2008. Maulvi Omar was arrested on 18 August 2009 when he was on his way to Orakzai Agency.[61]

TTP Finance

The TTP is a well-financed terrorist organization that draws its funds from sources including Al Qaeda, ransoms from abductions, bank robberies, volunteer donations, forced taxes and funding from the forces hostile to Pakistan. The most important source, however, is money collected through criminal activity. In October 2008 a Karachi English-language magazine, *The Herald*, published a report about the financing of the Pakistani Taliban through criminal activities.[62] The report disclosed that a number of tribal criminals have joined the Taliban to continue their activities and pay a vast amount of money to finance the Taliban's Jihad in return for their protection. In October 2008 Owais Ghani, the governor of the North West Frontier Province (NWFP), put the annual expenses of Baitullah Mehsud at about three billion rupees (US$4 million), while Brigadier Mehmood Shah, the former secretary of FATA, estimated the monthly budget was around 30 million rupees.

Armed robberies are an important source of income and TTP has formed squads to commit armed bank robberies in FATA and adjacent areas. Mainland terrorist outfits have also been organized to collect money through illegitimate means.[63]. In August 2008, for example, terrorists of Jundullah, a mainland terrorist outfit linked to TTP, revealed during an

investigation that they had robbed foreign banks and dispatched the
money to their headquarters in Wana. The money was used for weapons,
explosives and other necessities.[64] The TTP also sent trained people from
Wana to acquire jobs in security companies in order to facilitate robberies
in Karachi, so generating funds for the organization.[65] As a means of
speeding up the funding process, the TTP hired youngsters from Karachi,
many of whom belonged to Jaish-e-Mohammed, Harkat-ul-
Mujahideen, Harkat-ul-Jihad-i-Islami and other militant outfits. According to Pakistani security officials, the TTP-affiliated outfits were involved
in both large- and small-scale bank robberies, as well as kidnapping for
ransom in the city.[66]

Kidnapping is the TTP's most important source of income.[67] In August 2008 the Crime Investigation Department (CID) of Sindh arrested
three TTP financiers in Karachi.[68] Under interrogation they disclosed that
they have kidnapped individuals for ransom on behalf of their leaders in
Darra Adamkhel. In July 2008 a Christian named Lister Lobo was kidnapped from the Cantt area of Karachi, and was released only after his
family went to Darra Adamkhel and paid a ransom of 900,000 rupees. A
kidnapped a surgeon at a Peshawar hospital was released in exchange for
three million rupees. It would be incorrect to assume that these acts were
intended simply to spread terror or to make a political point. The abduction of high-profile dignitaries and foreign nationals, such as Chinese engineers (30 August 2008) and the Afghan ambassador to Islamabad (22
September 2008), together with his Pakistani counterpart (11 February
2008), has been an important source of finance. It is also interesting that
the Pakistani Taliban have managed to justify this practice on religious
grounds, claiming that: 'We have a fatwa that funding "jihad" through ransom money is justified.'[69]

Between July 2007 and December 2009 there were some 144 incidents of kidnapping or abduction in the NWFP and FATA that involved the
Pakistani Taliban or their allies. At first these were mostly concentrated in
North Waziristan and South Waziristan, generally targeting military personnel, policemen and government officials , but before long kidnappings
spread throughout the region and a wide range of civilians were also abducted. These included students and teachers, NGO and aid workers, a
telecommunications engineer, an oil company official, the owner of a car
rental company, a freelance journalist and a polo team. Groups of Christians and Shi'as were also taken. Political rivals belonging to the Awami
National Party (ANP), the Pakistan People's Party (PPP) and the JUI-F were
seized, as well as pro-government tribal elders. Among the nationalities
held were Afghans, Polish, Canadian, Iranian and Greek. The last of these

was seized in Chitral on 8 September 2009 and held in the Kamdesh area of Nooristan province of Afghanistan; the Taliban demanded a ransom of us$2 million dollars and the release of three Afghan Taliban leaders in return for his freedom.[70]

Drug money is another vital source of funding for the Pakistani Taliban. Pakistan is the key transit route for opium produced in Afghanistan. According to some estimates, 90 per cent of the Afghan opium produce is transported through routes in North and South Waziristan with the permission of the Taliban members, who control the drug agencies. A Taliban leader based in Mohmand Agency stated that the sale of drugs for serving the cause of 'jihad' is not *haram* (forbidden): 'this cash crop is God's gift to fight the infidels'.[71] Protection has also been provided to timber mafia and trucking mafia involved in smuggling: 'These groups have financed and supported the Maulana Fazlullah-led Taliban in Swat'.[72]

In Mohmand Agency the Taliban agents rely more on extortion. A close aide of the top local militant leader of the area admits that his organization is taxing traders, transporters, businesses and smugglers. The major source of their income comes from the transportation of marble from the quarry in Ziarat. Each truck is charged 1,000 to 2,000 rupees for 'safe passage' out of the region: 'Donating a few thousand rupees for the cause of the mujahideen should not be a problem for the marble dealers".[73] The Taliban also hold courts at the Pandyali seminary, Lakaro Tehsil's Lal Masjid, the Dawezai Zao madrasa and the Khwezau Khalodog madrasa, and collect money from court fees and fines. In Bajaur, northwest of Peshawar, the Taliban have imposed taxes on households ranging from a few hundred rupees to a hundred thousand rupees per month.[74]

Extortion has not been limited to cash. Petrol stations were forced to provide 100 to 150 litres of fuel per day for the Taliban vehicles: according to the owner of a fuel station located on the Khar-Munda Road, 'We were supplying them with free fuel, as they were in power and we have to do business here'. A Home and Tribal Affairs Department official also conceded that the militants now gather taxes that the political administration would previously have collected.[75]

The TTP's income in South Waziristan comes from taxation and fines on residents and transport operations. The militants' hold in North and South Waziristan has allowed them to appropriate much of the compensation provided by the government for the reconstruction of villages damaged during the military operation in January 2008. According to a local journalist, the Taliban kept almost half the compensation money, about 200 million rupees, while the remainder was distributed among the villagers.

According to the report, crime and ideology have formed a nexus. Among the Taliban there are those motivated by ideology as well as criminal elements involved in robberies and bank raids. The former need the latter to finance their 'jihad', and the latter need the protection of the former for their illegal activities.[76]

One of the most important external sources of finance for TTP is the funding received from countries hostile to Pakistan. While the Pakistani Taliban is less likely to accept any direct funding from such countries, such funds are channelled by foreign intelligence agencies through local contacts disguised as part of the Taliban or as one of their sympathizers.

In October 2008 three arrested TTP militants claimed that the Research and Analysis Wing (RAW), an Indian Intelligence agency, has been funding suicide bomb attacks in Pakistan, funnelling 680 million rupees through its links with the Afghan secret intelligence agency;[77] the issue remains controversial, however, as no concrete evidence could be established. The Indian and Afghan intelligence agencies have been accused of supporting TTP because its attacks have mainly been intended to destabilize the country and have been carried out within Pakistan. The three militants, who were arrested on 13 August 2008, admitted that they belonged to a group under Qari Hussain Ahmed Mehsud deputed to 'destabilize democratic Pakistan' with the sole purpose of the 'enforcement of Shariah' in the country.[78] To discredit Qari Hussain, Pakistan alleged that he worked both for RAW and the Afghan intelligence agency Riyast-e-Amniyat-i-Milli (RAM).[79]

Qari Hussain's three adjutants in the operation to manage suicide bombers were Farrukh Usman alias Shahjee, Tayyab alias Baba and Ustad. Farrukh Usman, Qari's deputy, was responsible for setting up attacks in Punjab, particularly in Lahore. He was the mastermind of suicide attacks on the FIA building, Naval War College, Model Town, Lahore High Court and a military bus in Sargodha. Another team under his control, including Bablu, Rehan, Ghulam Mustafa alias Asif and Abdul Rahim, was assigned to provide explosives once the suicide bombers had been prepared to perform the 'sacred feat'.

Tayyab alias Baba mainly operated in the twin cities of Rawalpindi and Islamabad, masterminding the bombings at the Aabpara Market and Marriott Hotel. The third person, known only as Ustad, is an expert bomb-maker who leads suicide bombers to the intended site of the blast. He is believed to be of Indian origin and 'works with a vengeance'.[80]

Shamim was the facilitator, whose task was to distribute funds to suicide bombers at the behest of Qari Hussain and Tayyab alias Baba. Since he is known to look like any other educated and well-dressed civilian and can easily assimilate with the urbanites, he was also entrusted with reconnoitring the target area. Khurram Ishtiaq alias Ibrahim was a well-trained militant whose role was to look after suicide bombers at a secret venue until they were led to where they were to carry out the attack.

Al Qaeda is believed to be the TTP's major donor. Since taking refuge in TTP strongholds in the FATA, Al Qaeda has been obligated to appease its hosts financially. In an interview Muslim Khan, a TTP member, admitted that Al Qaeda gave Baitullah Mehsud money and logistical advice.[81] Al Qaeda funds the TTP by various means, including cash and goods. Afghan and Pakistani businessmen who sympathize with Al Qaeda, usually in the United Arab Emirates, are given money to buy high-priced goods such as cars, which are then shipped to Pakistan and sold, often tripling Al Qaeda's investment. The businessmen take only a small percentage of the profits, while Al Qaeda distributes the remaining wealth among its allies.[82]

TTP Group Affiliations

The TTP is a complex combination of various Taliban groups and individuals from different Jihadi outfits. This complex grouping makes it difficult to assess whether those groups are officially a part of the TTP, or merely dissenters from a different Jihadi outfit that have joined the TTP. Nevertheless, a close study of TTP's structure provides an understanding of its affiliations and the differences between the various Taliban groups of FATA and NWFP and the mainland Jihadi organizations of Pakistan.

The Al Qaeda-TTP Nexus

The TTP and Al Qaeda maintain a close affiliation. In fact, Pakistan's Interior Minister accurately described the TTP as an extension of Al Qaeda: 'The organizations have close ties ... If Al Qaeda is to move in a tribal area, they have to look to the TTP to get refuge. The TTP is a host to Al Qaeda and is their mouthpiece.'[83] There is evidence to suggest organizational connections between Al Qaeda and the TTP.

Abu Kasha, a key link between Al Qaeda's Majlis Shura and the Taliban, possibly holds a senior position in the TTP.[84] In October 2008 Maulana Faqir Muhammad, Naib Amir (Deputy Leader) of the TTP, insisted in a video interview that the TTP closely supports the activities of Al Qaeda in Pakistan and Afghanistan because these Jihadi operations represent the 'will of all Muslims'.[85] When asked about the Taliban's interest in launching 9/11-style attacks on US soil, Faqir assured his audience that Al Qaeda 'can plan another such attack ... The Al Qaeda and the Taliban can do anything they want ... and we certainly have the desire to launch one.' Al Qaeda and the Taliban have also carried out various terrorist operations within Pakistan. An example of their operational collaboration was the bombing of the Marriott Hotel in Islamabad on 20 September 2008. Although 'Fidayeen-e-Islam', a previously unknown group, claimed responsibility for the bombing, it was believed that the Al Qaeda-Taliban nexus was behind the attack but had used a pseudonym to avoid public criticism, since the collateral damage, including civilian casualties, was immense.

Baitullah Mehsud strongly endorsed Al Qaeda's ideology of the global Jihad, including threats against the White House, New York and London. In his first-ever television interview, aired on 28 January 2008, Baitullah told Al Jazeera television network's Ahmad Zaidan:

> Our main aim is to finish Britain, the us and to crush the pride of the non-Muslims. We pray to God to give us the ability to destroy the White House, New York and London. And we have trust in God. Very soon, we will be witnessing Jihad's miracles.[86]

The TTP has also helped facilitate Al Qaeda's global operations. In August 2008 Maulvi Omar, the TTP's main spokesman, disclosed that the 7/7 bombings in London were planned from Bajaur.[87] British government investigation proved that the cell was a homegrown cell linked to Al Qaeda.

Al Qaeda has also proved itself to be a 'friend in need' to the Pakistani Taliban. In October 2007 Al Qaeda came to its assistance when Pakistani security forces launched a offensive against Taliban led by Maulana Fazlullah, the General Secretary of TTP. A report at the time concerning military operation in Swat disclosed, 'Some recent news reports suggest that Al Qaeda may also be supporting TNSM militants in Swat.'[88] This support could come as finance or as fresh recruits from the tribal region. A militant from Afghanistan fighting in Swat was reported as saying that without money from Al Qaeda they would not be able to fight. He had recruited a score of militants in North Waziristan to reinforce Fazlullah's followers in Swat. It is quite conceivable that Al Qaeda militants infiltrated the ranks of Fazlullah's fighters in order to establish a territory from where they could orchestrate their worldwide operations and a troubled Swat may well have suited their needs.

The Al Qaeda-TTP nexus presents a grave challenge to counter-terrorism forces worldwide. The TTP's leaders are all alumni of Al Qaeda training camps in Afghanistan under the Taliban. Al Qaeda now exerts more influence on the Pakistani Taliban than the Taliban in Afghanistan. While the Afghan Taliban are increasingly distancing themselves from Al

Qaeda and even signalling their intention to abandon it, the TTP is becoming closer to Al Qaeda. It offers shelter to top Al Qaeda leadership in its strongholds: Pakistani forces, for example, monitored the movement of Al Qaeda's deputy leader, Ayman al-Zawahiri, in TTP-protected Tribal Areas in the Bajaur Agency in September 2008. Given the fact that the Pakistani Taliban controls territories where Al Qaeda is hiding, regrouping and reorganizing, it must be the top priority for all those involved in the War on Terror to disrupt the nexus between two global terrorist outfits.

The TTP and the Afghan Taliban

The TTP is commonly thought of as a Pakistani branch of the Afghan Taliban with similar objectives, but they are indeed two different entities with different goals. For this reason the Afghan Taliban, led by Mullah Omar, have always openly disassociated themselves from the TTP. Despite this, a few Afghan militants have joined with the TTP. Qari Zia, for example, has been leading 1,000 fighters in the Mohmand/Bajaur region and was suspected of involvement in the assassination attempt on Asfandyar Wali Khan, the Awami National Party chief, in October 2008.[89] Similarly, after military operations against the TTP and other foreign militants in August and September 2008, the Pakistani security forces revealed that Taliban members from Afghanistan were entering Bajaur from Kunar province to fight against Pakistani forces.[90] Pakistan informed the US about this because the NATO-ISAF forces have not challenged the cross-border movement on this section of the Pakistan-Afghan frontier.

Since its inception, the TTP leadership has always pledged allegiance to Mullah Omar, who is recognized as the spiritual leader of Taliban on both sides of the border.[91] The TTP claimed that Mullah Omar appointed Baitullah Mehsud as the head of the Pakistani Taliban, but despite all the TTP's rhetoric, the Afghan Taliban never endorsed TTP activities against Pakistan. In fact, in January 2008 the Afghan Taliban publicly distanced themselves from the TTP and Baitullah Mehsud;[92] according to Afghan Taliban spokesman Zabihullah Mujahid,

> We have no concern with anybody joining or leaving the Taliban
> movement in Pakistan. Ours is an Afghan movement and we as a
> matter of policy do not support militant activity in Pakistan …
> Baitullah is a Pakistani and we as the Afghan Taliban have nothing
> to do with his appointment or his expulsion. We did not appoint
> him and we have not expelled him.[93]

The Afghan Taliban disowned the TTP at a critical time as it unleashed a wave of terror across Pakistan, indiscriminately killing thousands of security personnel and civilians. The Pashtuns inhabiting the FATA and the NWFP were the prime victims of the atrocities committed by the TTP and the Afghan Taliban feared that they would lose popular support among them owing to the TTP's actions. It was imperative for the Afghan Taliban to distance themselves from the TTP in order to secure their support base in the Pashtun-dominated areas of Pakistan.

In September 2008 the Urdu language newspapers of Pakistan published a report that the Afghan Taliban was unhappy with the TTP.[94] The Afghan Taliban continued to distance themselves from the TTP whenever the latter was involved in high-profile terrorist attacks in Pakistan. For instance, in July 2008, the Afghan Taliban sent a senior delegation to North Waziristan to persuade the TTP commanders to stop such attacks. A similar message was sent to Baitullah Mehsud after the suicide bombing at Wah Ordinance factory on 21 August 2008: approximately one hundred civilians were killed and sixty were injured,[95] and the TTP was quick to claim responsibility.[96] The Afghan Taliban believed that the TTP was tarnishing its own standing in Afghanistan by carrying out such terrorist attacks.

Another factor defining the rifts between the TTP and the Afghan Taliban is the former's policy vis-à-vis the 'Soft Taliban' factions in FATA, who are more focused on Afghanistan and do not necessarily support the TTP's terrorist activities in Pakistan. On 19 July 2008, for example, the TTP's Mohmand commander, Umar Khalid, killed the Muslim Khan, alias Shah Khalid, and his deputy Maulvi Obaidullah, two veteran Jihadis from Mohmand Agency who maintained close links with the Afghan Taliban movement.[97] Dozens of other militants from the Shah Khalid group and the TTP were also killed in clashes between the two groups in July 2008. The Shah Khalid Group was also linked to Lashkar-e-Tayeba and the killing of Shah Khalid exposed the differences between the TTP and the Afghan Taliban on the one hand, and between the TTP and Lashkar-e-Tayeba on the other.

In August 2008 the TTP killed Haji Namdar, the head of the defunct militant organization Amar Bil Maarouf Wa Nahi Munkar (also known as the Promotion of Virtue and Prohibition of Vice).[98] Haji Namdar did not support the TTP's strategy of waging war against the Pakistani security forces and was a 'hurdle in Taliban's entry into Khyber Agency'.[99] The outfit led by Haji Namdar, influenced by his religious beliefs, was more focused on eliminating social evils in his area. Haji Namdar also had close links with the Afghan Taliban and was a significant source of manpower for Afghan Taliban.

The Afghan Taliban consider the tribal areas of Pakistan to be important bases for guerrilla warfare against foreign forces in Afghanistan. The loss of key commanders like Shah Khalid and Haji Namdar would have displeased the Afghan Taliban, leading them to publicly disassociate themselves from the TTP.

The TTP and Mainland Jihadi Outfits

In late 2003 Pakistani security forces initiated military operations to clear the FATA of foreign militants, leading some of the Pakistani sectarian and jihadi organizations that had previously operated in the settled areas of Pakistan to move to the FATA to join the pro-Taliban and foreign militants in waging war against the 'pro-West' Pakistani Army. Although there is no evidence to suggest organizational links between the TTP, Lashkar-e-Tayeba and Jaish-e-Muhammad (JEM), individuals with links to the latter two organizations and to the LEJ did become part of the TTP. Jamiatul Furqan, a splinter group of JEM led by Maulvi Abdul Jabbar, however, is linked with the TTP and Al Qaeda. JEM's former commander, Asmatullah Shaheen Bhittani, has been based in South Waziristan, where he maintains between 150 and 200 fighters.[100] A large number of students from Islamabad's Red Mosque also joined Asmatullah in the aftermath of 'Operation Silence' in July 2007.

The militants from mainland Jihadi outfits among the ranks of TTP are known as the Punjabi and Urdu-speaking Taliban. The cadres and leadership of the LEJ who are fighting alongside the Taliban are mainly concentrated in Kurram Agency, Hangu and Darra Adamkhel, where they have killed thousands of Shi'as in sectarian clashes. Many of those who deserted mainland Jihadi outfits have also joined Al Qaeda in the FATA, led by Abu Ali Tunisi, a Jihadi from Tunisia based in North Waziristan.[101]

The combination of 'Urban Taliban' and 'Tribal Taliban' under the banner of the TTP is likely to pose a long-term security threat to Pakistan and beyond. The terrorists in FATA under the protection of the TTP have carried out lethal terrorist attacks in mainland Pakistan against local and foreign targets. A comprehensive strategy is required to disrupt the troika of the TTP, the Al Qaeda and the mainland Jihadi outfits.

Lashkar-e-Tayeba and Tehrike-e-Taliban Pakistan: Friends or Foes?

There is no evidence to suggest a formal organizational link between the TTP and LET, a proscribed terrorist outfit based in Pakistan and focusing on Kashmir. Conflicting ideologies and objectives explain the strong differences between the two groups: the LET adheres to the Ahl-e-Hadith school of thought, a local version of Wahhabism, whereas the TTP follows the Deobandi school of thought. The LET puts more emphasis on Jihad in the Indian-held Kashmir (IHK) with the aim of liberating the Muslim-dominated disputed territory from Indian occupation. In contrast, the TTP is primarily focused on Pakistan and, to some extent, Afghanistan. While the LET has labelled TTP's attacks inside Pakistan as *Fasaad* (Anarchy), it has not labelled them as Jihad.[102]

The differences between the LET and the TTP culminated in clashes in July 2008, when the TTP killed LET's commander, Shah Khalid, and kidnapped more than 60 members of the Shah Khalid Group. Clashes began with the occupation of a madrasa in the Khalodag village of Mohmand Agency.[103] The two groups were running separate training centres and had set up roadside checkpoints. After days of fighting, two senior Afghan Taliban commanders, Ustad Mohammad Yasir and Maulvi Sadre Azam, mediated and brokered a ceasefire on 17 July 2008, but fighting between the two groups soon restarted. The militants associated with Shah Khalid reportedly attacked one of Omar Khalid's senior commanders, Qari Shakil, when he entered Khwezo, a town considered to be a stronghold of the Shah Khalid group.[104] Qari Shakil, who belonged to Peshawar's Michni village, was injured in the attack. Omar Khalid's fighters, staying at a nearby training camp, were enraged and hundreds of them stormed into a house at Ashrafabad where Shah Khalid's men were present. In the aftermath of the bloody clashes in Mohmand, a member of the LET disclosed in an interview that their leaders are under threat from the Taliban.[105]

Clashes between pro-Baitullah and pro-LET Taliban led to internal splits within the TTP. After the killing of Shah Khalid, the TTP in Bajaur Agency split into two factions. Four important commanders, Maulvi Munir, Dr Abdul Wahab, Maulvi Abdul Hameed and Salar Masood, resigned from the TTP, announcing that: 'Innocent mujahideen were killed in Mohmand. This is against shariah. Mujahideen do not kill innocent people. Baitullah Mehsud-led TTP is "deviating" from the real cause of fighting the Americans inside Afghanistan. We took up the matter with Baitullah Mehsud but he did not take our concern seriously.'[106] Despite the strong ideological differences and disparity in their objectives, the TTP and various factions of the LET began to work together, operating both within and outside Pakistan. As of May 2010, LET operatives were active in Afghanistan.[107]

The TTP-*Muqami Taliban*

Mullah Nazir, who belongs to the Wazir tribe of South Waziristan, leads the Muqami Taliban. There is a long history of hostility between the Wazirs and Mehsuds and it was not until February 2009 that the Taliban ideology brought the two factions together. Mullah Nazir Wazir disagreed strongly with Baitullah Mehsud in early 2007 over the eviction from Waziristan of Uzbek militants, whom he viewed as a threat to pure Jihadi forces and as agents of the KGB, CIA and Mossad. He formed a Lashkar and initiated a military campaign to purge the Uzbeks from Waziristan, justifying his actions in a pamphlet entitled 'Tahir Yuldashev is a Foreign Agent', which was distributed in tribal areas;

Our Beloved Muslims and Countrymen,
    May Allah protect you. Your sacrifices and services for religion and nation are commendable. This is well known that the people of tribal areas are playing an important role in religious movements throughout the Islamic world. Your devotion and commitment with the Islamic movement of Taliban is not a secret. Moreover your sympathies with the fellow Muslim Mujahideen of Iraq, Palestine, Somalia, Chechnya and Kashmir are recognized by the world. It is right to say that all of these movements and groups are working actively with your moral support and prayers. We are also aware that working on the behest of Americans and Zionists, the government of Pakistan is putting all efforts into creating hurdles in the way of Jihad. But the brave and courageous people of tribal areas stood firmly against government's anti-Jihad policies ... The formation of 'Mujahideen-e-Haq'[108] on 19 March 2007 was also a part of our struggle to purify the Jihadi movement. We waged Jihad under the leadership of Mullah Nazir against Qari Tahir Yuldashev and his supporters in Wana and its neighbourhood. What were the reasons that compelled us to take this step? No doubt you people are unaware of these reasons and you would have some doubts about our step to wage Jihad against Tahir Yuldashev. Moreover, propaganda news reports have also created confusion over our drive against the Uzbek miscreants. With a firm belief in the greatness and superiority of Allah who is our Creator, we affirm that this letter would bring you all the facts and realities against the Uzbeks. We hope that, after knowing the truth, you will dispel all the doubts from your mind and accept our stance and support the step we have taken.
    As all of you are well aware, the people of tribal areas are very simple, truthful and very committed Muslims who follow Islamic orders along with their tribal values. History shows that tribal Muslims, especially from North and South Waziristan, have played a significant role in eliminating British rule from the subcontinent,

the formation of Pakistan, the Kashmiri freedom movement, the destruction of the Soviet Union in Afghanistan, establishing an Islamic government under Taliban, Jihad against Americans and their allies and then rehabilitation of foreign Mujahideen in tribal areas.

After the Taliban government's fall in Afghanistan, many foreign Mujahideen along with Uzbeks moved to our areas. Regarding them as Mujahideen and refugees, we provided them shelters and facilitated them with every need of life. Their security was our responsibility. We did everything one can do to serve our guest. We invited the anger of the Pakistan Army, which took stern actions when we refused to hand over the Mujahideen to the government or expel them from our territories. International institutions like the United Nations and European Union also turned against us. We were targeted with missiles and bombs to pay the price for hosting foreign Mujahideen. We had to carry the dead bodies of our martyrs, our houses were destroyed, our shops were demolished, our gardens were looted and our life became full of miseries. We faced all these difficulties only for our so-called and thankless Mujahideen and refugees. We were trying to act like 'Ansaar-e-Madina'. But Tahir Yuldashev and his supporters were not ready to behave like 'Refugees of Makkah''. They started stealing cars, carrying out abductions and bank robberies. Then we found that some computers had been stolen from the office of nadra. After investigations it was revealed that Tahir Yuldashev and his Jihadist companions were involved in these troublesome activities. When they were asked why they did so and why they were targeting Pakistanis, the answer was that those being killed are hypocrites, the wealth of Pakistanis is booty (Maal-e-Ghanimat) for us and the most superior jihad is against Pakistanis. Almost 800 people, including 200 locals, 80 Turkish and Punjabis, Arabs and Uzbek Mujahideen who left his group, are reported to have been killed by Tahir Yuldashev and his supporters. When these brutal beasts started to kill innocent people indiscriminately then well-wishers of Islam and Muslims asked these agents of the CIA, KGB and Mossad to leave our region otherwise they will be penalized under Islamic laws. These demands of 'Mujahideen-e-Haq' were sent to Tahir Yuldashev through Khalifa Siraj [the son of Jalaluddin Haqqani and a nominated commander of Emarat-e-Islami].[109] But he refused to fulfill any demand and closed all doors for talks. After this 'Mujahideen-e-Haq' consulted local Ulema and leading Ulaema of Pakistan and some from Saudi Arabia. After consulting all of these leading Ulema and getting a decree against Uzbeks, we started fighting against them. This struggle resulted in the end of brutality, cruelty and the night of darkness.[110]

Mullah Nazir's military campaign against the Uzbeks was successful and they were forced to leave Wana and Shakai, the strongholds of Mullah Nazir and his Waziri Taliban. Baitullah Mehsud offered help to the fleeing Uzbeks and provided them with shelter in the Laddha and Makeen areas of South Waziristan. When Baitullah invited all the Taliban factions to join the newly founded TTP, Mullah Nazir simply refused. Mullah Nazir later accused Baitullah of deviating from pure Jihad by carrying out more attacks inside Pakistan than in Afghanistan. Meanwhile, clashes between Mullah Nazir's group and the TTP led to several deaths on both sides.

The rift was resolved only in February 2009 with the formation of the Shura Ittehad al Mujahideen (SIM) to jointly fight their enemy.[111] A Taliban commander remarked on that occasion, 'We had understood Pakistan's divide and rule policy, and decided to get united and fight together against it in future. Pakistan caused more losses to the Mujahideen than the US. It handed over 700 Arab Mujahideen to the US and jailed our people.'[112] Senior Pakistani and Afghan Taliban commanders played a role in resolving the differences. A fourteen-member Shura was formed, headed by Baitullah Mehsud, Hafiz Gul Bahadur and Maulvi Nazir. Ten other people were drawn from Baitullah Mehsud's tribe, Gul Bahadur's Utmanzai Wazir tribe and Maulvi Nazir's Ahmadzai Wazir tribe. Mullah Nazir was nominated as the head of the new organization, but he was unwilling to accept.[113] The temporary alliance between Baitullah Mehsud, Maulvi Nazir and Gul Bahadur came to an end within a few days and the SIM was reportedly dissolved.

The TTP-Abdullah Mehsud Group

Abdullah Mehsud was a veteran of the Afghan Jihad who was involved in the kidnapping in October 2004 of three Chinese engineers, one of whom died days later. After Abdullah Mehsud's death in July 2007, Qari Zainuddin Mehsud became the head of the Abdullah Mehsud Group. He belonged to the Shuman Khel clan of the Mehsud tribe and was educated at a local mosque before leaving for Dar-ul-Uloom Faizoo, a madrasa located in Laki Marwat. He then went to Karachi to study in the madrasa of Maulana Taqi Usmani.[114] After time spent as a Khasadar (member of the tribal police) he went to Afghanistan and fought against the Northern Alliance. On his return to Pakistan, Qari joined the Taliban group led by Abdullah Mehsud.[115] It is believed that differences developed between Qari and Baitullah after the death of Abdullah Mehsud and led to violent clashes between the Baitullah and Abdullah groups. Close aides of Abdullah alleged that Baitullah had supplied information to security forces who were looking for him. Masood-u-Rehman took over the Abdullah Mehsud Group, but he was assassinated by Baitullah-led Taliban. Masood's son, Qari Zainuddin Mehsud, replaced his father and emerged as a challenger to Baitullah Mehsud from within his Mehsud clan.[116] Zainuddin and his small band of fighters took refuge in Shakai, a stronghold of Mullah Nazir, and later his family moved to Abotabad, fearing attacks from the Baitullah group.

In December 2008 differences were resolved between Baitullah Mehsud and Mullah Nazir, who reached an agreement by which Mullah Nazir was required to persuade Zainuddin Mehsud and his fighters to leave Shakai. Zainuddin sought a new alliance with Turkestan Bhittani, another anti-Baitullah commander in South Waziristan.[117] During his stay with Turkestan Bhittani, Zainuddin started targeting Baitullah's fighters and killed 30 of them.

In June 2009 the government decided to eliminate Baitullah Mehsud and encouraged Qari Zainuddin Mehsud to challenge Baitullah Mehsud's authority and the credibility of his status as a holy warrior by claiming that he was 'maligning Islam' by killing Muslims and bombing places of worship.[118] In an interview with the *Sunday Telegraph*, Zainuddin declared that Mehsud had betrayed both his religion and his tribe, and that Islam did not allow 'these bombings in mosques, in markets, in hospitals'.[119] In an interview with Geo TV, he accused the TTP chief of having links with India and Israel, acting 'against Islam as well as the country and if not eliminated now, militancy would surge and problems for the government would grow', and adding that he would support military action against him. Meanwhile Zainuddin established two centres in Tank and Dera Ismail Khan.

Qari Zainuddin Mehsud was assassinated at Dera Ismail Khan on 23 June 2009 by his long-time guard, Gulbuddin Mehsud, who came from the Makeen area of the South Waziristan Agency.[120] It was reported that the assassin had also been among Abdullah Mehsud's guards and had witnessed the killing of Abdullah Mehsud in Zhob by the security forces. Zainuddin's aide Baz Muhammad witnessed the attack and said that the gunman was acting on the orders of Baitullah Mehsud: 'It was definitely Baitullah's man who infiltrated our ranks, and he has done his job.' Misbahuddin Mehsud, who succeeded Qari Zainuddin, vowed to avenge the killing of the senior leaders of the Abdullah Mehsud Group.

The TTP-Turkestan Bhittani Group

The Hajji Turkestan Bhittani or Malik Turkestan Bhittani belongs to the Niamat Khel clan of the Bhittani tribe. He is a resident of Jandola village in the Tank frontier region, at the entry point to South Waziristan Agency. The Bhittani tribe resides in the area from the Gomal Valley in the south to Gabar Ghar Mountain in the north, including the territory between Waziristan and the Dera Ismail Khan district.[121] The Bhittanis are traditional rivals of the Mehsuds and the two tribes have remained engaged in violent clashes.

There are no reported links between Malik Turkestan Bhittani and any religious or secular political party in Pakistan, although he is known to belong to the Deobandi school of thought. Turkestan has performed Hajj and therefore is also known by the title Hajji Turkestan. He formerly served in the paramilitary force of the Frontier Corps (FC), from which he retired in 1998.[122] The FC is trained and manned by the Pakistani military and was established to help safeguard the Pakistan-Afghanistan border. There is no information currently available about Turkestan's education, although his service in the FC would suggest that he must have received a minimum education of eighth grade. As a tribal elder he has supported the government but has turned into a Taliban commander who opposes violence in Pakistan. Turkestan, however, believes in 'Jihad' in Afghanistan against the US and NATO troops.

Media reports describe Turkestan's initial association with the Taliban groups of South Waziristan Agency (SWA). He initially fought on the side of the Taliban and remained associated with Abdullah Mehsud, who recruited local tribesmen from the Mehsud tribe after his release from Guantanamo Bay and fought against Pakistani security forces during 2004. Many analysts describe Abdullah as a successor of the pro-Taliban militant leader, Nek Muhammad Yargul Khel from the Ahmadzai Wazir tribe of SWA, who was killed in a missile attack in the Shakai in June 2004.[123]

Some reports also state that Turkestan worked with Baitullah Mehsud for some time before they adopted opposing views on suicide bombings and terrorist attacks on the Pakistani security forces.[124] These media reports are mistaken, however, since the main ally of Baitullah Mehsud in the Bhittani tribe's area has always been Asmatullah Shaheen Bhittani, who took refuge with the TTP after his eviction from Jandola in 2007.

Turkestan rose to fame in October 2007 when he clashed with dozens of Taliban militants, affiliated with Asmatullah Shaheen Bhittani, who planned to destroy a bridge, built by the British, that linked Kari Wam, Niamat Khel and other hamlets within Jandola. The local Bhittani tribesmen used the bridge for foot and vehicular traffic, but the militants announced that the bridge was government property and should be destroyed. Tribal elders of the Bhittani tribe, led by Malik Turkestan, arrived along with their fellow tribesmen and tried to persuade the militants not to damage the bridge owing to its importance. The disagreement led to an armed clash in which one militant was killed and a few others, including Asmatullah Shaheen Bhittani, were injured. Two Bhittani tribesmen were also injured. This was the first reported instance of the local tribesmen resisting the restrictions imposed by the self-styled tribal militants.[125] In due course, Turkestan formed an Aman (peace) Committee known as the Niamat Khel Aman to maintain the peace in the Bhittani region.

Malik Turkestan and his Aman Committee not only prevented the Taliban militants from operating on the Bhittani tribe's territory but also put a check on the movement of Mehsud Taliban through Jandola to the North West Frontier Province (NWFP). During the Pakistani government's military operation against Baitullah Mehsud in January and February 2008, it was reported that Turkestan discouraged his tribesmen from assisting the Mehsud Taliban and the common tribesmen who were fleeing from the Mehsud tribe's area to NWFP via Jandola.[126] This incensed Baitullah Mehsud. Militants belonging to his group, led by Asmatullah Shaheen, attacked the Aman Committee on 24 June 2008 and took 27 members of the Committee hostage, including Turkestan's brother and nephew,[127] and briefly took control of the town of Jandola, Soor Kali and Kariwam. The Baitullah Mehsud group later killed most of the kidnapped members of the Committee.[128] Many families were forced to leave the frontier region of Jandola following this incident. Turkestan lost several family members and friends during the attacks and was fortunate to survive while operating in an area close to Baitullah's strongholds.[129] He later took shelter with paramilitary forces in Jandola.

In early 2009 Turkestan formalized an alliance with Qari Zainuddin Mehsud, the successor and leader of the Abdullah Mehsud Group. Turkestan described Baitullah Mehsud as an agent of American, Indian and Israeli interests, and also accused him of misleading local youth into attacks on fellow Muslims and the Pakistani security forces.[130] However, the death of Zainuddin Mehsud in June 2009 and his replacement by his brother, Qari Misbahuddin Mehsud, seems to have fractured the alliance. Misbahuddin Mehsud opposed the announcement of Ikhlas Khan Mehsud alias Waziristan Baba as the new head of the Abdullah Mehsud group, doubting his credentials as an established jihadi. Differences between Misbahuddin and Turkestan were highlighted by the absence of

Mehsud fighters from the battles between the Turkestan Bhittani and the Baitullah Mehsud groups in August 2009.

On 8 June 2009 Zainuddin and Turkestan held a *jirga* of Mehsud tribal elders in Tank, at which Turkestan condemned Baitullah's methods and urged the elders to fight against the leader of the TTP if he did not end his attacks on civilians and begin negotiations with the government.[131] After the assassination of Qari Zainuddin Mehsud on 23 June 2009, Turkestan spoke openly against Baitullah Mehsud and vowed to uproot the TTP from Waziristan: 'We reject Mehsud's policies and are willing to cooperate with the Pakistan Army as well as the American forces to fight against the TTP head'.[132] He told journalists that, 'After dealing with my opponents in South Waziristan, I will go to Helmand to reorganize my leader Abdullah Mehsud's group against foreign forces'. He reaffirmed his loyalty to Mullah Omar, but criticized Hakimullah Mehsud and Waliur Rehman Mehsud: 'They are neither Taliban nor Muslims, but earning Islam a bad name. I am also a Talib, but unlike Baitullah, Hakimullah and others who only kill Muslims and do nothing for Islam.'[133]

The TTP-Asmatullah Bhittani Group

Asmatullah Shaheen Bhittani has established his own Taliban faction affiliated with the TTP, the Asmatullah Shaheen Bhittani Group. He belongs to the Alim Khel clan of the Bhittani tribe and, like Malik Turkestan Bhittani, comes from Jandola village in the Tank frontier region. He is not believed to belong to any secular or religio-political party of Pakistan, although he may lean towards Jamiat Ulema-i-Islam-Fazl (JUI-F) since that organization belongs to the Deobandi school of thought, to which Asmatullah also subscribes. While Asmatullah has announced allegiance to Mullah Omar, he has dedicated little effort to 'jihad' in Afghanistan but has instead focused on Talibanizing the Bhittani tribe's area and implementing Taliban-style Sharia in the region.

Asmatullah joined the TTP in December 2007, representing the Bhittani component of the group, and has followed the TTP's move towards Al-Qaeda's ideology of subscribing to the global jihad. Although he did not complete his education at a local madrasa in the Jandola area, he has become one of the principal supporters of Tehrik-e-Taliban in the Bhittani area. He was initially associated with Abdullah Mehsud. Influenced by Taliban ideology and the emerging Taliban movement in South Waziristan Agency, Asmatullah started Talibanizing the Tank frontier region in 2004. In April 2006 he initiated a drive to recruit local tribesmen into his group to wage 'jihad' in Afghanistan. He imposed strict Taliban-style Sharia in the Bhittani tribe's region and exhorted the local tribesmen to keep a beard and pray five times a day. Those who failed to comply would face a 'social boycott' under which local hospitals run by tribesmen would not help them and their children would be barred from school. He also announced a series of other Islamic laws, without saying how they would be enforced, [134] and warned locals not to undertake 'un-Islamic' businesses and to avoid watching television and foreign media channels.

In 2004 and 2005 Asmatullah organized attacks against Pakistani security forces in the FR Tank region, which were conducting military operations against the Taliban elements in South Waziristan. Asmatullah's group was among those who held hostage around 300 security personnel in the SWA in September 2007 and made their release conditional on the withdrawal of troops from the tribal areas, as well as the release of fifteen of their comrades.[135] They also took responsibility for kidnapping ten Frontier Corps soldiers in Mohmand Agency.

In December 2007 he joined the Tehrik-e-Taliban Pakistan (TTP) in a move that could be seen as an attempt to strengthen his support base among the Taliban to fight his rival militant commander, Turkestan Bhittani, who is head of the Niamat Khel peace committee and a pro-government tribal elder.[136]

Asmatullah was part of the negotiation team, also including Baitullah Mehsud and Qari Hussain, who held unsuccessful talks in Ladha with a *jirga* comprising prominent tribal elders from all three subsections of the Mehsud tribe and a 21-member peace committee headed by Maulana Merajuddin, a JUI-F Member of the National Assembly, concerning the release of soldiers held hostage.[137]

The TTP's Military Capabilities

According to TTP's spokesman Maulvi Omar, the outfit maintains 100,000 fighting soldiers, only in tribal areas.[138] Such numbers, however, are usually exaggerated for propaganda purposes. Intelligence sources claim that Baitullah commands a highly trained militia of 20,000 to 25,000 fighters. In January 2009 Owais Ghani, the Governor of NWFP, stated that the TTP maintains 10,000 militants, but the local tribal chief put the number at between 8,000 and 10,000 well-trained fighters.[139] The core of this force is believed to be about 2,500 to 3,000 foreign fighters, mostly of central Asian origin.[140] The TTP cadres are expert at mountain warfare as most of them come from the mountainous FATA or the NWFP region in Pakistan. They have also shown expertise in the manufacture and use of IEDs.

Most of their weapons are those that were pumped into the NWFP and FATA region during the Soviet Afghan war during the 1980s. The TTP claims that there is a mass reservoir of weapons in the Pakistani tribal areas and in Afghanistan: 'We have enough weapons to continue jihad against the Americans till doomsday.'[141] The arms manufacturing industry in the FATA and the NWFP is another source of locally made weapons. Pakistani government sources claim that terrorists operating in the tribal areas also receive weapons from Afghanistan.[142] Weapons seized from the Pakistani security forces are also used by the TTP. According to Maulvi Omar,

> We have huge stocks of G3s and mortar shells. We have arrested 300 army men in Waziristan and seized a large amount of weapons from their custody, and with that, we can fight against the Pakistani security forces for 10 years. We also have armoured jeeps and other military vehicles.[143]

The possibility of the Pakistani Taliban acquiring nuclear weapons is a much-debated issue among security circles worldwide. In an interview with Al Jazeera TV, however, Baitullah Mehsud denied those apprehensions:

> Islam doesn't permit the killing of women and children, which nukes would inevitably do. Don't have thoughts about the use of nuclear weapons. America killed innocents in Japan – Hiroshima and Nagasaki. The fear right now is the use of American bombs against the Muslims as they used against the Japanese.[144]

The TTP's strategy seems to be centred on creating chaos and fear through suicide bombings. The purpose is to destabilize the government and force it to submit to their demands. The TTP never lets an attack on its positions in the tribal and settled areas go unchallenged. It is quick to take revenge by sending suicide bombers or by sponsoring bomb explosions. Security forces and law-enforcement agencies are targeted in these attacks, especially those that are spearheading military operations in tribal areas.

The Taliban has used a variety of tactics to enforce its control over the FATA. Their aim has not just been to spread terror in order to repress civilians, but also to assert their authority. Between July 2007 and 2009 the Pakistani Taliban was responsible for an estimated 136 suicide bombings, 316 rocket attacks, 119 remote-controlled bombs, 149 abductions, 69 beheadings, 12 misssile attacks, 272 time bombs, 239 IEDs, 44 hand grenade attacks, 444 shootings and 142 other acts.

The TTP uses its facilities in the FATA region for training in the art of guerilla warfare and suicide attacks. They also maintain training facilities for developing IEDs and training homegrown Jihadis from the Western hemisphere in the art of bomb-making. In 2008 TTP and its affiliated groups had eight training camps located in Darra Adamkhel where it is believed that foreign militants were providing members of the local Taliban with basic military training.[145] Potential suicide bombers were sent to South Waziristan for a further four months of training.

The TTP has often claimed responsibility, supported by videos, for killing and kidnapping hundreds of soldiers. It has been involved in high-profile terrorist attacks such as the assassination of Benazir Bhutto and the suicide attacks on Pakistan's former Interior Minister Aftab Sherpao, Asfand Yar Wali and Bashir Bilor of the Awami National Party, and many others. The TTP attempted to assassinate Prime Minister Yousuf Raza Gilani on 3 September 2008.[146] The TTP has also attacked the Inter Services Intelligence (ISI), Pakistan's premier external intelligence agency. As many as 43 persons have been beheaded by the TTP on the charge of spying. A number of foreigners have also been kidnapped by the TTP. For instance, in October 2008, Peter Stanczak, a Polish engineer working on a seismic survey for Geofizyka Kraków Ltd, was seized in the Attock district.[147] Two Chinese engineers were kidnapped by the TTP in September 2008.[148]

Many women have been charged with prostitution and beheaded. Several hundred girls' schools have been set on fire or bombed by the TTP in FATA, particularly in Swat.[149] The TTP has blown up thousands of video shops and net cafes. Barbers have been terrorized, and even kidnapped. Local and foreign NGOs have frequently been targeted. Young people have been warned not to wear western clothes, as they are considered 'un-Islamic'.

The TTP has targeted moderate and pro-government Taliban in the tribal areas. On 13 August 2008, for example, Haji Namdar, head of Amar Bil Maarouf Wa Nahi Munkar (Promotion of Virtue and Prohibition of Vice), was shot dead by a teenager at Takya Mosque in Khyber Agency; the TTP claimed responsibility for the attack.[150]

Hundreds of pro-government tribal elders have been killed by the TTP. In early 2008, when the government of Pakistan formed tribal militias (lashkars) against the TTP, the terrorist outfit kidnapped, beheaded and shot many tribal people linked to them. Faced with bombardment from aircraft and helicopter gunships and the prolonged military operation in Swat, Bajaur Agency and other parts of the tribal belt, the militants targeted the pro-government tribal elders and peace jirgas. In one such attack on an anti-Taliban jirga in Salarzai Tehsil, Bajaur Agency, on 6 November 2008, more than twenty tribal elders were killed, including Malik Fazal Karim Baro, the head of the area's tribal lashkar, and about

100 tribesmen were injured. In a similar attack on another anti-Taliban jirga in the Adezai area of Orakzai Agency, more than 110 tribal elders were killed. The militants in Chamarkand Tehsil of Bajaur Agency kidnapped eleven elders of a tribal lashkar in November 2008; eight of these were beheaded and their bodies dumped on the main road. These incidents were a clear message to the tribal people not to form lashkars against the Taliban. The TTP has also targeted the forces of peace in FATA, brutally killing 28 members of the Jandola Peace Committee in June 2008.[151] Since then there have been regular attacks on the members of peace committees.

Pakistan's Counter-Strategy against the TTP

Pakistan has adopted a combination of 'carrot and stick' and 'divide and rule' policies to contain the threat from the TTP. It has carried out significant military operations against the various sections of the TTP and entered into a number of agreements with the group to make them shun extremism. Pakistan's efforts to contain the TTP have been partially successful since locals in the FATA rose against the TTP in late 2008. Tribal militias have helped to hunt down the Taliban. Political administrations in some tribal areas have demanded that locals unite against the Taliban, and helped facilitate the process, and in other areas they have acted on their own.

In September 2008 the local population chased and killed a group of six militants who had brutally killed some eight policemen on duty at a police station in the Kingargali area of the Buner district of NWFP.[152] After that incident, the people of Buner raised a tribal lashkar to contain the activities of militants in their area. This action was followed by the people of the Maidan area in Lower Dir district, where many Taliban militants had taken refuge after escaping Pakistani military operations in Bajaur. The people united against the militants, setting up checkpoints on the main road, and managed to flush them out of the area after negotiations. Similar meetings were held in Mardan, Swabi, Hangu, Lakki Marwat and other parts of the NWFP.[153]

In the tribal areas, the first lashkar was formed in Salarzai Tehsil of Bajaur after the Taliban ambushed three tribal elders, Malik Bakhtawar Khan, Malik Shah Zarin and religious scholar Maulvi Sher Wali, on their way home after a meeting with government officials in Khar, where they pledged to raise a lashkar and sought government support for the purpose. The local tribesmen held the Taliban responsible for the killings and formed the lashkar under the leadership of Fazal Kareem Baro. The lashkar, however, was unable to flush out the militants from their stronghold in Mula Said Banda and the Darra areas of Salarzai Tehsil.

The tribesmen's initiative runs against the militant's claims that they have huge followings in areas under their control. The increasing numbers of tribal people standing up to the Taliban militants signifies that in many parts of the tribal areas people are seeking refuge from the Taliban's brutal grip. Popular support and community-based action is pivotal for Pakistan's counter-insurgency campaign in FATA. The government must encourage such uprisings against the militants by fully supporting the tribal lashkars logistically, economically and politically.

In addition the government has tried to win over TTP leaders in order to weaken it from within. This 'divide and rule' formula has successfully created rifts within the TTP. Moderate commanders of the TTP were taken into confidence, while isolating the hardliners. A peace deal in North Waziristan was struck with commander Hafiz Gul Bahadur in February 2008. Another peace deal was reached in South Waziristan with Maulvi Nazir, who assured the governor through tribal elders that he would not fight the Pakistani Army and would not allow anyone in his area to provide shelter to foreigners.[154] The peace deals created differences within the TTP, resulting in Baitullah Mehsud losing control over militants in North Waziristan. As a result, attacks on the Pakistani Army sharply declined in both North and South Waziristan during September and October 2008. Following the deadly terrorist attacks launched by the TTP in FATA, NWFP and mainland Pakistan, Operation Rah-e-Nijat (Path to Salvation) was launched in South Waziristan on 19 June 2009. It quickly yielded results and the army was able to clear 90 per cent of the area within three weeks. By capturing most of the population centres in South Waziristan and disrupting the terrorists' food supply line, the Pakistani Army busted the myth that this was a graveyard for empires and it would be a graveyard for the army.[155] The TTP reacted in desperation to the military victories and a number of indiscriminate suicide attacks were carried out during Operation Rah-e-Nijat. Despite the initial military gains in South Waziristan, however, the TTP is likely to remain a challenge for Pakistan. It has proved its resilience in the aftermath of each military operation. The outfit is adaptable and maintains second-tier leaders within its ranks to fill any slot if necessary.

The military operation in South Waziristan is more challenging for the Pakistani Army for various other reasons. Unlike their counterparts in Swat, the South Waziristani Taliban fighters have few equals in the art of mobile warfare. Some analysts attribute this to their fanaticism, ruthlessness, ability to withstand huge losses, familiarity with the terrain and mastery of the tactics and weapons of guerrilla warfare, thus making them a formidable enemy.[156] While Swat does not share a physical border with

Afghanistan, the South Waziristani Taliban is able to exploit a porous border with Afghanistan for reinforcement, and to escape Pakistan's military operations. The presence of a significant number of Punjabi Taliban and Uzbek fighters also strengthens the resolve and capabilities of the TTP in South Waziristan. With the ability to retreat strategically in South Waziristan, the TTP could prolong its guerilla warfare against the Pakistani security forces. Defeating a well-organized and brutal group like the TTP in South Waziristan will require patience, consistency and cooperation between Pakistan, Afghanistan, the US and NATO. There is certainly no quick victory and the cost to achieve it remains high.

TTP – A Long-Term Security Threat

The Taliban claims that they fight in the name of Islam; judging them by their actions and not just by their words, however, it is evident that their primary targets are ordinary Muslims, for which there is very little legitimate religious justification. Islam advocates that 'Seeking education is a duty for every Muslim male and female', but the Taliban does not seem to be convinced: some 350 schools were burnt and bombed by the Taliban in the restive Swat region between November 2007 and August 2008.[157] Since 2004 the Taliban has also been enforcing an extremely strict code of living, which has been imposed on the local population with the threat that offenders will suffer extreme forms of punishment.

Though patriotic in their rhetoric, the Pakistani Taliban poses an threat to the existence of Pakistan. They have attacked and killed thousands of Pakistani security personnel, and targeted and assassinated several Pakistani politicians, including the former Prime Minister Benazir Bhutto. Most importantly, the TTP and its affiliated groups are responsible for the deaths of thousands of Pakistani civilians in terrorist attacks. Between 2003 and 2008 casualties from Taliban-related violence numbered more than 20,000 civilians and security personnel. By comparison, Pakistani casualties during the 1965 war with its traditional rival India stood at 4,000. There is now a consensus in Pakistan that the internal threat posed by the Taliban is far greater than any external threat.

According to Maulvi Omar, the TTP's spokesman, 'this is unfortunate but we are fighting against them because they have become allies of the United States and killing their own people for dollars'.[158] It is quite obvious that the deaths of thousands of civilians in terrorist attacks launched by the TTP had nothing to do with the United States or its policies towards Pakistan. Similarly, a failed suicide bomber of the TTP justified the killing of fellow Muslims by stating, 'those who are not fighting against the government would be considered supporters of the government. They are not innocent at all if they don't come and join Taliban, they are liable to be killed, and we do not regret killing such civilians.'[159]

Internal Splits in the TTP

At the time of TTP's formation, it was predicted that the organization would fall apart within a few years. The power struggle between its various factions, opposition from the pro-government 'soft Taliban' and the TTP's brutal policies towards the local population have proved the prediction true.

In July 2008, within seven months of its inception, clashes between the pro-Baitullah Taliban and the pro-LET Taliban led to internal splits within the TTP. After the killing of Shah Khalid, the TTP in Bajaur Agency split into two factions. Four important commanders of the TTP, Maulvi Munir, Dr Abdul Wahab, Maulvi Abdul Hameed and Salar Masood, announced their resignation.[160]

In October 2008, even before celebrating its first anniversary, Baitullah Mehsud's violent policies against the Pakistani security forces, which were weakening the cause of the Afghan resistance against foreign forces, led to the TTP's second deputy leader, Hafiz Gul Bahadur, announcing his split away from the TTP.[161] This was the first major organizational blow to the TTP.

On 1 November 2008, the TTP offered a unilateral ceasefire. Talking on the telephone from an unknown location, Maulvi Omar revealed that the decision to lay down arms and hold talks with the government was taken in a meeting between Baitullah Mehsud and Taliban commanders from South and North Waziristan: 'TTP is not against Pakistan, rather, it is waging its struggle against the US imperialism'.[162]

Analysts believed that the TTP's offer to hold peace talks was a tactical move aimed at safeguarding their cadres, leaders and organizational structure, which had been heavily affected by the ongoing military offensives in FATA. The Pakistani government was warned that it should not provide the TTP with any chance to reorganize itself.

Despite all the organizational blows, the TTP poses a long-term security threat not only to Pakistan, but to regional and global peace as well. The TTP's foiled plot to launch a suicide attack in Barcelona in September 2008, and various suicide attacks in Afghanistan, is evidence of its regional and global agenda. In the past the TTP has also vowed to destroy the White House, New York and London. The TTP's increasing strength and consolidation in Pakistan would also strengthen Al Qaeda. Both of the terrorist outfits would be suitable partners in the common pursuit of global terrorism.

The TTP is pursuing its nefarious agenda of displacing the state by attempting to restrict its jurisdiction. If the government of Pakistan cannot neutralize these challenges militarily and politically, it will become increasingly irrelevant in much of what is still Pakistan today. This is the most serious challenge to post-1971 Pakistan: an armed and well-organized movement has entrenched itself in the tribal areas and now threatens to displace the Pakistani state from as much of its territory as possible. Stability and peace in Pakistan are crucial to winning the global war on terror. Unless the TTP groups are completely crushed, there will be no security for the entire region as it will remain unsafe from their violence.

In order to ensure regional security, the disruption of TTP's operations should be a top priority for regional and international counter-terrorism forces. It can be done through providing better training and the latest counter-insurgency equipment to the Pakistani Army. Pakistan needs international support in various fields to carry out its fight against this well-organized, non-state army, which poses a direct threat to all the stakeholders involved in the War on Terror.

Tehrik-e-Nifaz-e-Shariat-e-Muhammadi (TNSM)

Tehrik-e-Nifaz-e-Shariat-e-Muhammadi (Movement for Enforcement of Islamic Laws) was the first Taliban-style organization to be founded in Pakistan. Unlike the other Pakistani Taliban groups of FATA and NWFP that emerged in the aftermath of international intervention in Afghanistan in 2001, TNSM is a pre-9/11 Islamist group. Initially referred to as the 'tor patki' (Black Turban Movement), the TNSM was founded in 1992 by Sufi Muhammad, who had previously belonged to Jamaat-e-Islami (JI) Pakistan. Sufi Muhammad left the JI because he believed the existing democratic order was an 'un-Islamic system of the infidels' and supporting such a system was a great sin.[163] Sufi stated during a press interview in 1995, 'We want to see the imposition of shariah here and in the rest of the country and the rest of the world … The Jamaat-e-Islami wants to come into power in Islamabad. They are even ready to accept the American [brand of] Islam.'[164]

Members of the group are identified by their shoulder-length hair and camouflage vests worn over traditional shalwar kameez, which is the trademark of Sufi Mohammad. The TNSM views the Taliban regime in Afghanistan as an ideal system of governance: according to Sufi Muhammad, 'The *Sharia* system of governance is not currently in force anywhere in the world. Only the Taliban had enforced *Sharia* when they were in power in Afghanistan.'[165] The Swat district of the Malakand division was selected as a base area in which the ideological, political and military struggle to establish a Taliban state in Pakistan was to be conducted. The TNSM's headquarters was located at Bilal Masjid in Batkhela town of the Malakand Agency. During the time when Maulana Fazlullah was leading the TNSM, the Imam Dheri Markaz madrasa was used as the organizational headquarters.

Two Shuras, or councils, assist the head of the TNSM organizational structure.[166] Ulema Shura, with several Swati clerics, advise him on the religious policies of the group. Another Shura, known as the executive body, is the highest policy-making organ of the TNSM. The deputy leader is called the Naib Amir and there is also an official spokesman.

Ideologically, most of the TNSM supporters follow the Wahhabi brand of Islam. The motto of the organization is 'Shariah ya Shahadat' ('Islamic laws or martyrdom'). It rejects all political and religio-political parties, since they follow the Western style of democracy, and openly condones the use of force in Jihad.[167] A television interview with Sufi Muhammad after he struck a peace deal with the government in May 2009 reveals much about the ideology of TNSM. Sufi Muhammad termed democracy, socialism and fascism as un-Islamic because infidels invented them: 'I would not offer prayer behind anyone who would seek to justify democracy.'[168] This explained why he had refused to offer prayers behind Qazi Hussain Ahmad, the head of Jamaat-e-Islami (JI), or Maulana Fazlur Rahman of Jamiat Ulema-i-Islam Fazl (JUI-F): 'How can people who believe in democracy be expected to enforce the ideals of sharia.'[169] He rejects the constitution of Pakistan, claiming that there is no need for a constitution in a country in the presence of the Qur'an and Sunnah.[170] According to Sufi Muhammad's version of sharia, women are not allowed to leave their house for any reason other than to perform Haj.[171] However, a female patient was allowed to visit a male doctor to seek a cure for her ailments.

Though TNSM is mainly an Islamist outfit, a large number of communists active in Swat under the Mazdoor Kissan Party (Workers and Peasants Party) have attempted to penetrate the outfit. Where successful, the massive influx of communists has made the TNSM more like a movement of the common man against the ruling elite, which has failed to provide social justice and services. In some areas at least, it has 'pitted landless tenants against wealthy landlords and there are reports that big landowners were forced to leave the valley'.[172] The militants organized peasants into armed gangs that became their shock troops. The approach allowed the Taliban to offer economic spoils to people frustrated by lax and corrupt government even as the militants imposed a strict form of Islam through terror and intimidation. The leadership and cadre base of the TNSM consists in large part of men who have worked or continue to work in shops, or as day labourers, hawkers and peddlers. The TNSM top leader Maulana Fazlullah, for example, was a chair-lift operator. Unlike other Pakistani Taliban groups, the TNSM is not organized on a tribal basis. Most of the militants linked to the TNSM belong to poor families and have been waging a war against the 'Haves'. For that very reason, when Sufi Muhammad tried to persuade the local militants to lay down their arms after the Swat Peace Agreement in April 2009, they simply refused. Most of the foot soldiers of the Swat Taliban movement were afraid that if they lay down arms and returned to their areas, the powerful landlords would try to take revenge because the Taliban had forced them to leave the area.[173] This is not to say that the TNSM aims to empower the marginalized groups of the Swat valley. None of the group's demands are for the development of infrastructure, employment, conservation of natural resources or the development of socio-cultural institutions such as education, health care and transportation. Sufi Mohammad simply capitalized on the frustration of the people to launch his movement for the promulgation of his sharia code.

The movement launched by Sufi Muhammad was non-violent in nature, but after a time he lost control and the movement turned to violence in 1994. Sufi Muhammad had ordered his followers to stage a peaceful sit-in in Malakand, but some TNSM members blocked the Mingora–Peshawar road for seven days, cutting off the Swat valley from the rest of Pakistan.[174] The group started kidnapping government officials and even killed Badiuz Zaman, a Member of the NWFP Assembly. They also occupied the Kanju airport and other government buildings. Sufi Muhammad eventually persuaded his fighters to pull back from confrontation with the security forces. He was flown by military helicopter to everywhere in Swat and Malakand where his black-turbaned followers had blocked roads and taken positions on hilltops to fight the troops.[175] He then delivered speeches from the helicopter, directing his men to stop fighting and return to their villages. The FC also freed a number of government officials, including judges, policemen and district administration officials, who had been taken hostage by the TNSM fighters in Swat's Matta town. In an interview with a private television channel, Sufi Muhammad stated that he was opposed to the members of his organization resorting to killing people: 'They took these actions without informing me and after I came to know of them, I prevented them from doing so.'[176]

It would be incorrect, however, to regard Maulana Sufi Muhammad as a completely non-violent preacher.[177] In 2001 there were numerous reports that he had succeeded in assembling a group of around 5,000 young men from his native area of Malakand and convinced them to join the Taliban ranks in Afghanistan through his fiery speeches.[178] Sufi led thousands of his followers to Afghanistan via Bajaur Agency with an array of weapons, including swords, axes and bazookas. To their total surprise, the Taliban refused to welcome them and asked them to return to Pakistan after handing over their weapons.[179] Meanwhile a series of US air strikes against Al Qaeda and their hosts, the Taliban, were starting to cause heavy casualties. The Taliban, who had some sort of plan to escape the bombardments, disappeared and abandoned the TNSM cadres. Many were killed or seriously injured. Most were arrested by the new Afghan government.[180] Sufi Muhammad returned to face the question of how teenagers with no prior military training were expected to go into battle against the most powerful military machine in the world. Fearing an intense backlash, he was 'arrested' at his own request in November 2001 after returning from Afghanistan.[181] With Sufi Muhammad in jail, TNSM's capabilities declined significantly. Most of his supporters went underground after the Musharraf regime banned the TNSM on 12 January 2002, along with four other Jihadi and sectarian organizations.

There was a strong belief among the people of the Swat and Malakand districts that the earthquake in October 2005 was a punishment for their misdeeds. Maulana Fazlullah established an FM radio station at Imam-dairi, a small town in Swat district, from where he started to deliver teachings on the Qur'an and persuaded people to destroy their musical appliances, arguing that listening to music and performing other sinful acts caused the earthquake. According to the broadcasts, if believers did not give up their musical and electronics equipment, it would invite the anger of God.[182] Thousands voluntarily destroyed their electronic goods in just a few days and this chain of events has continued with only short intervals in between. Since the volunteers of the TNSM were at the forefront of the humanitarian relief work, the popularity of the group once again increased. [183] In the process of helping the quake-affected people, the TNSM re-established its stronghold in Malakand, Swat and Bajaur and started mobilizing its activists. However, unlike other banned militant organizations that deemed it necessary to rename themselves before resurfacing under new identities, the TNSM leadership decided not to abandon its previous identity.[184]

The War on Terror in Afghanistan, its spillover effects, and the emergence and rise of various Taliban groups in FATA inspired the TNSM to resort to violent tactics in order to achieve its objectives. A US Predator missile strike in Bajaur Agency on 30 October 2006, in which Maulana Fazlullah, then acting head of the TNSM, lost his younger brother Maulana Liaquat, a key leader of the organization who used to run the seminary, was the incident that caused the radical transformation of the TNSM from an extremist group into a militant group.[185] Three sons of Maulana Liaquat were also killed, along with 80 other madrasa students. A few hours after the missile attack, Maulana Faqir Muhammad announced that the deaths of the innocent madrasa students would be avenged by carrying out suicide bombings against Pakistani troops. A week later a suicide bomber struck at the Punjab Regimental Centre training school at Dargai. The attack, which killed 45 Army recruits, was subsequently claimed by the TNSM.[186] There has since been a significant resurgence in the activities of the TNSM, mostly targeting the country's security forces.

In the aftermath of Operation Silence in July 2007, the TNSM vowed to avenge the killing of 'innocent students and teachers' at Islamabad's Red Mosque. The Swat region, the stronghold of the TNSM, became a source of manpower for various terrorist groups.[187] The group established links with the Taliban factions of FATA to fight against a common enemy: the state and the security forces of Pakistan. In December 2007, with the formation of the TTP to unite all the scattered Taliban groups, the TNSM leaders were given key designations in the new organization: Fazlullah was designated as the General Secretary and Maulvi Faqir Muhammad was selected as the Deputy of TTP. By merging the TNSM with the TTP, Fazlullah was obliged to allow Taliban of Waziristan, Bajaur and other agencies to establish footholds in Malakand Agency. However, it must be noted that the mainstream TNSM led by Sufi Muhammad and the TTP are two entirely different outfits with different agendas and strategies. Fazlullah established links with the TTP at the time when he was the self-proclaimed head of TNSM. It is not clear whether Sufi Muhammad approved Fazlullah's decision to make the TNSM a part of the TTP. Because Sufi was then under arrested, he was distancing himself from the activities of his son-in-law, Fazlullah. While in confinement, Sufi directed his followers to lay down arms.[188] In March 2008 Sufi Muhammad denounced Fazlullah's terrorist activities in Swat Valley:

> They are doing no service to Islam by carrying out suicide attacks but rather damaging the cause for the enforcement of the Shariah in the Malakand region. We [TNSM] never intended to pick up arms for the enforcement of Shariah. We can't even think of killing people for the purpose. Peaceful struggle (within the parameters of the Constitution) had been our policy, and I will clearly tell the people to support peace overtures.[189]

Sufi called Fazlullah a 'rebel' and urged people to abandon him.[190] Further, Fazlullah was not a formally appointed head of the TNSM after the arrest of Sufi Muhammad. It was Maulana Muhammad Alam who was designated as acting chief of the TNSM by Sufi Muhammad. Fazlullah took control of the violent faction of the TNSM in the absence of Sufi Muhammad and linked up with the TTP and other terrorist outfits. Formal links between the TTP and the mainstream TNSM are not substantiated. There were clashes between the two outfits after Sufi Muhammad signed a peace deal with the government to end militancy in the region. According to the deal, Sufi Muhammad had to persuade Swati Taliban to lay down their arms, and in return the government announced the enforcement of Sharia in Malakand through the Nizam-e-Adl Regulation, approved by the National Assembly on 13 April 2009. However, Sufi Muhammad failed to disarm the Taliban.[191] Instead the TTP took advantage of the peace deal and covertly reorganized, starting a three-pronged assault on the state.[192] First, the Swat chapter of the TTP started large-scale recruitment and built bunkers in different parts of Swat. They then, in line with the Taliban alliances in FATA and the rest of Pakistan, reorganized their forces and and started extending their assaults from the north to the south of the NWFP. The Taliban's onslaught on Buner and Dir was part of this strategy. The Taliban next started consolidating their positions by securing control of strategic passes and side valleys of Swat, Buner, Shangla and Dir.[193] Sufi Muhammad attempted to persuade the militants to adhere to the peace deal, but the TTP threatened to assassinate him if he insisted that the Taliban should lay down their arms.[194] The differences between the two outfits culminated in violent clashes: at least two people were killed and another injured on 19 April 2009 in a gunfight between the Taliban and the operatives of TNSM in the Mamond Tehsil of Bajaur Agency.[195] Rizwan, a TNSM leader and son of Sufi Muhammad, described the incident as the result of a misunderstanding.

Before the TTP moved into Swat there was no evidence of foreign fighters in that area except for the presence of Kashmiri jihad-related mainland groups. Taking advantage of the peace agreement, the TTP brought in foreign fighters. It was the TTP, not TNSM, that vowed to welcome Osama in Swat.[196] There is no evidence to suggest any links between Al Qaeda and the TNSM, whose leadership never endorsed Al Qaeda's activities in Pakistan: in 2005 Sufi Muhammad said that what Al Qaeda was doing in Pakistan was *Haram* (forbidden).[197] But the TTP's links with the global terror outfit are not a secret. The events that unfolded after the peace deal of April 2009 proved that the Pakistani Taliban is divided.

The agreement reached between the TNSM, TTP and the government covered fourteen points:

1. Sharia law would be imposed in Swat, including the whole Malakand division.
2. The Army would gradually withdraw security forces from the region.
3. The government and the Taliban would exchange prisoners.
4. The Taliban would recognize the writ of the government and cooperate with the local police.
5. The Taliban would halt attacks on barbers and music shops.
6. The Taliban would not display weapons in public.
7. The Taliban would surrender heavy weapons such as rocket launchers and mortars to the government.
8. The Taliban would not operate any training camps.
9. The Taliban would denounce suicide attacks.
10. A ban would be placed on raising private militias.
11. The Taliban would cooperate with the government to vaccinate children against polio and other diseases.
12. The madrasa of Maulana Fazlullah in Imam Dherai would be turned into an Islamic University.
13. Only licensed FM radio stations would be allowed to operate in the region.
14. The Taliban would allow women to work without any fear.[198]

The government kept its word by imposing Nizam-e-Adl on the Malakand division.[199] The TNSM and the TTP, however, did not fulfill their side of the agreement. Attacks on security forces continued and this highlighted the futility of dealing with men who could not be trusted. There were indications that Sufi Muhammad was under immense pressure from the more hard-line militants, led by his son-in-law, to increase demands on the government. The truce was sabotaged from within and did not last for more than three months. The government had to change tactics and resort to all-out military action to stop the Taliban advancing towards settled areas of Pakistan.

Muqami Tehrik-e-Taliban

Muqami Tehrik-e-Taliban (Local Movement of Taliban) was formed on 30 June 2008 by two major Taliban militant groups operating in the North and South Waziristan Agencies. The declared objective of the Muqami Tehrik-e-Taliban is to merge their forces and effectively coordinate their efforts in fighting the ISAF-NATO and US troops in Afghanistan.[200] They also agreed that they would fight the Pakistani security forces if they were attacked. Hafiz Gul Bahadur was appointed the Supreme Commander, with Mullah Nazir as the Deputy Commander, while Mufti Abu Haroon was nominated as the official spokesman.[201] The militant group maintains affiliations with the Mullah Omar-led Afghan Taliban, the Tanzim Al Qaeda al-Jihad, the Libyan Islamic Fighting Group (LIFG) and the Islamic Jihad Union. Muqami Tehrik-e-Taliban's operations are presently confined to the Wazir tribal territory in North and South Waziristan agencies, although it is also active in hit-and-run operations in the adjoining provinces of Khost, Paktia and Paktika in Afghanistan.

The Muqami Tehrik-e-Taliban is ideologically akin to the Afghan Taliban. Both Hafiz and Nazir believe in the enforcement of Taliban-style Sharia in Pakistan, and have imposed Taliban Sharia laws in the areas under their control, but neither is attempting to Talibanize the NWFP and other agencies of FATA.

The Supreme Commander and head of the organization, Hafiz Gul Bahadur, is also supreme commander of the North Waziristani Taliban. The Deputy Commander, Mullah Nazir, belongs to the Wana area of South Waziristan Agency and is also supreme commander of the Ahmadzai Wazir Taliban. Both Hafiz and Nazir enjoy extensive support among their respective tribes and the Taliban rank and file.

The Taliban of the Ahmadzai Wazir tribe and Uthmanzai Wazir tribe had been operating in the South and North Waziristan Agencies, respectively, since 2003, although there was a lack of coherence in their policies as well as a characteristic absence of coordination between the two. Ahmadzai Wazir Taliban, led by Nek Muhammad,[202] was the first group to give refuge to foreign militants, including members of Al Qaeda, between 2002 and 2004. The subsequent military operations by the Pakistani security forces in 2003 and 2004 led to Al Qaeda and its affiliated foreign militant groups moving their infrastructure and forces to North Waziristan. Since mid-2004 Al Qaeda and foreign militants have been able to carve out a semi-sanctuary in North Waziristan with the Uthmanzai and Daur tribes. Military operations by the Pakistani government against the two tribes in 2005 and 2006 failed to dislodge foreign militants from North Waziristan. An attempt to solve the problem through political means resulted in the signing of the North Waziristan Accord in September 2006, which also failed to evict foreign militants from the area.

Similarly, historical jealousies and rivalries between various tribes in North and South Waziristan agencies continue to dilute any chances of coordination among the various Pakistani Taliban groups divided on a tribal basis. In March and April 2007 the eviction of militants belonging to the Islamic Movement of Uzbekistan (IMU) from Ahmadzai Wazir tribal territory by the Wazir tribe and Taliban led by Mullah Nazir became a bone of contention when the Uzbek militants took refuge with Baitullah Mehsud and used the Mehsud tribal territory to conduct attacks on Ahmadzai tribesmen. This infuriated both Nazir and the Ahmadzai tribesmen, who demanded that Baitullah evict the Uzbek militants.

Mullah Omar and the senior Afghan Taliban leadership, which had always wanted the Pakistani Taliban to concentrate their energies in Afghanistan and shun activities in Pakistan, resented the formation of the TTP. Mullah Omar subsequently disowned Baitullah Mehsud.[203] However, Baitullah Mehsud continued strengthening and consolidating the TTP. Given the Afghan Taliban's disapproval of the TTP, Hafiz Gul Bahadur and other prominent Taliban commanders distanced themselves from Baitullah and his TTP.

Another reason for Hafiz to distance himself from the TTP was the peace negotiations with the Pakistani government held between December 2007 and February 2008. Finally, in January 2008, both Hafiz and the government were able to revive The North Waziristan Accord was revived with minor changes in January 2008 and was signed on 17 February. The government suffered a critical setback in North Waziristan Agency in June 2009, however, when the Taliban formally scrapped the peace deal.[204] Hafiz Gul Bahadur, previously known as pro-government, termed this move 'a protest against the US drone attacks'.

Despite the peace accord, the two sides never enjoyed cordial relations and a lack of trust has always been apparent. The militants were running the tribal region based solely on what they wanted, leaving little space for the government and the law-enforcement agencies. In fact, the militants in North Waziristan had already started targeting the security forces before they formally scrapped the peace deal. During an attack on a military convoy in the second week of June, for example, students and teachers from the Cadet College at Razmak were kidnapped by Baitullah's men within Frontier Region (FR) Bannu, an area that Hafiz Gul Bahadur considers as part of his tribal fiefdom. It was suspected that militants loyal to Hafiz Gul Bahadur cooperated with Baitullah's fighters in the kidnapping.[205] An attack on a military convoy on 28 June claimed the lives of 30 Pakistani soldiers.[206]

On 30 June 2009 the government finally responded to the terrorists' provocations by launching air strikes against suspected positions of the

Hafiz Gul Bahadur-led Taliban in North Waziristan.[207] Hundreds of Utmanzai tribal families started migrating to relative safety in towns such as
Bannu, Lakki Marwat and Peshawar. Some of the families living in border
villages, such as Madakhel, Dattakhel and Lowara Mandi, even crossed
into the Urgoon area of neighbouring Afghanistan, where an Afghan official welcomed the displaced tribal families and gave each $300.[208]

Differences between the TTP and Muqami Taliban

From the formation of the TTP Baitullah Mehsud continually tried to mo-
nopolize power in the FATA and NWFP by eliminating any Taliban group or
militant leader intending to operate independently of the TTP. Fighters
loyal to Baitullah made multiple attacks on Mullah Nazir and two of his
close aides,,Commander Khanan and Metha Khan,[209] both of whom were
eventually killed in 2008.[210] Mullah Nazir himself faced several attacks, including a foiled suicide attack at his office in Wana. The killing of Nazir's
close aides generated fear within the Ahmadzai Wazir tribe, who understood the ramifications of what would happen if the Uzbeks and their local
supporters returned to the Wazir tribal area in the event of Nazir's death.

   Baitullah Mehsud also increased his activities in the adjoining North
Waziristan Agency. To counter these, on 30 June 2008 Hafiz Gul Bahadur
and Mullah Nazir announced the merger of their two Taliban groups (Ahmadzai Wazir and Uthmanzai Wazir) to form the Muqami Tehrik-e-
Taliban. According to Sadia Sulaiman, the formation of the Bahadur-Nazir
alliance could be described as a 'Waziri alliance' since both Nazir and Bahadur belong to the dominant Wazir tribe, which nearly encircles the
Mehsud tribe on three sides in Waziristan.[211] Mullah Nazir stated that the
group had been formed to 'defend the Wazir Tribe's interests in North and
South Waziristan'.[212] A tribal *jirga* of the Ahmadzai Wazir tribe later rati-
fied the alliance agreement, which according to them was aimed at forg-
ing unity against Mehsud.[213]

   While both Nazir and Bahadur are committed to attacks on the ISAF-
NATO and US presence in Afghanistan, both disapprove of the TTP's terrorist attacks in Pakistan.[214] This stance conforms to the broader policy of
the Afghan Taliban, who have always advised the Pakistani Taliban to shun
fighting Pakistani security forces and focus their resources on
Afghanistan.[215] However, some Taliban militants have recently moved
closer to Al Qaeda, which advocates conducting terrorist attacks against
the Pakistani government and staging global jihad.

Muqami Taliban's Sources of Finance

There is little documented evidence regarding the source of finance of the Muqami Tehrik-e-Taliban. One source states that the Taliban raise considerable amounts of money through levying taxes in the region. After signing the North Waziristan Peace Agreement in September 2006, one of the local Taliban's first steps was to levy 'taxes' in North and South Waziristan agencies and impose harsh penalties for various offenses. A pamphlet issued by the Shura (consultative council) of the Taliban of NWA was widely circulated throughout the Waziristan region.[216] This contained a 'tax schedule' under which every ten-wheeler truck entering the Waziristan region was required to pay Rs1,500 (US$25) for allowing them six-month road access, while six-wheeler trucks were asked to pay Rs1,000 (US$17) twice a year. Similarly, petrol pump owners were required to pay Rs5,000 (US$ 84) to the Taliban Shura every six months. The 'tax' is described as a 'donation' in the pamphlet, but there is no mention of how this money would be used.

Other sources of finances include levying taxes as protection money on timber and goods passing through North Waziristan en route to Afghanistan. There are also reports that the drug traffickers also pay protection money to get a safe passage through North Waziristan.

The Muqami Tehrik-e-Taliban leaders are known to provide semi-sanctuary to Al Qaeda and other foreign militant organizations. Hafiz Gul Bahadur and Mullah Nazir maintain close contact with the Al Qaeda leadership, which helps fund the Taliban movement as well as supplying terrorism know-how. Many expatriate tribesmen from North and South Waziristan working in the Gulf region send remittances to their families in the twin agencies; some of these are also Taliban sympathizers who send finances to the movement.[217]

The Operational Capabilities of Muqami Taliban

The Muqami Tehrik-e-Taliban is believed to be the single largest Taliban militant group in FATA and NWFP, rivalling the TTP in size. The fact that its leadership is host to Al Qaeda and abides by the Afghan Taliban's directives, however, has given it an advantage in access to IED technology and finance, making it stronger militarily than the TTP. Similarly, since it controls the entire border region adjoining Afghanistan, the TTP militants have to cross Wazir tribal territory to conduct cross-border attacks. This provides the Muqami Tehrik-e-Taliban with some control over the TTP's actions. There is support for the Muqami Tehrik-e-Taliban in both North and South Waziristan agencies. Similarly, there are considerable numbers of Wazir tribesmen living in the adjoining settled districts of NWFP. Some of these settlers are sympathizers of the Taliban movement and provide political, moral, financial and material support and manpower to the Muqami Tehrik-e-Taliban.

Most operations conducted by Muqami Tehrik-e-Taliban militants are hit-and-run attacks employing small arms and IEDs. Militants infiltrate the adjoining provinces of Khost, Paktia and Paktika at night or use unfrequented passages along the rugged Pak-Afghan border to conduct an attack and retreat immediately. They do not often engage in pitched battles, but attack in small numbers and disperse quickly. Their tactics are mainly centred on guerrilla warfare using small arms, rocket attacks, IEDs and suicide attacks. The training is mainly conducted in temporary or makeshift camps across the entire Waziristan region, and is limited to a few weeks or days since the tribesmen are already adept at using weapons.

The selected targets include US and ISAF-NATO troops, installations, Afghan security forces, pro-government tribal elders in Pakistan and alleged 'spies' working for the US forces in Afghanistan or Pakistan. There were reports of attacks on Pakistani security forces and their infrastructure in the wake of popular anger over the US drone strikes in North Waziristan.

Pakistan has viewed both Mullah Nazir and Hafiz Gul Bahadur favourably since both persuaded their groups not to carry out attacks in Pakistan or to Talibanize the NWFP. The peace agreements signed with both Wazir groups – the April 2004 Shakai Agreement and the September 2006 North Waziristan Agreement – were scrapped by the militants in June 2009 after US drone strikes targeting Mullah Nazir and other commanders turned Muqami Taliban against the Pakistani government and security forces.

Punjabi Taliban

The presence of Punjabi Taliban in the Waziristan region was reported in March and April 2007, when they helped Mullah Nazir to evict Uzbek militants of the Islamic Movement of Uzbekistan (IMU) from the Ahmadzai Wazir tribal territory. The IMU militants had started interfering in tribal affairs, local customs and traditions, and were involved in the targeted killing of tribal elders; they also killed some Arab militants who happened to be close aides of Nazir.

According to reports, the Punjabi Taliban mainly comprises members of mainland Pakistani groups and splinter or breakaway factions from

Kashmiri groups. These include Harkat-ul-Jihadi-e-Islami (HUJI), Harkat-ul-Mujahideen (HUM), Jamiatul Furqan (also known as Maulana Abdul Jabbar), a splinter faction of Jaish-e-Muhammad (JEM), and breakaway individuals of Lashkar-e-Tayyaba. The Punjabi Taliban is estimated to constitute about 2,000 people and most come from Rahim Yar Khan, Lahore, Multan, Sadiqabad, Bahawalpur, Dera Ghazi Khan and other parts of the southern and northern Punjab province.[218] They pay much higher rents to the locals for their houses and shops, and have started businesses mostly related to the food and pharmaceutical industries. It is claimed that 95 per cent of the Punjabi Taliban speak fluent Pushtu, the local language, even though it is not their native language. In some ways they are more lethal than the Taliban of South Waziristan and other tribal regions.[219] Trained by Al Qaeda, they pre-date the Taliban in the craft of terrorism and have enjoyed the patronage of the Pakistani state in waging a proxy war in Indian-held Kashmir.

The leader of HUJI, Qari Saifullah Akhtar, was linked to Al Qaeda and Mullah Omar, the leader of the Afghan Taliban, during Taliban rule in Afghanistan during the 1990s. Qari's fighters fought alongside and trained the Taliban in camps in Kandahar, Kabul and Khost. HUJI joined Osama bin Laden's International Islamic Front upon its formation in 1998. After the Taliban regime was ousted from Afghanistan, HUJI was dislodged from its base and its militants were scattered across Pakistan. Some settled in Waziristan, while others sought safe haven in the NWFP to continue training for raids in Kashmir.

Rashid Rauf, who was behind the foiled plot to blow up aircraft over the Atlantic Ocean in August 2006, was a member of Jamiatul Furqan. He escaped during an appearance in court, but was later killed along with Abu Zubair al-Masri, an Al Qaeda operative, in a Predator drone strike in the Mir Ali area of North Waziristan Agency on 22 November 2008.[220]

In another US Predator drone strike twelve members belonging to Al-Badr, a Kashmiri militant group with close ties to Jamaat-e-Islami (JI) and Hizb-e-Islami-Hikmatyar (HIG), were reported killed and fourteen were wounded on 13 September 2008 in North Waziristan Agency.[221]

Breakaway elements of Lashkar-e-Tayyaba (LET) have been operating in FATA and Afghanistan. In an interview with the Pakistani journalist Saleem Shahzad in November 2007, a former LET militant operating in the Pak-Afghan border region stated that

> In 2003, a gathering in Muredkey [the LET's Pakistani headquarters] was an eye-opener to sincere jihadis. Hafiz Mohammed Saeed [chief of the LET] introduced us to one Abdullah, a person wearing

a prayer cap and a small beard. He addressed the gathering and made the point that the Kashmiri jihad could not achieve its objectives and that it was a lame duck. He advised the mujahideen to sit quietly at home until new circumstances developed. This sort of advice turned people into our [Taliban] camp.[222]

Another splinter group of LET, the Shah Khalid group, was very active in the Mohmand Agency of FATA until July 2008, when Muslim Khan, alias Shah Khalid, and his deputy Maulana Obaidullah were killed along with dozens of fighters by Omar Khalid, the head of the Bajaur chapter of the TTP.[223] The Shah Khalid group was solely focused on waging 'jihad' in Afghanistan and avoided attacking Pakistani security forces. Omar Khalid wanted Shah Khalid to be subservient to him in the region, but the latter refused. The resulting fighting led to the elimination of the entire Shah Khalid group from Mohmand Agency.

The Punjabi Taliban was initially scattered throughout the Wazir areas of North and South Waziristan agencies, but they later spread into the Mehsud tribe's territory as well. There are reports that significant numbers are concentrated in the Shawal Valley bordering Afghanistan, where they were able to establish their infrastructure in mid-2008.

When asked to explain the goals, objectives and motives of the outfit, a member of Punjabi Taliban explained that the violence perpetuated by the outfit was a continuation of the Jihad waged against Russia, and now directed towards America. He confidently stated that the Jihadi forces could not be eliminated. In reply to why the Pakistani Army is now a target of the Jihadi forces, given their former good relations, especially during the period of the Russian invasion, he asserted that it has also lost its 'Islamic identity' since the operation against the Red Mosque. The army killed hundreds of children and 'most of the students who were killed in Operation Red Mosque came from earthquake affected areas'.[224] The Pakistami Taliban thus see themselves as agents for revenge.

When challenged with the notion that most Islamic scholars do not support violence, the interviewee explicitly denied this, saying that the government hand-picked the clerics who issued the Fatwas against suicide attacks, so explaining their lack of credence. He argued that the army has lost the confidence of the mainstream Ulema, especially after the Red Mosque incident. Apparently, the army disregarded the potential for a peaceful solution between the Ghazi brothers (the Red Mosque clerics) and the Deobandi Ulema. This widened the rift between the Ulema and the army. Footage of the Red Mosque operation and of other military operations in FATA has been made into a series of recruitment videos. Young boys are sent to the main training centre in Kari Kot, South Waziristan, and instructed how the Pakistani army and government are now mere puppets controlled by the American government. This has served as the main means of recruitment.

Questioned about the infiltration of foreign fighters, especially from Bangladesh, he said that the Bangladeshis enter Pakistan either through the Tableeghi Jamat platform or with the help of an ethnic political party of Karachi. While people entering through the former route tend to end up joining the Jihad in Afghanistan, the latter fight in Pakistan. He also stated that the Taliban has no presence in South Punjab, but the US, Hindus and the Zionists are conspiring to seize the uranium in Dera Ghazi Khan, and need an excuse to enter that sensitive area.

In reply to a question about whether there were any possible solutions to the instability in Pakistan, exacerbated by the violence perpetuated by the Punjabi Taliban, he claimed that American influence in Pakistan had to decrease substantially because, in his opinion, it was always the US that sabotaged peace efforts. As a sovereign state, Pakistan should determine its policies independently. Although he conceded that no single political or religious-political party can resolve the country's current problems, the government should listen more to the Ulema-e-Deoband (Scholars of the Deobandi sect), whom the Jihadi leadership hold in high regard, instead of continuing to harass and alienate them.

Tehreek Lashkar-e-Islam (LI)

Tehreek Lashkar-e-Islam (Army of Islam, or Horde of Islam) started its activities from tehsil (sub-district) Bara in the Khyber Agency of FATA. Its headquarters, first established in Bara, were demolished in a military operation against LI in June 2008. LI's other important bases were located in the Akkakhel, Nala-Malikdin Khel and Shalobar areas of Bara. Khyber Agency, LI's stronghold, is of high strategic value for Pakistan and the coalition forces in Afghanistan. The main artery connecting Peshawar to Kabul passes through the Khyber Pass. Furthermore, the US military sends 75 per cent of its supplies, including 40 per cent of its fuel, for the Afghan war through or over Pakistan. Under normal circumstances about 300 trucks with supplies for Western forces travel through the Khyber Pass crossing at Torkham every day, compared with about 100 through the Chaman crossing.

Tehreek Lashkar-e-Islam is also known as the Mangal Bagh group. The locals in Khyber Agency refer to the LI as 'Tanzeem'. The organization does not maintain any website. Founded by Mufti Munir Shakir of Karak district, the LI traces its roots to sectarian differences with the Barelvi sect in Khyber Agency. Both groups engaged in a vicious propaganda war against each other through makeshift FM stations, resulting in violent clashes between their followers in 2005, which led to the creation of organized militias (the Barelvis are led by Pir Saif-u-Rehman). The LI also engaged in pitch battles with another Deobandi organization, Ansar-ul-Islam. A fragile peace descended upon Khyber after the expulsion of Munir Shakir and Pir Saif-u-Rehman. The LI resumed and intensified its activities under Mangal Bagh, extending its war to include drug traffickers, smugglers and kidnappers as a means of winning popular support. Mangal Bagh's leadership provided a new momentum to Lashkar-e-Islam and it soon grew more militant and powerful. Lashkar-e-Islam came to prominence in April 2008 when it tried to extend its control from its base in the Bara area to the Jamrud region of Khyber Agency. The town of Bara soon became a battleground between Lashkar-e-Islam and Ansar-ul-Islam. Mangal Bagh forced the political administration of Khyber to abandon the Bara subdivision in early 2008 and a military operation was launched against both outfits in July 2008. The LI, however, managed to survive, since Mangal Bagh had left the area and strategically decided not to offer any resistance to government forces. Military action was suspended after the Bara region had been cleared of the militants linked to LI and AI. Soon after, however, Mangal Bagh returned to Bara from Tirah and resumed his activities.

The LI tends to portray itself as a religious- cum- social organization. The LI leadership has always vowed to eliminate social evils from society and not to involve itself in fighting against Pakistani security forces: . Interestingly, the LI's objectives are totally different from the TTP's. Lashkar-e-Islam's manifesto puts a complete ban on the entry of local and foreign terrorists in Khyber Aagency.[225] In April 2008, *Khabrain*, an Urdu daily newspaper, published the details of the Lashkar-e-Islam agenda for the Khyber Agency, which covered 26 points for implementation:[226]

1. Eradicating all *shirk* [polytheism/idolatry], *bid'at* [innovation in Islam] and all un-Islamic practices from Khyber Agency.
2. Permitting only Islamic-style graves.
3. Enforcing a total ban on the activities of local and foreign terrorists in Khyber Agency.
4. Providing [only] justified assistance to the security forces [of Pakistan] deployed in the area.

5. Banning any kinds of bribes to and from the mujahideen of Lashkar-e-Islam.
6. Punishing any activity disturbing the peace without Lashkar-e-Islam permission; punishment will be as per tribal norms.
7. Committing to defend the geographical and ideological frontiers of Pakistan.
8. Committing to prevent crime and punish criminals.
9. Enforcing a total ban on the sale of wine, on gambling, on counterfeit currency, on heroin factories, etc.
10. Enforcing a total ban on paid killers and kidnappers in the region.
11. Enforcing a ban on thieves, theft, and stolen cars.
12. Abolishing interest/usury in business transactions.
13. Forcing fugitives who reside in Khyber Agency to behave properly and to be accountable to the local residents.
14. Rehabilitating all mosques in Khyber Agency.
15. Committing to protect teachers, male and female students, doctors, and ulema.
16. Committing to resolve land disputes and ensure no land goes uncultivated.
17. Enforcing a total ban on non-shari'a practices such as magic, charms, etc.
18. Committing to ensure absolute peace.
19. Committing to ensure that women are modestly dressed according to Islamic norms when attending school, and to spread education among the people.
20. Committing to ensure collective prayers are offered after the *azaan* [call for prayer] is sounded.
21. Protecting women's rights and resolution of marriage-related matters as per sharia or tribal practices.
22. Committing to total eradication of un-Islamic practices during marriage ceremonies, such as music and celebratory firing into the air.
23. Banning women from going to mountains to collect wood for fuel; violators will be fined 10,000 rupees.
24. Banning women from going to doctors or hospitals unaccompanied by a male relation.
25. Enforcing the compulsory wearing of caps, according to tribal traditions.
26. Banning the sheltering of rapists, and totally banning homosexuals, in Khyber Agency.

The Lashkar-e-Islam established its fiefdom in Bara where it enforced its own version of the Islamic justice system. In a bid to expand their influence across the Khyber region, its fighters fought with Kokikhel tribesmen in Jamrud and Landikotal, which led to the closure of the Peshawar-Torkham highway between Pakistan and Afghanistan for four days. This highway is a main supply route for Coalition Forces in Afghanistan. After establishing its stronghold in parts of the Khyber Agency, dozens of Lashkar-e-Islam activists with rockets and other heavy weapons attacked Shaikhan village in the suburbs of Peshawar, killing ten people.[227]

In mid-2008 Lashkar-e-Islam militants appeared on the streets of Peshawar and kidnapped sixteen Christians in broad daylight. Its efforts to extend its control beyond Khyber led the Pakistani government to launch a military operation against the outfit. Many of its offices were raided and its hideouts were demolished. As a result, state control was restored in the Bara area as well as in the Tirah Valley of Khyber.

Although Mangal Bagh stated that the group was not to extend beyond Khyber, it seems likely that if the LI succeeds in getting rid of its opponents in Khyber, it will divert its attention to the other parts of the agency that are currently out of its reach.

Lashkar-e-Islam maintains almost the same organizational structure as the TTP. The Shura (Consultative Committee) is the supreme body of the organization and the central leader of the organization is called Amir. The Shura also nominates senior commanders as representatives of different areas. The financial department is termed the Bait-ul-Maal and a spokesman makes public the official statements of the outfit.

The Shura undertakes most of the policy decisions. Under the leadership of Mangal Bagh, however, the command structure was centralized. Mangal has maintained a strong authoritarian role in organizational matters.

Lashkar-e-Islam adheres to the Deobandi school of thought. Commitment to this ideology has led the LI leadership to undertake 'Jihad' against the non-Deobandis, who were referred to as evil powers by Mufti Munir Shakir, the founder of LI. Mangal Bagh and his supporters are opposed to moderate Sufi Pirs as they consider most of them exploiters. However, the LI's wider campaign against criminals, drug traffickers and smugglers is motivated less by ideology and more by the financial rewards from charging the locals for providing security from the local criminals. Therefore, the LI cannot be termed as a 'Taliban outfit' in the political sense.

Mangal Bagh has always claimed that the army and the paramilitary forces are like brothers to him. This was demonstrated when, even though

Pakistani forces destroyed their compounds, houses and seminaries during the military operation in Khyber Agency in July 2008, the LI militants remained underground and did not fire a single shot. The outfit has shown no flexibility, however, over the strict code of conduct introduced by the Shura. Within a few years the LI rid Bara of drug-traffickers, gamblers, kidnappers, car-snatchers and other criminals, a task previously impossible for the government.

Mufti Munir Shakir belonged to the Karak district and arrived in the Khyber Agency in 2003 after he was expelled from Kurram Agency because of his controversial views about those belonging to other sects. In February 2006, following bloody clashes with Ansar-ul-Islam, Muft Munir Shakir was persuaded by the government to leave the Bara area of Khyber.

Haji Amir Gul was appointed as the first Amir, but he resigned after ten days and was succeeded by Haji Gul Shah Kukikhel on 12 December 2005. Concerns were raised about his inefficiency and laziness, however, and he was forced to resign. Mangal Bagh succeeded him on 22 December and led the organisation for almost three years, preaching to the people on his private FM radio channel every day throughout this time.[228]

Mangal Bagh attended lessons with Ulema (religious scholars) but did not acquire any formal education,[229] although he is able to read Urdu newspapers and applications from those seeking his help.[230] He is articulate and able to quote from the Qur'an and Ahadith to make his point. According to those who listened to his nightly radio speeches, he speaks in a learned manner and at length.[231] Mangal Bagh belongs to the Afridi tribe, the biggest clan in the Khyber Agency. His family had a transport business operating a bus between Bara and Peshawar and owning one or two trucks. He has been variously described as a bus conductor or truck cleaner, but he maintains that he drove his own bus. It is reported that, as a young teen, he spent a time fighting against the Soviets in Afghanistan in the 1980s. He was briefly an active member of the Awami National Party, a secular Pashtun nationalist political party, and then joined up with Mufti Munir Shakir. His journey from a cleaner to a commander took only four or five years.[232]

Mangal Bagh's humble origins have made him anti-feudal and pro-people.[233] He loses no opportunity to criticize the Maliks, the hereditary tribal elders who are traditionally pro-establishment and receive all the benefits doled out by the government. He is keen to highlight the plight of the ordinary tribesmen and solve the problems confronting the common man. If he had his way, he would rob the rich to pay the poor, just like a modern-day Robin Hood. This explained his appeal to the young men, mostly unemployed, who make up the bulk of Lashkar-i-Islam.[234]

Mangal Bagh punished rich Maliks and other tribesmen who violated the tribal and Lashkar-i-Islam's code of conduct. A rich Malik was once ordered to host a feast with rice cooked with meat for the whole tribe. He even forced most of the candidates contending for the National Assembly seat from Bara, including the eventual winner and now federal minister Hamidullah Jan Afridi, to pay for a grand feast for voters, make speeches at a joint public meeting, agree to a code of conduct for electioneering, and pledge to spend all development funds honestly in consultation with Lashkar-i-Islam upon election as MNA.[235]

Mangal Bagh resigned on 25 November 2008 at a meeting held in Daro Adda Akakhel and was replaced as Amir by Haji Haleem Shah, who belongs to the Kamarkhel tribe of the Khyber Agency.[236]

The LI is largely dependent for its finances on funds collected locally, especially from those 'not walking the path of Siraat-e-Mustakeem [The path of righteousness]'. Major penalties have been imposed on those who do not offer prayers five times a day, who do not wear caps or who drink liquor. In April 2008 the LI issued a fourteen-point decree that peace would be brought to Bara tehsil through the imposition of heavy penalties on such crimes: a fine of Rs 500,000 (US$8,300) would be paid for murder, Rs 50,000 (US$830) for having a satellite dish and Rs 500 (US$8.30) for not offering prayers five times a day.[237] Fines of Rs 5000 ($83) were imposed on the owners of all kinds of video shops and cable operators.[238] Mangal Bagh made it customary in his area to wear a *topi* (Islamic hat) or be fined Rs. 100. Despite LI proclaiming to have an anti-crime agenda, its activists are involved in kidnapping wealthy people for ransom from Peshawar valley.[239]

Local donations contribute significantly of the total funding collected by the LI. It is important for a 'puritanical' group like LI to maintain a legitimate perception of popularity among the local population by not relying entirely on their donations. Bara shopkeepers pay LI a monthly fee, previously given to a bazaar committee, for providing security to the large markets in the town that used to sell foreign smuggled goods. Voluntary donations by the rich are another important source of funding: in May 2008 Mangal Bagh disclosed that pious and wealthy tribesmen had donated about 70 vehicles, almost all double-door pickups, for use by Lashkar-i-Islam volunteers.[240] LI activists have also been accused of extorting money from truckers moving goods between Afghanistan and Pakistan.[241]

There is no evidence to suggest foreign funding from Al Qaeda or from quarters hostile to Pakistan. However, the Pashtun diaspora worldwide donates substantial sums on the basis of ideological compatibility or as part of an alliance based on brotherhood of sect.

LI's Military Capabilities

The LI was reported in 2008 as having 120,000 men under arms and controlling almost all of Khyber Agency, except parts of Jamrud tehsil and a two-kilometre stretch of territory in the Maidan area of Tirah Valley.[242] This is unlikely to be correct, however, since the total of Pakistani troops deployed in the entire FATA region is no more than 100,000. It is certain, however, that most of the LI's foot soldiers are forced to join the ranks. The LI has made it compulsory for the locals to send at least one member of each family to join their war with Ansar-ul-Islam in the Tirah Valley: 'Every person in the tribal areas owns a gun and has fighting abilities. The LI forces each family to send one of their members to join their fight against their rival group. Those who refuse, risk having their homes demolished and a heavy fine is imposed on them.'[243] The report revealed that, while it used to be possible to avoid service by paying Mangal Bagh's men, this is no longer allowed: 'They compel our youth to join their fight or face penalties that may vary from losing their home, a heavy fine or going into exile.' Mangal Bagh also asked 'pupils in the [local] schools to participate in his war, which has started to eradicate crimes and establish law and order'.[244]

The LI seems to gain popular support by successfully presenting itself as an alternative to a political administration that has failed to ensure security and peace in the region. Before the LI took over, the state of law and order in Bara was so bad that anyone visiting the Khyber Agency would be lucky to escape kidnapping. It is now claimed, however, that it is safe for strangers to move freely in the entire Bara Tehsil and Tirah Valley. LI has also portrayed its sectarian war against the rival Ansar-ul-Islam as a religious obligation to purge the area from exploiting Pirs.

The LI in Khyber has also expertly exploited the immense power of propaganda using FM radio stations. Mufti Munir Shakir established a full-time FM radio station even before announcing the formation of LI. Since then, the outfit has exploited the media's power to forward its agenda among the locals. Extensive use of FM radio has led to Mangal Bagh and Munir Shakir being known as the 'Radio Mullahs'.

Jihadi outfits operating in Pakistan and Afghanistan have trained the top leaders of LI. For instance, Mufti Munir Shakir started his Jihadi career by joining the SSP, a proscribed terrorist group, and Mangal Bagh was trained in Afghanistan during the Soviet invasion in the 1980s. However, a majority of the foot soldiers associated with LI are untrained local tribesmen who possess a gun as a tradition and have been forced to join the ranks. Unlike the Taleban, Lashkar-e-Islam forbids suicide bombings.

The LI has picked battles with Ansar-ul-Islam and targeted some of the local sub-tribes of Bara. In April 2008 there was a skirmish with the powerful Kukikhel tribesmen of Jamrud because the Kukikhels wanted to engage in businesses that Mangal Bagh considered un-Islamic. As part of its larger campaign to 'purify' Khyber Agency from social evils, the LI has kidnapped, killed and stoned various criminals and prostitutes. The stoning and shooting of two men and a woman on charges of alleged adultery by the Lashkar-e-Islam was the first incident of its kind in March 2007. A huge crowd assembled to watch the executions after the event was announced over the mosque's loudspeakers.[245] The group also staged a public execution of two prostitutes in March 2008.

LI Relations with Other Organizations

Al Qaeda

The LI maintains no links with Al Qaeda or any of its affiliated organizations. Its manifesto puts a complete ban on the entry of local and foreign terrorists in Khyber Agency.[246] Unlike Al Qaeda, the LI is a local phenomenon with no global agenda. In an interview with a Pakistani journalist, Mangal Bagh stated that he has no intention of operating outside his native Khyber Agency.[247]

Tehrik-e-Taliban Pakistan

Unlike other Islamic militant groups of FATA, Lashkar-e-Islam is not pro-Taliban. The groups have different agendas: the TTP is bent on fighting against the US and NATO troops in Afghanistan, while the Lashkar-e-Islam aims to eradicate social evils from society.

In April 2008 Mangal Bagh disclosed that he was repeatedly invited by Baitullah Mehsud and his supporters to join the Tehrik-i-Taliban Pakistan (TTP), but he declined as he did not want to fight Pakistan's security forces and harm the country.[248] He said that his fighters had not been sent to fight alongside the Taliban in Waziristan, Swat and Darra Adamkhel. Unlike the TTP, Lashkar-i-Islam did not object to the presence of the Pakistan Army and Frontier Corps in Bara. Differences between LI and TTP became obvious in August 2008 when a TTP-linked group in Khyber killed Haji Namdar, a close friend of Mufti Munir Shakir and head of the defunct militant organization Amar Bil Maarouf Wa Nahi Munkar (Promotion of Virtue and Prohibition of Vice).[249] Since then the LI has become more critical of the TTP's 'Jihad'.

The presence of a TTP-linked terrorist group in Khyber Agency, however, formerly led by Maulana Mustafa Kamran Hijrat, an Afghan Taliban member close to the TTP leadership, presents a grave threat to NATO's supply lines into Afghanistan. Hakimullah Mehsud used to oversee the TTP's activities in Khyber and was believed to be involved in the assassination attempt on Haji Namdar. Militants linked to the Hakimullah group were involved in the hijacking of thirteen NATO military trucks from Khyber in November 2008. That was the first incident of its type carried out by the TTP. The LI has proved to be the only force that is stopping the TTP from crossing into Khyber: if they ever get into the area, the TTP could potentially choke off the Pak-Afghan highway and cut off vital NATO supply routes to neighbouring Afghanistan. This possibility became a reality in December 2008, when the TTP carried out multiple attacks on NATO logistics in Khyber and temporarily cut off the supply lines.

Afghan Taliban

Although Mangal Bagh admitted to fighting in the Afghan 'jihad' against Soviet occupying forces in Afghanistan in the late 1980s, there is no evidence to suggest that he sent fighters to support the Afghan Taliban. Mangal Bagh denies links with the Afghan Taliban, but defends the Taliban's resistance against the US-led coalition forces occupying Afghanistan.[250]

Ansar-ul-Islam

Ansar-ul-Islam (AI) is another Deobandi militant outfit operating in Khyber Agency. Strong differences over religious issues have led to severe animosity between the LI and AI. Lashkar-e-Islam regards Ansar-ul-Islam as evil and an arch enemy. Hundreds of people have been killed in sectarian clashes between the two groups. On July 2007 Maulana Fazlur Rahman, who leads Jamiat Ulema-i-Islam Fazl (JUI-F), sent a grand *jirga* to the Tirah Valley for talks with the two warring groups to bring about peace in the area.[251] The *jirga* failed to persuade them to accept peace and clashes resumed. On 22 July 2008, Ansar-ul-Islam reportedly sent assassins to target Mangal Bagh and other Shura members, but the plot was foiled and three persons armed with remote controlled explosive devices were arrested.[252]

Pir Saifur Rehman Group

The supporters of Pir Saif-u-Rehman, a Barelvi spiritual leader, are operating in Tirah under the name of Syed Akbar Group, also known as the Tanzeem Ahl-e Sunat Wal-Jamat. The Pir Saifur Rehman group follows Barelvi Islam, which encourages music and sees Prophet Mohammad (PBUH) as a semi-divine figure (a personage of light). In contrast, the LI follows the puritanical Deobandi form of hard-line Islam. Most of the Tal-

iban leaders in Afghanistan were educated at the Deobandi madrasa of
Haqqania located in Akora Khattak, Nowshera.[253] The conflict between
the two religious figures in the Bara area started with the trading of allegations. Pir Saif-u-Rehman migrated from Afghanistan in the 1940s and
settled in the Pakistani tribal area, while Mufti Munir Shakir moved to
Bara in Khyber Agency in 2003 after he was expelled from the tribal Sadda
Kurram Agency following an explosion in a mosque in which several people were killed. Mufti Munir Shakir, who is reportedly linked with the outlawed militant group Sipah-e-Sahaba Pakistan, belonged to Karak district.
Mufti Munir Shakir and Pir Saif-u-Rehman, both of whom have large followings in the area, set up illegal FM radio stations to criticise each other.
The two broadcasting sheikhs began warring on the airwaves in December 2005. Their opposing views polarized the people, leading naturally to
violence when the LI demolished a house belonging to Pir Saif-u-Rehman
on 28 March 2006. Twenty-six people died in the clashes, including Pir
Saif-u-Rehman's son Sayyed Anwar Badshah.

Mufti Munir Shakir and Pir Saif-u-Rehman were officially expelled
from Khyber Agency by the political administration: in February 2006 Pir
went to Lahore and Mufti left Bara. Fighting between their followers continued, however, and the following month more than two dozen deaths
were reported within two days in Khyber Agency.

Pakistan's Response to Lashkar-e-Islam

The Pakistani government has adopted a very ambiguous strategy in dealing with the LI. Large-scale sectarian clashes between the LI and AI that resulted in hundreds of deaths were neglected. In February 2007, after four
months of bloody clashes, the political administration expelled the leaders of LI and AI from Khyber Agency. After Munir Shakir's removal, however, the LI was allowed to reorganize and intensify its activities under the
leadership of Mangal Bagh. The government banned Lashkar-e-Islam in
June 2008, one month before a full-scale military operation was launched
against LI in its strongholds of the Bara area and Landi Kotal. Mangal Bagh
and his core group of key fighters, however, moved into Tirah ahead of
the operation. In the course of thirteen days about ten compounds, including the house of the LI chief, were dynamited. Most of these served as
regional headquarters for the LI and were abandoned soon after the launch
of the operation. The government halted the military operation on 4 July
2008 to allow peace talks between Mangal Bagh and Afridi tribesmen who
were worried that the security operation could continue indefinitely until
all the set goals had been achieved.[254] As a result of these talks, Mangal

Bagh signed a peace deal with the government on 10 July 2008, according to which the LI agreed not to interfere in the provincial metropolis and other settled parts of the province.[255] The LI was also ordered to limit its activities to the Khyber Agency. It agreed not to challenge the writ of the government in Bara or in any other area, or create hurdles for the political administration in the agency. It also agreed to the government's condition that there would be a complete ban on the display of weapons and its activists would not violate the ban in any way. In return, the government agreed to release the 92 persons taken into custody during the operation, including members of the LI and its ally Amar Bil Maarouf Wa Nahi Munkar. It was also agreed that a thirteen-member committee headed by the political agent would be formed: the members of the committee would identify the main barriers to maintaining law and order in the area and the political agent would then take responsibility for solving them.

The LI's peace agreement proved to be a tactical move by Mangal Bagh as his men reappeared in Bara within a few days of signing it. Mangal Bagh made his first appearance in Bara Bazaar on 27 July 2008 and his men were seen manning the main marketplace and elsewhere in Bara.[256]

Is Lashkar-e-Islam a Real Threat?

It must be recognized that the activities of the LI in Bara had nothing to do with the Taliban movement. The LI also maintains considerable local support. Nevertheless, this does not imply that the government should allow or tolerate a parallel system of administration to emerge. The LI must not be dismantled, but needs to be won over by the government in order to ensure a TTP-free Khyber Agency. If Mangal Bagh were to be eliminated, the TTP and Al Qaeda would enter Khyber Agency. Since the US and NATO forces in Afghanistan transport 75 per cent of their supplies, including 40 per cent of their fuel, through the Khyber Pass, any disruption due to a worsening law and order problem could have a negative impact on the counter-insurgency operations of foreign troops. The LI is a lesser evil, or a better alternative, to the TTP or anti-Pakistan Taliban. At least, the LI is not likely to fight against Pakistan or send fighters to Afghanistan. A pro-government LI would ensure a secured road to Afghanistan via Khyber for the benefit of travellers as well as the movement of NATO's supplies. In the worst-case scenario, if the LI joins the ranks of the TTP it would be catastrophic for the Pakistani government and the foreign forces in Afghanistan.

Tanzeem Ansar-ul-Islam (AI)

Qazi Mehboob-ul-Haq, Military Commander of AI
Tanzeem Ansar-ul-Islam (The Organization of the Supporters of Islam) is
often misunderstood as a Barelvi militant outfit led by Pir Saif-u-Rehman.
However, this is not the case. The AI is a Deobandi militant outfit operating in Khyber Agency. Although both groups follow the Deobandi school
of thought, the strong differences between the LI and AI over various religious practices have led to severe animosity. Speaking about the origin and
ideology of Ansar-ul-Islam, Qari Izzatullah, the General Secretary, said:

> Media outlets in Pakistan have been writing in their editorials that
> Ansar-ul Islam was founded by the re-grouping of followers of Pir
> Saif-ur Rehman after the latter had been evicted from Bara. But this
> is not true; Ansar-ur Islam is affiliated with the Deobandi school
> of thought whereas Pir Saif-ur Rehman is not. The Pir's support-
> ers are operating in Tirah under the name of Syed Akbar Group
> also known as the Tanzeem Ahl-e Sunat Wal-Jamat. Whereas Ansar-
> al Islam's core constitutes 99 per cent of Deobandis who have noth-
> ing in common with them.[257]

Tanzeem Ansar-ul-Islam was formed in June 2006 with the following objectives:

- Worship of Allah.
- Following in the footsteps of the Holy Prophet (PBUH).
- Rebelling against oppressors.
- Supporting the oppressed.
- Unconditional service to all of humanity.
- Guarding the sanctity of mosques and madaris, their teachers
  and students
- Striving for peace and removing the ills of society
- Striving for development of tribe and country
- Working for betterment of all sectors of Islam (Jihad, Tableegh,
  Zikr, etc).
- Educating the masses to help them seek a brighter future for
  themselves.

Lashkar-e-Islam regards Ansar-ul-Islam as an arch enemy, and believes
that those linked to AI have gone astray and do not follow the true
Islam. Similarly, the AI calls LI the 'trouble maker'. Hundreds of people

have been killed in clashes between the groups. The outfit vows to be defensive in terms of using force against LI: 'We consider it *haram* to shed blood of another Muslim who is also the proponent of Qalma. But still Islam allows every Muslim to defend himself by all means available to him.'[258]

Maulana Qazi Mehboob-ul-Haq, the first Amir of the group, oversees the AI's 'military campaign' against Lashkar-e-Islam. Qari Izzatullah Ham Khial is the General Secretary and policy decisions are taken in consultation with the Shura (Consultative Committee). Politically, AI is affiliated with Maulana Fazlur Rahman's Jamiat Ulema-i-Islam. Ansar-ul-Islam is a sectarian organization and harbours no ambitions to establish its writ outside its sphere of influence.

The Ansar-ul-Islam has been quite strong in parts of the Tirah valley in Khyber, but there is no presence in Bara, the stronghold of LI. By the time that Pakistani security forces launched Operation Sirat-e-Mustqeem in Bara, the AI had already been evicted from the region by the LI and so did not suffer any further losses.

The Ansar-ul-Islam has never been involved in suicide bombings or attacks on law enforcement agencies and security forces. It also has never intended to send fighters to Afghanistan to support Taliban's insurgency. There is no evidence to suggest that it has links with Al Qaeda or any other terrorist outfit present in FATA. In June 2008, the AI was banned under the Anti-Terrorism Act despite its pro-government rhetoric. While the AI does not present a long-term security threat, mediating between the warring AI and LI is crucial to ensure peace and stability in Khyber Agency.

Tanzeem Amar Bil Maarouf Wa Nahi Munkar

Haji Namdar launched the Tanzeem Amar Bil Maarouf Wa Nahi Munkar (Organization for the Promotion of Virtue and Prevention of Vice) in 2003. The group is based in Bara, Khyber Agency. During their rule in Afghanistan, which lasted more than six years, the Taliban set up a fully fledged department of Tanzeem Amar Bil Maarouf Wa Nahi Munkar to implement edicts that formed the basis of their strict religious rule.[259] The force that implemented those edicts was also known as the religious or morality police, and it mainly comprised young Taliban members riding pick-up trucks, flying white flags, and wielding sticks that were used to strike anyone defying those edicts. On occasion, the more over-zealous religious police would carry glasses to measure the size of men's beards, and arrest those with short beards. Violators were detained until their beards had grown to the proper size, before being released. Women failing to cover their faces also faced punishment.

At the time of its formation, the Tanzeem was affiliated to Al Qaeda and the Afghan Taliban, which recognized the strategic importance of the Khyber Agency in their Jihad against foreign forces in Afghanistan. The Khyber Agency is a vital transit point for NATO supplies going into Nangarhar province. Haji Namdar, a believer in the Salafi strain of Islam and a vocal supporter for the Jihad in Afghanistan, was their means of establishing a foothold in the Khyber Agency so that the Taliban and Al Qaeda could attack NATO supply lines:[260] 'Namdar went so far as to announce on his FM channel that anyone in the Muslim Ummah who was willing to fight against NATO and other Kafirs [infidels], and who had no safe haven or means, would be welcomed in Khyber Agency.'[261] He offered to train them and provide accommodation to their families, who could live in peace within their territory. Many Mujahideen came to the area, but it soon became clear that not all of them were coming with true intentions to fight for Allah. Many of the tribal elders opposed Haji Namdar, but as leader his word was final. Many of those who migrated came from Waziristan, Mohmand Agency and Bajaur Agency, as well as Turks, Arabs, Punjabis, Uzbeks, Tajiks and others.[262]

Foreign fighters were allowed to stay in Khyber and carry out operations under the protection of Haji Namdar. The Tanzeem successfully disrupted NATO supplies passing through the Khyber Pass. On 20 March 2008, twenty petrol tankers out of a convoy of forty were blown up at Torkham, the border crossing from the Khyber Agency into Nangarhar province. This led NATO to make a deal for some supplies to be sent through Russia, despite it being a far more arduous route.[263] The Torkham success was followed by a number of smaller attacks, and the Taliban's plan appeared to be going better than expected.

Haji Namdar, however, secretly switched sides after pressure from the CIA and Pakistani intelligence in April 2008, betraying the Taliban for a reward of US$150,000 paid in local currency.[264] Al Qaeda and the Taliban immediately called an emergency shura in North Waziristan to review the situation. Following the reported deal with the CIA, Haji Namdar ordered foreign fighters linked to Al Qaeda to leave his area:

> Haji Namdar gave them three warnings not to carry out these kinds of activities but unfortunately they continued. Ultimately, Emir Haji Namdar announced again on his FM station that anyone involved in these kinds of activities were not Mujahideen and would not be allowed to remain in Khyber Agency and he requested they

leave. He stated that he only wanted pure jihadis in the territory; not kidnappers, car-lifters and thieves.[265]

Further discord also developed between the Tanzeem and the TTP when several of Baitullah's fighters were arrested and expelled from the area after they ambushed a government convoy in Bara. Haji Namdar was also contemplating joining the new Taliban umbrella group established to oppose Baitullah Mehsud, announcing that he would not be involved in attacks against Pakistani security forces.

Haji Namdar and his outfit were now a hindrance to waging Jihad in Afghanistan, and so it was necessary for Al Qaeda and the Afghan Taliban to eliminate him. In May 2008 a Taliban faction linked to the TTP sent a suicide bomber to kill Haji Namdar, but he escaped unhurt. Hakimullah Group, a militant organization associated with the Taliban, claimed responsibility and said that the suicide attack on Haji Namdar was 'the result of [his] links with the government and the expulsion of Hakimullah Group by the Amar Bil Maarouf Wa Nahi Munkar'.[266] A second assassination attempt in August 2008 proved successful, when a young assassin sent by the TTP started firing during the morning *Dars* (lecture) and more than 20 bullets pierced Namdar's chest.

Following the death of its founder, the organization's Shura nominated Haji Hukam Khan to replace Haji Namdar. Efforts had to be made to reclaim the trust of Al Qaeda and the Afghan Taliban. The Tanzeem started dispatching fighters to Afghanistan to fight against coalition forces: in November 2008 the allied forces in Nagarhar province killed seven Tanzeem militants and three were injured in an air attack.[267] This particular incident proved that the Tanzeem was actively engaged in Afghanistan against the coalition forces.

Tanzeem Amar Bil Maarouf Wa Nahi Munkar maintained strong affiliations with Lashkar-e-Islam, another Bara-based militant group averse to the TTP. Haji Namdar and Mangal Bagh of LI admitted having a close affinity: in an interview Haji Namdar stated: 'we enjoy good relations with him [Mangal Bagh]. Certainly, in every hour of need we come to the rescue of each other. This support includes material in terms of arms and ammunition, exchange of men and morale.'[268] While the government of Pakistan has banned both of these groups, the Tanzeem and thousands of its armed fighters present a real threat to NATO and the ISAF forces in Afghanistan.

Conclusion

The situation in FATA is highly complex. Pakistan and the global counter-terrorism forces should formulate policies that provide a long-term solution to the highly complex and layered interplay of local, regional and international terrorist forces active in FATA. In order to formulate a comprehensive strategy to win the crucial battle in FATA, recognition of the complexities is essential. It must be recognized that the Pakistani Taliban is not a monolithic entity, but instead is fragmented. The TTP has been the most lethal group and has placed considerable emphasis on waging 'jihad' against Pakistan. Taliban factions under Mullah Nazir and Hafiz Gul Bahadur, however, have not been in favour of carrying out attacks in Pakistan: Mullah Nazir never became a full participant in the TTP and Hafiz Gul Bahadur distanced himself from Baitullah Mehsud after the Afghan Taliban Supreme Commander Mullah Omar condemned the TTP's activities in Pakistan. Other Pakistani Taliban groups, however, maintain a totally different agenda, including Lashkar-e-Islam (LI), led by Mangal Bagh, and Ansar-ul-Islam (AI), under Maulana Qazi Mehboob-ul-Haq. Another Taliban style group, the TNSM, also follows a different set of goals in Malakand Agency.

The different factions of the Pakistani Taliban are driven by various factors. For instance, the TTP gathers public support and legitimacy for its cause by portraying itself as an anti-American group, formed to defend the Muslim land of Afghanistan and wage defensive Jihad against Islamabad. Therefore, Pashtun religion and anti-Americanism can be described as a driving force behind the TTP. The MTT led by Mullah Nazir is also inspired by the idea of Jihad and Pashtun brotherhood. Islamist militias like the LI and AI, which are often mistakenly described as Taliban, are merely religious-cum-social organizations, driven to purify society for religious motives. The TNSM exploits these class differences for recruitment, and makes it more like a movement protesting against vast disparities in wealth and the failure of the authorities to provide justice, jobs and essential services like education and health. On occasion it has pitted landless tenants against wealthy landlords, some of whom have been forced to leave the valley.

The Pakistani Taliban groups are driven by a combination of religious, social, political and economic factors. Since they are divided into many small and dispersed networks, a subtler tactical strategy is required to secure FATA. A comprehensive strategy must address the varied interests of the Taliban alongside the use of force. Militarily, the US and other Western governments are required to enhance the Pakistani Army's counter-insurgency capabilities. It would be misconceived to question the Pakistani Army's will to fight against the Taliban in FATA because the real issue at stake is not a matter of will, but capability. The Pakistani Army is trained to fight conventional wars with India and it is not necessarily a counter-insurgency force. A strong, well-organized and specialized counter-insurgency force able to face the non-state militias and enforce the law must be built.

The militants must be deprived of legitimacy in all regions where they operate. The Pakistani Army has been reluctant to take decisive action against the Pakistani Taliban, fearing adverse public opinion and an equally lethal media hostility. At the time of their inception in 2004, the local population supported the Pakistani Taliban. The anti-American stance, the cause to liberate Afghanistan from 'foreign occupation', and the manipulation of Islam for their political objectives, provided much-needed legitimacy among the local population. For many, the Pakistani Taliban represented a religious movement, not necessarily hostile to Pakistan and not necessarily an enemy of the people. Despite the deadly terrorist attacks carried out across the country, the popular media was reluctant to call them 'terrorists'. Public sympathy and an apologetic attitude towards the Taliban and their ideology gave rise to the fear that the Pakistani Taliban might transform into a socio-political movement like Hizbullah in Lebanon.

In view of the events that have unfolded since the rise of Talibanization in 2004, however, it has become clear that the Pakistani Taliban has not been able to maintain the public support essential to launch a mass movement. The tide has turned, with the majority of Pakistanis, including the popular media, now regularly and vocally using the term 'terrorist' to refer to the Taliban. This loss of public support has significantly reduced the possibility that the Pakistani Taliban would transform into a socio-political movement.

What caused this shift? There is no one reason for the current failure of Talibanization in Pakistan, but a series of interrelated issues and events have altered public opinion and created a hostile environment for the Pakistani Taliban to advance their ideological and political agenda.

Pakistan, with the help of the international community, has been battling the Taliban on both the operational and ideological fronts since early 2004. The Pakistani government has implemented a comprehensive strategy to eliminate the effective fighting force, as well as to address the material grievances in the Taliban areas. More than anything, however, the Taliban's own tactical and strategic blunders have cost them vital public support. Their brutal tactics of beheadings and suicide bombings are an anathema to Pakistani society, and this has allowed mainstream religious scholars to attack the legitimacy of such tactics. The frequent and public use of these tactics demonstrated their commitment to adopting the radical positions of international jihad, but never took the religious and social realities of Pakistan into consideration. Additionally, the shift in the targets of suicide bombers, from security forces to the general public, turned supporters into angry opponents. Initially suicide attacks against the security forces were largely viewed as 'justified' by a large segment of Pakistani society because the Army and other law enforcement agencies were commonly misperceived as mercenaries fighting the unpopular US war on Pakistani soil. That substantially changed when the Islamist death squads started targeting public places, mosques and funerals. Even when the attacks were against 'legitimate' targets, the bombings caused considerable 'collateral damage' that wore down public support. It resulted in a huge strategic failure for the Taliban and their associates as they lost public sympathy.

Other incidents reinforced the strategic miscalculation. The assassination of former Prime Minister Benazir Bhutto, attacks on the Sri Lankan cricket team, the attack on the Marriott Hotel in Islamabad, the flogging of a sixteen-year-old girl in Swat, and the killings of leading religious scholars like Maulana Hasan Jan and Mufti Sarfaraz Naeemi, also served to undermine the Taliban's public support. The Pakistani Taliban and their associates have been strategically unwise in claiming such attacks as they occurred in Pakistan and immediately cast doubt on their claim to be fighting the 'foreign occupation' in Afghanistan only. The public have come to understand that these men want nothing less than the capture of Pakistan in order to create a cloak of darkness couched in religious zealotry. The people have seen the savagery with which the Taliban has treated innocent Pakistanis. Between 2003 and 2008 the casualties from Taliban-related violence, including both civilians and security personnel, numbered more than 20,000. By comparison, Pakistani casualties during the 1965 war with its traditional rival, India, stood at only 4,000. For these reasons, there is an emerging consensus in Pakistan that the internal threat posed by Taliban is far greater than any external threat.

The blunders mentioned above are surmountable, but the strategic objective of creating a mass movement capable of taking power in Pakistan seems increasingly remote, even more so given the fragmented nature of the Pakistani Taliban internal structure. Unlike the Afghan Taliban, the Pakistani Taliban is not a monolithic entity, although many are loosely united under the Tehrik-i-Taliban Pakistan (TTP) umbrella. Sectarian issues, geographic divisions, tribal politics and the fierce independence desired by various factions suggests that there is little chance the TTP can actually take power. Any victory, as remote as that seems, would take on the appearance of the pre-Taliban Afghanistan. Disunity among the Pakistani Taliban does not diminish its threat. A fragmented Taliban would always pose a serious threat with the chaos and instability created in the country, even if they might not be able to win the hearts and minds of common Pakistanis.

It would be safe to assume that the Pakistani Taliban has lost the capabilities for mass mobilization and advancing as an insurgent movement. This is not to suggest that Pakistan and the international community have gained a total victory over these elements. Al Qaeda, Taliban and their associated groups are likely to remain a primary threat to Pakistan and the rest of the world. However, since there has been a sharp decline in public sympathy for Taliban, the biggest obstacle to stopping the advance of militancy, the threat has become more manageable.

3

Terrorism and Karachi

The single strategy of severing NATO's supply lines from Pakistan
is the key to success. If the blockage is successfully implemented
in 2008, the Western coalition will be forced to leave Afghanistan
in 2009, and if implemented next year, the exit is certain by 2010.[1]

The target area is being shifted to the southern port city of Karachi,
where almost 90% of NATO's shipments land, including vital oil.
From this teeming financial center, 80% of the goods go to Torkharm
in Khyber Agency on their way to the Afghan capital of Kabul.
About 10% go to Chaman, then on to the northern Afghan city
of Kandahar. The remaining nato supplies arrive in Afghanistan
by air and other routes.[2]

To enforce the writ of law in Karachi, it can be done. The only way
is for political leaders to become role models. If political leaders
are willing to be a part of the crime-politics nexus, we cannot.
I was not keen to accept this job. If I accepted, I told them
I need a total free hand. If someone wants to interfere, I will not.
It is easier said than done. One must be a pragmatic practitioner.
There is no other city like Karachi.[3]

The Evolution and Impact of Terrorism and Crime on Karachi, 1998–2008

The megacity of Karachi is an important financial and industrial centre, yet its dynamic urban environment belies a complex political and security environment. Located in Pakistan's southern Sindh Province, Karachi or 'Kalachi-jo ghote' (pond of Karachi) was a small fishing village in 1729 and grew into a major trading hub during the British Raj.[4] Historically, Karachi had trading links with Asia, Africa and the Middle East. As the tenth largest city in the world – between 18 and 20 million people live and work there – Karachi's population is bigger than that of 100 countries.[5] About half the population of Sindh Province speak Mohajir or Urdu; the rest of the population includes those from Sindhi, Punjabi, Baluchi, Pashtun and other communities.

While Islamabad is Pakistan's political capital, Karachi is its economic hub.[6] As the nation's major port, Karachi was the lifeline for both Pakistan and landlocked Afghanistan until a second port at Gwadar became operational in March 2008. The The port of Karachi supplies between 80 and 90 per cent of goods needed by the NATO and other forces in Afghanistan.[7] Domestic and international trade and commerce boosts Karachi's economy, but also spawns an underworld undertaking a diverse range of organized and low-level crime. It is the most important transit point for the underground economy of smuggled goods that penetrates Afghanistan and Pakistan.

The city of Karachi faces unprecedented challenges because it is poorly regulated. Karachi has no mass transit system and the traffic situation is burdened with a further 600 new vehicles every day.[8] Despite its severe transportation and housing problems, the city continues to develop. The private sector contributes immensely to Karachi's economy and to the rest of Pakistan. Its overground and underground infrastructure is disorderly yet vibrant. Despite political instability, there have been significant international, regional and national investments in Karachi. A motorway is being built to link Central Asia, China and South Asia with the ports of Karachi and Gwadar. If the threat of extremism and terrorism can be contained, not only Karachi and Pakistan, but also the south and central Asian region, will grow at an unprecedented pace.

As a trendsetter from terrorism to industry and fashion, Karachi is dynamic and vital in many ways. The influx of migrant and diaspora communities as a result of globalization has made Karachi the most vibrant city in Pakistan. Its emergence as an important financial city as well as a criminal and terrorist hub reflects both the positive and negative effects of

globalization. Governing a city with diverse ethnic and religious communities, a multitude of political orientations and allegiances, and penetrated by criminal and terrorist groups, is a complex challenge.

The characteristics of Karachi's armed groups are divided into six interrelated variables: leadership; rank and file membership; organizational structure and functions; ideology and political code of beliefs and objectives; strategy and tactics; and linkages with other non-state and state actors.

Context

The Soviet invasion of Afghanistan in December 1979 gave a boost to extremism in Pakistan that was compounded by other global events, including the revolution in Iran and the Camp David agreement. Pakistan became the single most important frontline state in the fight against the Soviets and General Zia ul Haq, the former military ruler of Pakistan, used religion to mobilize the Muslims to achieve a political goal. Once the fight was framed in the context of a holy war, a Sunni extremist movement emerged. In order to remain in power, Zia used us and Saudi funds both to fight the Soviets and to Islamize Pakistan. While the protracted anti-Soviet multinational Afghan campaign (1979–89) militarized a segment of the Sunnis globally, Pakistan remained as its epicentre. Jihad in Afghanistan and Kashmir attracted many volunteers from Pakistan and overseas. Those from Pakistan who went to fight in Afghanistan and Kashmir were mostly from the Deobandi tradition.

As in the rest of Pakistan, there are two traditions of Islam in Karachi. The hard-line Deobandi and the 'soft' Barelvis have produced many political and religious parties as well as violent groups. The groups that subscribe to the Deobandi tradition range from the non-violent Tablighi Jamat to the violent Pakistani Taliban. Most Urdu-speaking Mohajirs are Barelvis, but a small percentage have converted to Deobandi. The Deobandis are mostly Punjabi or Pashtuns. Compared with the other communities, the Baluchis are not as religious-minded; a significant proportion of Baluchis are deeply influenced by the Communist nationalist tradition.

Many of the recruits for jihad come from the underdeveloped Seraiki belt in Punjab, a region that touches the borders of Sindh, NWFP and Baluchistan, and has spawned most of the militant groups, such as the Harkat-ul-Mujahideen created in Dera Ismail Khan in NWFP, the Laskhar-e-Jhangvi and Sipah-e-Sahaba Pakistan from Jhang (Punjab), and Jaysh-e-Muhammad from Bhawalpur (Punjab). Most of the fighters come from northern and southern Punjab: Muridke, for example, in Punjab produced Lashkar-e-Taiba. The threat to Sindh, particularly to Karachi, formerly spilled over from Punjab and Afghanistan, but since the 9/11 terrorist incident the threat has stemmed primarily from the Federally Administered Tribal Areas (FATA). Due to the distance between tribal Pakistan and Karachi, there is still a perception in some quarters that Karachi is safe and the threat from FATA is not acute.

Prior to the Soviet invasion, Zia was isolated and, as a military dictator, he had no support. Zia addressed his lack of support with the Islamization of society. He introduced sharia law and a zakat system. The

Shia community, fully encouraged by the Iranians, refused to pay zakat to the state, asserting that they are not for the state's brand of Islam. After the fall of the Shah, who was supported by the US, anti-American sentiments dominated Iranian politics. The sizable Shia population in Karachi came under Iranian influence. For the first time there was tension between the Shi'as and the Sunnis, whereas before there was no such differentiation in Pakistan. In response to Zia's announcement, the Shia community announced that 100,000 of them would gather in Islamabad to petition for the exclusion of the Shias from sharia law and the zakat system.

The birth of the Sunni movement in the early 1980s coincided with two events: the anti-Soviet multinational Afghan campaign in the early 1980s and the resurgence of the Kashmiri movement against Indian rule in the late 1980s. Pakistani and US security and intelligence services played a key role in supporting the Sunni movements and their madrasas. Coming from poor backgrounds with no exposure to mainstream education, young Muslims fell victim to a warrior vision of Islam crafted and manipulated by external forces. They believed that they were fighting for Islam and fellow Muslims against the 'kuffar', who were the Soviets. They also believed that, in the event of death, they would be honoured with the title of *shaheed* (martyr) and enter paradise.

The surplus pool of jihadists nurtured by the ISI, CIA and the Saudis scattered to other conflict zones after winning the jihad in Afghanistan. Some went to Tajikistan, Bosnia, Chechnya, Kashmir and to other conflicts that emerged in the 1990s. As there was no rehabilitation programme, some turned to crime and bank robbery, while others started to attack rival factions or kill Shias. Encouraged by international events, indoctrinated by virulent ideologies, and strengthened by military assistance, the Sunni movement, especially SSP and LeJ, grew in strength and influence.

The threat was compounded by the ongoing Saudi-Iranian rivalry. After the fall of the Shah in 1979, Iran and Saudi Arabia poured funds into Pakistan in an effort to influence the Sunni and Shia communities, respectively, with their religious ideologies. Their financial support helped to fund Shia and Sunni extremism, and led to the growth of political extremist and violent groups. With Saudi funding aimed at countering the growing Iranian influence, there was a shift in power to Wahhabi-Deobandi. Sponsored by the ruling family and the Saudi public, Saudi-linked preachers, schools and mosques proliferated in Pakistan. The country remains a playground as the Iranians and Saudis compete to fund Shia and Sunni groups. It was easy for the Sunni extremist ideologues to convince semi-literate youngsters with a skewed interpretation of events, given their limited understanding. Some mullahs and tribal leaders attributed their suffering to the Americans and maintained that the Pakistan government was the puppet of the US. The youngsters were instructed that it was their duty to fight to correct the situation. Without money, however, it would have been difficult for extremist groups to convince the youths to join their cause, and support for the new terrorist mission against the US, its allies and friends came from donors and criminals who were influenced by extremist ideology.

Even after the defeat of the Soviets, both the jihadists and their patrons, particularly the House of Saud, continued to sponsor the anti-Shi'a forces. Saudi sponsorship damaged the social fabric in Pakistan. Dost Ali, Superintendent of the police in Karachi, has commented that: 'When a Muslim got money, he called the other a non-Muslim. Then the dynamics of politics in Pakistan changed.'[9] Iran stepped up its support in response. As a result of this competition, Iranian and Saudi influence is evident thoughout Karachi, as Dost Ali points out: 'Pakistan's problem has been money. Whosoever gives it is our friend.'[10] Developments in Pakistan were affected by the growing Sunni-Shi'a divide throughout the region. While Sunni families ruled throughout the Gulf, the Shi'as constituted a significant segment of the population in Bahrain, Kuwait, Saudi Arabia and Qatar. With the rise of Iran, these monarchies perceived a threat from Iran and the Shi'as. The Middle Eastern regimes held the view that the US exploited the Shi'a-Sunni dispute under the guise of spreading democracy. The impoverished Shi'a communities looked towards Iran as their benefactor and patron: even in Dubai, the biggest hospital was sponsored by Iran and it provided free medicine. Saudi support for Sunni groups, meant to counter Shi'a influence, had an unintended consequence, spawning vibrant Sunni extremist movements worldwide, one of them led by Osama Bin Laden. Saudi Arabia's decision to host US troops in the first Gulf War was the final straw that broke the camel's back, and Bin Laden's hostility led to the Riyadh compound bombing in May 2003.

The mission of the Sunni extremist movement changed after the 9/11 attacks but their threat persisted. There has no halt to their attacks on the Shi'as, but the US became their primary enemy as the perpetrators of injustice in the Muslim world. In such an environment, Pakistan failed to control the expanding Sunni extremist movement that had developed its own momentum. According to Dost Ali, 'When the Jihadists started to exploit religious motivation to fight against the West, the Pakistan establishment said, "Please do not use that tool". But the successful side said, "Why should I not use that tool?"' Referring to the post-9/11 proliferation of groups seeking to attack the West, and drawing an analogy with KFCs and Pizza Huts, he added, 'As no one had copyright of this latest tool, there were many franchises … Each fulfilled their desires of accruing political and financial rewards, including going to heaven.'[11]

Throughout the 1990s there were attacks on the Shi'a community of Karachi by the Sunni extremist movement. Prominent Shi'a clerics and community leaders, businessmen and professionals, notably doctors, were murdered. As law and order deteriorated the police were forced to act. Before the Al Qaeda attacks in the US, the attacks in Karachi were largely triggered by the Shi'a-Sunni divide, as Tariq Jamil confirmed: 'The attacks of September 11, 2001, came when we were coping with sectarian terrorism … The situation in Karachi became worse in 2000–01.'[12] The tide turned against the West after 9/11 and the US attack against Afghanistan compounded the situation. The attention, focus and energy of the Pakistani extremists and terrorists was turned towards the West, as Tariq Jamil explained: 'Hitherto they believed that the Shi'as were against Islam. Now they believed that both the Shi'as and the US were against Islam.'[13] To meet this escalating threat, groups and individuals that had not worked together previously started to unite, and extremists from the north and south of Punjab, as well as jihadists from Karachi, all of whom had trained together, started to work together.

With public protests following the US-led intervention in Afghanistan, the jihadists saw their activities as representative of popular sentiment. Both criminals and terrorists fuelled the agitation that followed: 'They wanted to do something. As they saw themselves as the vanguard, they wanted to act. They attacked the US consulate in Karachi. The attack was not triggered by local conditions in Pakistan.'[14] After 9/11, the threat was largely driven by the global environment, principally by developments in Afghanistan and Iraq. To facilitate the movement of operatives out of Pakistan to target countries, Al Qaeda moved its most capable operative Khalid Sheikh Mohamed to Karachi. Thereafter, the threat in and from Karachi increased exponentially, since Al Qaeda mounted attacks there and also used it as a base from which to strike overseas. Timely US assistance enabled the Pakistani law enforcement, security and intelligence agencies to neutralize the Al Qaeda presence in Karachi. Nonetheless, the jihadist ideology persisted in radicalizing both tribal and mainland Pakistani groups. Presently the bigger threat to Karachi comes from like-minded Pakistani groups working with Al Qaeda and operating largely from tribal Pakistan: 'In parallel with the denial of political rights, there was no way to communicate with the state, it was better to communicate with God.'[15] A significant segment of the population turned to religion during the Musharraf period, and they were hence vulnerable to extremist indoctrination and terrorist recruitment. The Sunni extremist movement has developed its own momentum and now poses a threat to world peace and national security. Like the rest of Pakistan, Karachi suffers from Sunni extremism, nurtured over two decades.

The Karachi Landscape

Karachi is a microcosm of Pakistan. The city has been under massive demographic pressures since the partition of India in 1947. All Pakistan's ethnic communities have established a presence in Karachi, with Mohajirs (50 per cent), Sindhi (25 per cent), Pashtuns (15 per cent), both from NWFP and refugees from Afghanistan, Punjabi (10 per cent) and Baluchis (less than 5 per cent). The massive influx of Mohajirs (Urdu-speaking immigrants) from India happened between 1941 and 1951.[16] The Karachi population grew alarmingly by 432 per cent between 1941 and 1961.[17] Within Pakistan, migrants came from NWFP, Baluchistan and Punjab, settling in both Karachi and interior Sindh. As Pakistan's commercial and industrial hub, Karachi attracted people from all the surrounding regions, creating the country's racial melting pot.

The migrant communities in Karachi provided the required workforce and bureaucracy for Pakistan to develop economically and politically. When Karachi was declared the capital of Pakistan on 22 May 1948, the Constituent Assembly separated from Sindh to become a federally administered area. This decision fuelled the Sindhi supporters' anger towards the Mohajirs 'who they deemed as arrogant city-dwellers full of contempt for the sons of the soil'.[18] Although seeds of tension were planted between Sindhis and the Mohajirs, Karachi remained a secular city into the 1980s. To quote Laurent Gayer, a scholar on Karachi, 'In the 1980s, Karachi's urban crisis fuelled social antagonisms which turned into ethnic rivalries due to the particular social division of work in the city'.[19]

A culture of violence ensued after Karachi received a huge influx of Afghan refugees. Drugs and guns proliferated during and after the anti-Soviet Afghan campaign. Throughout the 1990s, Karachi's social fabric was threatened along ethnic and religious lines. Violence took the form of ethnic and religious conflict, and Karachi suffered a series of riots and ethnic clashes: Anti-Ahmedi riots in the early 1950s, anti-Pashtu riots in 1965, anti-Ahmedi riots in 1969–70, Sindhi-Mohajir riots in 1972–3, and ethnic clashes between the Pashtuns and Biharis in 1985, 1986 and 1987, and between Mohajirs and Sindhis in 1988 and 1990.[20] Terrorist attacks on mosques and political leaders were commonplace. The political elite found that they no longer had control over some parts of the city. To consolidate power and maintain uniformity within their communities, leaders played along with the ethnic and religious politics, and armed themselves by creating militias. This security vacuum created terrorist organizations and criminal syndicates that have grown in number and size. With the rise of ethnic politics, Karachi was demarcated along ethnic lines, and was dominated by ethnic groups such as MQM and Jaye Sindh. Sectarian violence further demarcated Karachi into Sunni and Shi'a areas controlled by such as the LEJ, SSP and Sipah-e-Muhammad Pakistan (SMP; Soldiers of the Prophet Muhammad). In a highly charged environment, Babar Khattack, the Karachi police chief, said, 'The political parties draw their strength by exploiting ethnic and religious similarities as well as differences. They highlight the similarities of their own and differences with their rivals.'[21]

Dubbed as Pakistan's 'southern urban jungle', Karachi is demarcated into planned (residential and commercial) and unplanned areas (illegal squatter settlements). In Karachi, 'housing conditions and access to utilities, to education and to health vary'.[22] In the planned areas, there is governance; in the unplanned areas, there is an informal underground economy and a political order influenced or controlled by leaders of ethnic and religious groups. East of the old centre, the 'notables, big landowners and merchants' live.[23] Karachi has nineteen towns, and each has a police officer of the rank of SSP or SP.

Crime in Karachi is not an easy phenomenon to understand. All the ethnic communities are involved in various forms of crime. Even when discussing the issue of religious extremism in Karachi, it is incorrect to say that the problem rests with the Afghan community or the Internally Displaced Peoples (IDPS): religion is a tool used by all who want to become stakeholders, be they Mohajirs, Punjabis or Pashtuns.

Nevertheless, the Afghan refugees and settlers are considered to be a major source of crime. Criminal activities in the Afghan settlements of Karachi are relatively high. Karachi hosts the largest concentration of Afghans outside Afghanistan (approximately 800,000), mainly settled illegally in the vicinity of Malir and Gadap towns in various housing schemes and bastis, such as Jangabad, Luqman Colony, Machar Colony, Yasrab Colony, Maymar Complex, Decent Complex, Al-Asif Square, Gulshan-e-Akakhel, Quetta Town, and New Sabzi Mandi.[24] There was a massive influx of Afghans into Pakistan at the time of the anti-Soviet mujahideen campaign. The number of refugees escalated in 1983 and grew steadily from 1985. Most relocated to Pakistan's bordering provinces, NWFP, Baluchistan, Sindh and Karachi, where the Afghan Pashtuns settled in Sohrab Goth, Qaidabad, Baneras, and Kemari, areas traditionally inhabited by Pashtuns. There was no proper settlement plan: Sohrab Goth, the largest settlement, for example, reached at least 100,000 at its peak.[25] The

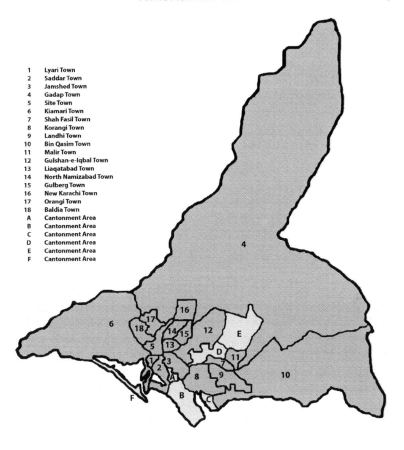

1 Lyari Town
2 Saddar Town
3 Jamshed Town
4 Gadap Town
5 Site Town
6 Kiamari Town
7 Shah Fasil Town
8 Korangi Town
9 Landhi Town
10 Bin Qasim Town
11 Malir Town
12 Gulshan-e-Iqbal Town
13 Liaqatabad Town
14 North Namizabad Town
15 Gulberg Town
16 New Karachi Town
17 Orangi Town
18 Baldia Town
A Cantonment Area
B Cantonment Area
C Cantonment Area
D Cantonment Area
E Cantonment Area
F Cantonment Area

area was congested, streets were narrow and police movement was difficult.[26] Traffic between Karachi and Afghanistan and Pakistan's frontier, notably FATA, increased. The increase in refugees was matched by the growth in the supply of weapons and narcotics from Afghanistan. Criminal syndicates engaged in narcotics and gun running expanded their influence within the refugee camps in Pakistan and beyond., Zakat funds collected from terrorist-infiltrated mosques moved to NWFP and FATA through the hawala system of money transfer.

The Karachi orbit includes many jihadist groups.[27] Only a few are militarily active and mount attacks. Most are politically active, however, politicizing, radicalizing and mobilizing the masses. The high threat groups are Al Qaeda (Qari Zafar Group), TTP, LEJ and SSP. The medium threat groups are Sipah-e-Muhammad Pakistan (SMP), Harkat-ul-Mujahideen al-Almi (HUMA), Harkat-ul-Jihad-i-Islami (HUJI), Tehrik-e-Islami Lashkar-e-Muhammadi (TILM), and Jundullah. Low threat groups are Harkat-ul Ansar (HUA), Jaish-e-Muhammad (JEM), Lashkar-e-Taiba (LET), Tehrik-e Nefaz-e Fiqh-e Jafria (TNFJ). The most active local groups are Sipah-e-Sahaba Pakistan (SSP) and its military wing, LEJ. The Harakat-ul Mujahideen (HUM) breakaway faction HUMA, Jundullah, and TILM have been dismantled, but their remnants are active.

In Karachi, LEJ has two factions, led by Asif Ramzi, operating primarily with Al Qaeda against Western and Pakistani government targets, and Akram Lahori, operating against the Shi'a. After their arrest members of Asif Ramzi's group were asked why they did not kill Shi'as. They claimed that while the Shi'as are their 'enemies', their agenda was 'ideologically bigger' and focused on 'playing the international game' against the US, as well as its allies. While Asif Ramzi's group only operated in Karachi, Akram Lahori's group operated throughout Pakistan. HUM splintered into HUJI factions led by Maulana Khalil ur Rehman operating in Karachi, and by Qari Saifullah Akhtar in NWFP and Kashmir. Another breakaway faction from the Karachi branch of HUJI, Harakat-ul Mujahideen al-Almi operated against Western targets. As the government is able to control their leaders, mainstream LET, JEM, HUA and HUJI do not pose a significant threat. Nonetheless, disgruntled members of these groups have joined Al Qaeda, Pakistani Taliban and other active Pakistani threat groups. Like SMP, TNFJ is a Shi'a group that is politically active only: it is not presently engaged in killing Sunnis.

The CID in Karachi has collected information suggesting that members of outlawed organizations have been receiving training in Wana as suicide bombers for attacks in Karachi. Training for the average suicide bombing, which includes being shown videos of suicide bombers in Iraq, Afghanistan and Palestine takes two weeks.[28] Notorious terrorists like Maulvi Abbas, Maulvi Azmary, Ustaz Jafar and Qari Zafar are training new recruits. They also have strong links with Al Qaeda, Afghan and Pakistani Taliban, and Pakistani groups in Karachi. The robust support network in Karachi then houses the trained bombers.

The Contemporary Terrorist Threat

Terrorism in Pakistan is not a new phenomenon.[29] Karachi experienced both ethno-nationalist and politico-religious terrorism during the 1990s and 2000s. Jaye Sindh (Long live Sindh), an ethno-national group with leftist leanings (communist nationalists), developed a well-structured militant cadre to fight MQM.[30] Driven by Sindhi nationalism, the armed activists of the group clashed with MQM, which represents the Mohajirs. After the Pakistani military started to fight MQM, Sindh support for Jaye Sindh diminished. Renamed Jaye Sindh Quami Mahz (JSQM), its organized armed wing reconfigured itself into a group of activists with arms, aimed primarily at targeting political opponents. For 'political and monetary benefit', some Jaye Sindh leaders split from the main group and formed several new groups.[31] Taraki Pasand is a faction that retained armed activists. Similarly, an MQM breakaway faction, Haqiqi group, retained armed activists. Although the Haqiqi group has a Member of National Assembly representing it, its activists engage in 'crime'.[32]

Attention shifted from fighting ethnic terrorism to sectarian terrorism in the mid-1990s. Terrorism became a grievous problem particularly after 9/11. A number of religious parties in Karachi, mostly drawing their membership from the lower income groups, provided moral, spiritual and financial support.[33] The police and the security agencies were unable to monitor many of these groups.

Traditionally, the Taliban has been supported by a segment of the Pashtun population in Karachi. The two main political parties supporting the Taliban are Jamiat Ulema-i-Islam – Fazlur Rahman Faction (JUI-F) and Jamiat Ulema-i-Islam – Sami-ul-Haq Faction (JUI-S). While the clergy of Jamia Binoria in Karachi influences the leadership of JUI-F, JUI-S is influenced by Dar-ul-Haqannia, Akora Khattak, Peshawar.[34] Jamia Binoria is the ideological headquarters of the Deobandi political, militant and terrorist outfits, while Maulana Fazlur Rahman, a Pashtun from Dera Ismail Khan, lives in NWFP. He patronizes Ansar-ul-Islam, a militant group active in Khyber Agency, and is a member of the National Assembly. Maulana Sami-ul-Haq, an ideologue, was known to guide the members of the Afghan Taliban leadership.[35]

Sectarian terrorism in Karachi steadily increased from 1994, initially sparked by clashes in Punjab and an incident described by Dr Sohaib Suddle, a criminologist who investigated it:

&&About 50 Shi'as travelling from Lahore to Islamabad were waylaid near Jehlum at sunset and 16–17 were killed and others were injured in 1994. It was a big incident. After that a bank was robbed … It was drilled into their minds. Their motivation was sectarian. They believed they were waging a jihad. They knew how to handle weapons.&&

Arguing that the law enforcement approach worked, Dr Suddle said, 'After we arrested them in Karachi, there were no sectarian killings for one year'. Although the Karachi police had managed to keep the attacks at a manageable level, no city in the world has suffered from sectarian terrorism over such a long period. The Shi'a-Sunni attacks resulted in the loss of 376 lives from 1994 to 2001. The number of casualties stands at 57 in

1994, 98 in 1995, 13 in 1996, 28 in 1997, and 8 in 1998.[36] Between 2001 and early 2010 there has been a total of 267 sectarian killings, divided fairly evenly into 132 Shi'as and 135 Sunnis. In some years, however, one community or the other has suffered particularly badly: in 2004, for example, there were 47 Shi'a killings and 3 Sunnis, whereas in 2006 this was reversed to 2 Shias and 49 Sunnis.

Of the multitude of terrorist threats facing Karachi, the threat from sectarian terrorist groups is protracted. Some organizations supporting the Taliban, Al Qaeda and their associated groups were proscribed after 9/11, but 'they remain active in Karachi'.[37] By law, their leadership and membership is 'under watch', but the police acknowledge that, 'We lack the capacity to effectively monitor the groups proscribed under schedule four'.[38]

After Pakistan assisted the US-led coalition in its campaign, it suffered from suicide terrorism. Karachi witnessed nine suicide bombings between 2002 and 2007 that killed 274 persons and maimed or injured 772.[39] The first vehicle-borne suicide bombing in Pakistan took place in Karachi on 8 May 2002, when a suicide bomber from the Harkat-ul-Mujahideen al-Almi (HUMA), the first terrorist group to be formed in Pakistan after 9/11, drove into the side of a bus outside the Sheraton Hotel: eleven of the fourteen killed were French naval technicians staying at the hotel. Three of the nine suicide bombings involved vehicles, three had explosives packed into a briefcase, and three suicide bombers wore belts and vests.[40]

The targets of the nine suicide bombers included US and European nationals, Shi'a worship places, Sunni (Brelvi) religious gatherings, and prominent political and religious leaders. The police identified the perpetrators and their masterminds in eight cases: some of the masterminds were arrested or killed, and others are currently being hunted. The terrorist groups responsible originated in Sindh, elsewhere in Pakistan, and increasingly in tribal Pakistan. The few foreign terrorist groups operating in Karachi, such as Al Qaeda, staged or instigated the most graphic attacks. In December 2002 HUMA bombed the Macedonian Consulate in Karachi and its operatives slit the throats of three Pakistanis.[41]

The most significant international act of terrorism before 9/11 was the killing of Gary Durrell of the Central Intelligence Agency (CIA) and Jacqueline Van Landingham of the US National Security Agency in 1995 when unknown terrorists opened fire on a van in which they were travelling on Sharah-i-Faisal Road in Karachi. In a similar attack, five workers of the Houston-based Union Texas were killed in Karachi in November 1997. Between 2002 and 2008, there were several other noteworthy cases of terrorism, including the kidnapping and killing of Daniel Pearl, two abortive attempts on the President of Pakistan in 2002 and 2003, and the attack on the Corps Commander's convoy in 2004. Al Qaeda and LEJ targeted Daniel Pearl, the first American to be killed after 9/11. Two new groups, HUMA and Jundullah, targeted President Musharraf and the Corps Commander, respectively. Both groups were linked with and deeply influenced by Al Qaeda. According to Mirza Saud of the CID in Karachi: 'The investigation into the attempt on the Corps Commander in Sindh revealed that the Jihadists saw not only the US government but the Pakistani government as a pro-US government institution. Furthermore, the investigation revealed that there were several new groups operating that we did not know.'[42] While previously unknown groups such as HUMA and Jundullah continued to emerge, Karachi was also vulnerable to the SSP, LEJ and other known groups operating both there and elsewhere in Pakistan.

Al Qaeda in Karachi

At the turn of the twenty-first century, Karachi hosted a vast extremist infrastructure for disseminating propaganda, fund-raising, procurement and other support activity, at the apex of which were the multiple terrorist groups engaged in operations both in Pakistan and overseas. Al Qaeda is at the tip and the operational leadership that mounted the 9/11 attack was operating out of Karachi.[43] Al Qaeda's organizational activities in Karachi can be divided into three phases: before 9/11; until the arrest of KSM, the mastermind of the 9/11 attacks; and after KSM's arrest. Even before Al Qaeda was founded in 1988, Maktab-il Khidamat, the predecessor of Al Qaeda, had maintained a presence in Karachi.[44] Those who came from all over the world to fight the Soviets first arrived in Karachi and every mujahideen group had offices and homes there. Even Osama bin Laden flew into Karachi in December 1979 when he first visited Pakistan. The Karachi station of Al Qaeda developed gradually as it evolved into a global organization,. With the exception of Central Asians, Chinese and Pakistanis, almost all the Al Qaeda recruits, members and leaders who went to Afghanistan to train had to stop over in Karachi. As Al Qaeda expanded in Afghanistan, it needed to receive recruits, funds and equipment from the outside world, while maintaining contact with like-minded organizations. It was important that Al Qaeda maintained its own logistical and operational cells in Karachi: after Al Qaeda set up its headquarters in Afghanistan (1996–2001), it always posted a senior leader in Karachi. Peshawar was crucial, but Karachi was critical. Al Qaeda needed to be in constant contact with its operatives to transfer funds and dispatch experts.

It was difficult for Al Qaeda to maintain contact with its global network from Afghanistan, a landlocked country with poorly developed communications and transportation infrastructure. Two of its most capable operatives, Abu Zubaidah and Khalid Sheikh Mohamed (KSM), alias Mokhtar, were assigned to Peshawar and Karachi, respectively: Al Qaeda could not have operated globally without a forward operational base in Karachi personally directed by KSM.

In this first phase, Al Qaeda maintained in Karachi a robust infrastructure, from safe houses and vehicles to a network of suppliers, couriers and supporters moving back and forth from Afghanistan, and for supporting Al Qaeda activities globally. It was also the base for training its members to conduct terrorist operations in urban settings and for rehearsing the preparations necessary for attacks targeting oil tankers, diplomatic missions and western flights. Under interrogation a senior Al Qaeda operative said that in July 2001 he received orders from Mohammed Atef alias Abu Hafs al Masri (Al Qaeda's military commander) to train Abu Hazim al-Sha'ir, Abu Hafs al-Kuwaiti and Abu Mus'ab al-Hashid as suicide bombers in Karachi before they left to attack targets in Singapore. They were trained for two weeks on how to reconnoitre a target, how to hide and operate in a western city, obtain information, read a phone book and use mass transit. He also taught them how to buy chemicals and components on the open market to produce explosives. Abu Hazim had been in East Asia the previous year and was in charge of a cell of three people.[45]

After Al Qaeda was dislodged from Afghanistan, Khalid Sheikh Mohamed, its most senior operational commander, relocated to Karachi to facilitate the travel of its operatives and also to mount attacks. He was joined by Ramzi Bin al-Shibh, the coordinator of the 9/11 attacks. For Al Qaeda to sustain its presence in tribal Pakistan, it needed to communicate with the outside world. A presence in Karachi ensured the flow of supplies, support, and recruits to FATA. Having lost its principal host, Al Qaeda had to reestablish contact with Pakistani and international groups. Karachi was also an important venue for the preparation of multiple operations, including attacks on targets inside Pakistan, as well as global operations, including the second wave of attacks against America's West Coast.

Al Qaeda moved several of its capable leaders and operatives to Faisalabad and Karachi to facilitate the exit of its members, and in some cases their families, to target countries.[46] Karachi, with international flight connections to the Middle East and Asia, was the most important city. A CIA interrogation report stated:

The following is from a senior Al Qaeda captive after leaving Afghanistan for Karachi with his wife at the beginning of the fasting month. He and his wife spent two or three weeks in Karachi at a house in the Ghulsan Iqbal area, where a lot of Jihadis were staying, including Sheik Abu Ahmad al Kuwaiti. At that time al Kuwaiti gave the captive an address to contact. In December 2001, four or five days before the captive left Karachi, several suicide bombers trained by Al Qaeda, such as M. Farik bin Amin alias Zaid alias Zubair, and Bashir bin Lap alias Lillie, arrived at the said house in Karachi. The captive said that Amin and Lillie were initially part of the Malaysia group led by Masran bin Asrhad alias Abd al Aziz al Malaysi, who was conducting a separate program for Muktar [KSM], who was under the control of JI [Jemmah Islamiyah]. Amin and Lillie were originally members of KMM [Kumpulan Militan Malaysia] and technically not part of JI.[47]

This Asian suicide cell was designated to participate in the second wave of attacks against the US. The Al Qaeda leadership was preparing them to hijack an aircraft originating in Malaysia and crash it into the Library Tower (now known as the Bank of America Building) in Los Angeles.

The Al Qaeda network in Karachi received and managed the funding it received worldwide, including the funds the organization continued to receive from the Middle East, both from the Gulf and the Arabian Peninsula.[48] Portions of that funding were allocated to supporting Al Qaeda operations worldwide, the newly established Al Qaeda headquarters in FATA, and the activities of its forward operational base in Karachi. The best-documented of these is the transfer of funds from Karachi to support attacks in Southeast Asia. Between January 2002 and August 2003 Hambali, a senior Al Qaeda leader and the Jemaah Islamiyah (JI) operations leader in Thailand and Cambodia, received a total of US$130,000 from KSM in Karachi. According to the CIA report:

Al-Qaeda sent the money to him without any condition and without any instruction. He was allowed to use the money the way he wanted. The prisoner indicated that the real power that he really had was as a money middle-man between Al Qaeda and JI, and mentioned that the money was very important for Jemaah Islamiyah in Indonesia.[49]

Based on Hambali's revelations, the CIA reported:

Since mid-2002, JI had a fund of US$ 55,000, which came from members of JI who were obliged to give five percent of their income to the group. In mid August 2003, the prisoner claimed that the arrest and raids could be said to have destroyed all JI savings and he could only depend on the money that came from Al Qaeda.[50]

When JI was severely weakened, Hambali's statement demonstrated that Al Qaeda still had funding and it was Al Qaeda's funding which made JI resilient. The report continued:

Al Qaeda was highly satisfied with the Bali bombing, and as a result, they provided additional money for the prisoner, again without any condition. In other words, Al Qaeda sent US$50,000 at the end of December 2002 and/or early January 2003 and the second sending was US$50,000 in February 2003. The prisoner took the US$100,000 since the end of December 2002 until February 2003, when he returned to Thailand from Cambodia at the end of February and/or early March 2003.[51]

Karachi was indispensable and remained the preferred location for KSM until Ramzi bin al-Shibh was arrested in Karachi on 11 September 2002, ten miles from the US Consulate.[52] KSM relocated to Rawalpindi. Despite the visible threat, second-tier Al Qaeda leaders continued to operate from Karachi. To ensure that communication with the Al Qaeda leadership was not severed, Al Qaeda's Head of Administration of Operations, Walid bin Attash alias Khallad, relocated to Karachi in January 2002 and remained there, working on multiple international and domestic operations, until his capture in April 2003.[53] When arrested, he was in the final stages of preparation for a coordinated simultaneous attack that would have involved flying an explosives-laden aircraft into the US Consulate in Karachi, and attacking Western residences and Westerners at Karachi airport.[54] A US Department of Homeland Security advisory said: 'Operatives were planning to pack a small fixed-wing aircraft or helicopter with explosives and crash it into the consulate.'[55] The Pakistani authorities recovered 330 pounds of explosives and a large quantity of weapons, including 200 detonators, 46 transmitters and 70 pistols. They also recovered maps of the Gwadar seaport and two airbases in Jacobabad and Pasni used by US troops operating in Afghanistan.[56]

Another Al Qaeda operational leader, KSM's nephew, Ammar al-Baluchi, alias Ali Abd al-Aziz Ali, was also arrested with Khallad.[57] He worked as a computer programmer in Dubai and was both a travel and financial facilitator for the 9/11 hijackers transitting in the UAE.[58] After 9/11, Ammar facilitated the attacks in Southeast Asia by moving funds and dispatching Majid Khan to the US to mount attacks. Majid Khan, who lived in the US, moved back to Karachi in 2002 to train as an operative.[59] In addition to travelling to Southeast Asia to fund attacks, Majid Khan planned to blow up petrol stations and poison water reservoirs in the US, and to kill President Musharraf in Karachi. Majid Khan and Ammar together planned to smuggle explosives to the US from Karachi using a Karachi-based textile import and export firm. At Ammar's request, Majid was supported by Aafia Siddiqui, an MIT biology graduate and PhD candidate in neurocognitive sciences at Brandeis University, who also lived in Karachi.[60] Forming a spirited logistical and a ruthless operational group, they ensured the survival of Al Qaeda in FATA and its ability to strike after the loss of Afghanistan. Against the odds, the Karachi cell members functioned as Al Qaeda's foremost operational base and carried out many acts, from murdering Daniel Pearl to facilitating major attacks in Karachi, Tunisia, Indonesia and worldwide. Despite the losses they faced, the cell members were highly motivated. KSM and Ramzi bin al-Shibh, for example, developed a plan to hijack an aircraft from Heathrow: even after their separate arrests, Ammer al Baluchi continued with the preparations until he was arrested.

Other cells operated in Karachi, including one led by Abu Faraj al-Libi, who later succeeded KSM. Another important operative was Ahmed Khalfan Ghailani, a document forger and travel facilitator.[61] A few hundred Afghan-trained foreigners lived in Karachi until the arrest of KSM in Rawalpindi on 1 March 2003, including Jack Thomas, an Australian operative who worked in Karachi from November 2002 to January 2003,[62] and Jose Padilla, a US operative who travelled from Karachi to Chicago to bomb high-rise buildings in the US.[63]

Many foreign terrorist groups maintained a presence in Karachi. From Arab to Asian groups, Karachi hosted a vast support infrastructure for recruits passing through before and after training, and operatives managing finance, logistics and terrorist operations. The groups rented and owned offices and safe houses, and also had access to madaris and businesses either owned or operated by them. The JI, for example, used Karachi both as a staging post for entering and leaving Afghanistan, and to groom a new generation of leaders. To legitimize travel to Afghanistan, the JI office in Karachi produced false documentation to show that a local religious school in Pakistan had accepted their recruits for religious studies, so providing the cover needed to account to their families and employers for their absences for between three and six months.

The recruits travelled by road to Kuala Lumpur for flights to Karachi, from where they were moved to safe houses in Karachi, Peshawar or Quetta and waited to be transported overland in batches into Afghanistan. To train a new generation of leaders in the Karachi madaris, Hambali established the Al Ghurabah (The foreigners) cell in 1999.[64] After undergoing initial education in Ulu Tiram madrasah and Lukmanul Hakim Islamic Boarding School in Malaysia, they received letters of recommendation to continue their studies in Pakistan. Afterwards some would take up 'field studies' in Afghanistan, deepening their knowledge of battle weaponry, or work in the administrative offices.[65] Abdul Rohim, the son of Abu Bakar Bashir, the JI leader, for example was an Al Ghurabah member in Karachi who worked in the Al Qaeda media office in Kandahar.

The Emerging Terrorist Threat

The pre-eminent threat to Karachi from outside Sindh stems from tribal Pakistan, notably from the Federally Administered Tribal Areas (FATA). Mirza Saud, the officer responsible for counter-terrorism in Karachi, said, 'Whatever happens to the Mehsuds in FATA will have an impact on Karachi. We host the largest population of Mehsuds in Karachi.'[66] Karachi has a Pashtu population (about four million) larger than that in Peshawar (about three million). There is considerable contact in terms of communication and the movement of people between FATA and Karachi. When an individual leaves FATA through South Waziristan, the first stop is Dera Ismail Khan, and then the main road leads to Karachi. Even from Swat, where the Taliban has established a presence, there is considerable traffic to Karachi. The tribal population was displaced by military operations in Waziristan and, while the neighbouring agencies received most of the displaced people, Karachi also received a significant population.

Operating under US pressure, the Pakistani military has used excessive force, militarizing a segment of the Mehsuds. This development has led to internal displacement, refugee flows, new recruits and support for an insurgency. According to an astute observer of the escalating insurgency, Dost Ali of the Karachi Police, 'Whenever you try to solve political problems through force, you face violence. The degree of force determines the degree of violence. The stronger you are, you will use more force. Over time, the weak will win. Everybody who cooperates becomes a friend.' The spillover effect has been profound.

Since 2007 there has been a significant threat from FATA. Videos and literature relating to extremist and terrorist propaganda from FATA are found in Karachi, including the book most widely used by the Jihadists, *Fazail-e-Jihad* (The Benefits of Jihad), which seeks to justify violence theologically.[67] Another book available in Karachi is *Islam or Fedai Hamle?* (Islam and Suicide Attacks?) by Mufti Abu Bashar Khasmi, most likely a pseudonym, and purportedly published in Dakha, Bangladesh.[68] Both books were included in list of banned titles produced for the Interior Ministry's campaign against extremism and terrorism in 2006. In addition to using Karachi to raise funds and gather new recruits, the Pakistani Taliban and Al Qaeda in tribal Pakistan are launching operations directly and through Pakistani groups in the mainland to hit targets in Karachi.[69]

The threat to Karachi from Jihadists and nationalist groups is likely to grow. For instance, the Baluchistan Liberation Army (BLA), an ethno-nationalist terrorist group operating in Karachi, carried out more than twelve sabotage attacks on electricity pylons, pipelines from the Sui natural gas fields and railway lines around Karachi and in Interior Sindh in 2007 and 2008.

Although Islamist terrorist groups present the greatest threat, the threat does not stem from politico-religious groups alone. The Muttahida Qaumi Movement (MQM), another ethno-nationalist group from Karachi, presents an enduring threat to the city, and the ongoing feud between MQM and Sunni Tehreek has claimed lives on both sides.

Terrorist groups in Karachi often target front-line security personnel. As law enforcement and intelligence services continue to hunt down terrorists and their supporters, these security officers are the ones whose lives are threatened daily. Four police officers were killed in Karachi in the last two weeks of March 2008, and a further two Intelligence Bureau officials were killed in the second of those weeks: according to the Karachi Police,

> these two events seem to be deliberate attempts to spread disaffection and undermine the morale of the law enforcing agencies as well as security agencies from acting effectively against anti-state inimical forces. These incidents appear to be the handiwork of the militant forces, who now feel emboldened due to transitory period.[70]

Events in Karachi are an indicator of likely future developments. The former prime minister, Benazir Bhutto, for example, narrowly escaped an assassination attempt in Karachi before she was killed in Islamabad on 27 December 2007. This was the worst of the fourteen terrorist incidents that took place in Sindh Province in 2007. The twin suicide attacks on the Benazir Bhutto welcome rally at Karsaz after midnight on 19 October 2007 resulted in the most fatalities ever seen in a single terrorist incident in Pakistan. A reported 130 were killed and 403 injured.[71] A further sixteen were missing, and presumed dead, so increasing the total number of fatalities to 146. These numbers include six dead police officers and twenty-nine injured. Most of the fatalities and injuries were caused by steel pellets. The first blast took place on the left side of the container truck carrying Bhutto as it crossed the Karsaz Flyover. The brunt of the blast was absorbed by a police car to the side, thus preventing serious damage to the truck. Two other cars were also damaged.[72] About one minute later there was a second blast that caused even greater damage.

The Karachi Police responded swiftly. The Deputy Inspector General (DIG) assigned to the investigation was later replaced by the DIG of CID. The crime scene was thoroughly inspected by the Investigation Team with the assistance of the Bomb Disposal Unit of the Special Branch. Circumstantial and material evidence collected ruled out the possibility of explosives installed in any vehicle because both vehicles were burnt and no evidence of explosives was found. Reports by the Bomb Disposal Unit, SIG of the Federal Investigation Agency (FIA) and FSL, material evidence collected from the crime scene, video footage and eyewitness accounts indicated that the explosions were the result of twin suicide bombings; this conclusion was also supported by FIA's SIG and other intelligence agencies. A striker sleeve, specifically used by suicide bombers as a manual-triggering mechanism to detonate explosive jackets, was recovered from the crime scene. According to the FIA's analysis, and further confirmed by the NWFP Police, similar striker sleeves of the same batch number had been recovered from ten previous suicide bomb blasts in the course of 2007.[73] Between them these blasts – in Peshawar, Dera Ismail Khan Quetta, Charsadda, Kohat, Rawalpindi and Karachi – had killed a total of 292 and injured 636.

The police were able to recover important evidence from the crime scene, including two heads, one with the face intact and some parts of the upper torso, and another severed head that was reconstructed with the assistance of doctors. Investigations revealed that the head with the face intact belonged to a Pakistan People's Party (PPP) activist, and not a terrorist. The severed heads received widespread media publicity. A reward of Rs5 million was offerd by the Government of Sindh for information leading to the arrest of the perpetrators, but to date no claimant has identified the second head.

Qari Zafar's group, the most feared group active in Karachi, is suspected of having conducted the bombing. Linked both to Al Qaeda and the Pakistani Taliban, it operates out of FATA, mounting suicide attacks especially in both Punjab and Sindh. Working under the supervision of Qari Hussain, the deputy of Baitullah Mehsud, Qari Zafar's training camps were in Wana. It is his task to prepare suicide bombers to attack foreign interests and law enforcement agencies in Pakistan. Qari Zafar built links with Amjad Farooqi's group operating in Karachi.[74] After Amjad's death, Qari Zafar strengthened his links with Matiur Rehman, alias Samad Sial, Amjad's assistant and successor. Matiur Rehman's group operated in Punjab and Sindh, particularly in Karachi. Formerly a member of Harkat-ul-Jihadi-Islami (HUJI), Matiur Rehman was involved in suicide attacks on President Musharraf in Rawalpindi.

These leaders, both from tribal and mainland Pakistan, together with foreign jihadists including Arab, Uighur and Uzbek mujahideen, developed a relationship of mutual cooperation and collaboration. Nek Muhammad, the leader of the Ahmedzai Wazir tribe in South Wazirstan, was the first to provide sanctuary to Al Qaeda leaders and members, and mobilized Pakistanis to fight against the Pakistani military. Since he posed a significant threat, Nek Muhammad was killed in a US Predator strike in June 2004. Baitullah Mehsud, the leader of the Mehsud tribe that lives side by side with the Ahmedzai Wazir tribe, succeeded him.

In light of previous suicide bombings in Karachi, the police shortlisted the Pakistani Taliban (Baitullah Mehsud Group), Al Qaeda (Qari Zafar Group), the LEJ, Harkat-ul-Mujahideen al-Almi, and hostile foreign agencies and miscellaneous groups as possible suspects.[75] The Sindh Police arrested Qari Saifullah Akhtar, the leader of HUJI, after CID Punjab released him on 13 March 2008.[76] A native of South Wazirstan, Qari Saifullah Akhtar, formed HUJI to fight the Soviets in Afghanistan but later established links with Al Qaeda, Taliban and several Pakistani groups. Akhtar was thoroughly interrogated during his remand period of fourteen days by the JIT, composed of members of all the security and intelligence agencies and law enforcement authorities, but the JIT could not establish his indirect or direct involvement in the Karsaz incident.[77] Following Bhutto's death in Islamabad, uncovering the identity of those behind the attempt in Karachi became of paramount significance. Working with other branches of government, the Sindh Police assigned the highest priority to identifying the perpetrators behind the Bhutto case.

The activities of several other terrorist groups that were otherwise unknown came to the foreground in 2007 and 2008. The police dismantled three terrorist groups and cells planning to mount attacks in Karachi and arrested seven members of Tehrik-e-Islami Lashkar-e-Muhammadi. Between 2002 and 2007 the hitherto unknown group, led by Wajahat,

killed fourteen persons belonging to minority communities – Christians
and Ahmadi, prominent businessmen and members of an NGO. A large
number of explosives, which the group intended to use for a spectacular
event, were also recovered. Immediately before the Day of Ashura the police, acting on a timely lead from the Federal Security Agency, were able to
destroy a terrorist cell planning to carry out a massacre of a Shi'a community by mixing cyanide in the Sabeels installed on the route of the main
Shi'a procession. Karachi police raided a hideout on 29 January 2008 and
encountered fierce resistance from Judnullah, a heavily armed and well-en-
trenched terrorist group, who killed two police officers and injured two.
During the prolonged encounter, the police killed three Jundullah members and arrested three more.[78] The police also recovered huge quantities
of heavy weapons and explosives, which the terrorists had acquired for activities in Karachi and to target sensitive military installations and can-
tonments. Members of this group were involved in an attack on the Corps
Commander's convoy in 2004 and carried out bank robberies in Karachi
in 2007 to fund the Pakistani Taliban. The US Consulate, Nishtar Park
blasts and Karsaz incidents undoubtedly indicate the ability of Al Qaeda,
the Pakistani Taliban and its affiliates to undertake big operations in
Karachi and Sindh. Despite the disruption of local terrorist cells, Karachi
will continue to experience periodic attacks of varying scales, especially
by groups operating out of FATA.

Stemming from developments both globally and within Pakistan,
two security threats are affecting Karachi. First, Pakistan's support for the
US fight against the insurgency in Afghanistan and tribal Pakistan is having an impact on the security of mainland Pakistan, notably in Karachi.
Secondly there is the threat of the Shi'a and Sunni rivalry in Pakistan and
the Middle East, which has not diminished. When hunted by the police in
Karachi, the Sunni terrorists and extremists who attacked the Shi'as relocated to tribal Pakistan. Other non-sectarian terrorists from Sindh also
joined or linked up with Al Qaeda, the Pakistani Taliban and the Punjabi
Taliban in tribal Pakistan. These individuals and groups from Karachi are
now fighting the Pakistani security forces in FATA and coalition forces in
Afghanistan. They present a long-term threat to Karachi and the rest of
Pakistan. Urdu-speaking Pakistanis from Sindh and a smaller percentage
of Sindhis united with Punjabis and Seraikis to fight both the coalition
forces and the Pakistani military under the banner of the Punjabi Taliban.[79] Abdul Rahman, a Punjabi, organized this non-Pashtu Taliban
grouping in FATA, but he and a group of Arabs were killed in Bahgar, An-
goorda, on 14 August 2008 as they crossed into South Wazirstan after fighting the coalition forces in Paktika. After being indoctrinated in global jihad

and learning tradecraft, the Sindhi and Urdu-speaking Pakistanis from Sindh are likely to return to Karachi to join terrorist and extremist groups there.

In the immediate future the threat to Karachi will stem from a diverse range of groups, including sectarian groups, Al Qaeda, the Pakistani Taliban and its associate groups, and ethno-nationalist groups. In the case of sectarian attacks, an escalation of police action might create a serious and violent backlash from the aggrieved community that leads to a widespread ethnic conflagration between the various ethnic communities. The terrorists, besides targeting Shi'a or Barelvi factions and political leaders, might increasingly attack police and military personnel and establishments. The recent incidents in Karachi and the rest of the country strongly confirm this trend. Both ethno-nationalist terrorist groups from Karachi and outside the city operate there. While MQM presents an enduring threat, the BLA may increase their attacks against state infrastructure as well as targeting foreign nationals, specifically the Chinese in Sindh.

Although not from groups, state sponsorship of terrorism still presents a challenge in South Asia. The geopolitical rivalry between India and Pakistan has led their intelligence agencies to support terrorism across their borders. Although the ISI sponsorship of terrorism in India has been globally highlighted, India too has actively supported terrorism in Bangladesh, Sri Lanka and Pakistan. In the 1980s India's foreign intelligence service, the Research and Analysis Wing (RAW), supported Jaye Sindh in Karachi. Similarly, the Pakistan government alleges that RAW has supported the BLA and MQM and the Karachi Police has assessed that: 'Foreign inimical powers might also exploit the situation by carrying out sabotage/terrorist activity in Karachi and interior Sindh to further aggravate the law and order situation. Recent bomb blast in Pathan populated area in Landhi, January 2008, strongly indicates this trend.'[80] Especially with Pakistani groups and those linked to Pakistan targeting economic targets in India, it is likely that RAW will consider expanding its support for threat groups that will hit Pakistan's economic hub.

Responding to Terrorism

The dedicated organization for fighting terrorism in Karachi is the Crime Investigation Department (CID) of the Provincial Police of Sindh. Created in response to the wave of sectarian violence, the CID built a modest capability before 9/11. It was the CID that investigated the kidnapping and beheading of Daniel Pearl, the first American to be killed by a terrorist group after 9/11. The event and the investigation demonstrated that associated terrorist groups trained, financed and ideologized by Al Qaeda could work together, and that the threat to the US and its interests will grow. A counter-terrorism specialist from the CID remarked that, 'For the first time, we saw different groups coming together. In Karachi, AQ, LeJ and other groups started to work together.'[81]

On the genesis of the CID in Karachi, Mashwany, a dedicated counter-terrorism operations officer, said,

> It took 10 days and 42 trucks to clear the garbage, mostly old files. When we started, some of us worked 18 hours a day. After dark, there were no lights. So we used candles. We had no computers but typewriters. We had neither phone cards nor national card registration. We operated against several odds. We still have no capacity to monitor communications. We had provided phone numbers for monitoring to IB and ISI. The phone users were picked up. Callers' IDs were blocked.[82]

The CID considers its inability to monitor communications a major impediment to its progress in the fight against terrorism. Mashwany added, 'If you are gagged and bound, it is a major weakness in the laws.'[83] According to Dr Suddle, then Inspector General of Police for Sindh Province, 'There is no institutionalized method for the police to share intelligence with IB or ISI. It is an individual relationship.'[84] Rather than fighting terrorism, the police in Pakistan fought ordinary, serious and organized crime for decades. From criminal sources and investigations, they considered criminals as men with no character and few moral values. While the police had the structures and doctrines to manage the criminal threat, the CID officer soon realized that the men they were hunting were unlike ordinary criminals. If physical torture were used, it would become personal and would send a message that 'I abused the prophet and Islam in front of me.' Their organizations were more powerful than criminal groups:

> A criminal never or rarely accepted his crime. But they took pride in it. Here it was 180 degrees reverse. You think he is lying. You think it is his ego talking. You think he is bragging. When we checked the ground realities, it was found true ... With a few exceptions, the terrorists had no modern education. But he had the ability to make a bomb using ordinary things and kill 100 people ... Although not all, many of them were discreet. When it came to betraying their colleagues,

some lied. They did not know the exact identities.

Unlike criminals, terrorists waged a continuous campaign. The police learned by trial and error and experience. Relying on intuition and gut feeling, occasional blunders were made. Javed Bukhari, for example, debriefed a terrorist who gave up only a partial story. The detainee could not be broken and he was released. Soon after, however, another officer arrested him and he finally gave the complete picture during the second interrogation.

Terrorism, extremism and crime in Pakistan can be fought effectively only by addressing the challenges both at the micro and macro levels. At the micro level, an intelligence-led law enforcement approach can reduce the immediate threat. Karachi is suffering from terrorism and extremism, as well as organized and low level crime, because Pakistan has not invested adequately in law enforcement. The Sindh police require resources (financial and manpower), robust intelligence, Internet forensic capability, IT support, equipment to monitor communications and other tools of the trade. Pakistan must qualitatively and quantitatively address a range of issues.

At the macro level, Pakistan needs to reconstruct the basic institutions: a credible judiciary, a responsive elections commission, an incorruptible police force, a forward-looking education system, and laws that accord equal status to women. 'When we do not have such institutions, they become the cause of disorder. Rather than become the solution, you become a part of the problem. People lose confidence. They adopt the laws of the jungle and ultimately take the law unto themselves.'[85] To stay ahead of terrorism and extremism, Pakistan needs an all-encompassing national and international strategy with clear-cut goals, objectives and means to achieve them. Due attention should be given to the economic, political and social aspects of the strategy. In order to be successful, these initiatives should complement one another. To achieve this, a nationwide consensus accompanied by strong political will is paramount.

Intelligence plays a central role in the fight against terrorism, and has proved to be exceptionally effective in Karachi. For instance, the ISI and IB have a responsibility to fight terrorism at a federal level, but Jundullah was broken by the Sindh Provincial Police, especially the CID, in Karachi with input from ISI. The Deputy Inspector General in charge of the CID in Karachi, Mirza Saud, said, 'We worked with them.'[86] However, it is necessary to establish close collaboration and coordination between the intelligence agencies and police forces throughout Pakistan. The Karachi police currently feel handicapped as they seldom get timely information from the intelligence agencies whenever the police request such information from intelligence agencies, since "it rarely receives such information in time".[87] In order to overhaul the present ineffective system, there is a dire need to set up a task force at the provincial and national levels, composed of members of law enforcement authorities and security agencies. Such an arrangement would remove unnecessary barriers between different organizations working towards a similar objective.

The US has generously supported the ISI, Pakistan's premier intelligence service, and the Frontier Constabulary, which is operating in FATA. 'The ISI received huge resources, both technical assistance and finance, from the CIA. However, the Karachi police received no foreign support in the form of equipment or resources. Karachi Police's budget for informant handling is a meagre US$6,000 per month.'[88] Adequate funds for obtaining information through sources should be placed at the disposal of the Provincial Police forces. Surveillance teams need to be raised. The present system for monitoring proscribed groups and 'suspects listed under IV schedule of ATA-1997' calls for serious pursuance and implementation by the provincial police forces: 'There is a definite need for reappraisal as the present system does not seem to be working effectively.'[89] Because their intelligence budget was minuscule, the Karachi police admitted that their intelligence network was gravely limited and so they came to know of threat groups operating in Sindh only after an attack, as Mirza Saud explained:

> Some groups are sleepers. Only after an incident we came to know of their existence. There may be others operating in Karachi … For instance, Wajahat from Harakat-ul Ansar formed Tehrik-e-Islami Lashkar-e-Muhammadi (TILM). They planned to kill Americans and Jews. As the Rotary founder was a Jew, Wajahat believed that only Jews can be members of Rotary Clubs. Lashkar-e-Muhammadi killed thirteen people of which eight were Christian ngo workers. Wajahat believed that Father Arnold paid money to spread Christianity. Wajahat developed his own manifesto and manual.[90]

Although it is known that Wajahat, a *khepia* (trader) by profession, travelled to both Dubai and Colombo, the details of what he did overseas are not available. He claimed that he stayed in Dubai for a year, establishing a buying and selling business, but this could not be verified as there was no security and intelligence liaison between the police forces in Karachi and Dubai. Under interrogation Wajahat was only asked questions relevant to the prosecution, not those that would be of value to the intelligence agency. Policemen were instructed at training schools and mentored by their superiors in building cases rather than collecting intelligence, which would have required different techniques.

There is 'no regular or close interaction or exchange of information on terrorism issues between the different provincial police forces'.[91] As there is no common platform for sharing and no mechanism for collaboration, there are gaps and loopholes, duplication of efforts, and wastage of resources and time. In the aftermath of the manifold increase in terrorism in the country in 2007, there is clearly a need to establish a specific counter-terrorism organization at the national level. Pakistan is in favour of emulating the UK model, by which New Scotland Yard merged two branches in 2006 to create the Counter Terrorism Command. Setting up such an agency in Pakistan may prove more effective in the long term.

Terrorists are increasingly resorting to novel methods of recruitment, communication and fund-raising via the Internet. The Pakistani police lack technical capabilities to monitor the Internet or forensic capability to investigate computers recovered from terrorists. There is a greater need to scrutinize and block Jihadi websites 'which seem to have extremely negative influence upon youths of the country'.[92] There is support within the Pakistani police for the creation of a permanent watchdog body.[93]

The Karachi police also lack a community engagement programme. The gap in trust between the law enforcement agencies and the general public needs to be bridged urgently. Until public confidence is restored, the law enforcement agencies, however efficient, would not be able to counter terrorism effectively without vital public support. According to a related report, 'the introduction of community policing in the country may be the best solution in this quest'.[94]

There is no programme in Pakistan to counter the ideology of extremist and terrorist groups. Feelings of hopelessness and ignorance in the Muslim world have been exploited by politically motivated individuals. Referring to the exploitation of Islam to legitimize terrorist and extremist activities, Dr Sohaib Suddle said, 'Since 9/11, it has become a menace. We need to give the right message of Islam. Mullahs that lead the prayers on Fridays or on any other day must be co-opted to join the mainstream. They are historically a marginalized group. They collected food items for survival.'[95] Although Pakistan has prepared a list of publications to be banned, terrorist and extremist groups are still disseminating propaganda with the aim of radicalizing the next generation. Darul Islam, an independent commercial organization established by some members of Ja-maat-al-Daawa, is selling Jihad CDs.[96]

While there is enthusiasm, there is a limited understanding of how to develop a counter ideology programme, or its potential impact. The police approached a few clerics and they agreed to preach against extremism, but nothing happened. The police did not trust their sincerity either.[97] While a few performers bold enough to promote peace received television and radio airtime, there are no sustained programmes to proactively build a society that abhors violence and extremism. Even in the printed media, no priority is given to efforts, either by Pakistan or other governments, to move in that direction. For instance, when Dar-ul-Uloom Deoband, the subcontinent's most prestigious madrasa, issued a fatwa against terrorism, it was buried on the inside pages.[98] The Karachi police understands the need to embark immediately on a national de-radicalization programme similar to that in Singapore, Egypt, Uzbekistan, Indonesia, Yemen and Saudi Arabia: 'In this regard, services of prominent religious leaders specifically from the Deobandhi faction and others of such ilk can be harnessed earnestly.'[99]

The criminal justice and prisons system in Pakistan is weak. Legally, there are many obstacles to reducing terrorism and crime in Pakistan. There is certainly a need for a better prosecution of terrorism cases, particularly in terrorism courts: 'Trials are long – it takes years for a case to be resolved.' [100] Frequent abuses of detainees are a result of the lack of a proper criminal justice system. When the system cannot dispense justice on the guilty, policemen in Pakistan are inclined to take the law into their own hands. Many of those who participated in the abduction, detention and murder of Daniel Pearl are walking freely on the streets of Karachi. It is also necessary to educate the judges, prosecutors and lawmakers about terrorism and counter-terrorism. Due to the lack of an effective witness protection programme, convictions in terrorism cases are almost impossible to achieve. People are asked to give evidence, yet the evidence collected by a police officer is not admissible in court. 'Crime and terrorism can also be contained by taking it to its logical conclusion – towards this end, the legal institution needs to be strengthened! More effective courts are needed!'[101]

To fight terrorism and crime effectively, more resources are necessary. The threat will persist without dedicated leadership at all levels: 'The formula to fight terrorism and crime effectively is to lead from the front. Then people will have faith in you. You should have the capacity to say no to orders coming from any quarter: friends, relatives or politicians.'[102] Referring to his style of leadership, Babar Khattack, Police Chief of Karachi, claimed, 'In one month, I reduced crime by 30 per cent. I have adopted a no-nonsense approach – recruiting better persons and monitoring the work of the officers. I have not faced political pressure. If you let political pressure affect you, you must draw the line. Public rely on your leadership.'[103]

In the absence of political will, the madaris system has not been reformed. Half of the 20,000 madaris (Islamic seminaries) in Pakistan represent the Deobandi tradition.[104] The Minister of Law and Parliamentary Affairs, Ayaz Soomro, said in July 2008 that madaris in Karachi are supporting terrorism.[105] The pace of Islamization increased in Pakistan during the anti-Soviet multinational Afghan campaign (1979–89) and madaris proliferated throughout the 1980s and '90s. It is through madaris that the extremist and terrorist groups exercise their influence on the community:

> Pakistani familes are large. A poor family of eight–ten children is vulnerable to recruitment. Due to poverty and the ignorance of parents, they send their children to madaris. A madaris is like an NGO where the children get free food, clothes, books and a place to stay. There is huge unemployment due to the lack of basic skills. If you are educated by the mullah, you cannot join a bank, the police or the army. Even if they have extremist ideas, after joining a mainstream institution, it will be diluted. In the case of madaris graduates, they simply do not have the skills to work. By sending children to a madaris, parents think that the children will become disciplined and good. Sending children to a madaris, where the curriculum is restrictive, is not like sending them to a British boarding school. As a priority, it is necessary to transform madaris and ensure that they are at par with the other established mainstream institutions of learning. To hate and kill is not in the genes and to take one's own life is not programmed.[106]

For instance, the Taliban maintains a strong ideological and operational support base in Karachi through the 'large Pashtun community, hundreds of Deobandi Madrasahs and banned terrorist outfits'.[107] Traditionally, the Deobandi madrasas in Karachi, especially Jamea Binoria, have provided the key leadership to the Taliban movement in Afghanistan and Pakistan, including Abdullah Mehsud, the Pakistani Taliban commander killed by Pakistani security forces in July 2007.[108] Jamea Binoria also exerts considerable influence on sectarian and terrorist outfits such as Sipah-e-Sahaba, Lashkar-e-Jhangvi and Jaish-e-Muhammad. Although Mullah Omar never studied at Jamea Binoria, or even completed his religious education, he was awarded an honorary degree. Jamea Binoria, was established in Jamshed Quarters in 1978. While it is politically affiliated with Jamiat Ulema-i-Islam, its jihadi affiliation is with Jamaitul Furqan, and its educational board is Wifaq-ul-Madaris Al Arabia. Its sub-branches consist of Tajweed-al-Qur'an, Hifz-ul-Qur'an, Books Department, Dar-ul-Aftaa, computer, publishing, administrative, library, foreign students and local students. The highest educational level its students can achieve is a doctoral degree and its annual expenditure is Rs 20 million. Most of the Sipah-e-Sahaba Pakistan members come from this madrasa. The school acknowledges that it lost nine 'martyrs' in Afghanistan, although the number may be higher. It is opposed to madaris reforms and the Women Protection Bill. Female students study at Madrsa Al Binat. There are five federations of madaris in Pakistan altogether, each representing its own sect or affiliation. It is high time that the present government addresses this issue, once and for all, with political sagacity. There is also a need for consistently strict legal action against perpetrators of religious hatred in the province.

There are appropriate economic solutions for dealing with political disputes. Genuine aspirations and grievances can be tackled by providing education for the masses and facilitating economic development. To this end, Pakistan can develop a plan to garner international support. On economic empowerment, Dr Suddle suggests that

> The global political economy is mainly benefiting only a few. The threat of terrorism and extremism cannot be handled by the Third World countries alone – they are the victims. The US, EU, Japan and China should step in. To resolve the issue, it is necessary not only to implement a range of measures like enforcing the law, but also correct the local and global reality. I do not believe there is no issue that cannot be resolved if there is a will.[109]

By addressing political, economic, and social challenges at the national and international level, Pakistan can help change the reality of the environment. As the threat globalizes, enlisting international financial and economic support to empower the marginalized countries economically will serve to reduce the threat.

Besides empowering the economically destitute, it is also necessary to empower the politically marginalized. Only a government that is truly representative of the people will receive public support. On political empowerment, Dr Suddle said:

> People must own whatever they have. Without a sense of ownership, there will be no real progress. Issues of governance remain unaddressed. Police and the criminal justice and prisons system must

be above board; perceived just and genuine grievances should be addressed with a certain degree of speed. Today, there is a lack of rule of law, and people feel a sense of hopelessness towards the justice system. Another grievance is economic injustice. Old fiefs that still persist must end. There should be equal opportunities. People must be able to dream that if you are okay on merit, nothing should stop you from reaching the top.[110]

Public support is crucial if the government is to harbour any hopes of defeating the contemporary wave of extremism and terrorism.

Governments lack an understanding of the larger picture – that there cannot be peace without restoring regional stability. Instead of using their already limited funds to destabilize each other, it is necessary for governments to use the money for economic and social development. As Pakistan and India face increasingly similar threats, both countries will need to share intelligence and conduct joint operations. Without support from neighbours, terrorism and crime cannot be fought effectively in the twenty-first century.

Global terrorism demands an international response. As a Muslim nation, Pakistan has the credentials to change the status quo. Global developments have contributed to the Muslims' rage. Developments in the Middle East over the Palestinian issue, in India and Pakistan over Kashmir, in Afghanistan following the intervention after 9/11, and Iraq after the invasion in 2003 increased the threat. In the midst of these events, threat groups exploited the simmering resentment in the Muslim world, including Pakistan. There is a widely held view in the Islamic world, particularly in Pakistan, that the international community, especially the US, is unfairly pro-Israeli. Seeking to stabilize conflict zones using peace processes and having the military work with local forces can help to reduce that threat. Fewer conflicts lead to a more harmonious social structure and reduce the tendency towards social disintegration.

Political-Criminal-Terrorist Nexus

Is there a nexus between criminal and terrorist groups? Terrorist groups have relied on criminal networks to transfer funds, obtain identity documents, especially for travel, and smuggle operatives and material. The US investigated whether Al Qaeda relied on criminal syndicates like D-Company to transfer money for terrorism.[111] Well-established groups such as Al Qaeda preferred to use their own front, cover and sympathetic organizations to support their activities. Quite early on, the professional terrorist groups realized the dangers of relying on financially motivated criminal groups that could be compromised by government security agencies.

Terrorist and criminal organizations have different motivations: terrorists are willing to sacrifice their lives for their beliefs, while criminals are motivated to acquire wealth and power for themselves. Given this difference, the nexus between these two economically and politically motivated groups is not widespread: it is an exception rather than the rule.

Terrorists prefer not to engage in crime to generate funds to mount attacks. They are conscious of retaining public support, especially from their ethnic groups or religious communities. They would not want to be isolated or marginalized by their supporters but would prefer to be viewed as heroes and freedom fighters. Terrorists are of the belief that if they engage in crime, they will lose public support. Furthermore, they will be exposed before they complete their mission. Engaging in criminal activity attracts the adverse attention of law enforcement authorities and the intelligence agencies. To ensure the success of their terrorist operations, the terrorist modus operandi is to operate discreetly until they mount the final attack. When terrorists are dispatched on a mission, the Karachi experience shows that they are sent out with sufficient money. There are several examples to illustrate the terrorists' reluctance to engage in high-profile crime. With a few exceptions, vehicles used for mounting terrorist operations are not stolen because the terrorists are aware that there may be a police record if a vehicle is stolen, and the police will be on the lookout for it.

There are terrorist groups in Karachi that engage in crime and those that steer clear of it. While terrorist groups that are financially unstable engage in crime to fund their operations, well-funded groups do not need to resort to crime. The Karachi case study reveals that there is a spectrum in the way terrorist groups fund their operations. Groups such as LeT and Jayash-e-Mohamed with significant public support, for example, do not engage in crime but instead highlight their socio-economic, educational and welfare activities, and appeal for donations. In contrast, groups such as LeJ, Jundullah and Tehrik-e-Islami Lashkar-e-Muhammadi, which have no public support, engage in crime. The terrorist shift towards crime is observed only when the political agenda is not sufficiently appealing to garner support. When these groups' sources of funding dry up, they turn to crime.

In contrast, there is a nexus between politics and crime. Tribes, ethnic communities and major political parties in Karachi have their own militia wings. This has significant implications for maintaining law and order. For instance, if a policeman arrests a Mohajir who is influential enough to speak to a Mohajir politician, he is likely to be released. The politician will speak to a senior police officer to seek the release of his constituent. The arresting policeman may be penalized or punished, or he may even be transferred to another police station, thus affecting his prospects for promotion and bringing hardship to his family. Policemen are cautious about arresting influential figures and tend to drop cases they perceive to meet with political interference. The worst-case scenario is that the policeman involved may be threatened or killed. Governing Karachi and maintaining law and order is complex. According to Mashwany, Superintendent of Police, CID Karachi:

> There was no political interference when it came to fighting terrorism. However, because political parties, including major political parties, were affiliated to religious groups or criminal groups, there was considerable intervention. For instance, the Shi'a groups were religious groups with a quasi-political orientation. Intervention was both political and violent. Politicians telephoned senior police officers or organized their supporters to protest to seek the release of their party or family members. Unless decisions were reversed, criminal groups targeted individual officers or threatened to target their families. In the face of resistance, some police officers were killed.[112]

Both nationalist and religious parties have their own formal or informal militant wings. Some militant wings or segments are self-financed and some others are funded through criminal activities. When voluntary donations decline, armed activists engage in extortion or other forms of crime. The militia of some nationalist and religious parties also engage in coercion, both explicit and implicit.[113] The business community may even provide support to parties, militias and other threat groups to protect their business interests. The financial elites have also been found to support the militant wings financially, but not because they sympathized with their ideologies. Several nationalist or religious parties give political protection to the groups engaged in crime. In some cases, such as MQM, the leadership approved and even directed the criminal activity. In most cases, however, the leadership was aware but condoned and tolerated it as it benefited the party.

In Sindh, the different ethnic groups are organized in tribes, with their own tribal structures, codes and leaders. The Mohajirs, as refugees and migrants from India, had no tribal system. To survive in Sindh, notably in Karachi, the Mohajirs organized themselves like a tribe. The MQM provided the leadership and the structure to fill this gap. Although the MQM has the support of only between 30 and 40 per cent of the Mohajirs, it successfully organized them, disciplining the Mohajirs as a community through sporadic threats and acts of violence. Significant portions of the Mohajirs work together to support the MQM. The MQM has a presence throughout Sindh, especially in cities like Karachi and Hyderabad. The political strongholds of MQM in Karachi are in Korangi, Landhi, Nazimabad, Orangi and Liaqatabad. The MQM also has significant influence in the Shi'a areas.[114] Today, the MQM is a significant political organization.

The MQM engaged in systematic fund-raising until 2005. Every shop – both Mohajir and non-Mohajir – had to make a monthly payment to the MQM: the smaller shops provided Rs 500–1,000 per month, while the larger shops provided Rs 1,000–2,000 a month.[115] MQM collectors said it was a tax that guaranteed their protection. A phone number was provided to contact the MQM for such emergencies. Careful records of donors were kept. The MQM's strategy of demanding money from every shop owner eroded the image of the group initially, but by 2005, the MQM had invested its funds wisely and built a steady support base, realizing the importance of protecting its name. Since 2005 the MQM has raised funds largely from big businesses, and in most cases the funds came voluntarily. Although the MQM as an organization appears to shy away from crime, its members and supporters engage in criminal activity that can be violent.

The militia wings attached to the major political parties in Karachi are the student wings, which are armed and are used to protect their leaders, members, supporters and their families. The political parties in this category are the Pakistan People's Party (Bhutto), MQM (Altaf Hussein), AMP (the party in power in NWFP Agency) and Jamaat-i-Islami.[116] With the exception of Jamaat-i-Islami, the militia wings of the other parties have become notorious for engaging in crime, although the party leadership may not have approved of the criminal acts, and they may have been committed by individuals. In the case of the tribal groups and ethnic communities, the only entity that does not have its militia wing is the Sindhs. The indigenous community of Sindh Province is one of the most peaceful and the Sindhs, as a community, are not involved in terrorist, criminal or sectarian organizations. Although there are recent exceptions, the Sindhs are a model community. Three factors are likely to have led to this: geography, distance and culture. Geographically, Sindh is not in direct contact with Afghanistan and NWFP Agency, areas with martial cultures and a tradition of fighting. It is isolated from conflict zones in terms of distance. The language barrier and cultural differences with Punjab and others also shields it from outside influences.

In traditional societies, each tribal or ethnic group maintains the militia group that protects it. With modernization, political parties replace partially or fully the tribal and ethnic structures. Pakistan is a society in transition and, as a nation that fails to modernize adequately, tribes, ethnic communities and political parties have maintained their militias. This practice has continued as Pakistan is incapable of disarming the militias. In many areas, government authority does not function beyond the major cities. Until law enforcement authorities and the government are able to exercise centralized authority, this state of affairs is likely to persist.

The crime-politics nexus in Pakistan is not only evident in the ethnic and religious political parties, but also in mainstream political parties. To maintain power, politicians, including those at the higest levels, maintain contact with criminals or use their youth wings to commit crimes. According to Dost Ali,

> The most civilized manifestation of a criminal is a politician. Politicians and criminals are strikingly similar and different. Politicians have the power to convince supporters to give money. Criminals are unable to convince but will use force to get money. The motto is that whoever gives money is our friend. Some politicians will work with criminals and use force. Some criminals will seek the patronage of politicians for protection. Criminals are not willing to work under ethical and moral formula. The conduct of some politicians, once in power, will be similar to the criminals.[117]

Although some mainstream parties, including the PPP, the Muslim League and AMP, expelled some of their members for engaging in crime, most splinter groups routinely engaged in extortion.[118] When asked if the writ of law can be enforced in Pakistan, Dr Sohaib Suddle said,

> It can be done. The only way is for political leaders to become role models. If political leaders are willing to be a part of the crime-politics nexus, we cannot. I was not keen to accept this job. If I accepted it, I told them that I need a total free hand. If someone wants to interfere, I will not. It is easier said than done. One must be a pragmatic practitioner. There is no other city like Karachi.[119]

Securing Karachi

Both terrorism and crime affect all sectors of Karachi society. Political, ethnic and sectarian divisions make securing Karachi a multi-dimensional, multi-pronged and a multi-agency task. One state actor, however good it may be, cannot accomplish this. It requires the integration of both state and non-state instruments. With 90–95 per cent of the infrastructure owned or operated by the private sector, the public-private sector partnership has become essential to secure Karachi. Furthermore, the partnership with the community has become even more crucial.

The key role of law enforcement and intelligence services is to detect attacks by groups that seek to disrupt social harmony, and that will have a negative impact upon law and order in Karachi. The Shi'a-Sunni attacks cannot be eliminated, but the threat can be managed. Similarly, the ongoing feud between MQM and Sunni Tehreek, which has claimed several lives on both sides, will persist. Both the Pakistan government and the provincial government of Sindh need to invest more in good governance. Until then, it should be accepted that peace and security cannot be established in Karachi. Disarming political and other groups, and restoring the rule of law, cannot be accomplished overnight. It will require the government to assure and provide security to political and other interest groups. As long as the police and other law enforcement authorities remain understaffed, there will always be violence in Karachi.

Maintaining ethnic and religious harmony is a key challenge as it can prevent terrorist attacks against religious and ethnic communities, as well as ethnic or religious riots. If inter-ethnic and inter-religious tensions are not checked effectively, all the communities will suffer. Only through integrating law enforcement with community engagement can the probability of an ethnic or religious backlash be reduced. An approach focused purely on law enforcement will not work. A permanent platform for dialogue and building good relations among political, religious and other leaders is required. Unless the different ethnic and religious groups have the opportunity to meet up periodically to bridge their differences and communicate with each other, the security and stability of Karachi will be jeopardized. Despite political and other differences, it is of paramount importance for leaders of different communities to meet and talk because most disagreements that degenerate into violence resulted from misunderstandings. Although leaders in law enforcement have a major role to play, securing Karachi is ultimately the responsibility of the elites of Karachi.

4

Mainland Pakistan Terrorist Groups

Many groups that began with local agendas have transformed into groups with regional and international agendas. As the international agenda was seductive and attractive, virtually none have returned to their domestic agenda. These Muslim nationalist groups developed transnational linkages and began to operate beyond their traditional territories. In addition, violent extremist groups such as Sunni Tehreek, Tehrik-e-Jafria Pakistan and Muttahida Qaumi Movement have formed that are ethno-nationalist and have overseas wings.

Lashkar-e-Taiba (LET)

On 26 November 2008 India was rocked by multiple terrorist attacks in the financial hub of Mumbai. The deadly attacks, which claimed more than 195 lives, were conducted by LET . The magnitude and impact of the Mumbai attacks brought this group, previously known only from its engagement in India-controlled Kashmir, to the world's attention. Did Al Qaeda, the chief proponent of global jihad, influence the perpetrators of the Mumbai carnage? In future, will the sub-continental terrorists prefer to attack the 'crusader and Jewish' targets identified by the global jihadists as opposed to 'Indian government and Hindu' targets? The Mumbai attack was unprecedented in its choice of targets. Four of the five pre-designated targets were frequented by Westerners. The Taj and Oberoi are international hotels patronized by Westerners while the Leopold Café is a favourite venue for tourists. Nariman House, a Jewish community centre, is popular among Israeli backpackers. The exception was Chhatrapati Shivaji Terminus, one of the busiest train stations in the world.

Previous attacks by Lashkar-e-Taiba had focused on Indian government targets. Why did a Pakistani group that is not affiliated to Al Qaeda mount an Al Qaeda-style attack? Was the target selection influenced by India's alliance with the US and Israel? Does the growing India-US-Israel axis influence the orientation of sub-continental Muslim groups to the point where even their target selection is dramatically changing? The method of operation was classic Al Qaeda style: a coordinated simultaneous attack against high-profile, symbolic and strategic targets aimed at inflicting harm and damage on the innocent masses. The terrorists differed from Al Qaeda in that they did not mount a suicide attack. Although they fully intended to die, it was a no-surrender or a fedayeen attack, a classic LET attack modus operandi.

The Mumbai attack was a watershed. It demonstrated LET's stark departure from a group that is anti-India to one that is both anti-India and anti-Westerners. LET's direct and operational role in the Mumbai attack surprised the security and intelligence services that are interested in the group. Founded to fight Indian presence in Kashmir, LET has evolved into a group operating against targets throughout India and has trained Pakistanis, Indians and other foreign nationals to target India. Today, its operations have globalized. Although it is premature to identify LET as an Al Qaeda-like outfit, LET has clearly crossed the line. It has adopted a larger agenda.

Until Mumbai, LET belonged to the category of Islamist nationalist groups. Groups such as Palestinian Hamas, Palestinian Islamic Jihad, Al Aqsa Martyrs Brigade, Moro Islamic Liberation Front, Moro National Liberation Front, Pattani United Liberation Organization, Free Aceh Movement, Al Badr and Hezbul Mujahideen remain Muslim nationalist groups. In contrast, groups in Egypt (Egyptian Islamic Jihad, Islamic Group of Egypt), Algeria (Salafist Group for Call and Combat), Libya (Libyan Islamic Fighters Group), Uzbekistan (Islamic Movement of Uzbekistan), Philippines (Abu Sayyaf Group), Indonesia (Jemaah Islamiyah) and many others that began with local agendas have transformed into groups with regional and international ambitions.

The evolution of LET from an anti-India militant outfit into a regional terrorist entity presents an interesting case study for understanding the patterns of terrorism in South Asia. LET was formed soon after Hafiz Mohammed Saeed, Zafar Iqbal and Abdullah Azam set up Markaz Dawa ul Irshad (MDI, Centre For Religious Learning and Social Welfare), its parent religious organization, in 1987 at Muridke, near Lahore in Punjab, primarily as a centre for religious preaching. The land at Muridke was purchased by Abdul Rehman Sherahi, an Arab Mujahid with Al Qaeda connections, who is the brother-in-law of Zaki-ur-Rehman Lakhvi. MDI soon distinguished itself as a hard-line fundamentalist organization following what is known as the Ahle-Hadith movement, an ultra-orthodox grouping of organizations that accepts the austere Wahhabi practices of Saudi Arabia.[1] Hafiz Mohammad Saeed was in charge of the military aspects (LET), Zafar Iqbal was head of reform-oriented education.[2]

Initially MDI's sole objective was to assist the Afghan mujahideen to liberate Afghanistan from the Soviet occupation during the 1980s and the MDI recruited volunteers to fight as mujahideen guerillas. After the Soviets pulled out, the group maintained close ties with the Taliban regime in Afghanistan, where it continued to train and educate its members until the US-led campaign forced them to relocate.[3]

The earliest reference to MDI dates from 22 February 1990, when it was reportedly launched during the inauguration ceremony of Maskar-e-Aqsa at Tango in the Kunar province of Afghanistan.[4] The same year, Maskar-e-Aqsa was established near Muzaffarbad in Pakistan to conduct training for the Kashmiri Jihadis.[5] Under the command of Abu Hafas, LET's Amir for Kashmir, LET cadres began to infiltrate into the Kashmir Valley. The first encounter between the LET and the Indian security forces took place on 26 August 1992 at Rishighund, but the formation of LET as the armed wing of MDI was announced only in 1993.[6] LET came to prominence when there was a large-scale infiltration of its cadres into Jammu and Kashmir in 1993, in collaboration with the Islami Inquilabi Mahaz, a militant outfit based in the Poonch district of Indian-controlled Kashmir.[7]

The sole objective of LET was to liberate Kashmir from Indian occupation and promote the creation of three separate independent Muslim homelands within India. The first one merges Kashmir with Pakistan, and the two others would be achieved by liberating Muslim majority areas in North and South India respectively. The means by which this is to be carried out, according to Hafiz Mohammad Saeed, is *jihad*: 'The jihad in Kashmir would soon spread to the entire India. Our mujahideen will create three Pakistans in India.'[8] This would be accomplished, he said a year later in an interview, by arousing (Indian) Muslims 'to rise in revolt … so that India is disintegrated'. In Hafiz Mohammad Saeed's own words, 'Kashmir is only our base camp. The real war will be inside India as we consider Himachal Pradesh (India) as the door to Jihad in India. Very soon we will enter India via Doda and unfurl the Islamic flag on Red Fort (New Delhi).'[9]

The LET 'agenda', as outlined in a pamphlet titled 'Why Are We Waging Jihad?' includes the restoration of Islamic rule over all parts of India.[10] The pamphlet reportedly describes jihad as being obligatory for taking back Spain, where the Muslims ruled for 800 years, the whole of India, including Kashmir, Hyderabad (in the Indian state of Andhra Pradesh), Assam (India), Nepal, Burma, Bihar (India), Junargarh (India), the parts of Palestine occupied by Israel, Hungary, Cyprus, Ethiopia and Russia.[11]

LET's primary area of operation is the Jammu and Kashmir region, which includes areas in Indian- and Pakistani-administered Kashmir. The group is known to have been active elsewhere in India, for example in New Delhi, Mumbai and Hyderabad.[12] LET was involved in the attacks on the Indian army barracks in the Red Fort at Delhi in December 2000.[13] Indian officials have also blamed the group for a series of bomb blasts in Mumbai in 2002–3, alleging it to be working in conjunction with SIMI, an Indian-Muslim students' group.

In August 2003 Maharashtra police unearthed an LET base in Mumbra, in the Thane district, and arrested some terrorists in connection with the blasts in Mumbai. Mumbai has a substantial Muslim population and seems to have become a base for militants who receive assistance from local residents. On 13 August 2001 the police in the Indian state of Uttar Pradesh arrested two LET terrorists, Altaf Hussain and Salim Qamar, from the high-security cantonment area of Lucknow. Police recovered more than 12 kilograms of RDX, and other arms and ammunitions. The next day the police shot and killed Imran, a Pakistani citizen and an LET area commander, in Ayodhya. Police believed that all three belonged to a group that was planning to explode bombs in temples and pilgrim sites in Ayodhya. Investigations revealed that both Altaf Hussain and Salim Qamar were working as mechanics in Saudi Arabia when they came in contact with LET activists and were persuaded to join. It was Imran who took them to Muzzafarabad in Pakistan-administered Kashmir (Azad Kashmir) via Karachi, where they were trained to use AK-47s and to make bombs. Significantly, the Maharashtra police, who then arrested some suspects in a raid in Mumbra, also knew about the presence of Imran. In a statement on 14 August 2001, the Thane Police Commissioner Surendra Shangari said that LET is 'looking to establishing bases in Mumbra to carry out terrorist activities in Mumbai and at an international level'.[14]

The LET presence in Hyderabad was part of a plan to expand its activities into south India. The organization reportedly received considerable support from the communally sensitive Hyderabad. Its presence was brought to public scrutiny with the bomb explosion at the Saibaba temple in Dilsukhnagar. From the investigations it was learnt that an LET operative Abdul Kareem alias Tunda, a native of Rae Bareli in Uttar Pradesh, and Javed Nasir, a former Pakistani soldier, trained LET cadres, recruited from Calcutta, eastern Uttar Pradesh, Bihar and Hyderabad, in the manufacture and use of explosives.[15]

A letter recovered from a terrorist killed after an attack on Hindu pilgrims to Amarnath in August 2001 read, 'Lashkar-e-Taiba: We are fidayeen. I am a fidayee and in the name of Allah we will continue to kill and be killed till such time we destroy India and we overcome India.'[16]

The main base of LET and its parent organization, JD, at Muridke has been the centre for many activities, including factories and an iron foundry, as well as residential complexes. In December 2001, however, LET shifted its headquarters from Muridke to Muzaffarbad in Pakistan-administered Kashmir. All the other offices of the LET have also been moved to areas in both the Indian-held Jammu and Kashmir (IHK) and Azad Kashmir.

LET's organizational structure is linked to that of its parent group, MDI, now known as Jamaat-al-Daawa (JD). Most of the leadership work in dual capacities in both organizations: for example, LET, as the militant arm of the JD, carries out jihad for the organization, while JD provides the ideological base.

On 23 December 2001 the Central Shura of Markaz Dawa ul Irshad held in Lahore appointed a new General Council of fourteen members. Maulana Abdul Wahid Kashmiri was appointed as the leader of LET, with Zaki-ur-Rehman Lakhvi as the 'Supreme Commander' for Jammu and Kashmir. Most of those appointed came from the Indian-occupied state of Jammu and Kashmir and Azad Kashmir. Indian intelligence observers believe that this was done to give a 'pure Kashmir colour'[17] to the LET, and give validity to its claim that it is no longer a Pakistani group, since it is now based in Azad Kashmir.[18]

Even though Hafiz Mohammad Saeed has dissociated himself from the LET officially, he retains *de facto* control over the organization. LET has subdivided the Kashmiri region into districts, with each district commander in charge of military operations within his areas of responsibility. Within Pakistan, the outfit has a network of training camps and branch offices, which undertake recruitment, fund-raising and military training for its cadres.

Under the 'Supreme Commander' for Jammu and Kashmir, LET has regional commanders for areas such as Srinagar, Bagh, Doda and Muzaffarabad. At its peak, LET formed four groups in the Indian state of Jammu and Kashmir: Al-Madina in charge of Srinagar district and its adjoining areas; Babul Hind Force for south Kashmir, including Anantnag district; Azam Jehad for areas in Doda and parts of Udhampur district; and Al-Mansoorian for Jammu. Al-Mansoorian is also tasked with attacking the security forces and other soft targets.[19]

The major source of LET's finance has been the Kashmiri community in the Persian Gulf and the United Kingdom, Saudi dissidents, Islamic NGOs and Pakistani and Kashmiri businessmen.[20] The Indian Army alleges that,

> Groups like Lashkar (LET) and Jaish (Jaish-e-Mohammad, JEM) generally run on donations from rich Gulf and Saudis or on Pak Government support ... The militant groups generally get the guns and other arms and ammunition from the Government sources across the border ... They don't need to purchase it (arms and ammunitions) at all from open market. And they manage funds locally also. It is either consensual donations or extortion from local businessmen or ransoms. This is apart from hawala channels ...[21]

In the past, one of the major sources of the group's finances has been the collection of funds through donation camps and public appeals. The group put donation boxes in many cities across Pakistan. On 14 October 2003 the US Treasury Department issued orders to freeze the US accounts of Al Akhtar Trust, a charity reportedly being run by Jaish-e-Muhammad (JEM) in Pakistan, 'providing a wide range of support to Al Qaeda and Pakistani-based sectarian and jihadi groups, specifically Lashkar-e-Taiba, JEJ, and Jaish-e-Muhammad. There were also reports about the associates of the trust attempting to raise funds in order to finance obligatory jihad in Iraq.'[22]

During the festival of Eid in November 2003, the LET was reported to have received charity contributions, mostly in the form of the hides of the sacrificed animals, which were sold to raise Rs 710 million (about US$15.7 million). In the same month there were reports that the JD was continuing to collect donations despite the government ban.[23] It set up several camps in Chauburji, Samanabad, Allama Iqbal Town, Shadman and Baghbanpura seeking donations and selling JD publications, posters,and other material. A poster displayed at the camps exhorted, 'Help the Mujahideen with your money. They are defending your ideological and national frontiers with their blood.' Ramadan is a good time for jihadi groups and seminaries to seek donations as this is when a large number of Muslims pay their Zakat (annual charity) and Fitrana (poor dues related to the Eid feast).[24] Similarly, *South Asia Tribune* reported during the same month that LET was able to raise funds worth Rs 1.4 billion from the Muslim community in Britain (especially from the 675,000 Pakistani Muslims out of a total Muslim population of 1.6 million) in the name of Eid sacrifice.[25]

LET has also invested in legal businesses, such as commodity trading, property and the production of consumer goods.[26] The *Friday Times* reported in January 2003 that:

> The Jamaat-ud-Dawa (JD), formerly known as Lashkar-e-Taiba, is snapping up properties across Pakistan. Sources told the weekly that recent real estate purchases by the jd amount to about 300 million Rupees (about US$6.7 million). It has reportedly bought four plots of land in Hyderabad division (Sindh Province) and six others in various Sindh districts. The total price tag is about Rs.200 million (about US$4.5 million). Recent purchases in Lahore have cost the JD Rs.100 million (about US$2.25 million).[27]

In addition to donations from Pakistani communities overseas and money collected from donation camps inside Pakistan, the LET also solicits funds through a website, under the name of Jamaat-al-Daawa, that also provides information on the group's activities.[28] In February 1999, major newspapers in Pakistan carried this advertisement:

> Jihad is the divine order and the Kashmir issue will only be resolved by it. To express solidarity with the oppressed Kashmiri Muslims and the Mujahideen who have been waging a war against the Indian forces, donate your one-day income to them. To join Jihad, contact the camps of Mujahideen-e-Lashkar-e-Tayyaba. Telephone no 142-7636902, 7231106, and 7666878. Fax: 042-7636928. Bank Account no: 2011816001, Faisal Bank, Mall Road, Lahore.[29]

LET maintains ties with religious and military groups around the world, from the Philippines to the Middle East and Chechnya,[30] and uses these sources to generate funds. For example, its UK network allegedly raised funds for jihad in Kashmir, as was revealed during the deportation trials of Shafiq ur Rehman, a cleric at a mosque in Oldham, Lancashire, as well as from the admission of Mohammed Sohail, who was working for the British firm Railtrack and also running the Global Jihad Fund 'to facilitate the growth of various jihad movements around the world by supplying them with sufficient funds to purchase weapons and train their individuals.' There are reports that Lashkar-e-Taiba and Jaish-e-Muhammad used to collect as much as £5 million (US$7.4 million) each year in British mosques in the name of Islam.[31] There are also reports that the LET has strong links with the Saudi Islamists, as well as with some members of the royal family,[32] but there is no evidence to substantiate these claims.

Leadership of the LET

Professor Hafiz Mohammad Saeed was the founder and leader (Amir) of the group. Saeed's family migrated from Hyderabad soon after the partition of the subcontinent in August 1947, and settled in the Janubi village in district Mianwali in Punjab Province. Saeed's mother used to teach the Holy Qur'an to her seven children. Saeed was a good learner and memorized the Qur'an: his favourite verse was 'Wajahidu Fee Sabilallah' ('Wage a holy war in the name of God Almighty').[33] Mohammad Saeed graduated from the Government College at Sargodha under the University of Lahore in the Punjab Province. He then went to King Saud University, Riyadh, Saudi Arabia, for a Masters in Islamic Studies and in Arabic Lexicon. His first job in Pakistan was as a research officer for the Islamic Ideological Council. Since retiring as professor of Islamic Studies from the University of Engineering and Technology (UET) in Lahore, where he was a colleague of Zafar Iqbal, he has devoted himself to his organization. Saeed married the daughter of his maternal uncle, Hafiz Mohammad Abdullah Bahawalpuri, a well-known religious leader and renowned Ahle Hadith scholar, with whom he has two children. His second marriage was to the widow of Abu Musa, who was killed in Srinagar in 2002.

Mohammad Saeed is a strong opponent of western-style democracy and calls for jihad to replace it with an Islamic Caliphate: 'The need for jihad has always existed and present conditions demand it more than ever'.[34] Saeed is also known for his pro-Taliban, anti-India and anti-US rhetoric. For instance, in a 2003 taped message played on Kashmir Day,[35] Saeed dared the Indian Prime Minister to increase the Indian army presence in Kashmir ('We will have more Indians to kill') and attack Pakistan ('What has to happen in ten years may as well happen now'). Similarly, Saeed warned the US Ambassador to leave Pakistan after she had criticized the Pakistani government over alleged infiltration into Indian-administered Kashmir: 'The holiest soil on earth is that of Pakistan and we cannot tolerate the unholy presence of Nancy Powell on our holy land. Her presence keeps us away from Allah's blessings. Pakistan should cleanse itself from her unholy existence.'[36] In another public speech Saeed said, 'The US bombing of Afghanistan and Iraq is an attack on the Muslim fraternity. You will go to hell if you do not wage jihad against the US.'[37] In an article released on the eve of the *ijtima* (Congress, or annual congregation) at Pattoki, near Lahore, in October 2003, Saeed wrote,

> Our big crime is that we did not change with the change in the [international] situation. All the governments stood by the United States when the us army attacked Afghanistan and launched its operations against the mujahideen. We were also expected to follow this policy. We were at least expected to keep silent. But, we openly described that as us terrorism. We sent the message of jihad to each and every city and town. That is why we have been designated as terrorists of Kashmir. O rulers! You have not understood us. You stood by the United States yesterday and you stand by the United States today . . . I ask the Muslims to wage jihad against the infidels everywhere, in Afghanistan, Kashmir, Palestine and Chechnya. I have to follow the word of my Allah. I do not accept the us New World Order. I cannot bow my head before them. I consider India, Israel, and the United States the enemies of Islam.'[38]

Hafeez Saeed has also criticized ex-President Pervez Musharraf for taking sides with the US: 'We shall not submit to you or your government but only to Allah. We will not allow you to besmirch the holy duty of jihad and the holy warriors know how to deal with such rulers.'[39] During his address at the All Pakistan Ulema Convention held in Lahore in July 2003, Hafiz Saeed accused President Musharraf of preventing clerics from organizing a successful jihad against America: 'We do not fear America. We can defeat it through jihad very easily, but General Musharraf is holding us up. He has become the biggest enemy of jihad, and if we can get him out of the picture, we can take care of the infidels.' He further said that it was the clerics' duty to 'liberate' Kashmir, Palestine and other occupied Muslim territories, and to prepare themselves and their students for 'the great jihad'.

Seemingly undeterred by the crackdowns on anti-government clerics, Hafiz Saeed continued with his fiery speeches and vitriolic diatribe against the Pakistani government. During the annual religious festival of Eid in November 2003, Hafiz Saeed exhorted 150,000 worshippers to support jihad in Kashmir and threatened the destruction of the US:

> Jihad is inevitable for the glory of Islam. The jihad process is continuing in Kashmir, Bosnia, Palestine and Iraq. Jihad has made Jews and Christians worried. They call Jihad terrorism. We will continue jihad without any fear or pressure and will not stop it on the asking of anybody.[40]

Because of his anti-government policies, the Pakistani government has attempted to restrict his activities and movement. He has been put under house arrest under the Maintenance of Public Order (MPO) several times, and the government has also asked the heads of all educational institutions, especially government institutions, not to allow Hafiz Saeed or his organization to hold public meetings or Friday congregations in their institutions. Hafiz Saeed remains undeterred, however, saying that he will never shirk Jihad, and will continue it till the freedom of Kashmir; there would be no peace until the sun of liberty and freedom rises in Kashmir. The government also banned Hafiz Saeed from taking out an Independence Day rally on 14 August 2004.

Hafiz Saeed's Jamaat-al-Daawa made a show of strength in March 2006 with a rally of 20,000 in Lahore in connection with protests against the publication of caricatures of the Holy Prophet (peace be upon him). Saeed called upon Muslims not to tolerate any insult to the Prophet (peace be upon him) and not to become slaves of the United States.[41] He also said that the Muslims should make a United States of Muslims and get out of the UN.[42]

The radical stand Saeed has taken extends to his family members as well. His only son Talha looks after the affairs of LeT at its base camp in Muzaffarabad. His brother-in-law, Abdul Rehman Makki, is his close partner and holds an important position in the Markaz at Muridke. Saeed's son-in-law, Khalid Waleed, is also associated with the LeT's organizational set-up in Lahore. [43]

In December 2001, after the group was proscribed by the US, Saeed announced his resignation, saying that from then on he would devote his time to preaching religion, and that Maulana Abdul Wahid Kashmiri from Poonch district in the Indian-held state of Jammu and Kashmir, had been appointed as the new commander of the group's militant wing.[44]

Saeed was arrested by the Pakistani authorities on 31 December 2001 and charged with making inflammatory speeches and inciting violence.[45] After a review board of the Lahore High Court refused to extend the three months detention period, however, he was released on 1 April 2002.[46] He was re-arrested on 15 May 2002, shortly after two attacks in Kashmir in which more than 30 people were killed, including 25 Indian soldiers and their families. He was released in October 2002 and reportedly kept under house arrest. He is now believed to have gone underground.

[47] [48] *LeT's International Links*

Although its rhetoric was originally anti-Indian, its anti-Western rhetoric has grown significantly since 11 September 2001. The mastermind of the Mumbai attacks, Zaki-ur-Rehman Lakhvi, also directed LeT military operations outside India. Since 2003 he has dispatched trained operatives, both Pakistani and foreigners, to Chechnya, Bosnia and Southeast Asia, also sending them to assess the situation in Iraq and, since 2004, to attack US forces there. Although LeT operatives have been arrested in the US, Europe and Australia, LeT was not a priority group for the international community since it did not align itself with Al Qaeda and refrained from operating in Afghanistan. Although LeT as a group kept away from Al Qaeda, LeT leaders and members maintained relations with Al Qaeda at an operational level, for example helping individuals from Al Qaeda and other foreign groups active in Afghanistan. In Faisalabad, an LeT leader provided housing to Abu Zubaydah, the first prominent target to be captured by the Pakistani police, working together with the US intelligence community.

Operational Characteristics of LET

LET militants normally operate in small groups of three or more persons, an operational strategy that allows them to conduct high-risk Fidayeen attacks against Indian security forces. Many kinds of arms and explosives, including AK-47 assault rifles, light and heavy machine guns, mortars and rocket-propelled grenades have been used in their operations. Interrogations of captured LET cadres have revealed that group members were proficient in bomb-making using various kinds of explosives. The interrogation in February 2003 of a LET cadre arrested in India revealed that LET was planning to use radio-controlled 'toy planes' in order to carry out small-scale 9/11 type attacks in Jammu and Kashmir. It reportedly acquired a 'fleet' of four dozen planes, each capable of carrying 10–15 kilograms of RDX for carrying out attacks on army posts or helicopter gunships of the Indian Air Force. Two of these were recovered from the Rajouri district of the Jammu region. The 'toy planes', which could hit a target within a range of 300 metres, were reportedly being assembled at the group's main base at Muridke.[49]

LET uses guerilla-type warfare to wear down and demoralize opponents who are much stronger militarily. The group is known for its well-planned and executed attacks on Indian security force targets and for the dramatic massacres of non-Muslim civilians. The LET also indulges in what it calls 'the war of nerves'. More important than the number of casualties inflicted on the security forces, the psychological impact of their attacks has helped to demoralize the army.[50] The intention is to gain publicity, generate fear and extract allegiance and support from the local population. Non-Muslim civilian massacres are meant to be some sort of ethnic cleansing in the state of Jammu Kashmir. This has also helped the group frighten away from the Kashmir valley many of the Kashmiri Hindu population.[51]

LET cadres often prefer to die in an encounter with security forces rather than be caught.[52] According to Khalid Walid, a senior LET officer, the LET cadres prefer death to capture as a matter of policy: 'Only those of our men are captured who faint during the fight. Otherwise, we fight until death and do not surrender at any cost.'[53] The LET is believed to be opposed to suicide bombings, but in many of the 'fidayeen' attacks, where, for example, a handful of fighters would burst into an Indian army barracks with guns blazing, there was little chance of the attackers surviving. LET subscribes to the notion that if its fighters are killed, they are believed to have embraced Shahadaat (martyrdom) while fighting in the name of Islam.[54] The LET cadres use 'hit and run' tactics when attacking military installations, airbases and police stations. LET hit squads typically move in small groups of less than ten; 'fidayeen' (faithful) suicide squads work in smaller groups of between two and five members.

For its recruits, the LET conducts either a twenty one-day basic course (Daura Aam) or a three-month advanced course (Daura Khas) on guerrilla warfare and commando training. This advanced course teaches the use of small arms, survival and ambush techniques. The newly enlisted soldier discards his old name and begins to use a *kuniat*, an Arabic-style nickname reminiscent of the *kuniats* belonging to the companions of the Prophet; this he holds until his death. The recruits are required not to shave or trim their beards, and to keep their hair long. The LET members also wear shalwars above their ankles.[55] It is alleged that the Pakistani military has provided training for the group.[56]

Abdullah Abdullah, an LET recruit arrested by the Indian security forces, said in an interview to the Inter Press Service in Jammu that he underwent advanced courses in guerrilla warfare, including weapon and explosives training, for about ten weeks alongside fifty other youths at the Al-Aqsa training camp. He also attended classes where he was influenced to wage jihad in Kashmir to 'liberate' fellow Muslims. The senior instructor in charge of the training was Nasser Javed, a Pakistani who had fought in Afghanistan against the Soviets and later against the Northern Alliance, before returning to Pakistan to help with the jihad in Kashmir.[57]

Farhan Ahmad Ali, an Indian from Moradabad, Uttar Pradesh, who was arrested in New Delhi in August 2002, was also trained at Al-Aqsa. Ali told his interrogators that he was recruited by a local LET cell when he was working at Salmiya, Kuwait. He flew to Pakistan for weapons training in February 1998 and stayed in an LET guest house in Islamabad with some 70 other recruits before being moved to another facility at the Yateemkhana Chowk in Lahore. There were at least eight Arab recruits: five from Saudi Arabia, and one each from Egypt, Yemen and Morocco. Soon after, the group was dispatched to the Al-Aqsa training camp, where in the course of a week he learned how to use various types of automatic weapons, lob hand grenades, and how to make and deploy improvised explosive devices. According to Ali, the camp at Al-Aqsa was an exclusive facility for residents of Arab countries: some 1,000 Arabs, along with four British converts to Islam and one Romanian, were in training at the camp when he was there.[58]

The LET encourages close fraternity among the cadres. Once inducted into the LET, cadres are drawn into a pattern of communal life epitomized by shared common meals, with all the young men using their fingers to pick food from a big, shared bowl or parat.[59]

The LET has been widely blamed for massacring Hindu civilians in the Kashmir region and other parts of India, for destroying Hindu temples and for carrying out attacks in tourist and business areas, notably at the Gateway of India and Zaveri Bazaar in Mumbai in August 2003. The LET, however, always denies the killing of innocent civilians: for example, re-acting to the massacre of 35 Sikh villagers in March 2000, allegedly by LET on the eve of a visit to India and Pakistan by then US President Bill Clinton, LET described it as a 'grave injustice' to associate this killing with it. Hafiz Saeed further said, 'We do not kill civilians, only aggressors. We don't believe it right to kill even a non-Muslim unless he is an aggressor.'[60]

The LET has carried out attacks on Indian security forces, such as border police and infantry patrols, and planned others against high-profile Indian leaders, including Deputy Prime Minister L. K. Advani, Gujarat Chief Minister Narendra Modi and Pravin Togadia of the Vishwa Hindu Parishad (VHP), a Hindu fundamentalist group that believes in the genocide of Muslims, Christians and Sikhs.[61] There have also been reports in the Indian media about LET's plans to kill important sport personalities, like Sachin Tendulkar and Souray Ganguly.[62] The Indian government has claimed to have foiled LET attempts to target software companies in Bangalore.[63] Indian analysts have also identified an increasingly worrisome possibility of an LET attack on US diplomatic missions and naval ships visiting Indian ports.[64]

LET draws support from those following the religious orientations of its parent organization, MDI/JD, which subscribes to the Ahle Hadith movement. Consequently it has found support among many of the Ulema in Pakistan and even in India,[65] especially among the hard-line Muslim communities in Kashmir, Andhra Pradesh, Tamil Nadu, Karnataka, Maharashtra and Gujarat. The LET is the only terrorist group based in Pakistan with support bases across India.[66]

The exact strength of LET cadres is not known, but the organization has at least several hundred members in Pakistan, Kashmir and India. The Terrorism Knowledge Base (TKB) produced by the US-based National Memorial Institute for the Prevention of Terrorism (MIPT) puts the total number of LET cadres at approximately 300.[67] The US Naval Postgraduate School (NPS) puts the total strength of LET at 'several thousand members in Azad Kashmir, Pakistan, in the southern Jammu, Kashmir and Doda regions, and in the Kashmir valley'.[68] The US State Department also estimates the number of LET members at several thousand.[69] The *Friday Times* reported that between January and June 2003 the various terrorist groups recruited more than 7,000 youngsters aged between eighteen and twenty-five from various parts of Pakistan: the outfits with the highest profile, the

LET and Jaish-e Muhammad (JEM), claimed to have recruited more than 3,350 and 2,235 boys, respectively.[70] In 2003 the LET's website claimed that, 'Around 800 youngsters had embraced martyrdom while fighting the Indian army last year.'[71] Similarly, Willie Brigitte, who was arrested in Australia and deported to France on suspicion of having links with terrorist organizations, and having received training at a LET camp in Pakistan, reportedly admitted that he had indeed received training in Pakistan, where there were nearly two or three thousand other mujahideen in camps operated by LET and Abdul Qadeem Zaloom, a Saudi-based person with links to Al Qaeda.[72]

Most are recruited through government schools and from unemployed youth: nearly 80 per cent of the cadres are from Pakistan and some were Afghan veterans from the Afghan wars.[73] It is known that LET cadres were killed in the northern Afghan city of Mazar-e-Sharif in October 2001 during the US-led war against the Taliban.[74]

LET has managed to attract thousands of committed young men. The driving force behind its massive success in recruitment is deceptively simple. It uses its impressive organizational network, which includes schools, social service groups and religious publications, to create a passion for jihad.[75]

The LET mainly utilizes public means to recruit young people to join its ranks and fight against 'occupation' in the Indian-held Jammu and Kashmir (IHK). Many factors, such as poverty, unemployment, the desire to acquire fame, problems with parents at home and religious passion, have been suggested as being responsible for the steady stream of recruits for the cause of jihad. Enlistment offers honourable living and an honourable death – martyrdom for Allah.[76] LET makes effective use of publications, websites, local prayer leaders, audio and video cassettes, CDs, badges and T-shirts in promoting the jihadi culture. The publications of LET and its mother body, JD, are distributed free of charge, especially during public rallies. These publications feature jihadi ballads, interviews and illustrated profiles of young jihadis, verses from the Qur'an, and letters from readers to inspire others, particularly the youth. The aim is 'to spur the passion of jihad when holy warriors are presented as heroes of Islam'.[77] According to Anis Jillani, head of the Society for the Protection of Children's Rights in Islamabad,

> the most steady stream of warriors comes from the seminaries run by various outfits. The seminarians are indoctrinated over a long period of time since they join at a much younger age. When they grow up, they are sent to jihadi outfits where they are imparted

guerrilla training to fight in Kashmir. Such boys join the jihadi outfits in huge numbers, though exact figures of recruitment from the
seminaries are not available.[78]

LET recruits those who are prepared to abandon their lives in the
mainstream to join the jihad and those who have been rejected by society.
As a matter of policy, however, only those whose parents give them permission to fight in Kashmir are allowed to do so. Recruits are also required
to convince their families about the importance of their mission.[79]

The group uses local Kashmiri cadres only as helpers and guides, so
restricting both the armed operations and the leadership to non-local
cadres, generally Punjabis.[80] LET is secretive about how many cadres it de-
ploys in Kashmir at any given time. The Amir (Hafiz Mohammad Saeed)
decides how many mujahideen need to be sent to the (Kashmir) Valley.
This depends on the number of deaths that have taken place, operational
requirements and the capacity of the organization inside Kashmir to ab-
sorb the new fighters. It is known, however, that the LeT recruits and trains
many more men than it actually requires to fight in Kashmir at any given
time.[81] Even after LET's camps were shut down following Musharraf's as-
surances to US President George Bush, Saeed continued touring Punjab
province to reorganize the group and recruit more jihadis, despite the disapproval of the Pakistani establishment.[82] The LET has continued to maintain extensive ties with religious or military groups around the world,
ranging from the Philippines to the Middle East and Chechnya. Many terrorist suspects from outside Pakistan have stayed at Muridke and in LeT
training camps.

In October 2003 the interrogation of Hambali, the operations commander of Jemmah Islamiyah (JI), led to the arrests of his brother Gungun
and other Indonesian, Malaysian and Singaporean members of the JI
studying in two madrasas in Karachi. At one of these madrasas, run by the
LET, Hafiz Mohammad Saeed was recruiting students from outside Pakistan through his teaching.[83]

In the same year the LET was reported as collecting funds in Pakistan
for its 'martyrs' who had died in the jihad against the Americans in Iraq.
There were also reports about LET recruiting and training volunteers in
different parts of Pakistan to assist the Iraqi suicide volunteers. Reports
indicated that groups like Harkat-ul-Mujahideen (HUM), Jaish-e-
Muhammad (JEM) and the LET sent trained cadres to Saudi Arabia disguised as Haj pilgrims to infiltrate Iraq. The speeches at the annual
convention of the Jamaat-al-Daawa (JD) at Pattoki in October 2003 revealed the JD's short-term political goal to unite the Muslim ummah in

the Muslim world around the anti-American agenda. This could be done only by following the Qur'an and Sunnah in letter and spirit. Hafiz Mohammad Saeed declared, 'I do not accept the US New World Order. I cannot bow my head before them. I consider India, Israel, and the United States the enemies of Islam.'[84] In his address, Abdul Rehman Makki said that new crusades have started: 'We would beat [President George] Bush and his camp followers the way Salahuddin Ayubi beat the ancestors of George Bush in the desert of Sinai'.[85] In another speech, Saeed stated, 'The US bombing of Afghanistan and Iraq is an attack on the Muslim fraternity. You will go to hell if you do not wage jihad against the US.'[86]

LET has been critical of the peace moves between the governments of India and Pakistan. Professor Saeed asserted several times that attacks would continue despite the ceasefire between the two countries across the Line of Control: 'Musharraf's priority may be peace in this region but our priority is freedom from India. We do not need peace at the cost of our freedom. If Musharraf and his men are also sincere, they would press India to resolve the core issue first.'[87] While openly opposing the bus service across the border between Muzaffarabad and Srinagar, he declared, 'We must continue to liberate Junagarh and Hyderabad from the evil clutches of Hindu Brahmins'.[88] Regarding Musharraf's overtures to recognize Israel, Hafiz Saeed opposed such moves, saying that if the government recognized Israel, it would threaten the ideological basis of Pakistan's existence.[89]

Countering the LET

The Pakistani government has consistently denied that it has given any support to LET. However, the group's alleged involvement in the attacks on the Indian Parliament on 13 December 2001, together with the Jaish-e-Muhammad, caused an escalation of tension between India and Pakistan, with both sides deploying a million troops along the border in preparation for what could have been a major war. India wanted Pakistan to hand over twenty terrorists, one of them reportedly being Hafiz Mohammad Saeed, the leader of LET.[90] Under pressure to take positive measures in order to ease the tension, President Pervez Musharraf ordered a crackdown on the militant groups operating from Pakistan, including the LET, and followed this on 12 January 2002 with a ban on the groups under Pakistan's Anti-Terrorism Act.[91] Pakistan police rounded up a few hundred Islamic militants across the country.[92]

The US officially designated the group as a Foreign Terrorist Organization on 26 December 2001 and froze its accounts. Pakistan followed this by similarly freezing LET's assets in Pakistan on 15 January 2002.[93] Anticipating government action, Saeed 'relinquished' his post as Amir of the LET on 24 December 2001. LET closed its offices in Pakistan and shifted to Azad Kashmir. On 2 October 2003 the US renewed its listing as a Foreign Terrorist Organization. Russia outlawed the group on 4 February 2003, while Canada listed the group in the 'Regulations Amending the Regulations Establishing a List of Entities' on 18 June 2003. Australia banned the LET as a 'terrorist group' in November 2003. In the same month the Pakistani government placed Jamaat-al-Daawa (JD) on its terrorism watch list.

Following the Mumbai attacks in November 2008, the United Nations Security Council's Al Qaeda and Taliban Sanctions Committee added the names of a host of Pakistani organizations and individuals, including Lashkar-e-Taiba and Jamaat-al-Daawa. Abiding by the United Nations' resolution, Pakistan launched a massive crackdown against LET and JD. On 9 December 2008 security forces arrested Zaki-ur-Rehman Lakhvi, an operational commander of LET and an alleged mastermind of the Mumbai attacks.[94]

The United States government verified that Pakistan's security and intelligence services were not behind the Mumbai attack. India, too, has confirmed this finding. In the past, the Indian government has been quite liberal in accusing the Pakistani government regarding terrorist attacks in India. Over time, both New Delhi and Islamabad are likely to realize the need for them to fight a common threat, both ideologically and operationally. In the coming decade, enlightened leaders of both India and Pakistan should strive to resolve the outstanding national issues such as Kashmir, and build robust security and intelligence partnerships to meet future challenges. The Mumbai carnage has demonstrated that the pre-eminent national security challenge facing both India and Pakistan is terrorism, and not each other.

Lashkar-e-Jhangvi (LEJ)

Lashkar-e-Jhangvi is the most lethal urban terrorist group based in mainland Pakistan. This group is also known as Lashkar-i-Jhangvi, Lashkar-e-Jhangvie, Laskar-e-Jhangvi, Lashkare Jhangvi, Lashkar-e-Jhangwi, Lashkar-i-Jhangwi, Jhangvi Army and Lashkar Jhangvi.[95]

The LEJ or the 'Army of Jhang' is a Sunni Islamist organization that commits terrorist acts. Traditionally, the group has acted against individuals or groups belonging to the Shi'ite community in Pakistan. Its main objective is to transform Pakistan into a Sunni state, just as Iran is a Shi'a state. The LEJ believes that Shi'ites are heretics or infidels of Islam, and the main obstacle to the establishment of an orthodox caliphate. Since 11 September 2001 and the American coalition's attack on the Taliban in Afghanistan, members of LEJ have also been involved in attacks against Christians and foreigners in Pakistan. LEJ is driven by political, religious and ideological objectives.[96]

LEJ was formed in 1996 (or, according to one source, on 23 September 1997)[97] by a breakaway group of radical sectarian extremists of the Sipah-e-Sahaba Pakistan (SSP), which was trained by the Molvi Younas Khalis Group in Afghanistan.[98] The LEJ was unhappy with the SSP's decision to tone down its militant activities and move into mainstream politics, and accused the parent organization of deviating from the ideals of its co-founder, Maulana Haq Nawaz Jhangvi, who was assassinated in 1990, allegedly by a Shi'a terrorist group. It is from Maulana Jhangvi that the LEJ derives its name. It was formed under the leadership of Akram Lahori, Malik Ishaq and Riaz Basra.[99]

The LEJ was formed in Jhang, a small town in Punjab. The group rapidly expanded its power base and established around 500 offices across Pakistan, scores of madaris, and its cadres grew to 100,000. Most of the suicide attacks in Islamabad and Karachi have been attributed to LEJ. According to Pakistani Intelligence sources, LEJ is the only terrorist outfit known to be operating and carrying out terrorist attacks in Islamabad. On 17 March 2002, for example, LEJ terrorists targeted a Protestant church in Diplomatic Enclaves, a highly secured area of Islamabad. Five people were killed and forty others (mostly foreigners) were injured. In July 2002 Pakistani police killed one of the alleged perpetrators and arrested four LEJ members who confessed to the killings and said the attack was in retaliation for the US attack on Afghanistan.[100] Similarly, LEJ is thought to have been behind the bomb attack at the Luna Capresse, an Italian restaurant in Islamabad, on 15 March 2008. Trish Gibbs, the second highest-ranking US embassy official in the country, and chief of FBI operations in Pakistan, is believed to have been the actual target of the Luna Capresse attack.[101]

Karachi remains a stronghold of LEJ. It is believed that the fracturing of LEJ into the Riaz Basra and Qari Hai factions, and their consequent rivalry for funding, was the precursor to the main area of sectarian murders shifting from Punjab to Karachi, the major source of funds for militant groups. The move also seemed wise given the Punjab police's successful crackdown on LEJ activists. In 1999 there were twelve sectarian killings in Karachi and eighteen in 2000. The number shot up in 2001 to 58, and by June 2002 there were already almost 30 victims.[102]

LEJ's mother organization, SSP, set up seventeen clandestine branches abroad, located in the UAE, England and Canada. The LEJ still maintains links with ssp. Although they deny having any organizational links, they share the same sectarian belief system and world view, and their cadres come from the same madaris and from a similar social milieu.[103]

leJ has links with Harkat-ul-Mujahideen (hum) and Jaish-e-Muhammad (jem). Many leading LeJ terrorists were trained at hum camps, especially the Khalid Bin Waleed camp in Afghanistan. Both ssp and leJ fought alongside the Taliban militia against the Northern Alliance. All three groups are closely linked in their fight against the Shi'as, both in Afghanistan and Pakistan. leJ and ssp cadres played an active part in the massacres of Shi'as by the erstwhile Taliban regime in Afghanistan. leJ members also underwent weapons training in several camps in Afghanistan, while the Taliban helped shield leJ leaders when Pakistani authorities were hunting them down.

It was only in the mid-1990s, after the worst wave of sectarian clashes and tit-for-tat targeted killings in Punjab and Karachi, that the authorities finally recognized that the sectarian groups were getting out of hand. Police and law enforcement authorities launched a crackdown against the sectarian terrorist groups. By then the ssp had made inroads into the hard-line Islamic militia of the Taliban, which introduced a strict Sunni Islamic system in Afghanistan. A security official familiar with the working and hierarchy of sectarian groups commented that: 'The Taliban were and still are natural allies of Pakistan's Sunni militants. They are against Iran and brutally targeted the Shi'a Hazaras in Afghanistan. For them, it was a natural ideological bonding on the basis of anti-Shi'a rivalry.'[104]

leJ has confirmed links with Al Qaeda. It is believed that the outfit has been involved or assisted in several high-profile attacks on Westerners in Pakistan, including the January 2002 kidnapping and murder of *Wall Street Journal* reporter Daniel Pearl. The connection became evident from two attacks in which the leJ was believed to have been involved: one on 8 May that killed eleven French technicians and three others outside the Sheraton Hotel, and another against the us consulate. Never before had leJ purposefully targeted foreigners (except, of course, Iranians, but those attacks were a factor of the Sunni-Shi'a rivalry). The Western targets, and the reported use of suicide bombers, bore the hallmark of Al Qaeda. It is believed that leJ banded with two other extremist groups, Jaish-e-Muhammad and Harkat-ul-Jihad-i-Islami, to form the Pakistani wing of Al Qaeda known as Lashkar-e-Omar.

In 2005 police recovered cyanide, other toxic chemicals and laboratory equipment stored in an leJ safe house in Karachi. The incident lends credence to the report that Al Qaeda operatives, working with the leJ, moved its chemical stores and shipments of gold out of Afghanistan to reestablish operations from Pakistan.

Interestingly, LeJ also forged a strong operational relationship with the Islamic Movement of Uzbekistan (IMU) during the Afghan Jihad, when both organizations were fighting the Northern Alliance on behalf of the Taliban. Further evidence pointing to a relationship emerged from investigations into the LeJ's endeavours to train female suicide bombers to attack the female quarters of Shi'a mosques. Pakistani intelligence reports revealed allegations that Aziza, a woman cadre of IMU, had been imparting fidayeen training.[105]

LeJ became a part of 'Brigade 313', a coalition of five Jihadi outfits formed to avenge the US invasion of Afghanistan in 2001. The number 313 was drawn from the strength of the Prophet's army in the first battle of Islam fought at Badr.[106] The coalition comprised Lashkar-e-Taiba, Jaish-e-Muhammad, Harkat-ul-Jihad al-Islami, Harkat-ul-Mujahideen al-Almi and Lashkar-e-Jhangvi, the last two of which are Deobandi organizations patronized by Al Qaeda.

It has been reported that Al Qaeda financed a series of bombing operations suspected to have been carried out by LeJ in Pakistan. In 2006 generous funding from Al Qaeda, and drug money from the Taliban, helped LeJ to reorganize itself.[107] LeJ also smuggles arms and ammunition from the North West Frontier Province into Punjab across the Attock River using two bridges near Taunsa and Bhakkar.

Some reports suggested that in 2002 the LeJ split into two factions, headed by Riaz Basra and by Majlis-i-Shoora Qari Abdul Hai, alias Qari Asadullah, alias Talha. Ostensibly the factions parted following differences over the resumption of LeJ's activities: while Basra favoured the resumption of attacks against Shi'a targets in order to force the government to comply with the outfit's demands, Talha opposed the plan as he reportedly felt it was suicidal for the organization in view of the increased attention on terrorist activities after 11 September 2001.[108] It is also said that the Qari Abdul Hai group of LeJ was directly involved in hunting down Riaz Basra in May 2004. According to some reports, Basra was trapped when an informant, probably from the Qari Abdul Hai group, lured him into a trap set by the police.[109]

By 2001 the LeJ had been involved in at least 350 violent incidents, but the organization then had to contend with severe setbacks after more than 30 LeJ militants, including senior leaders, were killed in numerous shootouts during 2002. These included Riaz Basra, who was killed along with three associates near Mailsi in Multan on 14 May, and LeJ chief Asif Ramzi, who was slain with six accomplices near Allahwala Town in Karachi. The slayings of Basra and Ramzi dealt a severe blow to the LeJ and Sipah-e-Sahaba Pakistan.

The LEJ reorganized in January 2004. The killing of the SSP's leader Maulana Azam Tariq motivated LEJ's scattered cadres to form a squad to get even with the 'Shi'a assassins'[110] Maulana Tariq was gunned down on his way to Islamabad in October 2003 and the SSP blamed Shi'a groups. The new squad, named the Al-Badr squad, also included members from two other banned groups, the Tehrik-e-Khuddam-ul-Islam and Jamaat-ul-Furqaan. At first the Al-Badr squad was limited to the Jhang district, the stronghold of the SSP.

Lashkar-e-Jhangvi started a new recruitment drive in 2006. Hundreds of Jihadis were recruited to form new cells at the district and provincial levels. Pakistani Intelligence agencies reported that the 'notorious terrorist' Matiur Rehman was behind the reorganization of the Lashkar cells.[111] Rehman is believed to have links with Al Qaeda and is one of the prime suspects in the London airline plot. He is also believed to have been involved in the murder of Daniel Pearl, the multiple assassination plots on President Pervez Musharraf and Prime Minister Shaukat Aziz, and the attack on the US Consulate in Karachi in March 2006. According to intelligence reports, Abdullah Faryad, the LEJ president in Ditta Khel (FATA), was told to help Rehman in the reorganization. Sheikh Ahmed Saleem, an Arab member of Al Qaeda, gave money to Qari Idrees, an LEJ activist based in Sahiwal, to recruit militants for the new cells, assisted by Abu Khabaib, an Arab explosives expert who was killed in a US Predator drone strike in 2008. Abdul Wahab Rashad, wanted for killing more than ten Shi'as in Shah Najaf Mosque, Rawalpindi, and a close associate of Riaz Basra, also helped in the reorganization, together with Nasimul Haq and Salahuddin from Quetta, Muavia from Hangu, Shoaib Khan and Usman Ghani from Hyderabad, and Jamil Khan from Karachi.[112]

The Leadership of LEJ

Riaz Basra, the first 'Salar-e-A'ala' (Commander-in-Chief) of LEJ, was born in Jhawarian, a village near Sargodha. Basra began his education at the school in Jhawarian, then moved on to Sargodha and finally to a madrasa in Lahore.[113] He joined Sipah-e-Sahaba Pakistan in 1986 and soon became a fiery activist. He was the president of the SSP in Sargodha when he first met Maulana Haq Nawaz Jhangvi. In 1988 Basra was appointed Central Secretary (broadcast and publications) of SSP. In the same year, he contested Nawaz Sharif in the elections and gained 9,000 votes. Basra also fought in the Afghan Jihad and thereafter walked with a limp. Basra remained a challenge for law enforcement authorities for twelve years, but on 14 May 2004 he was killed by the police at Mailsi, in the Vihari district of Punjab. He was wanted in connection with 300 cases and there was a reward of Rs 500,000 for his capture.[114] Akram Lahori, who replaced Basra as Salar-e-A'ala, had been a member of ssp since 1990. Following an internal disagreement with the parent organization in 1996, he founded lej along with Malik Ishaq and Riaz Basra and together they launched terrorist activities in Punjab. After securing support from the erstwhile Taliban regime, Lahori established a training camp in Sarobi, Afghanistan.[115] According to police, Lahori was involved in 38 cases of sectarian killings in Sindh, including that of Shoukat Raza Mirza, the Managing Director of Pakistan State Oil. In addition, Lahori was also involved in the massacre at Imambargah Mehmoodabad and in the murder of Iranian cadets in Rawalpindi. Lahori was captured in June 2002 and was sentenced to death on 26 April 2003 by an anti-terrorism court in Karachi. Under interrogation Lahori confessed that he was involved in 30 cases of sectarian killings in Punjab, including the incident involving 24 persons who were attending a Majlis in Mominpura. Lahori also revealed that his group planned to kill Interior Minister Moinuddin Hiader, but due to tight security measures, murdered his brother Ehtishamuddin Haider instead.[116]

Amir of lej in Karachi, Qari Abdul Hai was Basra's trusted lieutenant and succeeded Lahori, but he was arrested during a raid in Muzaffargarh in Punjab on 29 May 2003. Asif Ramzi, the second-in-command of lej, was killed while attempting to make an explosive device in Karachi in December 2002. Another senior member, Qari Ataur Rahman alias Naeem Bukhari, was arrested for his role in the murder of Daniel Pearl. It is not clear if Hai passed on the lej leadership to anyone else or if he continues to head the outfit while in detention.[117]

Organizational Structure

lej is organized into small cells, each of approximately five to eight cadres, that operate independently of each other, so ensuring increased security for individual cell members. It is an amalgam of loosely coordinated subunits in various parts of Pakistan, particularly in the districts of Punjab, with autonomous chiefs for each sub-unit. Riaz Basra reportedly controlled the lej's units in Lahore, Gujranwala, Rawalpindi and Sargodha. Malik Ishaq, currently under detention, was the chief of the units in Faisalabad, Multan, Bahawalpur and in the Bhakkar district.

The Majlis-i-Shoora (Supreme Council) is the highest policy-making body of the group. The entire leadership of the lej consists of Afghan veterans who fought against the Soviet forces in the 1980s. The security agencies' occasional successes against the LeJ forced the top leadership to remain underground. Rather than risk arrest by engaging in attacks themselves, they trained new recruits and directed operations.

Although LeJ maintains a violent sectarian identity, some of its leaders have contested elections hoping to gain legitimacy for their cause. In 1988 Riaz Basra, for example, stood against Nawaz Sharif in an election.[118] Jamiat Ulema-i-Islam, led by Maulana Fazlur Rahman, is also known to be supportive of LeJ. Maulana Haq Nawaz Jhangvi, the founder of SSP, was himself a member of JUI. Many JUI leaders not only welcomed the creation of SSP, but also ran a campaign to support it. Maulana Hasan Jan, then central leader of JUI-F (Peshawar), in particular was very active in this respect.[119]

Most LeJ cadres are drawn from the numerous Sunni madrasas in Pakistan. LeJ has reportedly secured considerable assistance from other Deobandi organizations and cooperates with both political and terrorist wings in conducting its activities.[120] The outfit drew its support mainly from Sargodha, Jhang, Bahawalpur, Multan and Muzaffargarh in the central and southern Punjab and Karachi in Sindh.

The active cadre strength of the LeJ has been estimated at slightly less than 300.[121] Most of these cadres are either under arrest in Pakistan or were based in the various training camps in Afghanistan, from which they regularly came to Pakistan to carry out terrorist activities. Despite large-scale arrests and the deaths of its members, the outfit is never short of cadres and keeps fielding new agents to evade arrests.

Sources of Finance

Collecting hides of sadrificial animals on the eve of Eid-ul-Azha was a major source of income for LeJ until the government took action to ban the group from this practice in 2006.[122]

LeJ also generates funds through abductions for ransom and bank robberies. In July 2006, for example, Lahore police arrested two LeJ activists who were planning to kidnap people from three of Lahore's richest families.[123] Investigations revealed that Shahid from Narowal, also known as Hammad and Billi, was involved in several atrocities, murders and abductions. His accomplice, Shahbaz, had committed three murders in Sialkot, Pasroor and Mandi Bahauddin, and had taken Rs 20 million in ransom for various abductions. Shahid was arrested from Chungh/Raiwind and Shahbaz was caught from Mozang.

The LeJ enjoyed the support of both the ruling Taliban regime in

Afghanistan and the Saudi regime. LEJ also managed to set up seventeen clandestine branches abroad, located in the UAE, England and Canada, and these, together with Saudi Arabia, have remained a major source of party funding. Evidence of private Arab funding was disclosed with the arrest of several LEJ cadres responsible for the May 1997 killing of Ashraf Marth, a senior police officer who had arrested the killers of Agha Mohammed Ali Rahimi, the Iranian Cultural Attaché in Multan. A substantial portion of LEJ's funding is reportedly derived from wealthy benefactors in Karachi.

LEJ Operations

The outfit is one of the most secretive sectarian terrorist groups in Pakistan. It has never exposed itself to the public or media except when claiming responsibility for any attack or killing. Individual LEJ cadres are reportedly unaware of the number of cells in existence that are similar to their own, or the structure of operations. After carrying out an attack, LEJ cadres often disperse and then reassemble at the various training camps to plan future operations. The outfit uses terror tactics with the aim of forcing the Pakistani state into accepting its narrow interpretations of the Sunni sectarian doctrines as official doctrine. In August 2003 the renowned journalist Massoud Ansari interviewed a terrorist associated with LEJ. Talking about the operational strategy of the group, the terrorist said,

> whenever a group decides to conduct an operation, they split up to avoid detection by intelligence agencies. When we go for a target, there is a frontline – comprising the hit men – and a second front that provides support. While the second line does reconnaissance, the actual assassins remain invisible.[124]

Lashkar-e-Jhangvi successfully exploited the loopholes in Pakistan's security system and the group has been able to penetrate the police. The police force came under suspicion, for example, after a policeman's badge was found among the bodies at the site of an explosion at the Hyderi Mosque, Karachi, on 7 May 2004. The man's body had disintegrated under the impact of explosives strapped to it, leaving just the badge intact. At the same time, it was discovered that Akbar Khan Niazi, a constable originally from Mianwali, had been absent from the police training college in Baldia Town for two days. Investigations revealed that Niazi was previously a member of Jaish-e-Muhammad, and later joined LEJ. He was obsessed with martyrdom and waging jihad against infidels.[125] He had fought alongside the Taliban in Afghanistan before joining the police in 2002 with the purpose of serving as an informer for his group. Similarly, the investigation into a suicide bombing in Quetta in March 2004 revealed the involvement of yet another police official. Ghulam Haider, a police constable in Quetta, was accused of an attack on a Shi'ite procession that left 48 people dead, including six policemen. The blast in Quetta was attributed to the outlawed LEJ.

LEJ is thought to be more lethal with its use of suicide bombings as a tactic to achieve its targets. In the aftermath of the government's crackdown on LEJ, and later the military action against Islamists in the tribal areas of Pakistan, LEJ let loose a reign of terror countrywide with its suicide attack squads. The outfit, with an extensive experience of carrying out suicide attacks in urban areas, is also believed to be behind most of the suicide attacks targeting foreign nationals in Islamabad. The group has also used suicide bombings for promoting sectarian strife, starting in July 2003, when a suicide bomber killed more than 45 Shi'as gathered for a Muharram procession in Quetta.

Lashkar-e-Jhangvi is also believed to have trained female suicide bombers. In June 2005 the law enforcement agencies arrested two female would-be suicide bombers from Swat. In October 2004 the Intelligence agencies had arrested Gul Hasan, a key member of LEJ, who was involved in suicide attacks at two Shi'a mosques in Karachi. During interrogation he disclosed that the group was planning to launch suicide attacks by using female bombers and that many female members of the group had been trained for this purpose.[126] Among these were two of his nieces, Arifa and Saba, aged twenty amd twenty-two respectively, who were trained to carry out suicide attacks without the consent of their parents. Both Arifa and Saba were studying at a local school in Lyari Town, Karachi, when Gul Hasan persuaded them to quit education and go on a 'holy mission'. They left their home on 29 June 2003 without informing their parents. Gul Hasan's wife, who was also a member of LEJ, facilitated their escape so that they could train as suicide bombers. Their unfortunate father blamed Gul Hasan for destroying his daughters.[127]

Besides suicide bombings, LEJ frequently uses various tactics including target killings, bombing and sabotage. Terrorists linked to LEJ also use police uniforms for their operations in order to secure easy access to mosques and to help their escape after committing a terrorist act.

LEJ militants are recruited from Pakistani madrasas and trained in camps located in mountainous areas of Pakistan and Afghanistan. Before the government's crackdown on the LEJ in the 1990s, the group maintained training centres in Kabirwal, Khanewal district. LEJ activists, along with members of Jaish-e-Muhammad and Harkat-ul-Mujahideen, received training at various camps, including one at Sarobi dam, Kabul, that was exclusively used by LEJ. Qari Asadullah, a top LEJ cadre, reportedly supervised training at this camp in collaboration with the Taliban regime.

Aside from attacks on Pakistani Shi'as and Iranians, LEJ is also known to have targeted leaders of the Pakistani establishment and western interests. The three most high-profile targets have been President Pervez Musharraf and two former Prime Ministers of Pakistan, Nawaz Sharif and Mir Zafarullah Khan Jamali. Attempts to assassinate Sharif began in 1998: the closest they came to success was in January 1999, when LEJ militants attempted to blow the bridge on the Lahore–Raiwand road while Sharif was passing. Eid Muhammad, the LEJ explosives expert, was alleged to have rigged Chaklala Bridge, Rawalpindi, with explosives in an attempt to assassinate President Pervez Musharraf on 14 December 2003. An attack on Mir Zafarullah Khan Jamali was also foiled with the arrest of a LEJ cadre on 1 April 2004.[128]

LEJ also selects targets with significant economic value, such as petrol stations. It has openly claimed responsibility for numerous massacres of Shi'as and targeted killings of Shi'a religious and community leaders. Between 2000 and 2002, LEJ assassinated more than 70 doctors and 34 lawyers, various Ulema (religious scholars), teachers and students of seminaries, leaders and activists of politico-religious parties and officials of various government and private institutions. LEJ has also carried out numerous attacks against Iranian interests and Iranian nationals in Pakistan.[129]

LEJ is suspected of being involved in the kidnapping and subsequent murder of US journalist Daniel Pearl in 2002, a series of car bomb attacks in 2002 and the murders of four US oil workers in 1997 in Karachi.[130]

Difficult times for the sectarian groups started in earnest when Islamabad sided with the US in its war on terror. On 12 January 2002 General Pervez Musharraf announced a new policy that banned both Shi'a and Sunni extremist groups. Hundreds of sectarian militants were subsequently rounded up. The Pakistani government classified LEJ as a sectarian terrorist group on 14 August 2001,[131] and the US designated LEJ a Foreign Terrorist Organization on 30 January 2003. Canada followed in late June 2003, classifying LEJ as a prohibited organization and a terrorist group.[132]

The outfit had suffered significant attrition, including the loss of several top leaders and other cadres, following a crackdown initiated by the Nawaz Sharif government in 1998. Sheikh Haq Nawaz Jhangvi was sentenced and hanged in February 2001 for terrorist offences relating to the murder of an Iranian diplomat in Lahore on 19 December 1990. Most of its top leadership has gone underground, but they remain active in training new recruits and directing operations.[133]

On 15 October 2001 the Sindh government announced rewards for the arrest of twelve proclaimed offenders involved in heinous sectarian terrorist attacks: seven absconders belonged to LeJ, while five were activists of another proscribed terrorist outfit, the Sipah-e-Muhammad Pakistan (SMP). A cash reward of Rs 1 million was offered for each of three LeJ terrorists: Qari Abdul Hai alias Qari Asad alias Talha, Atta-ur-Rehman alias Nadeem Bukhari, and Asif Ramzi. A cash reward of half a million rupees was fixed for each of another three: Asif Ramzi alias Chotto alias Hafiz, Muhammad Rashid and Lal Muhammad alias Lal Bhai alias Faqeer. A Rs 250,000 cash reward was offered for Muhammad Umer alias Haji Sahib.

In November 2003 Pakistani law enforcement agencies compiled a list of 107 sectarian terrorists wanted by the Punjab police: 63 were members of LeJ, 43 from the banned Shi'a organization Sipah-e-Muhammad (SM), and one from Tehrik-e-Jafria. Fifty-six names on the list, of whom nineteen were from Shi'a organizations, were in the 'grey' category, meaning that there is some evidence suggesting that they may be linked to terrorists, but it is insufficient to prove guilt.

Despite facing significant attrition at the hands of law enforcement forces, LeJ did not give up. In December 2008, LeJ was accused of involvement in a plot to kill former president Pervez Musharraf, masterminded by Sheikh Omar, the jailed killer of Daniel Pearl. The plot was pre-empted when prison officials recovered a large number of mobile phones, SIM cards and other equipment from Sheikh Omar, who was planning to assassinate Musharraf with the help of LeJ militants with whom he had been in contact by telephone during his imprisonment. His mobile phone records revealed that Omar had also been in touch with Atta-ur-Rehman alias Nadeem Bukhari, a key LeJ operative arrested by the Karachi police on 5 June 2007 in connection with the Daniel Pearl murder case. A search of the barracks at Sukkur Central Jail, where Atta-ur-Rehman was being held, recovered a mobile phone and three SIMs he had been using to stay in touch with Omar and other LeJ accomplices in Karachi and Rawalpindi.[134]

During the ensuing interrogations, Atta-ur-Rehman revealed that Sheikh Omar had already directed LeJ operatives to target Musharraf, either in Rawalpindi or in Karachi, preferably using a suicide car bomber. Musharraf's movements had been monitored while he was travelling between his Army House residence in Rawalpindi and his Chak Shehzad farmhouse on the 1-A Park Road in the Islamabad suburbs. They had planned to blow up the bridge on Shara-e-Faisal during his next visit to

Karachi at the precise moment when his convoy would arrive there from Quaid-e-Azam International Airport. After the assassination plot was uncovered Musharraf decided to leave for a short trip to London on 22 November 2008, his first since his resignation as president three months before. Owing to grave concerns for his security, Musharraf was compelled to remain at the Army House even after resigning as Chief of Army Staff.

Up to February 2010 the security forces had arrested 97 members of the LeJ and killed eight. It is believed that 81 members were still active, four had absconded and four were underground.

LeJ: The Future

The Pakistani government believes that the LeJ and the other sectarian extremist groups remain a serious threat, especially since they also pursue an anti-West agenda. Its association with the Kashmiri militant groups, however, not only enhances its power and influence, but also makes it harder to make a distinction between outlawed militants and so-called Kashmiri freedom fighters. Despite the arrest of hundreds of militants linked to LeJ, police officials estimate that thousands of trained sectarian militants still operate in the country. Sunni militants have joined hands with Kashmiri extremist groups, such as Jaish-e-Muhammad and Harkat-ul-Mujahideen, and their splinter groups are known to operate with Al Qaeda and Taliban forces in Pakistan: 'They can handle weapons, rockets, bombs. But the fearsome aspect is that they are not afraid of death.'[135] For them, killing Shi'as is a gateway to paradise. The danger of the LeJ remains: there is no evidence to suggest that it has, in any way, mitigated the intensity of its resolve to attack Shi'ites, Christians and Western targets, especially American, in Pakistan.

As the militant, or more accurately the 'death squad', wing of the SSP, LeJ's fortunes seem very much intertwined with that of its parent. Since they share similar political objectives and urban support base with the SSP, and LeJ's cadres are drawn from SSP-run madrasas,[136] the fate or destiny of LeJ cannot be divorced from the experiences of the SSP. As Christine Fair alludes, while the LeJ has its own structure and is believed to have only 300 or so cadres (although the US State Department puts the figure at about 100)[137],– its support base is rooted to the members of the SSP, numbering between three and six thousand.[138]

Since it primarily funds itself through criminal activities, such as protection rackets and robbing Shi'a banks and other businesses, the authorities should monitor this group's activities and links very closely as it is likely to continue these activities in order to survive.

LEJ has also shown remarkable resourcefulness in sourcing for funds, benefiting from funding channelled through Karachi to the group's 'treasury' by Saudi and other wealthy Arabs.[139]

Perhaps most importantly, LEJ continues to pose a threat to prominent Shi'a or SSP opponents. Massacres of political and/or religious adversaries cannot be ruled out. The type of operation that the group carries out – a lone cadre or a few cadres armed with automatic assault rifles opening fire in Shi'a mosques or during Shi'a religious celebrations and weddings – will most probably be retained in the short term. Alternative scenarios of terrorist attacks perpetrated by this group could include executions or assassinations of Shi'a professionals, such as doctors, lawyers and teachers, leaders of opposing political parties, lobbyists and scholars.[140]

In the long term, the LEJ's capabilities will likely be significantly reduced by the Pakistani authorities' crackdown, coupled with the American counter-terrorist campaign worldwide and its support for Pakistan in this 'global war on terror'. During Operation Enduring Freedom in October 2001, for instance, LEJ lost its most important training base at Sarobi in Afghanistan, although it still has important training bases in Pakistan at Muridke and Kabirwala.[141] Fortunately for the counter-terrorism forces, all these bases have come under close scrutiny by the ISI and have most likely undergone significant cuts in manpower.

On the other hand, some voices in Pakistan have doubted that LeJ was actually behind many of the attacks in the country, claiming that the government blamed the attacks on the LEJ to give itself 'a perfect reason' to liquidate the group. These 'doubters' could potentially be underestimating the threat posed by the group. Indeed, LEJ and SSP both have full access to a wide array of armaments, including many variants of the Kalashnikov family of AK rifles. According to Christine Fair, they also have rockets, landmines, explosives and other forms of weaponry made available to the group as a result of imports from Afghanistan and China.[142] Many existing members of the group have also received advanced bomb-making instructions and acquired mountain guerrilla warfare capabilities. Thus, while acknowledging the generally positive consequences of US and Pakistani involvement in the war against terrorism, it should not be forgotten that the LEJ is still a force to be reckoned with and should henceforth be monitored closely.

Harkat-ul-Jihad-i-Islami (HUJI)

Harkat-ul-Jihad-i-Islami (Islamic Movement for Holy War) is a transnational terrorist outfit based in Pakistan. Its organizational structure and network extends beyond Pakistan and Indian-held Kashmir to Chechnya, Uzbekistan, Xinjiang China and Bangladesh.[143] According to Pakistani intelligence, HUJI-Bangladesh (HUJI-B), while having come from the same parent organization, is effectively an independent operation concentrating on North Eastern India. In August 2004 some media reports claimed that HUJI had mutated into Harkat-ul-Mujahideen al-Almi.[144] It is speculated that HUJI started operating under this new name after the Pakistani government banned various militant outfits in mid-2004.

The outfit seeks to wage defensive Jihad against the non-Muslim aggressors: the HUJI has called itself 'the second line of defence for all Muslim states'.[145] It also seeks to impose the supremacy of Islam on the whole world.

Maulana Irshad Ahmed was the founder of HUJI, and Maulana Ahmed Umer was appointed the first vice Amir. Qari Zarar, who was also among the founding members, separated from HUJI and later formed his own organization, Harkat-ul Ansar.[146] In June 1985 Maulana Irshad Ahmed was killed at Shirana in Afghanistan in a clash with the Soviet forces. He was replaced by Qari Saifullah Akhtar, who reshaped the administrative structure of the outfit and established worldwide contacts with Jihadi outfits.[147] Akhtar was described as the 'operational head of Al Qaeda in Pakistan'.[148] He remained at the head of HUJI until he was arrested by law enforcement agencies on 26 February 2008.

Since HUJI is a transnational entity, its organizational structure is proportionally larger. When the Taliban was in power, its central secretariat was located in Kabul, and has since been moved to Waziristan and Bonir. The following departments are the most important in the organizational structure: Dawat-o-Irshad (preaching); military and training camps; finance; organization; and media and publications.[149]

Until 2004 Harkat-ul-Jihad-i-Islami maintained branch offices in 40 districts of Pakistan, including Sargodha, Dera Ghazi Khan, Multan, Khanpur, Gujranwala, Gujrat, Mianwali, Bannu, Kohat, Waziristan, Dera Ismail Khan, Swabi and Peshawar. It also had an office in Islamabad.[150]

HUJI has brought in many mujahideen to fight in Indian-controlled Kashmir. According to its publications in Pakistan, some 650 HUJI mujahideen were killed in battle against the Indian army: 190 came from either side of the border in Kashmir; nearly 200 came from Punjab, 49 from Sindh, 29 from Baluchistan, 70 from Afghanistan, 5 from Turkey, and 49 collectively from Uzbekistan, Bangladesh and the Arab world. Its publications frequently mentioned HUJI commanders fighting wars in Chechnya, Uzbekistan and Sinkiang. When its men were seen first in Tajikistan, some observers mistook them for fighters from Sipah-e-Sahaba Pakistan (SSP), but they were in fact under the command of a Punjabi commander, helping Juma Namangani and Tahir Yuldashev of the Islamic Movement of Uzbekistan in the Ferghana Valley. Harkat-ul-Jihad-i-Islami used to be entrenched in Korangi, part of Landhi Town, Karachi. The HUJI opened thirty seminaries inside Korangi and a further eighteen elsewhere in Karachi. The largest seminary in Korangi was Madrasa Khalid bin Walid, where the presence of 500 Burmese under training once gave Korangi the nickname of ' mini-Arakan'. They were later trained in Afghanistan and directed to fight against the Northern Alliance and against the Indian army in Kashmir.[151]

Many links have been drawn between HUJI-Pakistan and HUJI-Bangladesh (HUJI-B), but the reality is that the outfits are not as closely related as commonly perceived.[152] While both seem to have originated from Harkat-ul Ansar (HUA), they have split into two distinct organizations.[153] More importantly, HUJI's official literature does not mention any operational office or desk for or in Bangladesh.[154]

HUJI has international desks or departments covering the following regions: Uzbekistan, Afghanistan, Tajikistan, Chechnya, Burma, and Jammu and Kashmir. Its command structure, in descending order, covers the following positions: Patron; Patron in Chief; Central Amir (Head); Manager, Finance; Patron, All Jammu and Kashmir; Deputy Amir; Manager, Dawat-o-Irshad (preaching); Chief Commander, Jammu and Kashmir; Manager, Party Affairs; Committee for Families of Martyrs; Launching Commander; Student Wing (Al Jihad Student Movement); Amir, Burma; Amir, Uzbekistan; Amir, Afghanistan; Chief Commander, Tajikistan; and Manager, Chechnya.

HUJI strictly follows the Deobandi version of Islam and the group's main ideology is covered in ten precepts:[155]

1. God is our defender. Muhammad (PBUH) is our Prophet. Islam is our way of life. Kaba is our direction. Qur'an is our book. Sahabah (the Prophet's companions) are the standards for the precision. We are the followers of the four Imams of the Ahle Sunnet. Martyrdom for truth is our aim.

2. According to the Qur'an's commandment (verse Al-Tubah: 33), HUJI's primary objective is to establish the supremacy of Islam in the world.

3. To enable the renaissance of a new Islamic era and to regain the powers, which we only believe to be for Jihad and Dawwat [preaching].

4. We will struggle to free the Muslims of the world from the confinement of the 'east and west" and we will also struggle ideologically and practically to form a 'United Muslim Power'.

5. This organization is completely a religious and constructive party that opposes the un-Islamic western style of politics.

6. To follow the Qur'anic verse Alanfal: 59 (which says to always be ready with your capacity and strength) and always prepare for jihad far and wide at any time. For this purpose, [we] will establish such madaris, institutions and training centres which will produce youths who are brave, patriotic and ready to sacrifice their lives for the sake of Jihad.

7. We will be the second defence line for every Muslim country.

8. We will not stop our struggle until all occupied regions 'of the Muslims' are freed and all minorities are free and secure too.

9. For the sake of restoring and protecting God's Honour and Dignity, we are always ready to sacrifice our lives.

10. Islam is the only code of life, which provides the solutions to every problem and has the potential to establish a society based on the principles of 'Justice and Peace'.

Military Capabilities of HUJI

A Pakistani counter-terrorism expert stated in August 2004 that HUJI consisted of 4,000 fighters by the time the Afghan jihad came to an end in 1988. It had lost only 26 fighters during the first eight years of the Afghan jihad, and lost 17 fighters between November 1988 and November 1989.[156]

HUJI seeks to attain its objectives by provoking popular sentiments against 'infidels occupying Muslim lands and leaders of Muslim countries under tremendous influence of aggressors'. Moreover, the outfit lays great stress on conforming to the sect and Sharia, in order to gain more support from aspiring Deobandi youth.[157]

In its operations HUJI has been known to use the following tactics: suicide bombings, which have been used in attempts to assassinate key political figures; target killings; and hit and run attacks, which have frequently been employed in Afghanistan, Kashmir and Tajikistan. The main targets selected were high-profile government officials in Pakistan, the security forces in Indian-controlled Kashmir, and the state infrastructure and officials in Central Asian states.

During the Taliban rule in Afghanistan, HUJI had six training camps at Kabul and Khost, where most of its militants were trained. It also had a training camp in Indian-held Kashmir. Despite the presence of seven hundred thousand Indian soldiers in Kashmir, HUJI was able to run a training camp there for thousands of young Kashmiri men.[158] It is believed that HUJI militants also received training at Al Qaeda camps in Afghanistan during the 1990s.[159]

Funds were collected from grassroot offices as well as from sources abroad. The militia had accounts in two branches of the Allied Bank in Islamabad.[160] As well as collecting funds from all over the country, the organization has made a handsome profit from the sale of arms to smaller Jihadi organizations. Its representatives are also very active collecting funds in countries abroad.[161]

As mentioned above, HUJI was among the pioneer Jihadi outfits formed to fight the Soviet Union in Afghanistan. Funds poured in from Saudi Arabia, Pakistan's Inter Services Intelligence (ISI) and America's CIA.[162] After the Soviet withdrawal and the tragic events of 9/11, however, the US, Saudi and Pakistani governments rethought their policies towards Jihadi outfits active in the region. There is speculation that Arab governments are no longer supporting or funding HUJI, based on the fact that in October 2007 the UN Security Council Committee introduced a worldwide ban on Al Haramein Foundation, which was thought to be the major source of funding for HUJI and other Islamist militant organizations.[163] Qari Saifullah's repatriation from Dubai in October 2004 also signalled the closing of the Saudi channel of escape and support for the Deobandi jihadis.

Similarly, the Pakistani government banned several militant groups, including HUJI, in the wake of the September 11 attacks. The cosy relationship between the Pakistani military and the radical outfits it once used as proxy fighters has turned sour. HUJI, or any other Jihadi outfit, is no longer authorized or allowed to raise funds publicly in Pakistan.

Relations with Other Organizations

The Taliban Connection

During the Afghan Jihad, HUJI developed strong relationships with the Afghan mujahideen, particularly the Taliban. The outfit gained more strength with the introduction of the Taliban rule in Afghanistan, and many of its individuals enrolled in the Taliban army and administration. It is worth mentioning here that three Taliban ministers and twenty-two judges belonged to HUJI.[164] In difficult times, the HUJI fighters stood together with the Taliban and approximately 300 were killed fighting the Northern Alliance, after which Mullah Omar gave HUJI permission to build six more *maskars* (training camps) in Kandahar, Kabul and Khost, where the Taliban army and police also received military training. It eventually became the biggest jihadi militia based in Kandahar, located at the heart of the Taliban-Al Qaeda strategic merger.[165]

The group is also suspected to have strong links with Taliban militants in the Federally Administered Tribal Areas (FATA). After the fall of the Taliban in late 2001 Qari Saifullah Akhtar fled from Kandahar to South Waziristan, where he was provided with a safe hideout.[166]

Mainland Pakistani Outfits

Because of their common origin in the Banuri seminary, Harkat-ul-Jihad al-Islami and Harkat-ul-Mujahideen of Maulana Fazlur Rahman Khalil were merged in 1993 to improve their operational performance in Kashmir. The new outfit, known as Harkat-ul Ansar, was the first to be declared a terrorist organization by the United States after one of its commanders formed an ancillary organization, Al Faran, and kidnapped and killed Western tourists from Kashmir in 1995.[167]

HUJI also had close links with Jaish-e-Muhammad, led by Maulana Masood Azhar. In the aftermath of the Pakistan government's ban on Jihadi outfits, however, grave differences developed between the outfits and there were soon rumours that many senior leaders of HUJI were set on joining Jaish-e-Muhammad. Some media reports also revealed that Jaish-e-Muhammad attempted to take over HUJI offices. The HUJI senior leadership formed a committee to counter the issue and prevent further defections. Despite similar Deobandi backgrounds, differences between the organizations still exist and mediation by leading Deobandi clerics has been unsuccessful.[168]

Kashmiri Outfits

After the Soviets left Afghanistan, most of the Jihadi outfits looked towards Indian-controlled Kashmir as a new battleground. The first group of sixteen HUJI militants (four Kashmiris and twelve Pakistanis) infiltrated Kashmir in early 1992.[169] HUJI is called Harkatul Jehad Brigade 111 in Indian-held Kashmir. It was at first opposed by the Wahhabi elements there because of its refusal to criticize the grand Deobandi congregation of Tableeghi Jamaat and its quietist stance. In time, however, its warriors were recognized as 'Afghanis' and it finally had more 'martyrs' in the Kashmir jihad than any other militia. By 2005 HUJI had lost 650 militants in Kashmir, of which 190 came from Indian- and Pakistani-held Kashmir, 200 from Punjab, 49 from Sindh, 29 from Baluchistan and 70 from Afghanistan. Its resolve and organization were recognized when foreigners were seen fighting side by side with its Punjabi warriors. Its management is semi-autonomous but subservient to the central organization. It has its centres in Kotli, in Pakistan-held Kashmir, and a base camp in Muzzaffarabad.[170]

huji after 9/11

Qari Saifullah Akhtar and his group were tested after the events of 9/11 as the world started to close in on them. Following the us attack they were evicted from Afghanistan and then jihad in Kashmir was placed under the international microscope. Most importantly, the Taliban/Al Qaeda and Pakistan became estranged. Qari Saifullah Akhtar and his group faced the dilemma of choosing between the Taliban/Al Qaeda and Pakistan: Saifullah himself and part of his group apparently chose the former.[171]

The Pakistani government responded by banning huji on 11 January 2002.[172] Qari Saifullah Akhtar was arrested in Dubai in August 2004 in connection with his involvement in attempts on the lives of President Pervez Musharraf in 2003 and Prime Minister Shaukat Aziz in 2004.[173] On 26 February 2008 he was again arrested for questioning regarding the assassination attempt on Benazir Bhutto in Karachi on 19 October 2007.[174]

Jundullah-Pakistan

Jundullah (Army of God) was one of the several small, but highly organized, splinter groups that emerged in different parts of the country after 9/11. Jandullah can be best described as a product of the nexus between 'Al Qaeda-Taliban-mainland Jihadi' outfits. The outfit was created by the mastermind of 9/11, Khalid Sheikh Muhammad, under the patronage of the Taliban commander Nek Muhammad.[175] Khalid Sheikh Mohamed was arrested in Rawalpindi in 2003 and handed over to the Americans, after which Jundullah went wild.[176] 'Jund' means gang and is synonymous with most names taken by the jihadis to name their organizations, such as 'Sipah', 'lashkar' and 'jaish'. In 2007 another Jundullah sprang up in Baluchistan, attacking Iranian security personnel inside Iran. There was a widespread rumour that Pakistan was facilitating American mischief inside Iran through this Baloch Jundullah, but this organization had nothing to do with the Jandullah that is linked to Al Qaeda and whose members have been involved in carrying out terrorist attacks in Karachi.

Jundullah was formed in Karachi and carried out most of its key operations there. It is also believed to have been involved in a bomb blast in Quetta[177] and have links to FATA. Although Jundullah was not part of any criminal syndicate, its structure was very similar to those operating in Karachi: the only difference lies in the fact that Jundullah was ideologically motivated.[178]

Karachi police and other law enforcement agencies knew little about Jundullah's political and ideological mindset. The reason for this lack of information is the apparent indifference of these institutions towards such terrorist groups. Relying on the available information on Jundullah and the history of its links with other organizations and groups, however, it is not difficult to assert that Jundullah was ideologically very close to Takfiri thought.[179]

According to police sources, Jundullah's organizational structure was based on three levels of ranks: militants; administration; and preaching and training.[180] The militants' section was responsible for the planning and fulfilment of terrorist activities. The administrative section provided the financial resources, and its activists were involved in criminal activities such as bank robbery, dacoity, kidnapping for ransom and stealing cars. In addition, this section provided logistical support for various terrorist activities. The preaching and training section sought out recruits and trained new members in the Pakistani tribal areas. Police sources claim that this section of Jundullah used Karachi's mosques, seminaries, tea cafés and restaurants for training purposes, trapping unemployed youngsters in their net. The group was headed by an Amir (Commander), assisted by a Naib-Amir (Vice-Commander). The Al Qaeda and Taliban leadership in FATA acted as a patron of Jundullah.

The outfit was seeking to force the Pakistani government to stop supporting the US-led war on terror. Given its strong links with Al Qaeda and the Taliban, Jundullah is believed to have been a part of Al Qaeda's global Jihad, which seeks to drive out 'infidels' from Muslim lands. Although the founder of Jundullah and its other activists have had links with Jamaat-e-Islami and other banned organizations, the group had no direct organizational or ideological links with any other political or religious party. However, they did have links with the local Taliban and Al Qaeda in South Waziristan.[181] Jundullah had close links with tribal militants commanded by Mulvi Haji Bashir, who was a trusted commander of Baitullah Mehsud.

Jundullah drew its primary support from Karachi's disillusioned youth, inspired by Al Qaeda and residing in the areas of Shah Faisal Colony, Model Colony and Landhi. Several Jundullah terrorists were formerly members of the Muttahida Qaumi Movement (MQM). The organization survived a series of arrests because of its ability to draw on its large support infrastructure. The operation against Islamabad's Red Mosque in July 2007 provided Jundullah with hundreds of willing suicide bombers, most of whom are also former students of Islamabad's Lal Masjid.[182]

Ata-u-Rehman, who was designated as the Amir (Commander) of Jundullah, was born on 14 May 1970 in Model Colony Karachi. He passed his matriculation from the federal board in 1984 and entered Karachi University in 1987, eventually gaining a Masters degree in statistics. He started his political career by joining the All Pakistan Mohajir Students Federation, the student wing of the MQM, led by Altaf Hussain. After some time, he left APMSO and joined Jamiat Tulaba-e-Islam, the student wing of Jamiat-Ulema-i-Islami. He then formed his own group, consisting of twelve persons,[183] but left this group as well and disappeared for some time. When he reappeared it was with a new organization, Jamat-ul-Muslimeen. He started to wear a black turban. Ata-u-Rehman was arrested in May 2004 and is still in custody.

Shehzad Ahmad Bajwa alias Umer, the Naib-Amir, and Musab Aruchi, who is the nephew of Khalid Sheikh Mohamed and held an important position in Jundullah's leadership, were also arrested in May 2004.. The arrests were part of a government crackdown after Jundullah's attempt to kill the Pakistani Army Corps commander in 2004. About 85 per cent of the Jundullah rank and file were arrested within 24 hours. Musab Aruchi was turned over to the US soon after his capture.

Some members, however, managed to remain at large. Qasim Toori, Tayyab Dad and Ustaz Khashif escaped to Wana, South Waziristan, to regroup. Qasim Toori was a former policeman who had been forced to leave the service after he was accused of being involved in the rape of a 14-year-old boy at Shah Faisal Colony Gate, Karachi.[184] He returned to Karachi in 2007, together with Tayyab Dadd and some new recruits. They rented several safe houses and conducted three major robberies for the Pakistani Taliban and possibly for Al Qaeda, reporting to an Egyptian member of Al Qaeda, Haji Mumthaz, who worked with Baitullah Mehsud. Toori had one million rupees (US$16,200) on his head, but he was eventually arrested in Karachi on 29 January 2008 during a raid on a militant hideout to rescue a hostage; Tayyab Dad was arrested but died in hospital Two policemen were killed in the raid.[185] Ustaz Khashif is reported to be in hiding in Wana.

Dr Akmal Waheed, an orthopedic surgeon, and his younger brother Dr Arshad Waheed, a heart specialist, are said to have provided medical treatment to the members of Jundullah. They were associated with the Pakistan Islamic Medical Association and were heavily involved in relief work in Afghanistan after the US-led intervention. They later treated several high-profile Al Qaeda leaders in South Waziristan, and are said to have raised funds for Al Qaeda and helped several Arab families return to their countries of origin. Both brothers were arrested in 2004 for their alleged involvement in the attack on the Corps Commander's convoy. They were sentenced to eighteen years in prison by an anti-terrorist court for 'causing disappearance of evidence by harbouring and providing medical treatment to activists of the banned Jundullah group'. The brothers said they had expected such a verdict as 'it was part of the government policy to appease the United States'.[186] Following protest marches held in Lahore and Karachi, they were both released in 2006 by the Supreme Court. Dr Arshad Waheed returned to South Waziristan with his family in order to treat those affected by the war, but was killed by a US air strike on Wana on 16 March 2008.

Jundullah derived funds from criminal activities such as kidnapping, bank robbery, and car and motorcycle theft. During questioning, captured Jundullah terrorists claimed that Mulvi Haji Bashir has acquired a fatwa (decree) that gathering money through illegitimate means for Jihad is lawful in Islam.[187] They confessed that they had robbed foreign banks and dispatched the money from criminal activities to their headquarters in Wana, from which their needs for weapons, explosives and other necessities were being met.[188] Baitullah Mehsud, then the leader of Tehrik-e-Taliban Pakistan, sent trained people from Wana to acquire jobs in security companies and so facilitate the committing of robberies that would generate funds for his organization.[189]

Jundullah's first major operation was a fund-raising and weapons-gathering raid on the Gulistan-i-Jauhar police station a few days after they robbed a bank in the same area. A senior police officer said that: 'The primary target of the attack was to give a message of their presence and collect weapons, as they were reluctant to purchase weapons fearing that they could be exposed'.[190]

Car theft was another important economic source for Jundullah: according to police records, Jundullah was suspected of involvement in the theft of 120 cars between 2004 and 2007. Ata-u-Rehman admitted to being responsible for six of these, three of which were used in the attack on the Corps Commander Karachi.[191]

The possibility of Al Qaeda funding Jundullah cannot be ruled out since Al Qaeda's top leader, Khalid Sheikh Mohamed, and his other Arab contacts were involved in Jundullah's formation.

Military Capability of Jundullah

During investigations by the Anti-Violent Crime Unit, Karachi, Jundullah members disclosed that around 600 Jundullah militants were present in Karachi.[192] Not all the youngsters recruited by Jundullah were idle and unemployed. Some were educated and trained in information technology: Tayyeb Dad, a computer professional, had been in charge of Jundullah's IT.

Jundullah followed Al Qaeda's strategy of carrying out high-profile and symbolic attacks to achieve its objectives, notably the assassination attempt on the Corps Commander Karachi, General Ahsan Saleem Hayat, on 10 June 2004. Multiple tactics have been used in its operations, including shootings, targeted killings, bomb blasts and suicide bombings. The frequent changes in tactics made it difficult for law enforcement agencies to detect patterns that might identify Jundullah as a suspect in an unclaimed attack. The deputy superintendent of the Karachi Anti-Violent Crime Unit, Wasif Qureshi, has said that terrorist groups active in Karachi mostly use traditional tactics: the LeJ, for example, is considered an expert in shootings and bomb blasts, and investigating agencies can easily identify attacks that the LeJ were behind, and this helps them pursue further investigation. Jundullah used the tactic of shooting and targeted killing while attacking a Ranger mobile in the area of Ferozabad on 19 March 2004. They then used the same tactic to attack Corps Commander Ahsan Saleem Hayat on 10 June 2004. Between these two similar attacks, however, they used bombs for the attack on the Marina Club on 10 April and that near the Pakistan American Cultural Centre on 26 May. It is believed that Jundullah specialized in using hand grenades, which were employed on 15 January 2004 for an attack on the Pakistan Bible Society.

The group followed Al Qaeda's tactic of using mentally and physically unstable people to launch suicide attacks. In January 2008, for example, law enforcement personnel took into custody two brothers, Abu Abdullah and Gohar Muhammad, both physically unfit, who had been instructed to carry out suicide attacks.

Following the successful operation against Jundullah in the Shah Latif Colony on 29 January 2008, law enforcement agencies recovered two rocket launchers, twelve bombs, twenty-five hand grenades, three pistols, six Kalashnikovs, four bags of ball bearings and twenty-five suicide jackets. This revealed that the group was preparing for suicide bomb attacks in the city. Jundullah's expertise in suicide bombing can also be demonstrated by their killing of the US diplomat David Foey near the US Consulate on 2 March 2006, which, according to the special public prosecutor for Sindh, Rehmat Ali Randhawa, involved three people. Usman Ghani and Anwar-ul-Haq were given the death sentence for their involvement in the attack. Training in small arms and other weapons was given in camps run by Al Qaeda in the rugged tribal district of South Waziristan.[193] Some members of Jundullah have also attended the Taliban's training camps in Shakai.[194]

Jundullah Defeated

On 10 June 2004 the group went ahead with their biggest operation by attacking a convoy of vehicles in which the former corps commander, Lieutenant-General Ahsan Saleem Hayat, was travelling. Ten people were killed, including six soldiers and policemen, and twenty-one were injured. Soon afterwards the police arrested ten members of Jundullah, including Ata-u-Rehman and Shehzad Ahmad Bajwa. In Feburary 2006 Ata-u-Rehman, Shehzad Ahmad Bajwa, Aziz, Danish Imam and Khurram Saifullah Shoaib Siddiqui received death sentences, while the rest were given life sentences. Five named terrorist, however, remained at large. Nearly two years after the trial, police raided a house in Sector 17-A of Shah Latif Town, a residential area on the outskirts of Karachi. After a heavy exchange of fire, which resulted in six casualties, police managed to arrest Qasim Toori and the other militants there.

In 2004 the Interior Minister, Faisal Saleh Hayat, said that Jundullah consisted of no more then nineteen people, of whom twelve had been arrested.[195] The arrests of May 2004 and the outcome of the gun battle on 29 January 2008 were both major blows to Jundullah. Law enforcement agencies regarded the latter as a major victory over terrorist networks in the city, and claimed that Jandullah had been dismantled.[196]

Al Qaeda (Qari Zafar Group)

The group led by Qari Zafar originated from Lashkar-e-Jhangwi (LeJ). Qari Zafar founded the group after LeJ's key leadership was killed by the police or arrested. The group became involved in criminal activities in Karachi to raise funds. Qari Zafar established a close relationship with the Al Qaeda leadership hiding in FATA. It is also known that he used the infrastructure and members of LeJ to extend and strengthen the Al Qaeda network in Karachi.[197] The outfit came to prominence when three of its important militants, Shahid, Farhan and Ghani Subhan, were arrested in Karachi on 16 February 2007. The main objective of the Qari Zafar group is to establish a Taliban-like Islamic state in Pakistan.[198]

The original name of Qari Zafar, the founder and head of the group, was Muhammad Zafar; he was also known as Zafar Iqbal, Qari Sahib and Hussain Bhai. He was born in Sanjhoro village of Sanghar district in Sindh province. His family originated from the Hassar district of India and moved to Sanghar district after the partition. Qari Zafar moved to Karachi in 1985 and enrolled at the Dar-ul-Aloom in Binori Town, one of largest Deobandi madrasas in Asia. He started his Jihadi career by joining Harkat-ul-Mujahideen. In 1991 he travelled to Kunar province in Afghanistan to spend 40 days at a training camp.[199] He sided with the Taliban in their drive against the Northern Alliance in the 1990s. It was during his stay in Afghanistan that his fluent Arabic helped him to develop a close and personal relationship with the Arab mujahideen linked to Al Qaeda.[200]

Following the fall of the Taliban in Afghanistan, Qari Zafar fled to South Waziristan, where he was welcomed by the local Taliban. While based in the tribal areas, Qari Zafar unleashed a wave of terror against Pakistani security forces and the rival Shi'a sect and was involved in many sporadic terrorist attacks inside Pakistan. Under Qari Zafar, the group established strong links with other Deobandi outfits such as the LeJ, Harkat-ul-Mujahideen and Jaish-e-Muhammad. The Qari Zafar group was also accused of providing manpower for Al Qaeda's operations in the major cities of Pakistan Karachi was known to be the stronghold of the Qari Zafar group, but it relocated to FATA following the arrest of its key members in February 2007. The military operations in Wana dispersed the threat throughout Pakistan.

The head of the group, the Supreme Commander, controlled small units consisting of ten to fifteen members. More than fifteen terrorist cells were working in different cities across Pakistan, including those in Karachi and Hyderabad, all of them linked in some way or other to Qari Zafar in Wana.[201] After the cells in Hyderabad and Karachi were revealed during the interrogation of suspects, these cells went underground.[202]

The key members of the Qari Zafar group included Mohammed Shahid alias Kashif, Mohamed Farhan alias Nasir and Ghani Subhan alias Rashid. All three had joined the LeJ after fighting on different fronts against the Northern Alliance.[203] Their profiles demonstrate how Al Qaeda mobilized jihadists from different groups. Shahid, from the upper middle-class neighbourhood of Latifabad in Hyderabad, was recruited by Qari Akbar, a local jihadist who set him to robbing Shi'a households.[204] Arrested for robbery, he spent one and a half years in jail, after which he jumped bail. Shahid joined the SSP in 1993, and then went to Khost and trained in the Khalid bin Walid camp, where he met Qari Zafar. He served in Afghanistan and Indian-held Kashmir, where he spent four months in

2003 at a Harkat-ul-Mujahideen camp. After that he moved on to Wana, where he developed his knowledge in explosives.

Mushtaq, another local jihadist, recruited Farhan, who was also from Hyderabad.[205] Farhan was sent for a 40-day training course with Shikho at a Harkat-ul-Mujahideen camp in Kabul, where he met Qari Zafar and Qari Shahzad.[206] At the request of Qari Zafar, Farhan moved to Wana, taking with him 60kg of ball bearings for making suicide bombs.[207]

Ghani Subhan went to Kabul in 2001 and was injured fighting alongside the Taliban.[208] He was close to the Taliban leadership and joined forces with Nek Muhammad. After the latter's death, he joined Fakir Muhammad, leader of TNSM in Bajour Agency.

Muhammad Anwar, Qari Zafar's younger brother and an Al Qaeda-trained explosives expert, and Ustaz Abdul Hameed also held important positions in the leadership.

Qari Zafar's group adheres to Al Qaeda's ideology of global Jihad against infidels and establishing an Islamic government in Pakistan. Al Qaeda is believed to be a major donor to the group.[209] Further funding comes from bank robberies and looting wealthy Shi'as.

The group serves as Al Qaeda's logistical support base in Karachi. In order to carry out a terrorist operation in Karachi or any other major city, the terrorists are trained in FATA and return to their sanctuaries after hitting the target.[210] The cadres in Karachi come from small local cells and provide logistical support to them before disappearing from the scene. Sometimes weapons and explosive materials are brought from FATA. The car used in the suicide bomb attack on the US Consulate in Karachi, for which Anwarul Haq has been sentenced to death for his involvement, was prepared with explosives and transported from Waziristan to Karachi.[211] Kalashnikov rifles, TT pistols, hand grenades and suicide vests are frequently used by the group. Training also involves the use of videodiscs in which an Arabic-speaking man explains how to prepare a suicide bomber and how to inflict harm on a huge number of casualties.

On 16 February 2007 the Karachi police arrested Mohammed Shahid, Mohamed Farhan and Ghani Subhan in the middle-class neighbourhood of Gulistan-e-Jauhar.[212] They had an AK-47, two TT pistols, three hand grenades and a suicide bomb jacket, and were planning to target the Shi'a Chehlum procession in Karachi and to kill anti-terrorism court judges, police and intelligence officers conducting counter-terrorist operations.[213] In addition to planning to use a car bomb against the Intelligence Bureau office in Karachi, the cell had been monitoring the movements of MQM leaders Farooq Sattar and Mustafa Kamal. Two officials of the Intelligence Bureau were killed in a raid on Qari Zafar's house in Karachi. Muhammad Anwar and an Arab were arrested and the police recovered huge quantities of explosive materials.[214] Qari Zafar was declared a most wanted terrorist by Sindh police and a bounty of Rs 5 million was placed on his head. There are reports, however, that he was killed in a US drone strike in February 2010.

Tehrik-e-Islami Lashkar-e-Muhammadi (TILM)

Pakistan's decision to side with the international community in the 'War on Terror' gave birth to multiple clones of Al Qaeda throughout the country. These newly emerged Islamist groups perceived the policies of the Musharraf government as 'pro-US'. One such group, Tehrik-e-Islami Lashkar-e-Muhammadi (TILM), came into being in 2002 and comprised former Jihadis from leading Sunni Jihadi outfits like Jaish-e-Muhammad and Harkat-ul-Mujahideen.[215] It should be differentiated from an already existing group in Pakistan, Lashkar-e-Muhammadi, a Shi'a terrorist outfit aimed at targeting Sunnis. TILM's activities reached fever pitch in September 2007, when they murdered Liaquat Hussain, the Vice President of the National Bank of Pakistan, the businessman Dara Feroz Mirza and a physician, Dr Hameedullah, within ten days.

The outfit was formed to rid Pakistan of 'nefarious Zionist and Christian influences and turn Pakistan into a pure Islamic Amarat/Emirate on true Islamic lines with Jehadi manifesto'.[216] The group prepared a detailed manifesto in which they addressed all sections of society, and warned them to adhere to the Islamic call of Jihad and rid society of all Jewish and Christian influences. The TILM manifesto carries dire warnings for the ruling classes, members of law enforcement agencies, the armed forces, NGOs, businessmen, professionals and Ulema supportive of the Musharraf regime. The manifesto carried clear-cut threats of severe attacks against them if they did not desist from acting as agents of the un-Islamic foreign powers. After the Red Mosque incident, their main objective was to target Pakistani politicians who acted on behalf of Americans and supported the operations against the Mujahideen and madrasas in Pakistan.

TILM was formed in Karachi and most of its leadership and members came from the lower middle-class suburbs. The arrest of three TILM members in Lahore in April 2008, however, demonstrated that the outfit also maintained a presence or support base in Pakistan's cultural capital.

TILM attracted a very small number of recruits and consisted of only fourteen members. Following arrests by CID Karachi and the Lahore police in February and April 2008, only two remained at large.[217] TILM is thought to have been a strict follower of the Deobandi sect since its founding members belong to Jaish-e-Muhammad and Harkat-ul-Mujahideen, and maintained close links with the Taliban.

Reportedly, Wajahat alias Babar was the central leader of TILM.[218] Other key members included Muhammad Asif and Amar Hassan, who provided finances and vital technical knowledge of bomb making as well as ideological support.[219] Muhammad Hasan Amir, a Pakistani businessman based in the UK, provided sufficient funds for Wajahat to launch TILM in 2002.[220] He later moved to Karachi and is still at large.

TILM had links with Mullah Dadullah of the Afghan Taliban through Maulana Sirajuddin Haqqani, the son of Jalaluddin Haqqani.[221] These connections were revealed when the group members looted 150 walkie-talkie sets from a shop in Japan Plaza, Karachi, and tried to dispatch the equipment to FATA for use by Mullah Dadullah.[222] The TILM also stole walkie-talkie sets, laptops, blankets, shoes and other goods for the Haqqani group, using the Taliban commander Tahir as a go-between. A list of items requested by the Taliban was recovered from one of the group at the time of his arrest.[223]

TILM was mainly dependent on robberies from banks and multi-national companies. Asif Iqbal alias Kay Area Wala was responsible for raising money through bank robberies: he was involved in robbing the Habib Bank in Korangi and, before his arrest, was planning to rob the Soneri Bank in the KIA area of Karachi.[224]

TILM members acquired training from Afghanistan during the Afghan Jihad.[225] In order to prepare explosive devices, a separate laboratory was set up in a rented building in Korangi.[226] The group had in its possession literature for sophisticated circuits/switches used in preparing remote-controlled bombs. TILM members used to kidnap their victims, torture them, and kill them by injecting venom.

TILM members were also involved in target killings aimed at punishing NGO workers, specifically Christian organizations and those associated with the Rotary Club or Freemasons, politicians who were perceived as anti-Islam and pro-West, and any members of law enforcement agencies, the armed forces, businessmen, professionals and Ulema who were supportive of the Musharraf regime.

In early 2008 the Criminal Investigation Department (CID) of Sindh mounted an operation to arrest ten dangerous terrorists of TILM. The group eluded arrest on 18 January, but after prolonged and discreet surveillance the CID was finally able to arrest seven members of the militant group in a raid in Korangi on 15 February 2008.[227] The operation was deemed to be a significant success since those arrested included Zubair, Asif Iqbal and Muhammad Atif, three of its most dangerous terrorists.

Abdul Wahid alias Zubair lived in Shah Faisal Colony and worked as a furniture maker. His family have had links to the Afghan Jihad since 1990: one brother died there in 1995 and another was killed while learning to make a bomb in a Korangi graveyard in 1998. Zubair was linked to the banned Harkat-ul Ansar.[228] Asif Iqbal, Wajahat's brother-in-law and cousin, was then working as a mechanic in a textile mill. Muhammad Atif, who had joined Jaish-e-Muhammad when it was newly formed by Maulana Masood Azhar in 2000, worked as a butter supplier.

CID recovered a wide range of deadly chemicals and weapons, including a sub-machinegun, four TT pistols, a .223 rifle and ammunition. Bomb-making equipment included 30 detonators, four prepared bombs and all the chemicals necessary for morefrom TILM members.

The CID investigations led to three further arrests in Karachi on 26 February.[229] Several raids were mounted across the country, hunting TILM members. The FIA and other agencies were alerted and their help was also sought. This led to three arrests, identified as Samiullah, Arshad alias Assad Lalu and Muhammad Hassan Amir alias Ali, in Lahore on 14 April 2008. The Lahore police claimed that they had been members of Jaish-e-Muhammad, but had formed their own 'Tehrik-e-Islami Lashkar-e-Muhammadi' after they developed differences with the JEM and other militant organizations.[230]

Wajahat alias Babar, the group leader, is still at large and is believed to be hiding in Dubai or Nepal.[231] CID Karachi has been able to arrest most of the group's members, except for Wajahat and Amar Hassan.

Sipah-e-Muhammad Pakistan (SMP)

For decades, Pakistan's Shi'a and Sunni communities lived side by side without developing any major problems. The conflicts between Shi'as and Sunnis began to escalate from the 1980s in the wake of two epic movements taking place in neighbouring Iran and Afghanistan. The Islamic revolution of 1979 in the overwhelmingly Shi'a Iran inspired many Pakistani Shi'as to demand more rights for their minority. The second was the decade-long war waged by the Sunni Afghan Mujahideen against the Soviet occupation forces in Afghanistan.[232]

Sipah-e-Muhammad Pakistan (SMP), which translates as 'Soldiers of the Prophet Muhammad', is a violent Shi'a sectarian group founded in 1993–4 to protect the Shi'a community and fight the Sunni militant groups in Pakistan. Its principal opponents are the Sunni political organization SSP and the LEJ, SSP's military wing. Addressing a press conference at the time of its formation, the SMP leaders announced, 'We are tired of picking up corpses. Now, God willing, we will clear all accounts. We will erase the name of Sipah-e-Sahaba from the annals of history.'[233] The SMP emerged with a significant following in Jhang and Punjab.[234] SMP fighters became heavily involved in anti-SSP campaigns and targeted killings. They specialized in drive-by shootings against worshippers at Sunni mosques and in assassinating Sunni leaders and clerics.

In its ideology and goals, the SMP is very similar to the Shi'a political movement Tehrik-e-Jaferia Pakistan (TJP) and some analysts claim that, as with the example of the SSP and LEJ, the SMP is the military branch of TJP.[235] The aim of the TJP and SMP is to transform the Shi'a majority areas in northwestern and northern Pakistan into a separate province to be called Karakoram. In their view, a society based on 'pure Islam' will come into being only by defending the social, political and religious rights of Shi'ite Muslims in Pakistan, and by coordinating the activities of Shi'ite organizations around the world. Following the tenets of the Iranian revolution, the TJP and SMP also endorse Islamic egalitarianism and social justice.[236] The SMP is associated with Tehriq-e-Jaffria, Pakistan (TJP), the Milli Yekjehti Council (MYC), the Imamiah Students Organization (ISO) and Pasdaran-e-Inqalab, Iran.

Ghulam Raza Naqwi, a Shi'a scholar, is the Saalar-i-Aala (head) of SMP. Naqwi has been accused of allegedly orchestrating the murder of 30 Sunni Muslims. He became notorious for transforming Thokar Niaz Beg, a village in the suburbs of Lahore and SMP's headquarters, into a no-go area for Pakistani police, who tried to break into this Shi'a stronghold at least four times.[237] The Pakistan government announced a reward of Rs 2 million (about US$25,000) for his arrest. Naqwi was arrested in 1996 and is currently in prison. He was accused of – though not formally charged with – the attempted murder of Maulana Azama Tariq, the leader of the Millat-i-Islamia Pakistan (MIP, formerly SSP), on 22 August 1994.[238] Another high-ranking SMP leader, Munawwar Abbas Alvi, is also in prison, awaiting charges for the murder of Maulana Azama Tariq on 10 June 2003.

Maulana Mureed Abbas Yazdani and Ghulam Raza Naqwi created the SMP in the period 1993–4 after they became convinced that the TJP would not allow its young cadres to engage the SSP in combat. The SMP's strongholds include the Northern Areas (Gilgit and Baltistan), Jhang, Lahore, Khanqah Dogran and Karachi. It is estimated to have a cadre base of 30,000 Shi'a followers, but most of these are supporters and sympathizers, rather than actual combatants. Many are former members of the Tehrik-e Nefaz-e Fiqh-e Jafria (TNFJ) and the TJP.[239] However, the precise nature of the connections and the interactions between SMP and TJP are unclear.

At the head of the SMP stands Shi'a cleric Allama Rai Jafar Raza, with Malik Hasan Ali Noorka as senior vice-president. The group's headquarters in Thokar Niaz Beg were eventually cleared by the police and the organization went underground.

The SMP reportedly maintains close links with the Shi'a regime in Iran and relies to a great extent on help from Iran's intelligence services. Voluntary contributions from Pakistan's Shi'a community provide a further source of income for the group.[240]

The group undertakes retaliatory attacks against Sunni civilians and political leaders, Pakistani administrators and moderate Shi'a leaders. The methods used include drive-by shootings, mainly gunning down worshippers at Sunni mosques, and assassinating Sunni and Shi'a leaders. Bomb attacks are also common. Following the 2006 outbreak of conflict between Shi'as and Sunnis in Kurram Agency, SMP's training camps located in Shi'a majority areas of Parachinar have started operating again and a number of Shi'a youth have been trained to fight against the local Taliban (pre-dominantly Deobandis) and the Sunnis of the area.

An attempt was made to resolve the sectarian conflict in May 1995. The Milli Yekjehti Council (MYC) was formed with the participation of eleven religious/sectarian outfits, including the TJP and SSP.[241] Its principal goal was to foster sectarian harmony in Pakistan. The MYC adopted a seventeen-point programme of conduct, to which Sunni and Shi'a groups could refer to in the event of religious misunderstanding and social tension. However, the creation of MYC caused internal rifts within SMP. The radical segment of the outfit would not consider any compromise with radical Sunni outfits like SSP and LeJ. Maulana Mureed Abbas Yazdani, a key leader of SMP, accused Ghulam Raza Naqvi of reconciliation with SSP and compromising his religious principles.[242] Subsequently, Sipah-e-Muhammad was divided into two groups, led by Ghulam Raza Naqvi and by Allama Mureed Abbas Yazdani.

The Yazdani group emerged as the more radical faction of SMP. In August 1996 Allama Mureed Abbas was assassinated in Rawalpindi. Police investigations revealed that the murder was the consequence of differences with Ghulam Raza Naqvi's group over joining MYC. The police arrested the murderer, who confessed to the crime.[243] The period following the October 1999 military coup in Pakistan saw a decline in sectarian violence. In February 2001, at a meeting of the MYC, the SMP and SSP announced their willingness to shun all differences and to withdraw their cases against one another. (In the past the groups had blamed each other for the killings of their respective leaders and members.) In the same month it was reported that the SMP was seeking to become a member of the Grand Democratic Alliance that had been formed to launch a movement for the restoration of democracy in Pakistan. However, despite these apparent gestures towards peace, the SMP remained the major suspect for the attack on an SSP-controlled mosque in which nine Sunni worshippers were killed and twelve others were injured on 12 March 2001.[244]

The internal differences had seriously weakened the SMP and it had no response. when President Musharraf banned both Tehriq-e-Jaffria Pakistan (TJP) and its Sunni counterpart, the SSP, on 14 August 2001. Their military wings, the SMP and the LEJ respectively, were proscribed on 15 January 2002.[245] Pakistan's law enforcement agencies launched a massive crackdown on the Sunni and Shi'a politico-military outfits from 15 August 2001. Approximately 200 leaders and activists of the LEJ and SMP were arrested. On 16 August the Punjab police filed court cases under the amended Anti-Terrorism Act against the detained activists. Other arrests took place in Faisalabad, Jhang and Toba Tek Singh districts.[246]

Concurrently, the State Bank of Pakistan (SBP), through a circular issued on 23 August 2001, ordered all banks and financial institutions in the country to freeze the SMP's accounts with immediate effect. Since the outfit was operating predominantly underground, however, official sources indicated that there may not have been any accounts under its official name. The SBP confirmed reports that the TJP and SMP were not maintaining accounts with banks or financial institutions anywhere in the country.[247]

For all practical purposes, the SMP stopped operating in 1996 after Ghulam Raza Naqvi was arrested. Its cadres are now decentralized and reportedly operate on their own. The lack of financial resources and training are also key factors in SMP's relative demise. Though pro-violence Shi'a activists continue to support the Sipah-e-Muhammad, the TJP is choosing more and more to distance itself from the militants, At present, the TJP has restricted itsand cooperation is restricted at present to providing legal assistance and advice to arrested SMP SMP cadres.

Harkat-ul-Mujahideen al-Almi (HUMA)

Harkat-ul-Mujahideen Alal-Aalmi (HUMA), meaning the International Movement of Mujahideen) was, is the first terrorist group to be created in Pakistan after 9/-11. It was formed some time in the year 2002, after parting ways with Harkat-ul-JehadJihad-ei-Islami the latter on a dispute over organizational affairs. It was reported by According to The Friday Times that, there was reportedly some pressure on the HUMA after its proscription in Pakistan in November 2001 the HUJI was under pressure to merge with the Jamiat-ul-Mujahideen, another Jihadi group based in Pakistan, after it was proscribed in November 2001. However, this plan met with stiff internal resistance from within the HuM and the dissent led to a group breaking away from the parent outfit and calling itself the Harkat-ul-Mujahideen Alal-Almi.[248] HUMA's foremost objective was to target American and Western interests in Pakistan, more precisely in Karachi. The Harkat-ul-Mujahideen Alal-alami Almi is believed to be following the hard-line Deobandi ideology, since it emerged as an offshoot of the proscribed Deobandi terrorist group HUJI.

Mohammad Imran was the organization's chief at the time of its formation, with Muhammad Hanif as his deputy and the chief of militant wing. Mohammad Waseem, a former inspector in the Pakistan Rangers, held an important position. All three were arrested by the Karachi police in July 2002; they were given life sentences by the Anti-Terrorism Court on 14 January 2008 for their involvement in a failed attempt to assassinate President Musharraf.[249] Kamran Atif, a former Harkat-ul-Mujahideen member and Afghan Jihad trainer, is presently heading HUMA in Karachi.[250]

Harkat-ul-Mujahideen al-Almi is an associated group of Al Qaeda and maintains close links with the Afghan and Pakistani Taliban. Saud Memon, the key financer of HUMA, worked closely with Al Qaeda and was a close friend of Abu Faraj al-Libi.[251] Murtaza, who was arrested in Karachi in June 2004, was reportedly in charge of supplying weapons to HUMA and was in contact with Al Qaeda.[252] The group also has links to separatists fighting Indian rule in Kashmir and to Harkat-ul-Mujahideen led by Maulana Fazlur Rahman Khalil.[253]

The head of HUMA is called the Supreme Commander and he is assisted by a deputy. A Shura (consultative committee) oversees all the operational activities of the outfit. The head of militant wing takes orders from the Supreme Commander, and these are finally approved by the Shura. The finance secretary is responsible for collecting and managing funds for HUMA: at the time of HUMA's formation in 2002, the finance secretary was Muhammad Ashraf Khan. Several arrested members of HUMA named Saud Memon, the Al Qaeda facilitator who played an important role in the Daniel Pearl killing, as their chief financial backer.[254] Al Qaeda is also thought to be the key financier of HUMA's operations in Karachi.

HUMA is part of Al Qaeda's larger strategy to establish like-minded groups in Pakistan in order to force the Pakistani government to withdraw

its support for the war on terror. HUMA seeks to achieve its goals by targeting Western and American interests (financial, diplomatic and religious) in Karachi. In June 2004 the police recovered a book called a *hidayat
nama* (book of instructions) from a HUMA linked terrorist arrested in
Karachi. This provides a set of guidelines instructing them, for example,
not to divulge information if they are arrested, to avoid meeting family
members and not to discuss operational matters with them, not to keep
organizational literature and militants' addresses on their person when
travelling, always to use code names, and not to rely on Punjabis.[255] The
booklet also instructs militants on how to conduct themselves in public
and what measures to take before and after they are arrested. It starts with
the Islamic concept of martyrdom, and says that this should be every Muslim's foremost goal: 'Don't discuss personal matters with your companions. You are chosen in the way of Allah and family relationships and
friendships should become insignificant in the way of God.' The intrigu-
ing direction to militants – especially Arab and Afghan – against trusting
Punjabis is thus explained, 'Don't rely on Punjabis if on mission or in transit, because most intelligence officials are from Punjab'. The booklet also
instructs militants to be law-abiding, especially as far as vehicular documents are concerned, and not to lose their temper with traffic police and
police at checkpoints, especially if lawmen insult members of their family, a tactic apparently employed routinely by law enforcement officers.

It is believed that in the 1990s, when HUMA's top leadership was associated with HUJI, they were trained at Al Qaeda camps in Afghanistan.[256]
HUMA introduced the first vehicle-borne suicide bombing in Pakistan in
2002.[257] On 8 May 2002, a suicide bomber belonging to Harkat-ul-Jehad-
e-Islami (HUJI), but operating under the banner of HUMA, rammed a car
laden with explosives into the side of the bus carrying French technicians
in front of the Sheraton Hotel. HUMA has also been involved in high-profile assassination attempts. In May 2003 the group used explosive devices
to mount attacks against 21 British and US petrol stations in Karachi.[258]

Successes against HUMA

In September 2002 the police arrested fourteen members of Harkat-ul-
Mujahideen al-Almi, including Sharib and Mufti Zubair Ahmed, in a
crackdown in Karachi. Officials stated that Sharib was also suspected of
masterminding the Sheraton Hotel suicide bombing that killed eleven
French naval engineers and three Pakistanis, including the attacker. Sharib
was also wanted over a plot to assassinate President Pervez Musharraf in
April in Karachi.

In April 2006 the Karachi police arrested Mohammed Junaid, allegedly HUMA's operations chief, after a gun battle.[259] Junaid was already wanted in connection with several attacks on the police and a 2003 bombing at a private club in Karachi that injured nine people. The government had offered a reward of Rs 500,000 for information leading to his arrest. Police launched a raid as Junaid and an accomplice were shifting weapons from a hideout. The two allegedly opened fire on the police; his accomplice escaped but Junaid was arrested. Police recovered one AK-47 assault rifle, two grenades and a pistol.

The exact number of terrorists linked to HUMA is not known. HUMA's organizational network has been seriously disrupted after the police and law enforcement agencies captured its key leaders and several of its members. Although a number of HUMA terrorists may still be at large, HUMA is no longer believed to be a security threat to mainland Pakistan.

Jaish-e-Muhammad (JEM)

Maulana Masood Azhar officially launched Jaish-e-Muhammad (The Army of Muhammad) in Karachi on 31 January 2000, after he was released by the Indian authorities as part of the 'terrorists-for-hostages' swap negotiated following the hijacking of an Indian Airlines Airbus on 24 December 1999. Before the formation of JEM, he was General Secretary of Harkat-ul Ansar (HUA), which was formed in 1994 by the merger of Harkat-ul-Mujahideen (HUM) and Harkat-ul-Jihad-i-Islami (HUJI). Azhar was arrested while on a mission in Jammu and Kashmir, using a Portuguese passport under the pseudonym Essa Bin Adam.[260] By the time Azhar was released, the HUA had already been included in the US list of Foreign Terrorist Organizations (FTOS). This act compelled HUA's constituent groups to resume their pre-merger identities as HUM and HUJI.

The main cause for Masood Azhar's decision to create the new group, JEM, was disagreement with Fazlur Rahman Khalil, the chief of HUM, over the management of funds. Khalil was also getting increasingly uncomfortable with Azhar's virulent anti-Shi'a tendencies. Azhar announced the formation of Jaish-e-Muhammad (JEM) from the Dar-ul-Uloom Islamiah mosque in Binori Town, Karachi, one of the largest religious seminaries in Pakistan, and one of the most influential centres of hard-line Deobandi Sunni Muslim ideology in the world. Nearly three-quarters of Harkat-ul-Mujahideen (HUM) members defected to JEM.

JEM enjoyed the endorsement of the chiefs of three Pakistani religious schools: Mufti Nizamuddin Shamzai of the Majlis-e-Tawan-e-

Islami (MT) and the teacher of the Jamea Binori Town; Maulana Mufti Rashid Ahmed of the Dar-ul Ifta-e-wal-Irshad; and Maulana Sher Ali of the Sheikh-ul-Hadith Dar-ul Haqqania. These endorsements are important as they signify the popular support enjoyed by this group. According to Mufti Nizamuddin Shamzai, the 'new jihadi organization' came into existence as a result of the decision of the Ulema, who would be patronizing it with the sole purpose of organizing the Mujahideen to respond effectively and extending support to the Kashmiri Mujahideen in their struggle against Indian rule.[261]

Jaish-e-Muhammad intends to liberate Kashmir from India and unite it with Pakistan. Its objectives also include the 'destruction' of America and India.[262] Like the HUM, the HUJI and the LET, JEM projects Jammu and Kashmir as the gateway to India and retains the ambition to liberate Muslims in other parts of India after the liberation of Kashmir, in the subsequent phase of its jihad. For this purpose, it aims to work for unification of various Kashmiri militant groups. Its agenda on jihad also includes taking control of the Babri Masjid in Ayodhya in the Indian state of Uttar Pradesh, and other religious sites at Amritsar in Punjab and New Delhi. JEM believes in broadening the struggle by taking the battle to the people of India. Its strategy also envisages carrying out attacks deep inside India rather than focusing only on Kashmir.

JEM is based in Bahawalpur, Peshawar and Muzaffarabad (Azad Kashmir). The group, however, conducts terrorist activities and operations primarily in the state of Jammu and Kashmir, India. The only instance of its operations outside Jammu and Kashmir was the attack on the Indian Parliament in New Delhi on 13 December 2001. JEM maintained training camps in Afghanistan and reportedly ran bases in Azad Kashmir, Doda and southern regions of Indian-occupied Kashmir. The central office of the JEM, formerly in Islamabad, was moved to Bahawalpur since it was convenient for Masood Azhar to operate organizationally from his hometown.[263] JEM also reopened many previously closed offices, including that at Quetta, which reportedly controls foreign funds and liaises between JEM leaders and its field commanders. This office maintained three different accounts with Habib Bank: account number 4245774 for local currency, account number 0550-17-41 for US dollars, and account number 0565001-38 for UK pounds respectively.[264] These accounts have all been frozen or closed.

Jaish-e-Muhammad (JEM) maintains a centralized hierarchical structure, at the head of which is the Amir. It has a network of organizing units in various provinces such as Punjab, Karachi, Rawalpindi, and Gujjarkhan. There are functional departments such as those responsible for propaganda, finance, military affairs, Azad Kashmir affairs and publications. It has sector commands (different territories organized as sectors) and camps (training/logistics), each manned by commanders.

It appears that the Amir and his council oversee the ground operations through the chief commanders and launching commanders. The launching commander only reveals the plans to the operational unit at the very last possible moment to ensure operational secrecy. As disclosed by the Indian Police following investigations into an attempt by JEM to strike targets in New Delhi, 'the exact target would have been disclosed to them by headquarters a short time before the actual strike'. [265] Command and control of the ground units appears to be very tight.

Most of the JEM's material resources and its cadre have been drawn from the militant groups Harkat-ul-Jihad-i-Islami (HUJI) and Harkat-ul-Mujahideen (HUM).

Al Rasheed Trust, one of the many ostensibly humanitarian relief organizations that received extensive financial backing from some Western and Saudi intelligence agencies during the Afghan jihad, was suspected to be a funding source for the group. The Al-Rasheed Trust, based in Karachi, and was originally set up as a welfare organization. In the 1980s it was co-opted to channel Saudi Arabian funds to the Afghan mujahideen, paying compensation to the families of those killed in the Afghan jihad. After the Soviets withdrew the Trust's focus shifted to Kashmir. After his release Maulana Masood Azhar was put in charge of handling the Trust's assets. Although Azhar maintained the Trust's links with the Taliban, he expanded the concept of jihad to include Kashmir. The Trust has openly funded the Kashmiri mujahideen and paid compensation to their families. [266]

JEM has a wide network of fund-raisers and has established various sources of financial support. Osama bin Laden, for instance, has been suspected of providing funds to support JEM's activities. In addition, according to a press report in early 2003, even after the group was banned, its accounts seized and assets frozen, JEM's finances were still being collected and handled by five men identified as Hafiz Tariq Masood, Qari Eshan and Shabaz Haider in Lahore, and Qari Abdul Hafeez and Mohammad Tariq in Sheikhapura. [267] The report stated, 'These men were the key to the Jaish's organisational gains in Lahore, where the group has established 21 local offices in a short span of three years'. It also mentioned that the outfit has a network of donors from different countries. [268]

On 14 October 2003 the US Treasury Department issued orders to freeze the US accounts of Al Akhtar Trust, a charity reportedly being run by JEM in Pakistan and providing a wide range of support to Al Qaeda and

Pakistani-based sectarian and jihadi groups, specifically LET, LEJ and Jaish-e-Muhammad. JEM collects funds through donation requests in magazines and pamphlets and fund-raising/donation camps. It has also invested in legal businesses, such as commodity trading, property and the production of consumer goods.[269]

Masood Azhar was reported to have received assistance in terms of training and other logistics from the then Taliban regime in Afghanistan and from Osama bin Laden. Azhar himself met Osama in Afghanistan and spent some time in one of his camps before announcing the formation of JEM in January 2000. JEM was reported as receiving extensive patronage from the former Taliban regime of Afghanistan, and was able to build on the contacts it made through the Binori madrasa in Karachi. Osama bin Laden and his Al Qaeda drew supporters for the school, and many of the Taliban leadership were among its alumni. Many of the HUM cadres who subsequently joined JEM were trained in Afghanistan training camps, especially the Reshkhor camp. The JEM was expelled from Afghanistan following the conviction and subsequent execution of some of the JEM militants on charges of rape and murdering a Shi'a family in June 2000.[270]

Leadership

Maulana Masood Azhar was born in 1968 to a rich land-owning family in Bahawalpur, Punjab.[271] He received his Islamic education at Jamia Uloom-i-Islami, a leading religious university in Binori Town, near Karachi.[272] Azhar passed the *almia* (Islamic) examination in 1989. Jamia Islamiah membership consists of Arab nationals, Sudanese and Bangladeshis, as well as Pakistanis; all share the Deobandi ideology and many were recruited for the Afghan jihad. While at Jamia Islamiah, Azhar was influenced by the work of Harkat-ul-Mujahideen (HUM) leaders in the Afghan jihad. Azhar met Maulana Fazlur Rahman Khalil, the Amir (Chief) of the HUM, who invited him to participate in *tarbiat* (training) at a camp in Afghanistan. Rahman later asked him to publish a monthly magazine for the HUM. Following this, Azhar began publishing *Sada-i-Mujahid* ('Knock of the Mujahideen'), which was distributed free at public meetings and Friday prayers from August 1989.

Azhar became the General Secretary of Harkat-ul Ansar (HUA), when it was formed from the merger of Harkat-ul-Jihad-i-Islami (HUJI) and HUM. Azhar visited Kashmir to ensure cooperation between the chief commanders of both outfits, ascertain the situation, boost the morale of the cadre and resolve any differences between HUJI and HUM. Travelling on a Portuguese passport, Azhar flew to Delhi from Dhaka, Bangladesh, on

29 January 1994. He was seized by the Indian army on 11 February and jailed for his alleged involvement with Kashmiri militants. On 4 July 1995 a newly formed outfit known as Al-Faran abducted six foreign nationals (two Americans, two Britons, a German and a Norwegian) from the upper reaches of Pahalgam Valley in Jammu and Kashmir. The abductors demanded the release of Masood Azhar and several other top militants detained in Indian-occupied Kashmir. One of the Americans managed to escape after four days. To underscore the seriousness of their demands, Hans Christian Ostrø, the Norwegian hostage, was beheaded.[273] The Indian government refused to negotiate. The remaining hostages are still unaccounted for and are feared dead.[274]

Indian Airlines flight IC 814 (with more than 180 persons and crew onboard) was hijacked on 24 December 1999 by five Pakistani nationals believed to be from Harkat-ul Ansar (HUA), including Masood Azhar's brother, Ibrahim.[275] After landings in India, Pakistan and the United Arab Emirates, it was eventually flown to Kandahar, Afghanistan. The eight-day hijacking, during which one passenger died, ended after India released three jailed Muslim militants, Masood Azhar, Sheikh Omar Saeed and Mustaq Ahmed Zargar. The released prisoners and the hijackers, under the protection of the Taliban, fled from Afghanistan to Pakistan.[276]

US intelligence and military sources believe that Azhar may have spent time in Afghanistan, possibly with Osama bin Laden, before he reappeared in Pakistan. Azhar reportedly fought alongside bin Laden's Al Qaeda against the US troops in Somalia in 1994 and had participated in the training of Al Qaeda's supporters in Yemen. The Americans discovered boarding passes from IC 814 in terrorist camps in Afghanistan. On 31 January 2000, Masood Azhar announced the formation of Jaish-e-Muhammad (JEM) with himself as the Amir. His new group emerged from the split he orchestrated with Harakat-ul-Mujahideen (HUM).

There were reports in the Shi'a media that, as well as holding an office in the HUM until December 1999, Azhar held a position in the SSP, a Sunni extremist group, and was known for his strong anti-Shi'a views.[277] Azhar is considered a protégé of Maulana Azam Tariq, who was the chief of SSP until his assassination in September 2003. During his detention in India, Azhar used to send articles clandestinely to the Al Rashid Trust for publication in *Zarb-e-Momin*.

Although not officially one of Jaish-e-Muhammad's (JEM's) leaders, Omar Saeed Sheikh was one of the important agents who operated in association with the JEM. He is also known to be associated with several other Pakistani jihadi organizations.[278] Sheikh was captured by the Americans and Pakistani authorities in January 2002, soon after the murder of Daniel

Pearl, and sentenced to death in early 2003. He appealed against his death sentence but his appeal has not been heard by the Pakistani Supreme Court to date.

Omar Saeed is considered to be the epitome of 'the classic politically aware Islamic activist'.[279] The son of a wealthy self-made immigrant from Pakistan to the United Kingdom, he graduated from the London School of Economics where he studied applied mathematics, statistics, economics and social psychology in the early 1990s and joined the Islamic Society.[280] Sheikh's perceptions of the West were influenced by a series of documentary films about the oppression of Muslims by Christian Serbs in the former Yugoslavia. These films often portrayed the oppressors as 'agents of the West' (*kufr*). When he visited Pakistan with his father, Sheikh distributed films of the war in Bosnia and made contact with Islamic militants in Lahore, including members of Harkat-ul-Mujahideen, who encouraged him to take up arms. In 1993 he attended training camps around Khost and at the Khalid bin Waleed camp, both near the Afghan-Pakistan border.[281] He is believed to have played a key role in the killing of the *Wall Street Journal* reporter Daniel Pearl.[282]

JEM's Organizational Links

Al Qaeda

Maulana Masood Azhar reportedly fought alongside Al Qaeda forces against US troops in Somalia in 1994 and participated in the training of Al Qaeda's supporters in Yemen. Many of the HUM cadres who joined JEM received training in camps in Afghanistan, especially in Rishkhor, near Kabul.[283] Masood Azhar described the US-led coalition operating against the Taliban in Afghanistan as 'murderers and predators', and announced that the war between the 'infidels and Islam had begun'.[284]

After its formation in January 2000, JEM reportedly became a member of the Army of Islam, a clandestine group raised in Pakistan with the support of the official establishment to fight against the Soviet troops in Afghanistan during the anti-Soviet jihad. Under this umbrella organization JEM maintained links with Harakat ul-Mujahideen (HUM), LET, Al Badr and Al Qaeda.

Jamiat Ulema-i-Islam Fazl (JUI-F)

JUI-F is a mainstream radical and reportedly pro-Taliban political party in Pakistan. JUI-F chief, Maulana Fazlur Rahman was a personal friend of Mullah Omar and Osama bin Laden. Maulana Masood Azhar maintains extensive contacts with Maulana Fazlur Rahman.

Lashkar-e-Omar

Lashkar-e-Omar, which surfaced in Pakistan in 2002, is believed to be a clandestine conglomerate of 3 militant groups: Harkat-ul-Jihad Islami (HUJI), Harkat-ul-Mujahideen (HUM) and JEM.

Operational Capabilities of JEM

JEM has several hundred armed cadres located in Azad Kashmir and the Doda region of Indian-occupied Kashmir. Following Maulana Masood Azhar's release from detention in India, it was reported that three-quarters of Harakat ul-Mujahideen members defected to the new organization. JEM also managed to attract a large number of urban Kashmiri youth from Jammu and Kashmir, and Afghans and Arab veterans of the Afghan war.[285] The group uses light and heavy machineguns, assault rifles, mortars, improvised explosive devices and rocket grenades.[286]

The high-profile attacks it has organized, such as those against the Jammu and Kashmir Legislative Assembly and the Indian Parliament (October 2001 and December 2001, respectively), demonstrate that the group is capable of planning, coordinating and executing operations involving sensitive and even highly protected targets. This has been a factor of the level of training received in Afghan training camps. The group appears to be well versed in using modern information and communication systems, including mobile and satellite phones, and the Internet.

In a statement issued in Srinagar on 4 February 2002, a JEM spokesperson asserted that the group had enough ammunition in its possession to fight against India for the next five years.[287] Indian security forces believe that the JEM, with its small but committed network, is capable of conducting daring attacks both under daylight and night conditions.

JEM's strategy has been to engage Indian military forces with armed attacks and lure youths in Kashmir to the cause of liberating Kashmir. JEM militants are usually deployed in small numbers to carry out attacks against Indian forces using bombing, sabotage, armed insurgency and guerrilla tactics of hit-and-run attacks on police and security forces. Most of its attacks have been so-called 'fidayeen' (no surrender) attacks: militants storm high-security targets, such as a base, camp or convoy, and kill as many personnel and civilians as possible before they are killed by retaliatory action. In other cases, they kill and injure as many as possible before attempting to escape.[288]

JEM cadres were trained in camps owned by the group in Azad Jammu and Kashmir and in Punjab at Kahuta, Hazira, Rawalkot, Pallandri, Aliabad, Putwal, Sialkot, Zaffarwal, Dudhniyal and Kel, in camps north of the Kargil area in the state of Jammu and Kashmir in India.[289]

JEM also operated a large training camp for between 800 and 1,000 recruits at Balakot in the North West Frontier Province (NWFP), which was run by Yousuf, a Christian convert to Islam from Sindh who is married to Azhar's sister.[290]

According to a report prepared by Pakistani intelligence in early 2003, the Batrasi and Syed Ahmad Shaeed training camps at Mansehra and Balakot, respectively, were still functional even after the group was banned in January 2002.[291]

JEM usually targets Indian security forces, their camps, convoys and permanent establishments. There were also instances of targeting vital civilian installations and high-profile public places like the Legislative Assembly of Jammu and Kashmir in Srinagar, the Indian Parliament in New Delhi, and places of historical importance such as the Red Fort, New Delhi.[292] The group has also targeted political leaders, including the Indian Prime Minister, according to investigations into earlier incidents and the interrogation of captured terrorists.

According to a report in April 2000, Mufti Asgar, the Chief Launching Commander of JEM, claimed that all of India's vital installations were within the striking range of JEM's explosive experts and cadres, and that many hardcore commanders were firmly entrenched in Srinagar, the capital of Jammu and Kashmir.[293]

State Response

Concerted government action was undertaken only after 11 September 2001. Scores of JEM cadres, including area commanders, launching commanders and district commanders were killed or taken into custody, mostly by Indian security forces. Many were convicted for various offences in both India and Pakistan. However,

The Indian government banned Jaish-e-Muhammad under the provisions of the Prevention of Terrorism Ordinance (POTO, now POTA) on 25 October 2001. The United States ordered the freezing of its accounts and termed it a Foreign Terrorist Organization in December 2001. In view of the changed geopolitical environment that had developed since 11 September, President Musharraf was under immense pressure to take action against the group, along with others like the LET. He banned both organizations and Maulana Masood Azhar was taken into custody. Even though New Delhi wanted Islamabad to hand over Masood Azhar to India, the Pakistani authorities refused, claiming that, since he is a Pakistani national,

Azhar would face trial in Pakistan.

A wave of police detentions followed in Pakistan. During December 2001 and January 2002, all of JEM's offices were sealed and most of the group's leaders and workers, including four brothers of Masood Azhar, were arrested.[294] Criminal cases were registered against most of those arrested, but the Pakistani government, on the orders of the Lahore High Court, released Azhar, who was then placed under house arrest. Lahore's High Court Multan bench later refused to prosecute Masood Azhar on charges of making an anti-India speech.

Canada blacklisted JEM in October 2002, placing it in the list of organizations and individuals on whom substantial financial curbs have been placed, and prohibited Canadians from raising funds for them.[295] On 14 November 2003, the Pakistani government banned the group operating under the name of Khuddam-ul-Islam, sealed off its offices, and started a search for its leader, Masood Azhar.[296] The State Bank of Pakistan also froze the group's assets. Defending the decision, the Pakistani Prime Minister said that the government had taken the right decision to ban the extremist organizations that had relaunched themselves under different names after they were banned the previous year: 'Whoever transgresses the law . . . will be punished.'[297]

Shortly before its assets were seized, however, JEM withdrew funds from its bank accounts and reportedly invested in legal businesses such as commodity trading, real estate and consumer goods production. Similarly, Khudam-ul Islam (JEM's new identity) withdrew its funds before its accounts were frozen by an order dated 12 December 2003.[298]

To escape the crackdown imposed by Pakistani authorities since 2003, JEM contemplated shifting its offices to Jammu and Kashmir (J&K) instead of operating mainly out of Pakistan. It publicly stated that it would confine its activities to J&K, and suspend terrorist attacks in India (other than in Indian-occupied Kashmir).

On the operational and tactical front, JEM was likely to continue using 'fidayeen' suicide attacks as its primary modus operandi, even though security measures were stepped up following Pakistan's declaration of war on terrorism in January 2002. The implication is that attacks, especially suicide attacks, could continue against security establishments and vital installations in Jammu and Kashmir.

On 16 September 2003 JEM warned that it would target Indian leaders in suicide attacks that would be 'shocking for India'. JEM spokesman Wali Hassan Baba told the Associated Press news agency in a telephone conversation that the attacks would be in retaliation for the killing of Shahnawaz Khan alias Ghazi Baba, the 'operational chief' of JEM, by Indian security forces in Srinagar on 30 August 2003.[299] JEM remains a clear and present danger to the security of India, in particular. Its resolve to achieve its objectives has not abated and there is no reason to think that the threat posed by this group is any less dangerous than it was several years ago.

However, JEM poses a threat not just to India, but to Pakistan as well, not least because Pakistan has banned the organization from carrying out its activities. Indeed, one of JEM's operatives is believed to be behind the attempted assassination of Musharraf in December 2003. Thus, in the short term at least, this organization will pose a security threat to the South Asian region and its activities should be monitored even more closely by intelligence, law enforcement and academics covering this region.

Sunni Tehreek (ST)

Sunni Tehreek (The Sunni Movement) was founded in 1990 by Muhammad Salim Qadri. He was born in 1960 in Pan Mandi near Nanakwara in Karachi. He started his political career as an activist of the All-Pakistan Mohajir Students Federation (APMSO), the student wing of the Mohajir Qaumi Movement (MQM).. When Dawat-e Islami, a non-violent Barelvi missionary organization, was founded in 1980, he became its leader in Saeedabad and his rise began from there. His incendiary speeches soon ensured a place for himself in Dawat-e Islami and Jamiat Ulema Pakistan. In Karachi, he became known as Salim Saidabade. He stood unsuccessfully as a candidate for Jamiat-e-Ulema Pakistan in the 1988 general elections for the Sindh Assembly.[300] In 1990 he broke away from Dawat-e-Islami and formed Sunni Tehreek as a reaction against the growing influence of Ahle-e Hadith and Deobandi organizations. He was placed under house arrest three times, and served time in jail on four occasions on assorted charges, including murder. At the time of his death in May 2001, several cases registered against Qadri at various police stations were still pending.[301]

Sunni Tehreek claims to be non-political and follows a four-point agenda: to safeguard the interests of the Ahle-e-Sunnat;[302] to protect Ahle-e-Sunnat mosques; to protect the common people from false beliefs; and for the administration to hand over the Ahle-e-Sunnat mosques and shrines to the Barelvis.[303] Sunni Tehreek's main headquarters, Markaz Ahle Sunnat, is located in Karachi, while sub-offices have been established in a number of cities.

ST complains that the Deobandi and Ahle-e-Hadith sects have a monopoly over Pakistan's administration, government posts, and religious and government institutes. The Barelvi sect is minimally represented and asserts that the Ahle-e-Sunnat cannot achieve their rights until they have adopted the ways of the Ahle-e-Hadith and Deobandi organizations.

[304]In April 2006 Sunni Tehreek faced a major blow when its entire leadership was cleanly eliminated in a suicide attack at Nishtar Park, Karachi. All of its key leaders were killed in the attack, which was attributed to the Deobandi terrorist outfit Lashkar-e-Jhangvi. In order to fill the leadership gap, a six-member committee was formed (comprising Shahid Ghauri, Engineer Abdur Rehman, Qari Khalilur Rehman, Shahzad Munir, Sarwat Ejaz and Khalid Zia), but almost all of them were unknown quantities and many believed that it would take a long time for the ST to pick up the pieces.[305]

ST receives support from other Sunni Barelvi organizations, such as Jamat Ahle Sunnat and Anjuman Naojawanan-e-Islam, and from the leaders of Jamiat Ulema-e-Pakistan. ST operates throughout the whole of Pakistan, but Karachi is the main hub of its activities. ST does not have a provincial structure; instead conveners at the divisional level are answerable directly to the Amir at the centre.[306] There is a strong network of fourteen divisions and districts in Sindh, Baluchistan and Punjab provinces, with divisional centres at Hyderabad, Sukkur, Nawabshah, Multan, Bahawalpur, Bahawalnagar, Lahore, Sahiwal, Mian Chunnu, Sialkot, Gujrat, Turbat, Quetta and Jafarabad.[307] Several departments, including the ambulance centre, computer institute, students' wefare, jahez (dowry) fund and food distribution programmes, are under the supervision of the Khidmat Committee. There is a mosque and a madrasa attached to the secretariat. ST maintains a website and publishes the Urdu weekly *Zarb-e-Islam*.[308]

The ST follows the teachings of Imam Ahmed Raza from Bareilly, Uttar Pradesh, after whom this school of thought is named, and believes that all the Deobandis and Wahhabis are *Kaafirs* (infidels).[309]

The ST rooted itself deeply in some parts of Karachi and other urban centres of Sindh. According to the Election Commission of Pakistan, in the 2002 elections the Sunni Tehreek secured more than 90,000 votes from Karachi but did not win a seat.[310] The middle-class urban localities in Karachi, for example Saeedabad, Shah Faisal Colony, New Karachi, Liaquatabad, Burns Road, M. A. Jinnah Road, Korangi and Gulbahar (the former Golimar), are the traditional ST strongholds of ST and also provide religiously motivated youth to work for the group.

The Barkati Foundation of Karachi is believed to lead the funding of ST.[311] Markaz Ahle Sunnat and the hospital in Saeedabad have been constructed with Barkati Foundation funds. Members give monthly donations and money is also collected through different funds.[312] Some media reports also claimed that the organization continued to flourish under Abbas Qadri owing to the ample funds it could access from members of the rich business community of Karachi, especially the Memons, who were looking for protection from jihadi-sectarian organizations that were constantly 'demanding' money for their 'cause'.[313] The outfit also makes a sufficient amount by collecting hides on the eve of Eid-ul-Azha: the ST collected 70,000 hides in 2007.[314] The average price of a hide falls between Rs 1200 and Rs 2000 (US$20–32). Zakat (charity) is another source of funding: the Sunni Tehreek's Ahle Sunnat Khidmat Committee collected Rs 1.275 million in 2006.[315]

There is no evidence available to suggest ST's links with any foreign organization or government.

Although ST has been involved in sectarian killings and clashes, there are no reports available about the military or armed wing within the outfit. It is believed that most of the ST's violent activists are individuals who joined the group after deserting the Muttahida Qaumi Movement (MQM), a violent political party headed by Altaf Hussain. These individuals from MQM did not join ST because of their religious zeal, but for strategic purposes. According to a report published by the Lahore-based English daily *The News*, an understanding developed between Sunni Tehreek and the MQM workers when a police operation against MQM was launched in the 1990s under Benazir's government. To save themselves, numerous MQM workers joined the ranks of ST. This new influx strengthened ST against Deobandis and Wahhabis, and incidents between the two factions increased.[316]

Right after its inception, Sunni Tehreek styled itself as a violent sectarian organization and began to target the SSP and LeT. There were clashes with these two groups in Karachi, Hyderabad, Sahiwal (Punjab) and Nawab Shah, in which seventeen Sunni Tahreek workers were killed by 1998. The total toll in these clashes was 47. Sunni Tehreek's main targets were Ahle-e-Hadith and the Deobandi mosques, maintaining that Ahle-e-Sunnat mosques had previously been encroached upon.[317] Target killing of Deobandi and Ahl-e-Hadith leaders is the ST's most frequently used tactic.

On 12 January 2002 President Musharraf banned various Jihadi outfits including three sectarian groups – the SSP, Tehrik-e-Jafria Pakistan (TJP) and the TNSM – and put the Sunni Tehreek on notice. In the same year, the ST engaged in electoral politics when it fielded some of its leaders in the general elections: Iftikhar Bhatti contested two National Assembly seats, while Dr Abdul Qadeer contested a provincial assembly seat. Both men lost and accused government-backed parties of rigging the elections;[318] both were also to lose their lives in the Nishtar Park suicide bombing.

Muttahida Qaumi Movement (MQM)

The MQM originated as an ethnic student organization at the University of Karachi in March 1978. The Mohajir Quami Movement (MQM) was built around the core of the All Pakistan Mohajir Students Organization (APMSO), which itself was formed on 11 June 1978. The student movement later turned into an influential political party of Sindh, the Muttahida Quami Movement, which frequently used terror tactics to achieve its political objectives.

MQM was formed to safeguard the rights of post-partition Urdu-speaking migrants from India to Pakistan, whom it would like to see recognized as constituting a 'fifth nationality'. Mohajirs constituted 7.44 per cent of the Pakistani population, but their settlement in business hubs, notably Karachi, gave them influence well beyond their numbers. This created resentment in other ethnic groups and the administration of Zulfikar Ali Bhutto enforced a quota system at university and governmental level in order to accommodate them. The Mohajirs, who preferred the former special treatment, resented this affirmative action. The MQM was thus able to gain strong support among Mohajirs at an early stage of its formation.

MQM evolved into a mainstream political party that claims to represent the 'working, middle class and poor masses of the country who are presently down-trodden, disadvantaged and exploited by the two percent ruling elite'.[319] MQM aims to establish a 'genuine democracy by struggling against the prevalent feudal system of Pakistan, which is the main obstacle in the progress of the country and the prosperity of her people'.[320] The cherished goals of MQM are the eradication of political authoritarianism, abolition of the feudal system, promotion of cultural pluralism, devolution of power to the grass-root level, and the achievement of maximum provincial autonomy. The party maintains a strong internet presence and various websites have been designed and regularly updated.

The MQM mainly draws its strength from the urban areas of the Sindh province dominated by Urdu-speaking Mujahirs. After the 2002 general elections the MQM tried to extend its network beyond the limits of urban Sindh, but the party did not win over many owing to its role in ethnic violence in Karachi and the track record of its involvement in terrorism. Political analysts believe that by acting as it does, the MQM leadership has chosen to remain a party of urban Sindh's Urdu-speakers and that, in spite of claims to the contrary, it will primarily stay as an ethnic party.[321] Apart from their political motivations, MQM has a hardened militant wing that has been involved in all manner of crimes and terrorist activities, including target killings.

Leadership of MQM

The founder and leader of MQM is Altaf Hussain, who was born in Karachi in 1953. His early education was at the government Boys' Secondary School on Jail Road, Karachi. He passed his F.Sc examination from City College and was admitted to Islamia College. While a student at the University of Karachi he started his political career by forming the All Pakistan Mohajir Students Organisation (APMSO). MQM, launched on 18 March 1984, was renamed the Muttahida Quami Movement (MQM) on 26 July 1997. Altaf Hussain has acquired iconic status among Sindh's Urdu-speakers, but he does not enjoy the same position in the rest of the country: by the late 1990s more than 260 criminal cases involving Altah Hussain, many involving acts of terrorism, were under investigation or had come to court.[322] Altaf Hussain has lived in Britian since 1992 and has become a British citizen. His party governs five cities and the populous Sindh province. Altaf Hussain micro-manages the MQM with an acute attention to detail from his headquarters, or 'International Secretariat', in a red-brick office block opposite a supermarket on Edgware High Street, London.

Altaf Hussain holds the right to approve or reject any decision taken by the Coordination Committee, whose members in August 2008 included Imran Farooq, the Convenor, Ishrat-ul-Ibad Khan, the Governor of Sindh province, and Mustafa Kamal, the City Nazim (Mayor) of Karachi.[323] Zones (at district level), sectors (at regional level) and units (at town level) have been established under the central committee.[324] MQM has divided Karachi into 22 different sectors. On 19 June 1992, in response to a clean-up operation launched against MQM, Altaf Hussain issued orders to terminate the organizational structure to avoid arrests. A coordination committee was formed in March 1993 under Ishtiaq Zaheer, one of MQM's founding members, to continue organizational work. Altaf Hussain's secretary in London conveys his messages to the Coordination Committee.

It is important to understand that MQM's militant structure grew alongside its legitimate political structure from its inception. These entities meet only at the level of Altaf Hussain, but it is the militant wing that gives the political wing its leverage in politics through its actions. One of the most effective terrorist cells of MQM, the Khaliq Taqi Butt group, consisted of Javed Akram, Javed Saqib, Majeed Dhobi and fifteen others. This group was tasked to carry out target assassinations of police officers and members of rival political parties in the Old city area, Liaqatabad, Lions area, Clifton Colony, Defense and PIB. The Farooq Dada group, which consisted of Anees Turk, Ameen Sattar and ten others, was involved in the killing of a captain of the Pakistan Rangers and the SHO and four other policemen in Baldia town. Other terrorist cells formed under the umbrella of MQM include Fahim commando group in Federal B area, North Karachi, New Karachi and Nazimabad, the Mubeen Toonta group in Malir and Model Town, and the Javed Michal group, active in Shah Faisal Colony and Al-Falah Society.

Khidmat-e-Khalq Foundation is the charity front of MQM and the All Pakistan Muttahida Students Organization (APMSO) is the student wing.

The members follow instructions from London rather than from the coordination committee. An information centre has been established in Karachi for better coordination among those in charge of sectors and units at a district level and to the members. Instructions from the London Secretariat are sent to the information centre, which is responsible for disseminating it to the 22 sectors in Karachi. If a special operation has to be carried out, Altaf Hussain personally conveys instructions to his trusted lieutenants. Various codes have been used to maintain the secrecy of communication.

MQM's funding initially depended mainly on voluntary donations from its members. After the municipal elections of 1987, however, there was a growing tendency for the MQM leadership and activists to collect funds through illegal means. Contractors were forced to pay heavy sums to get contracts from the Karachi municipality. MQM was also involved in bank robberies from 1988: the activists were told that MQM is a representative of the poor, so there is nothing wrong with looting money from banks and rich people.[325] At the same time, MQM's members also started collecting Bhatta (forced tax) from the commercial areas of Karachi. The sector leaders were given a target to collect a specific amount of money, depending on the economic status of the area. MQM's activists also collected forced tax from wealthy individuals and industrialists in Karachi. The group has also been involved in kidnappings of rich industrialists, contractors, constructors and politicians.[326]

Overseas units of MQM established in the Gulf States, Saudi Arabia, America, Canada, UK and other European countries are considered to be a major source of funding for the party.

MQM: *Reformist or Terrorist?*

Altaf Hussain promotes the MQM as a secular party, a claim validated by
the statement he made soon after the tragic incident of 9/11 in New York.
MQM organized a huge public rally in Karachi in support of the war against
terrorism on 26 September 2001 and another against religious extremism
and fanaticism in the name of Islam on 15 April 2007.[327] The MQM has experienced a radical transformation from an ethno-nationalist group to a
mainstream political party that believes in the eradication of political authoritarianism, the abolition of the feudal system, the promotion of cultural pluralism, devolution of power to the grass-root level and to the
achieving of maximum provincial autonomy.[328] MQM strongly and vocally
opposes the violent, hardline Islamist outfits.

However, Altaf Hussain is believed to be an extremely impulsive man
who can alter a 'principled' stand in an instant, and often for no obvious
reason, unless one takes into account his well-known tendency to use terrorism as a tool of political blackmail.

The National Memorial Institute for Preventing Terrorism (MIPT),
funded by the US Homeland Security Department, considers the MQM as
a terrorist organization and brackets it with dozens of other Pakistan-
based militant outfits. According to the MIPT database, MQM has approximately 3,000 militants in its ranks.[329] MQM's militia is highly experienced
in operating in urban areas, which gives them an advantage over other
militant or terrorist groups. Equipped with the latest weapons and extensive experience, the MQM militia poses a real, constant threat to Karachi.

The MQM has used a multi-pronged strategy to achieve its political
objectives, including the use of force, creating terror, establishing itself as
a political party and charity work. Waging a smear campaign against its
opponents and limiting their physical ability to conduct political activities
on the streets of Karachi is the hallmark of MQM's strategy. It also under-
mines the MQM's claim to being a party of middle-class, educated Pakistanis who want to challenge the feudal political culture. In fact, its style
of politicking might be consolidating the image of the MQM as an organization that finds opposition unpalatable.[330] MQM has been involved in target killings of its political opponents, government officials, private citizens
and. more surprisingly, its own members who decided to quit the party.
The first to fall was Azim Ahmed Tariq, one of the founding members of
MQM, who later developed some differences with Altaf Hussain. MQM ostensibly mourned his death and various official agencies were held responsible. On the floor of the Sindh Assembly, however, the former chief
minister of Sindh, Muzaffar Hussain Shah, declared that Azim Tariq was

killed by two MQM activists, Hashamuz Zafar and Khalid Maqbool Siddiqui.[331] The activists of MQM firmly believe in the slogan 'Death to Altaf's traitors'. The MQM is reported to have frequently used target killings, torture cells, grenade attacks, kidnappings and robberies. Among its main targets have been eminent citizens, politicians and law-enforcement personnel, government officials, journalists and the former Governor of Sindh, Hakim Saeed, an internationally renowned scholar and social worker.[332] The MQM is believed to have training camps in India. The government has repeatedly called upon the organization to close them and recall Javed Langhra, a key member of MQM's terrorist cell, and others. Altaf Hussain responded with the accusation that such an allegation against a party was not only a crime, but it was also violating the security of the country.[333] By the 1990s MQM was looking further afield for training, including with Sri Lankan Tamil separatists and South African mercenaries. Saulat Mirza, a key member of MQM, admitted in 1998 that between 80 and 100 MQM members were in South Africa for commando training in order to carry out disruptive activities in Karachi. Links with South Africa began when MQM members started fleeing to South Africa to avoid arrest after clean-up operations were launched against MQM's terrorist cells in 1993, during which hundreds of its workers were killed by police or arrested on charges of terrorism. Contacts were established with South African underworld gangs in order to acquire shelter in the country.

In the aftermath of the 2002 general elections, MQM won most of the seats in Urban Sindh and formed the government in Sindh province. Ishrat-ul-Ibad, a key member of MQM and reportedly involved in various murder cases, was appointed as Governor of Sindh. The party maintained its political strength in the February 2008 elections, and emerged as the fourth biggest political party in the National Assembly by winning 25 seats.

Tehrik-e-Jafria Pakistan (TJP)

Allama Arif Hussain al-Husseini, Allama Syed Sajid Ali Naqvi and Allama Hasan Turabi were among the founding members of TJP. Allama Arif Hussain al-Husseini was highly influenced by Iran's Shi'a Islamic Revolution and studied the Iranian revolution and the life of Ayatollah Khomeini. Allama Husseini was assassinated on 6 August 1988 in Peshawar. In the aftermath of the proscription of TJP by the Pakistani government in January 2002, the group started operating under the banner of Tehrik-e-Islami Pakistan (TIP), with Allama Syed Sajid Ali Naqvi as its elected head, while

Anwar Ali Akhunzada was appointed as the central General Secretary. Akhunzada was assassinated by the LEJ in November 2001 in Peshawar. Maulana Muhammad Sibtain Kazmi replaced Anwar Ali Akhunzada as TIP General Secretary. Allama Syed Sajid Ali Naqvi is the current head of the TJP and Allama Hasan Turabi is the Sindh president of the Tehrik-e-Islami.

The TJP traces its origins to the establishment of Tehrik-e Nefaz-e Fiqh-e Jafria (TNFJ, Movement for the Implementation of Shi'a Law) in March 1979, a religious pressure group formed in response to General Zia ul-Haq's Islamization policies, which favoured Pakistan's Sunni majority. The objectives of the TNFJ were to formulate an Islamic constitution based on Shi'a principles as expounded by Iran's spiritual leader, Ayatollah Khomeini, unite the Shi'a community, protect Shi'a rights in a Sunni-majority state, and actively involve Shi'as in Pakistani politics. The TNFJ adopted 'an aggressive, confrontational style of politics' in its early years, especially after the formation of the Sunni SSP in the early 1980s.[334] The organization split in 1984, with a moderate, traditionalist group going one way, and a more militant reformist faction another. Both groups regarded themselves as pro-Khomeini. In 1987 or 1988 the TNFJ changed its name to the Tehrik-e-Jafria Pakistan and registered as a political party. It is generally believed that Pakistan's Sunni clergy considered the former name offensive and that this led to a religious backlash. It was reported that the name change was at the behest of Allama Arif Husseini, who wanted to take a more moderate stance and extend membership to non-Shi'as. The move reportedly gave rise to several splinter groups, including the Sipah-e-Muhammad Pakistan (SMP), a violent anti-Sunni faction.

The TNFJ/TJP remained the main political organization for Shi'as throughout the 1980s and most of the 1990s, but there are indications that there were growing divisions within the party from 1995.[335] The Shurae Wahdat-e Islami (Council of Islamic Unity), a Shi'a umbrella organization claiming to represent all Shi'a political activism, was created in August 1998, thereby usurping a role previously claimed by the TJP. There were reports of increasing dissatisfaction among the party''s affiliated groups with the leadership style of Allama Sajid Naqvi, who was described as the 'undisputed patriarch of Shi'a politics in Pakistan'.[336] Many resented the absence of a consultative process within the party's decision-making machinery and preferred a leadership based on discussion and agreement, rather than one based on a single individual. TJP hard-liners were increasingly unhappy with the moderate positions taken by the party, while moderates were unhappy with its inability to check the increasing anti-Shi'a militancy in Pakistan. The fact that the Shurae Wahdat-e Islami generated very little media attention seems to indicate that the council has never really established itself.[337]

The TJP was banned for three years by the Pakistani government on 12 January 2002. TJP started working under the banner of the Tehrik-e-Islami Pakistan (TIP), but this was also proscribed in 2003. TJP decided to lay low for a time, but the organizational structure was not altered and political activities were openly resumed after a brief hibernation. The TJP joined the Muttahida Majlis-e-Amal (MMA), an alliance of six religio-political parties. The central command of this group also formed new groups to function as front outfits. TJP office-bearers were reportedly accommodated in the new Azadari Council and Haideri Foundation.[338] In August 2003 differences emerged within the MMA and there was speculation that TJP would quit the alliance. However, the leadership rejected that speculation and stated their optimism for the bright future of the alliance.[339] On 10 July 2005 the TJP resumed its activities after the three-year ban on the party was lifted.[340]

The pronounced objectives of the TJP are the creation of a society based on 'pure Islam', the protection of social, political and religious rights of Shi'ites, the propaganda of Shi'ite ideas, the coordination of all Pakistani Shi'ite organizations and the fight against imperialism.[341] The TJP also vows to fight 'America and Zionist imperialism', and to follow the path shown by Ayatollah Khomeini, the ideologue of the Islamic revolution in Iran. As a result, TJP claims that Shi'a religious ideas and Shi'a religious activities should be used to fight global imperialism, in particular that of the United States of America. They also believe in Islamic egalitarianism and social justice.

TJP created a political committee to plan future strategy in a given situation and to negotiate with political leaders of national stature, but the leadership, most of whom are religious scholars, dispensed with the committee as a signal that the TJP was, and will remain, a religious organization. TJP members have been elected to the Pakistani Parliament. The TJP calls itself a 'peaceful and democratic' political force.

The TJP has several affiliated organizations, including Sipah-e-Abbas, Sipah-e-Ahl-Bait and youth bodies such as the Imamia Students Organization (ISO), Mukhtar Students Organization (MSO) and the Imamia Organization. Since 1994 the Sipah-e-Muhammad Pakistan (SMP), a splinter group of the TJP with a significant following in Jhang has emerged as a prominent Shi'a terrorist outfit involved in operations against Sipah-e-Sahaba Pakistan. It is generally believed that Maulana Mureed Abbas Yazdani created it in 1993 after he was convinced that the TJP would not allow its young cadres to physically counter the SSP. The

Shi'a youth had been asking the TJP to take notice of what they called the excesses of the SSP, whose members were alleged to be targeting some of the Shi'a beliefs. Although Allama Hamid Ali Musawi did not endorse the move, Maulana Mureed Abbas Yazdani created the Sipah-e-Muhammad Pakistan (SMP), with its headquarters at Thokar Niaz Beg, in 1993 and it adopted a more militant stance against the SSP than the TJP would allow. The SMP is estimated to have a cadre base of 30,000 Shi'a followers, although most of these are supporters and sympathizers, rather than actual combatants.

TJP maintained strong links with Hizb-e Wahdat, Afghanistan's militant Shi'a party, based in the Hazara region.[342] Media reports indicate that thousands of predominantly Shi'a ethnic Hazaras were massacred by ethnic Pashtun Taliban fighters following the capture of the northern Afghan city of Mazar-e Sharif in August 1998.[343] The thousands of Hazaras who took refuge across the border in Quetta were bent on revenge. Citing Pakistani police and intelligence sources, the report states that the Pakistani Shi'as' 'sympathy for their fellow believers killed in Afghanistan added a new motivation to the sectarian battle' in Pakistan, and that 'a natural alliance … is building between the fully trained Hazara guerrillas and the [Shi'ite] militant groups of Pakistan'.[344]

The TJP is a staunch supporter of Hizbullah, the armed resistance group in Lebanon, and has organized mass rallies in support of Hizbullah during the Israel-Lebanon crises. Allama Sajid Naqvi held a meeting with Hizbullah's Secretary General Sayyed Hasan Nasrullah in Lebanon on 26 May 2005. There is, however, no evidence to suggest organizational links between Hizbullah and TJP.

TJP is also a member of the Shi'a Ulema Action Committee Pakistan (SUACP), Pakistan's largest and strongest body of Shi'a clerics.

Under the leadership of Allama Syed Sajid Ali Naqvi, TJP became well organized, effectively representing the interests of the Shi'a community with a significant following in the Jhang district of Punjab. The Shi'a majority Northern Areas, Sikardu, Gilgit Hunza and most of Kurram Agency in FATA are considered to be the traditional strongholds of TJP. Apart from its religious structure, TJP has a political committee that oversees its political activities, such as contesting elections. The command structure comprises the President, Central Secretary General, provincial heads and district leaders.

TJP raises money through donations from the Shi'ite community in Pakistan and from certain commercial groups. It has also reportedly received funds from Iran, probably in the hope of using the TJP as a vehicle for an Iranian-style revolution in Pakistan, and is reported to have links with the Iranian clergy.

The TJP has been accused of planning the target killing of the SSP's top leaders, including Maulana Azam Tariq, who was shot dead by unknown gunmen near Islamabad on 6 October 2003,[345]

SMP's training camps were located in Shi'a majority areas of Parachinar, Kurram Agency. When the Shi'a-Sunni conflict in Kurram Agency broke out in 2006, the camps started operating again and Shi'a youths are being trained to fight against the local Taliban (pre-dominantly Deobandis) and Sunnis.

Since becoming a member of the Muttahida Majlis-e-Amal in 2002, TJP has joined mainstream politics in Pakistan. The TJP was also able to vote some of its parliamentarians into power in the general elections in 2002. Following increased pressure from the Sunnis, the TJP has preferred to adopt a more reconciliatory and accommodating posture than in the past when it appeared more assertive and threatening towards the government and Sunnis. Similarly, together with the other groups within the MMA, the TJP was an active member of the Movement for Restoration of Democracy in Pakistan, which called for a general election in February 2008. The TJP's participation in that election demonstrated the intellectual maturity of the TJP's leadership, whereas the radical Jamaat-e-Islami boycotted the general elections. TJP also shuns terrorist violence, and is believed to be distancing itself from Shi'a terrorist groups, such as the SMP.

It can be safely surmised that TJP will continue to remain a mainstream political party since it requires support from moderate Sunni religious parties, including several MMA components, in the wake of growing sectarian violence along the western borders of Pakistan owing to Al Qaeda-driven ideology among the Pakistani Taliban.

5

Instability in the Region: The Wider Effect of Militancy in Pakistan

... we also have to help make the case that the biggest threat to Pakistan right now is not India. It's actually militants within their own borders. And, if we can get them to refocus on that, then that's going to be critical to our success, not just in stabilizing Pakistan, but also in finishing the job in Afghanistan.[1]

At the end of the day, we may have to consider the Taliban to be an intrinsic enemy of the us and a new international pariah state. We are not there yet and we do not want to be there. We will continue our policy of trying to mitigate Taliban behavior where and when its ill advised policies cross our path.[2]

The Pakistani Threat to India

With increased globalization, India and China will be among the leading global economies in the coming decades. Political and military might naturally follow economic power. However, both India and China currently face many challenges. The predominant non-conventional national security challenge facing both India and China stems from terrorism. Without internal and regional security and stability, these two major powers will not be able to sustain their superpower status.

India will face an enduring threat from three sources in the foreseeable future: in order of severity, the threat will stem from radicalized segments of the Indian Muslim community, radicalized segments of the Pakistani and Bangladeshi Muslim communities, and finally the Pakistan state and nation.

Let us ignore political correctness in this analysis. India is the world's largest democracy, and managing a nation as diverse as India is complex and requires visionary leadership. This accounts for its failure to effectively redress the Babri Masjid and Gujarat riots. In a globalized world, not only are Indian Muslims angry about these tragedies, these events in India are among the principal sources of inspiration for terrorists even outside the subcontinent: the Bali bombers, for example, cited these ugly events as inspiration for them to kill 202 tourists and workers in Indonesia in 2002.

The greatness of a nation rests in its ability to look after its minorities. Although India has produced a Muslim President, the genuine aspirations and grievances of its Muslim community must be addressed. The vast majority of the Indian Muslims are tolerant and moderate. After the Mumbai attacks, they grieved and suffered with the rest of the Indian population. They expressed their disapproval of the attack by publicly condemning the attack and denying use of their cemetery for the burial of the perpetrators. India should not find comfort in that response, but strive to correct the bigger challenge it is facing.

In India, as a direct result of the brutality of the Hindu rioters, a tiny minority of the Muslims remains deeply affected. Their suffering and anger has translated into resentment and action. As a result, they tend to seek retribution and revenge. They have organized themselves into cells and groups who are willing to kill and to die. Multiple bombings in Mumbai on 3 December 1993 killed 350 and injured nearly 1,000 innocent Indians. Although the Mumbai attack in November 2008 specifically targeted foreigners, the scale and magnitude of the Mumbai attack in December 1993 was greater. After the attack, the masterminds and perpetrators linked up and started to work with like-minded groups and individuals across India's borders.

According to a report published in June 2009, India has the largest number of indigenous terror organizations in the world.[3] Even if all the support and sanctuary across the Indian border should end, the Indian Muslim terrorist groups are sufficiently motivated and endowed with resources to destabilize India. Groups such as Lashkar-e-Taiba (LET), which originated in Pakistan, have successfully manipulated the grievances of Indian Muslims. In doing so, the LET has created a strong network of Indian Muslims within India. The LET has been able to network with several Islamist extremist organizations across India, especially in Jammu and Kashmir (J&K), Andhra Pradesh, Tamil Nadu, Karnataka, Maharashtra and Gujarat.

Why are some Indian Muslims willing to kill their fellow citizens through such drastic measures and dismantle their own economy by targeting hotels and other commercial sites? According to Ryan Clarke,

> Terrorism in India can be attributed to pervasive and systematic discrimination against Muslims in Indian society. Muslims die earlier, are less healthy, and do not have the same access to education as their Hindu counterparts. The main reason for these events is the selective nature of Indian justice when it comes to prosecuting acts of communal violence. For example, India relentlessly pushes for the extradition of Dawood Ibrahim from Pakistan for his involvement in the 1993 Mumbai attacks while Narenda Modi, who was in power during the 2002 Gujarat riots in which thousands of Muslim innocents were killed, remains at the helm in the state and is still a bigwig in the Bharatiya Janata Party (BJP). Contradictions such as these serve as powerful motivators. Also, evidence is starting to emerge that a segment of Indian Muslims are beginning to identify with the Kashmir dispute, something that could prove disastrous if not addressed.[4]

Terrorism in India can also be defined as a reaction to the rise of Hindu terrorism. The menace of Hindu terrorism in India dates back to January 1948, when Nathuram Godse, an activist of Hindu terrorist group Rashtrya Sevak Sangh (RSS), assassinated India's renowned secular leader Mahatma Gandhi. One should also not forget the tragic incident of the Samjhota train blasts in 2007, in which more than 80 people were killed and the majority of victims were Pakistanis. Interestingly, Indian authorities blamed the attack on the ISI-backed LET. It was in late 2008 that the world came to know about the involvement of an Indian Army officer, not just in the Samjhota Express blasts, but also in other terrorist attacks in India. The network comprising a serving Indian Army lieutenant colonel, Prashad Srikant Purohit, and ten other people including a Hindu monk and a nun were linked to a former Indian Army major, Ramesh Upadhyay, who represents Abhinav Bharat, a banned Hindu terrorist outfit working for the greater cause of 'Hinduvata'. Colonel Purohit also confessed to training Hindu terrorists who had been taken to attack Muslims, and told investigators that he not only trained the Samjhota Express terrorists, but also supplied them with the explosives to do the job. The main motivation was to cause an armed conflict between Pakistan and India, so that anti-Muslim passions could be nurtured in India, leading to violence.[5]

India will need first to recognize that it has a serious problem at home. Indians have been living in denial of homegrown extremism and its by-product, terrorism. In addition to changing the status quo, India must develop community programmes to engage the Muslim population, dismantle Hindu extremist groups and prosecute politicians linked to violence and extremism. As a true multi-ethnic and multi-religious nation that strives for greatness, there should be no space for ethnic and religious politics that are divisive and create divisions among ethnic groups. The first step towards resolution is the recognition that India faces a domestic problem from its very own Muslim community.

Muslims in Pakistan and Bangladesh

Muslims in the countries that are its immediate neighbours do not perceive India as a friend. Although India is the home for more Muslims than either Pakistan or Bangladesh, they do not see India as a just or righteous power. The violent partitions and riots associated with the country have created bitter memories of the 'Hindu-led India'. The distrust and suspicion of India is largely what New Delhi has done to them in the years that followed partition. Regardless of its accuracy, most Pakistanis harbour a deep resentment against India for forcefully occupying Kashmir, intervening in East Pakistan, dismembering their nation, and for the proxy war in Pakistan's Baluchistan province.

Even after Bangladesh was created with Indian assistance, many Bangladeshis today resent India. Most Bangladeshis remember India's assistance in providing sanctuary, finance, training and arms to Shanti Bahini terrorists in the Chittagong Hill Tracts in Bangladesh. The Indian intelligence outfit's Research & Analysis Wing (RAW) is deeply involved in the problem.[6] In 1975 the RAW was instructed to assist the Chakma rebels with arms, supplies, bases and training, which was conducted in the border camps in Tripura. Specialized training, however, was imparted at Chakrata near Dehra Doon. Shantu Larma's Shanti Bahini members were flown to Chakrata and then sent back to Tripura to infiltrate the Chittagong Hill Tracts. A RAW office and its operatives at Agartala monitored the progress of the trainees. In 1976 the Shanti Bahini launched its first attack on Bangladeshi forces. A new insurgency had been born and India's secret war in the hills of Bangladesh had begun.[7]

Similarly, Indian intelligence had collaborated with a separatist organization known as Bangabhumi or Banga Sena, which called for the creation of a Hindu republic in south west Bangladesh and also proposed a homeland for the Hindus who migrated to India from Bangladesh from the basins of the Padma, Meghna and Madhumati rivers after communal riots.[8] They claimed to have a right to settle in their own motherland. Bangabhumi was planned to comprise the districts of Khulna, Jessore, Kushtia, Faridpur, Barisal and Patuakhali, which constitute almost one-third of Bangladesh and cover approximately 20,000 square miles. The border of Bangabhumi runs in the north along the Padma, in the east along the Meghna, in the west along the India-Bangladesh border and in the south along the Bay of Bengal. The declared capital of the state is at Samanta Nagar, which has no apparent existence. The headquarters of Bangabhumi is located in Calcutta. When India alleged that ISI was training Pakistani youth along the border with India, Pakistan alleged that RAW is training and recruiting Hindu zealots from Bangladeshi organizations. According to Pakistani sources, around 10,000 Hindu youths have been trained in camps located along the border districts of Bardhaman, Alipur, Durgapur and Bahrampur. There are also camps inside Bangladesh in the districts of Jessore and Khulna.[9]

There is very little India can do in the short term to improve its relations with the Muslim communities in its immediate neighbourhoods. India should invest more in caring and empowering its own Muslim minorities in order to correct the genuine grievances and aspirations, and invest more in correcting the perceptions or misperceptions about India. Because India's bureaucracy is antiquated, this is likely to take a generation. Although most Indians believe that they have not done anything wrong, India should seek to modify its own thinking and behaviour. It will require simple acts such as inviting and enabling Pakistani goodwill and friendship delegations to visit India. Similarly, Indian Muslim delegations should visit Pakistan to clear any misperceptions of deliberate discrimination against Muslims by the Indian government. Governments and leaders should drive the building of genuine and sincere bridges between

people. Changing the physical and psychological reality will require changing both the thought process and resource allocation at the top.

The attitude and orientation of Pakistani and Bangladeshi Muslim
leaders towards India is a reflection of its population. Unless there is a
change in the thinking of the Muslims in its neighbourhood with reference
to India, there will never be peace in India. Indian terrorists and extremists will continue to find refuge and resources in Pakistan and Bangladesh.
Unless the Indian state works towards turning a new page in its relationship with neighbouring countries, terrorist groups across the region will
continue to use bilateral animosity to perpetuate their activities. Terrorists
groups in the South Asian region succeed because of the existence of a
high level of acrimony and mistrust between states. Furthermore, local
terrorist and extremist groups active in Pakistan and Bangladesh will continue to support them. Groups such as Harakat-ul Jihadi-Islam
Bangladesh (huji-b) and multiple groups in Pakistan, including let and
Jaish-e-Muhammad (jem), perceive that it is their right to attack India.
Increasingly, these governments are incapable of controlling their own terrorists. Although India constantly blames Pakistan for every terrorist, Pakistan also suffers from the victimization of terrorism. For instance,
Pakistan has lost more security personnel and civilians than India since
2005. India has failed to recognize that Pakistan faces a more serious threat
from terrorism than India. As borders are porous, India has also failed to
recognize that greater instability in Pakistan means greater instability in
India.

Pakistani State and Nation

Investigation into the Mumbai terrorist attacks in November 2008 revealed
that the perpetrators of the Mumbai attack were from Pakistan. The Pakistani government was not behind the terrorist attack in Mumbai, yet it is
highly unlikely that Pakistan will hand suspects over to India or to a third
country. Even if they are prosecuted and sentenced in India, the reality is
that there are many like-minded groups and cells that will continue to
plan, prepare and execute attacks of similar scale in the near future.

The key to Pakistan's claims regarding its terrorist and extremist
groups rests in increasing its capital and capacity to deal with such groups.
With international assistance, the law enforcement capacity to deal with
these groups can be built and strengthened. The more important of the
two – political capital and enforcement capacity – for confronting let, jem
and a host of other groups is political capital. Without an adequate resolution to the Kashmir dispute – a festering wound between India and

Pakistan – there will be no genuine peace between the two countries. The political leadership in Pakistan will not be able to justify to its people why its assets in Kashmir need to be dismantled. As long as the dispute over Kashmir is unresolved, Pakistan will maintain groups such as LET and JEM. Pakistan has built a defensive and an offensive posture vis-à-vis India, and India has built a Pakistan-centric foreign and national security policy. This status quo will only change when the international community, especially the US and the UK, mediates in this crucial dispute that has brought India and Pakistan to war. Today, the dynamics of the conflict is different – both countries are nuclear rivals.

How can India manage and reduce the threat of terrorism? In dealing with its neighbours, India has not been strategic. The anti-India perception of its neighbours is not limited to Pakistan and Bangladesh. Without exception, all its neighbours feel the same way. India's subsequent behaviour to its neighbours has caused India to be perceived as a foe. Whenever there is a terrorist attack in Sri Lanka, most Sri Lankans refer to the terrorist training provided to the LTTE and other terrorist groups by the central government of India. The first batch of Tamil Tigers was trained at Establishment 22 in Chakrata, north of Dehra Dun in Uttar Pradesh. The second batch of Tamil Tigers was trained in Himachal Pradesh. Seven subsequent batches were trained in Tamil Nadu, including the batch that trained Tenmuli Rajaratnam alias Dhanu, the female suicide bomber woman who killed Rajiv Gandhi. New Delhi constantly denies its role publicly, but privately some Indian leaders admitted to it. Irrespective of geopolitical realities, India's role in covert and overt interference with its neighbours has come into question. India's covert and overt role in Nepal tilted the balance of power and has strengthened Hindu fundamentalist movements. RAW and other Indian intelligence agencies had links with the armed Madhesi groups, which started an armed rebellion against the government in the aftermath of Nepal's Orange Revolution in April 2006.[10]

Unless and until India normalizes its relations with Pakistan over Kashmir and other bilateral disputes, Pakistani soil will be used to wage terrorism against India. There is no easy solution other than to resolve these long-standing conflicts that cause seething anger and action across the divide. The easiest way is a tit-for-tat response, or to accuse and blame each other. However, the most intelligent response is for the leaders of India and Pakistan to sit down and discuss how best to address each other's concerns. The US Administration can play a strategic and long-term role to mediate and negotiate a resolution. Failure to do so will mean an increase in the threat not only to India and Pakistan, but also to the world at large. An unstable and insecure South Asia would only serve terrorist forces, which desperately desire to consolidate footholds in the region. With an increase in the threat from India to Pakistan, Islamabad would be compelled to move its troops on the Afghanistan-Pakistan border and in FATA to the Indian border. This means greater freedom for Al Qaeda, Pakistani Taliban, Afghan Taliban and their associated groups operating against US and coalition targets in Afghanistan, Pakistan and the rest of the world. As tribal Pakistan is the epicentre of global terror, the withdrawal of Pakistani troops from FATA will have major implications on global security. Even with Pakistani troops stationed in FATA, a failure on Pakistan's part to stop a mass-casualty attack on Indian soil originating from FATA could trigger an Indian response that may lead to an escalation. Therefore, a good Pakistan-India relation is crucial.

The Jundullah Factor: Iranian Connections

Jundullah, which is also known as the People's Resistance Movement of Iran (PRMI), is an armed group that has been declared as a terrorist entity by the Iranian and Pakistani governments. PRMI can be described as an ethno-religious outfit seeking to safeguard the rights of the Sunnis (ethnically Baloch) of Iran. The Iranian Baloch perceive themselves as the heirs of an ancient tradition, which is distinctive from Iran's Persian population that comprises the Islamic Republic. The Iranian Baloch often identify themselves with the larger Baloch community that resides in Pakistan and Afghanistan. This is referred to as 'Greater Baluchistan', because tribal and family lines traverse all three countries. The Baloch historical narrative is shaped by a collective sense of oppression and victimization by the imperial machinations of regional and colonial powers that have led to the division of the Baloch nation. The Iranian Baloch are followers of the Deobandi school of thought. They are economically downtrodden and are treated as second-class citizens. Persian-speaking Iranians dub them as sympathizers of Pakistan and Arabistan (a term used for Saudi rulers). The overwhelming majority earn their livelihood by smuggling goods and narcotics via land borders with Pakistan and along the coast to the Gulf States. The Iranian Jundullah group is engaged in armed resistance against Iranian border security forces, which are accused of perpetuating atrocities against the Iranian Sunni Baloch community. The areas under strong influence of Jundullah are Siestan-Baluchistan, Gulestan, the Baloch-belt of Khorrasan and Kirman.

Jundullah (PRMI) justifies its acts of violence by stating,

In such conditions, faced by the Baloch people of Iran, it is not easy
for us to live peacefully. Yet, we have been able to maintain our
independence in such an important geopolitical centre and battlefield. We have a moral right to defend ourselves, our community,
our nation and our country.[11]

PRMI maintains strong Islamic tendencies. Abdul Malik Reiki, the
founder of group, who was arrested by the Iranian authorities in February
2010, has been a member of Tableeghi Jamat, a Deobandi missionary organization. The group claims to follow Sharia rules to execute its strategy
and achieve its objectives: according to Abdul Malik Reiki, 'we have executed 200 Iranian hostages after trying them under Sharia and finding
them guilty of crimes against Jundullah, in particular and the Sunnis and
Baloch in general.'

Given its pro-Sunni rhetoric, it is speculated that PRMI is an anti-
Shi'a outfit, but Abdul Malik Reiki once refuted the allegations by calling
it propaganda by the Iranian government.[12]

Although little is known about Jundallah's origins, it is believed to
have emerged in 2003. According to Reiki,

Before declaring war against the Iranian state, we sent a delegation
of tribal notables to the Iranian government demanding equal
rights as enjoyed by the Shi'a majority of the country. Once the
government refused to consider these demands, the Jundullah
members took to the mountains and declared war to secure the
rights of Sunnis and Baloch living in Iran.

Reiki's personal grudge against the Iranian government – his brother was
executed on charges of drug trafficking – is another factor behind the formation of Jundullah. This provoked Reiki to start an armed struggle
against the Iranian regime.

For some time Jundullah-Iran was confused with the Al Qaeda-
linked, Karachi-based Jundullah, which was involved in a failed assassination attempt on the Karachi Corps Commander, Lt. Gen. Ahsan Saleem
Hayat, in June 2004. However, this is not the case. Jundullah-Iran is a separate entity with no links to Al Qaeda or the global Jihadi movement. For
these very reasons, the Iranian Jundullah changed its name to People's Resistance Movement of Iran (PRMI).

Jundullah is trying to fight militarily against the predominantly Shi'a
Iran owing to perceived oppression derived from their disadvantaged ethnic and religious position in the country.[13] Both PRMI and its leadership

have officially claimed that the organization does not believe in separatism or secessionism.

The group has previously conducted bold attacks against high-profile targets, especially government and security officials. In a May 2007 telephone interview with *Rooz*, an Iranian online newspaper, Reiki defended Jundallah's use of violence as a justified means of defending Baloch and Sunni Muslim interests in Iran. The attack on a bus carrying members of the Revolutionary Guard in February 2007 was perpetrated to draw attention to the plight of his people, whom he describes as Iran's poorest and as the victims of genocide. Significantly, Reiki declared himself an Iranian, and claimed not to harbour separatist aspirations: PRMI's goal is to improve the life of the Iranian Baloch.[14]

Jundullah's main area of focus is the Iranian province of Sist n-o-Balochest n, which is located in the southeast of the country where the borders of Iran, Pakistan and Afghanistan meet. Sistan's capital is Zahedan and has a population of 420,000 inhabitants. Unlike the majority of Iranians, who belong to Shi'a sects of Islam, the ethnic Baloch community in Sistan is overwhelmingly Sunni. Jundullah is also reported to operate under the banner of Fedayeen-e-Islam (those who sacrifice for Islam).[15]

Abdul Malik Reiki, the founder of Jundullah-Iran, is an Iranian Sunni Baloch of limited education.[16] After finishing primary education, Reiki joined a seminary in Iran but was expelled because of his political views. He later started preaching but had to give up because of unfavourable circumstances: in his words, the 'tyranny of the Iranian government' changed his life, compelling him to stop the practice of Prophets – that is, preaching – and take up arms against the repressive Iranian regime.[17] Before his arrest Reiki was living on the Iranian border near Pakistan and his men constantly carried out attacks inside Iranian territory. Reiki's parents also fled their home, fearing persecution, and started living in the mountains along with their militant leader's extended family.[18]

On 23 February 2010 Iranian security forces captured Reiki when the airliner taking him from Dubai to Kyrgyzstan was forced to land at Bandar Abbas. Reiki was travelling on an Afghan passport, allegedly provided by US operatives.[19] Although Iranian officials were reluctant to acknowledge this, reports suggest that Pakistani intelligence agencies helped the Iranians to arrest its most wanted militant.[20]

Iranian authorities and some analysts allege that Jundallah may have ties to the global terrorist organization Al Qaeda and its Pakistani support structures, especially the Taliban operating in the Pak-Afghan border region. These allegations are based on Jundallah's reliance on religious symbols and its discourse in expressing its nationalist aspirations and deep-seated resentment toward the Shi'a-dominated Iranian state. In February 2007, however, the organization issued a statement in which it categorically denied any links with Al Qaeda or any other Islamist group:

> We categorically announce that we have no relationships and links with Al Qaeda, Taliban and other fundamentalist groups. We categorically announce that we do not have any kind of relationships with foreign countries, including the United States of America and the United Kingdom. We do not receive any support, arms, ammunition, training and financial help from any country. In such conditions, it is not easy for us to live peacefully. Yet, we have been able to maintain our independence in such an important geopolitical centre and battlefield.[21]

Although the financial sources of PRMI are not known, the Iranian government alleges that the US government provides funding to the organization to carry out acts of sabotage and hostage taking within Iran.[22] Similarly, there is a hunch that the PRMI may be benefiting from the narco-trade money since Sistan Province is known to be an important drug route for the Afghan and Pakistani narco-cartels. Nonetheless, ransom money from hostage taking may also be a contributory factor in their financial resources. Abdul Malik Reiki once attempted to contact elements in Saudi Arabia in order to acquire financial support, but it is not known whether he succeeded.[23]

The Iranian government accuses the US of supporting PRMI (Jundullah) militants.[24] In April 2007 the Speaker of Iran's Majlis-al-Shura (Parliament), Gholam Ali Haddad-Adel, accused the US of trying to put pressure on the government in Tehran by supporting Jundullah's anti-Iran activities: 'The best indication of United States' support to a particular terrorist group is that one of the leaders of this terrorist group was given the opportunity to speak on VOA [Voice of America radio station] after committing the crime.' More interestingly, the VOA introduced Abdul Malik Reiki as the 'leader of the Iranian people's resistance movement'. Experts believe that the arrangement is reminiscent of how the US government used proxy armies, funded by other countries including Saudi Arabia, to destabilize the government of Nicaragua in the 1980s.[25]

Similarly, on 3 April 2007 ABC News reported that the US had been secretly advising and encouraging a Pakistani group (Jundullah-Iran was continuously mistaken with Jundullah-Pakistan before the Iranian Jundullah changed its name to People's Resistance Movement of Iran). Abdul Hamid Reiki, the brother of Abdul Malik Reiki admitted during interrogation by an Iranian court in Zahedan in July that Jundullah was trained and financed by the us.[26] Reiki, however, denied receiving external support from the us but acknowledged that his group accepts 'moral and political support' through diplomatic channels from many countries including the us and Saudi Arabia.[27] The us and the Britain were also blamed by Iran for their alleged involvement in the 18 October 2009 suicide attack in Sistan that killed thirty-six, including six Islamic Revolutionary Guards commanders.

There were also allegations regarding Pakistan's support for Jundullah/PRMI, which Pakistan has always denied. In the aftermath of the suicide attack in Sistan, Iran accused elements within the Pakistani intelligence of assisting Jundullah. The attack also heightened tensions between the two countries. Significantly, immediately after the 18 October attack, a senior Revolutionary Guards commander publicly demanded that his force be given permission to confront terrorists inside Pakistan.[28] On 30 November 2009, Revolutionary Guards in two jeeps entered Pakistani territory, probably in hot pursuit, but were arrested by the Pakistani security forces. Significantly, despite numerous border incidents, the two countries followed a policy of containing the problem. For example, within hours of this border event, Islamabad and Tehran tried to play down the event. 'The guards were handed over to the Iranian authorities because it was found that they crossed into Pakistan mistakenly', a spokesman for Pakistan's paramilitary Frontier Corps explained.[29] Mutual trust and cooperation, even after the terrorist attack of 18 October, inflicted a massive blow to Jundullah in the later days. Pakistani intelligence agencies intensified their efforts to help Iranians in hunting down Abdul Malik Reiki: with the help of Pakistani intelligence agencies, the Iranian authorities were able to arrest their most wanted militant in February 2010.

Operational Capabilities of Jundullah

As of August 2008, Jundullah's membership stood at 600.[30] Reiki also claimed in an interview that hundreds are willing to join Jundullah, but the organization is unable to admit them, as it is not economically viable to have too many members.[31]

The basic strategy of Jundullah is draw international attention to the alleged human right abuses against the Sunni Baloch population by the Iranian government. Jundullah poses itself to be a defensive organization that has been established to fight for freedom and democracy in Iran and to protect the Baloch people as well as other religious and ethnic minorities in the country.[32]

The outfit usually adopts terrorist tactics in its fight against the Iranian government, including kidnapping, executing and beheading Iranian officials. More than 200 Iranian soldiers and officials have been killed or kidnapped by the group. PRMI's tactics also include raids on the posts of border-security forces, killing or injuring security personnel, and looting their arms and ammunition. Jundullah has also beheaded ordinary Iranians it has kidnapped. Jundullah carried out its first vehicle-born suicide attack inside Iran in December 2008.

Jundullah-Iran is believed to maintain training camps in Pakistani territory. In April 2007 the Iranian authorities arrested 90 alleged members of the Jundullah, two months after the former blew up a bus carrying members of the Revolutionary Guard. During investigations, the detainees confessed that they had been trained for the mission at a secret location in Pakistan.[33]

Jundullah as a Threat to Pakistani-Iranian Relations

Historically, Tehran and Islamabad have jointly collaborated in suppressing Baloch nationalism, often through brutal military crackdowns. Both countries see Baloch nationalism as a serious threat to regional stability and the territorial integrity of both states. The ongoing negotiations over the construction of a proposed gas pipeline – the Iran-Pakistan-India (IPI) – would deliver Iranian natural gas to Pakistan and India through the Iranian and Pakistani Baloch territories. Hence, the IPI project is another point of concern that brings both sides together on the threat posed by Baloch nationalism and the emergence of groups such as PRMI/Jundallah. The Iranian and Pakistani authorities have arrested hundreds of PRMI militants from the Baloch territories of both countries: in April 2007, for example, Iran arrested 90 members of this group and confiscated a large quantity of weapons and explosives.[34] According to Abdul Malik Reiki, 700 of Jundullah's supporters and activists, including 70 commanders, are in Iranian custody, and that some are executed through special summary courts.[35]

The Iranian government believes that Jundullah is based in the Pakistani territory bordering Iran. In several cases, Jundullah kidnapped Iranian security personnel and government officials from Iran, and fled to their hideouts in the Pakistani side of Baluchistan. Pakistani forces had to execute extensive operations for the safe release of Iranian hostages from Jundullah-Iran. Constant efforts are being made by Pakistan to dismantle Jundullah.

In June 2008 Pakistan handed over four Iranian nationals to put an end to the dispute raging over 'the presence of an Iranian terrorist organization operating out of Baluchistan'. The most important of these was Abdul Hamid Reiki, who had been detained in a Quetta jail.[36] However, Iran appears to be apprehensive as the terrorist group is strengthening in terms of lethality and is intensifying its activities against Iran. It is believed that Jundullah has undergone a significant level of radicalization since its formation. The suicide attack carried out by Jundullah in Iran in December 2008 signified the group's radical shift from its traditional tactics. Before launching its first suicide attack, Jundullah mainly resorted to hit and run operations, taking hostages and other subversions against the state of Iran. The televised beheadings of Iranian soldiers by Jundullah validated the claim that the militant movements in neighbouring Afghanistan and Pakistan have also influenced Jundullah to resort to more lethal tactics.

In conclusion, Jundullah presents a real threat to Iran's internal security. Pakistan can ill afford to benignly neglect the presence of Jundullah on its soil. For both countries the compulsions for security cooperation are numerous. Their common borders, trade routes, religion and the common ethnicity essentially translates into a compulsion that dictates that the neighbours develop shared, if not common, security structures. Therefore, combating Jundullah through joint efforts is imperative if Pakistan and Iran are to ensure security, stability and prosperity in the region.

6
The Suicide Terrorist Threat in Pakistan

If he is an infidel, he trusts the sword,
If he is a faithful, a soldier fights sans sword.[1]

Muslims of Pakistan: your salvation is only through Jihad.[2]

Jihad in the way of Allah will continue across the entire world
till the Day of Judgment. No power in the world can stop the way
of jihad in the world.[3]

In the wake of the US-led War on Terror, Pakistani society witnessed the most brutal form of socially, politically and religiously motivated violence in the form of escalated suicide terrorism.[4] Pakistan became one of the prime victims of this form of terrorism. The 'Death Squads' of various interlinked terrorist outfits pushed the country into mayhem. Suicide bombers targeted security forces, political leaders and civilians indiscriminately. There was an isolated attack in 1995 and then none until 2002 and 2003 (one each), 2004 (five), 2005 (two) and 2006 (six). In stark contrast, however, Pakistan was described in 2007 as the country third worst hit by suicide attacks, following Iraq and Afghanistan.[5] In addition to ambushes, roadside bomb blasts and target killings of political leaders, nearly 60 suicide attacks were reported during 2007 alone. These attacks killed approximately 770 people and injured 1,574 others.[6] Among the suicide attacks, 37 specifically targeted security forces and installations. More surprisingly, in the first quarter of 2008 Pakistan even surpassed war-torn Iraq and insurgency-hit Afghanistan in terms of the number of suicide bombings. At least eighteen suicide attacks were conducted in Pakistan between 1 January and 1 March.[7] Most suicide attacks between 1995 and 2009 took place in Pakistan's volatile Federally Administered Tribal Areas (FATA, 114) and North Western Frontier Province (NWFP, 30). Other areas affected were Punjab (34), Islamabad (14), Sindh (7), Baluchistan (7) and Azad Kashmir (2).

There is anecdotal evidence to suggest that the phenomenon of suicide attacks in Afghanistan and Iraq has been primarily motivated by the presence of foreign forces in these two Muslim countries. In September 2007 a report by the United Nation's Assistance Mission to Afghanistan (UNAMA) validated that the occupation, or the perceived occupation of Afghanistan by foreign forces, is the primary motivating factor behind suicide attacks. The report noted that suicide assailants in Afghanistan and their supporters seemed to be mobilized by a range of grievances, including a sense of occupation, anger over civilian casualties, and affronts to their national, family and personal sense of honour and dignity arising from the conduct of counterinsurgency operations by allied forces.[8].These motivations are linked to the presence of foreign forces. Many suicide bombers in Iraq were reported to be themselves foreigners. Yet the wills and final statements left by the bombers indicate that they felt a strong claim on Iraq as a Muslim land, and believed that their act was a powerful tool of liberation. Prior to the US invasion, Iraq never suffered from suicide terrorist attacks, but suicide terrorism has escalated rapidly following the US invasion.[9]

Since there is no foreign occupation in Pakistan, why has the country become a hunting ground for 'death squads'? Is this really a manifestation of rising Islamic extremism in Pakistan, or an expression of revenge against the government's countermeasures, which are perceived to be extensive? Is suicide bombing a strategy that desperate militant groups use against a stronger enemy, or a phenomenon motivated by extreme poverty and a sense of deprivation? Does the presence of international forces in Afghanistan serve as a motivational factor for suicide terrorism in Pakistan? Among the various modus operandi utilized by the terrorist organizations in Pakistan, why has suicide bombing become the dominant tactic?

This chapter seeks to answer these questions. It is primarily focused on exploring the actors and the motivating forces behind suicide terrorism in Pakistan, and concludes that the phenomenon of suicide terrorism in Pakistan is complicated and multi-dimensional. Diverse elements contribute to shape the destructive trend of suicide terrorism, which poses a new security threat to the entire world. A multi-pronged strategy, involving efficient intelligence, precise military operations, public awareness campaigns and a comprehensive de-radicalization programme would be required to counter the threat of suicide terrorism in Pakistan.

Agents of Suicide in Pakistan

Al Qaeda – the Trendsetter

The tactics of suicide bombings, beheadings and killing of tribal elders was not a social norm in Pakistani and Afghan societies. The arrival of Al Qaeda in Afghanistan in 1996 under the Taliban regime and the dissemination of its violent/militant ideology helped in radicalizing the predominantly Pashtun Taliban militants on both sides of the Pak-Afghan border. Al Qaeda carried out its first suicide attack in Afghanistan when it assassinated the veteran Afghan Tajik leader Ahmad Shah Massoud on 9 September 2001, thus eliminating the last stumbling block in the way of Taliban rule over the entire country.[10]

Al Qaeda also carried out the first suicide attack on the soil of Pakistan. On 25 November 1995, a pickup truck filled with explosives was rammed into one of the entrances at the Egyptian Embassy in Islamabad, and resulted in the death of fifteen people and injured fifty-nine others.[11] Al Qaeda did not claim direct responsibility for the attack; responsibility was later claimed by the Egyptian-based Islamic Jihad.[12] However, evidence suggests that Al Qaeda was involved in the attack.

Funds for the bombing operation were raised by Al Qaeda's second in command, Ayman al-Zawahiri, on a fund-raising trip to the US in 1993, where he pretended to be a doctor raising money for refugees in Afghanistan.[13] Furthermore, immediately after the incident, Pakistani authorities arrested Ahmed Said Khadr as a suspect responsible for a terrorist attack; Khadr is thought to be a founding member and key financier of Al Qaeda.[14]

Since 19 November 1995 Al Qaeda, in collaboration with the Pakistani Jihadi groups, has frequently used suicide attacks to achieve its strategic goals and eliminate its desired targets in Pakistan. Especially after the Pakistani government decided to side with the international community in the war on terror, Al Qaeda and its associate groups replicated the tactics of suicide bombings in Pakistan. The second suicide attack in which Al Qaeda was directly involved took place in December 2003, when there was an attempt to assassinate President Pervez Musharraf in the garrison city of Rawalpindi. Reports claimed that this was masterminded and financed by Abu Faraj al-Libi, the chief operational commander of Al Qaeda, who was deeply connected to al-Qaeda's North African cells before becoming involved in Pakistan. According to Amir Mir, a journalist and expert on Al Qaeda, it was noted as the first field operation of Abu Faraj al-Libi.[15]

Pakistan suffered 139 suicide attacks between 2002 and 2008. The wave of attacks also signified the revival of Al Qaeda and its associates. They were forced to give up their power bases and flee to the Pak-Afghan border area as a result of the war on terror launched by the US-led coalition forces in October 2001. Most attacks were attributed to Al Qaeda and its affiliated groups in Pakistan. Al Qaeda specifically targets the army, the paramilitary forces and the police, while it carefully selects the odd politician when it wants to 'speak' to the United States. Since the organization has been able to find sanctuaries and vital training facilities in FATA, Al Qaeda will continue to remain a drivring force behind suicide terrorism in Pakistan.

Although Al Qaeda is regarded as the trendsetter with regards to the phenomenon of suicide terrorism, the problem largely remains indigenous. This was acknowledged by Rehman Malik, Pakistan's Interior Minister. In a statement issued in the aftermath of the deadly double suicide attacks at Wah Ordnance Factory in September 2008, Malik revealed that the suicide bombers, handlers and financiers are all Pakistanis.[16] However, there are some exceptions: Al Qaeda used a bomber of Saudi origin, for example, to target the Danish embassy in Islamabad in June 2008.[17] Similarly, Pakistani law enforcement agencies believe that the Uzbek militants hiding in FATA have also been involved in various suicide attacks across Pakistan.[18] Local suicide bombers of various terrorist outfits have been able to target high-risk infrastructure as sensitive as the FIA building and the ISI secret interrogation centre in Lahore. Arguably, it would not be possible for foreigners to mingle with crowds, approach targets in high-risk security areas and detonate suicide bombs without being noticed by others. Their ethnicity in itself would make them the object of attention.

Al Qaeda-Affiliated Groups

The statistics on suicide attacks inside Pakistan validate that erstwhile Jihadi organizations were involved in most suicide attacks within Pakistan. Law enforcement investigations also indicate that suicide bombings are the work of multiple militant and terrorist outfits directly linked to Al Qaeda. These groups include the LeJ, TTP and other Taliban groups active in FATA, and breakaway factions of various Jihadi outfits.

The LeJ is one of the most sophisticated and lethal groups that carry out suicide attacks. LeJ was the first sectarian terrorist group in the world to use suicide bombings. The group carried out its first suicide attack in Quetta in July 2003, targeting a Shi'a procession. LeJ was launched in 1996 as a splinter group of the SSP, which is a Sunni Deobandi offshoot of the Jamiat Ulema-i-Islam. Initially the group was focused on eliminating the rival Shi'a sect, but eventually the group went through a radical transformation from merely a sectarian group to an Al Qaeda-affiliated anti-West terrorist outfit. The political objectives of LeJ are no longer limited to targeting Shi'as, but it aims for the eventual transformation of the country into a Taliban-style Islamic state. The organization seeks to further its political agenda by targeting Western interests in Pakistan and rival Shi'a sects. In the aftermath of the 9/11 terror attacks, LeJ became the group of choice for hard-core militants intent on pursuing their jihadi agenda. Its leadership comprises mostly those who have fought in Afghanistan, first with the Mujahideen against the Russian troops, and then with the Taliban against the US-led allied forces. In addition, LeJ perpetrated a reign of terror with its suicide attack squads after it was dislodged from mainland Pakistan in 2000. The outfit, with extensive experience in carrying out suicide attacks in urban areas, is also believed to be behind most suicide attacks targeting foreign nationals in Pakistan's capital Islamabad.

The LeJ also maintains a strong presence in Punjab province. According to Pakistani Intelligence sources, LeJ is the only terrorist outfit known to operate and carry out terrorist attacks in Islamabad. On 17 March 2002 LeJ terrorists targeted a Protestant church located in the

Diplomatic Enclaves, a highly secured area of Islamabad: five people were killed and forty (mostly foreigners) were injured. In July 2002 Pakistani police killed one of the alleged perpetrators and arrested four LEJ members in connection with the church attack. The LEJ members confessed to the killings and said the attack was in retaliation for the US attack on Afghanistan.[19]

The group has also used suicide bombings as a tool for sectarian conflict in Pakistan. Countless suicide attacks against the Shi'as in Pakistan have been attributed to LEJ. They began utilizing their lethal tactics against the rival Shi'a sects in July 2003, when a suicide bomber killed more than 45 Shi'as gathered during a Muharram procession. This was the first time LEJ had selected Quetta as a battleground for its sectarian war. There were two specific reasons for this decision.

First, Pakistani security and law enforcement agencies had successfully disrupted LEJ in the previous couple of years by either capturing or killing its key leaders. Riaz Basra, the founder and operational head of LEJ, was killed during a shootout near Multan in Punjab in May 2002, and the police arrested his lieutenant and right-hand man, Akram Lahori, in June. Subsequently, the group was reorganized by a member who came from Quetta.[20] Security experts believe that this individual opted for Quetta to launch the first suicide attack against the rival sect because of his inside knowledge of the city.

Second, in 2003, many Taliban militants were released from the detention centres in Afghanistan and joined LEJ. Most of them had been detained and tortured by the Shi'a-dominated Northern Alliance. Perhaps, to avenge this humiliation, they decided to target Shi'as in Quetta, which is near the Afghan border.[21] As of June 2009, the LEJ terrorist outfit has launched thirteen suicide attacks specifically targeting Shi'a communities in Pakistan.

LEJ is infamous for its secrecy, lethal nature and unrelenting pursuit of its targets. It is also believed that female suicide bombers have been trained. In June 2005 law enforcement agencies successfully arrested Arifa and Saba, two female would-be LEJ suicide bombers, after an extensive search. Their existence had been revealed when intelligence agents arrested their uncle, Gul Hasan, a key member of LEJ, in October 2004. Under interrogation he told how he had persuaded them to run away from home and train for their 'holy mission' in order that LEJ might carry out a new strategy of launching suicide attacks by using female bombers.[22]

The second type of groups involved in suicide attacks are Taliban organizations linked to the Al Qaeda network based in the FATA region. Pakistani intelligence agencies claim that suicide bombers trained by the

Tehrik-e-Taliban Pakistan mostly target the security agencies. At least ten suicide bombings had been traced to the tribal areas by December 2007.[23] After the formation of the TTP, an umbrella organization for various Taliban factions in FATA, the Al Qaeda-linked Taliban has been vocal in claiming responsibility for various deadly suicide attacks targeting security forces, politicians, mosques, Jirgas and funerals. TTP has trained several hundred suicide bombers to conduct attacks within Pakistan.

The suicide bombers recruited and trained by the TTP and other Taliban factions are also sent into Afghanistan to target the American and NATO forces stationed there. An anonymous Taliban commander told the BBC Urdu network in January 2008 that Pakistani Taliban groups sent more than 140 trained suicide bombers to Afghanistan between 2006 and 2008. The majority were Pashtuns who belonged to the rural areas of NWFP and FATA, but more than 40 bombers were from Punjab province and belonged to various banned Jihadi outfits.[24] A United Nations report also stated that the tribal areas of Pakistan remain an important source of human and material assistance for suicide attacks in Afghanistan.[25] The report disclosed that 80 per cent of suicide bombers in Afghanistan come from the Waziristan agencies of the volatile FATA region. Many would-be suicide bombers from tribal belt of Pakistan have been arrested in Afghanistan in recent years. Fourteen-year-old Shakir was one of the Pakistani bombers who went to Afghanistan for a 'noble cause' and was later apprehended by the Afghan intelligence agency on 20 March 2008. Shakir, who belonged to Barwand village in North Waziristan, was recruited and trained by a local cleric of the madrasa where he had gone to learn about the Qur'an.[26] His recruiters from the Pakistani side of the border handed him over to Afghan handlers to provide further training and to deliver him to the actual target. Shakir was arrested when he was on his way to the target in a car filled with explosives. This particular incident highlighted the interconnection between the Taliban insurgents on both sides of the Pak-Afghan border. Although young Shakir was recruited by a local cleric in North Waziristan, he was trained by an Afghan cleric and a medical student from another Afghan city. Even though most of the suicide bombers in Afghanistan have been recruited and trained in Pakistan, this does not necessarily suggest that all of them are Pakistanis: most are Afghans who have spent time as refugees in Pakistan.

Another militant commander accused of being involved with carrying out suicide bombings on the Pakistan security forces is Maulana Fazlullah. He was formerly the chief of the banned TNSM and is the current head of the TTP Swat chapter.[27] The picturesque Swat valley in the NWFP, with its rolling hills, gushing streams and scenic vistas, used to be described as Pakistan's Switzerland. However, suicide bombings and the steady erosion of state authority have made this idyll a conflict zone where radical Islamists are pitted against the Pakistan Army. Since 22 October 2007, when the military began its operations in Swat, more than 300 Pakistani soldiers have been killed at the hands of Fazlullah's well-equipped private Taliban militia. In 2008 Swat was the area worst hit by suicide operations, in which 11 suicide bombers were involved in the killing of 101 people and injuring 294 others.[28] It is pertinent to mention that Fazlullah was initially fighting to enforce Sharia law in Swat. During the course of time he aligned himself with the Taliban movement of FATA, which was basically formed to wage Jihad against the 'occupying forces' in Afghanistan. Fazlullah has already threatened to extend his hold over a larger part of the NWFP, getting closer to Islamabad in the process, which is just 160 km from Swat.

Investigations also revealed the involvement of radical madrasas in suicide attacks. All the suicide bombers identified in this chapter studied at different radical Deobandi seminaries in Pakistan. Abid Hunzala of Rahimyar Khan, who bombed a Pakistan Air Force bus in Sargodha on 1 November 2007, studied in Islamabad's infamous Jamea Faridia, the Red Mosque, which was besieged by the Pakistani security forces in July 2007 over its alleged links to global Jihadi outfits. Hunzala was arrested from Lal Masjid during an operation against its clerics, which ended on 12 July 2007. He was later released with other prisoners. The sources said the Sindh CID had already identified Hunzala as a potential bomber on 23 September 2007, almost a month before the attack in Sargodha.[29] Similarly, the sixteen-year-old suicide bomber who assassinated Allama Hasan Turabi, a renowned Shi'a scholar, was a student of Jamea Khalilia located in Musa Colony, Karachi. Hafiz Yunis, who blew himself up after an unsuccessful attempt to hit Islamabad airport on 6 February 2007, studied at a madrasa in Southern Punjab. Imran alias Mansoor, a would-be suicide bomber arrested from Mohmand Agency in October 2008, was a student at the Jamea Binoria, Karachi, which is infamous for its links with LEJ, JEM and other militant outfits.[30] Likewise, Qari Shahid Ali, a would-be suicide bomber who was planning to target the former federal minister Azam Khan Hoti, was a student in Maulana Zubair's madrasa in Tarangzai, Charsadda.[31] The fact that all of the suicide bombers identified so far had madrasa backgrounds exemplifies the fact that the religious seminaries in Pakistan provide an ideal breeding ground for potential suicide bombers.[32]

Motivating Forces behind Suicide Terrorism in Pakistan

The motives behind suicide terrorism in Pakistan are mixed. It is commonly thought that religion is the sole motivation behind suicide attacks. In the context of Pakistan, however, this is not always the case. Religion is not the single and primary motivational factor behind suicide terrorism. Suicide terrorism is a multi-dimensional phenomenon. Diverse factors contribute towards motivating a suicide bomber. These factors can be cultural (revenge), religious (desire for a higher place in paradise), social (glorification of a suicide bomber), political (occupation of Afghanistan and Pakistan's pro-West policies) and economic (motivated by monetary benefits).

The individual desire for revenge can be described as the reason for the availability of volunteers willing to perform suicide terrorism in Pakistan. Investigations by law enforcement agencies indicate that suicide bombers are not fanatical individuals, but rather they make a clear choice prior to their involvement in terrorist activities. 'Minders', who are constantly in search of potential bombers, carefully recruit them. These recruiters usually target teenagers and young men in their early twenties. The conflict zones of FATA, NWFP and radical Islamic seminaries provide ideal hunting grounds for the recruitment of potential suicide bombers. These locally hired bombers are often either disgruntled or dismayed over the deaths of their loved ones due to military operations. Most suicide bombers in Pakistan are from the Pashtun-dominated FATA and the NWFP. Massive military operations launched in FATA by the Pakistani military from 2003 to evict foreign militants resulted in the death of civilians and the destruction of property. Large-scale collateral damage ultimately resulted in the production of hundreds of suicide bombers across the FATA and NWFP.

In the context of Pashtun society, the element of religion has always been subservient to culture, and thus revenge dominates the common behaviours. The Pashtun code of honour, otherwise known as Pashtunwali, requires family members to seek revenge for relatives that are killed.[33] The concept of *Badal* (revenge) means that every Pashtun who has lost a family member is on the warpath, led by revenge. Pashtuns believe that revenge takes time: as one Pashtun proverb describes, 'Badal badal we, ko agha saal kala pas humvi' ('I took my revenge after a hundred years, and I only regret that I acted in haste').[34] Indeed, it may take generations to retaliate. Retribution will be the focus of the family's life until honour is recouped.[35] This mode of thinking among the Pashtuns correlates to the fact that most suicide bombers in Pakistan come from Pashtun tribes and seek revenge after losing family members and loved ones in successive military operations by the Pakistani army or US drone attacks. Almost all of the suicide bombers who have been arrested or identified so far referred to two particular incidents as sources of their motivation: the US missile strike on Bajaur in October 2006, in which more than 80 people were killed, and the operation against the Red Mosque in July 2007, which claimed more than 100 lives.[36] Pakistan's military operation and the resulting collateral damage is not the only factor motivating revenge-seeking suicide bombers. US drone strikes in FATA and adjacent areas are also to be blamed. According to a statement made by a Taliban commander,

> Our recruiters spend more than three months to find a potential suicide bomber. But a single US drone/missile strike makes the task very easy for our recruiters. After each US strike inside our tribal areas, numbers of youth seeking revenge for the loss of their family relative approach our local commanders and register as suicide bombers.[37]

The spate of suicide bombings after the Musharraf government's mishandling of the Red Mosque incident in July 2007 resulted in the deaths of more than 100 women and children. This demonstrates that regime heavy-handedness correlates with increased suicide terrorism. Though there was widespread support for the security operation, its actual conduct has been deemed heavy-handed. Security experts believe that the issue could have been resolved without using any extensive force. The continuing effect of the Red Mosque operation was felt throughout the rest of 2007, as the country suffered from 47 suicide bombings in the last six months of the year. Before that, there had been only fourteen suicide attacks within the sixty-year history of Pakistan. In February 2008 a leading Al Qaeda-linked terrorist, Qasim Toori, revealed the presence of more than 600 suicide bombers in Karachi and how most of them were former students of the madrasa adjacent to the Red Mosque.[38] Similarly, on 20 March 2009 the Pakistani Taliban issued a video in which they vowed to avenge each and every individual martyred during the operation against the Red Mosque. During the footage, the Taliban claimed the responsibility for various suicide attacks in the aftermath of 'Operation Silence' against the Red Mosque. 'Martyrdom statements' of all the suicide bombers asserted, 'This is the revenge of Red Mosque'.[39]

The suicide bombers who targeted Wah Ordnance Factory in August 2008 were also sent to target the 'Englishmen' who were manufacturing arms in the factory for use by the Pakistani army to carry out military operations in FATA. One of the two suicide bombers, however, opted not to go through with the plan after realizing that the victims would be poor Pakistani workers and not 'Englishmen', as the recruiters originally told him. The bomber was later arrested when trying to escape from the scene.

The use of force without any remedial steps to alleviate social and political issues alienates civil society, and the perceived 'tyranny' provides terrorist masterminds with fodder for their propaganda against the government, motivating potential suicide attackers. Large-scale 'collateral damage' during military operations in FATA and its adjacent area suggests that the Pakistani government's countermeasures are mostly based on the extensive use of force in dealing with the terrorist organizations.

The recruiters also misuse religion to motivate disgruntled and revenge-seeking youth to become suicide bombers. Recruiters encourage these aspiring bombers by emphasizing the 'higher place' as a *shaheed*, or a martyr who receives the opportunity to enjoy life in heaven. The religious content in the testament tapes appears in references to the divine compensation in the afterlife and also to the holy Qur'an, where it asserts that martyrs remain physically alive even after death. For many impoverished teenagers, this may seem like an attractive option compared to a life of constant deprivation with little hope of change. It is also known that suicide bombers have been issued with 'tickets to paradise' from Baitullah Mehsud. One such letter was recovered from Mir Janan, a fourteen-year-old would-be suicide bomber arrested in September 2008 from Nowshera. The letter promised the young Janan that 'ngels will pick you for heaven immediately after pressing the button of the suicide jacket'.[40] Similarly, a nineteen-year-old would-be suicide bomber, who was arrested by the police in March 2007, disclosed thrilling details about the religious motivation of suicide bombers under training: an Uzbek trainer used to tell them not to forget to bow their heads while triggering the explosion, because one cannot enter paradise if one's head remains intact with the body.[41] This suicide bomber was the cousin of the infamous Taliban commander Abdullah Mehsud, and also a member of LEJ. Later he was released in a prisoner exchange programme with the Taliban.

Social prestige enjoyed by a suicide bomber in FATA is another important motivational factor. Most young suicide bombers tend to become fascinated by the booming Jihadi atmosphere in FATA where Mujahid (Holy Warrior) and Shaheed (Martyr) enjoy social prestige, status and pride. According to some reports, after the suicide mission has been accomplished, the TTP usually issues 'martyrdom certificates' to the family of a suicide bomber.[42] These certificates are considered to be a matter of great social prestige. Suicide bombers in FATA are glorified as the saviour of Islam against the tyrant regimes of America, Israel and their puppets, the Pakistani government and security forces.[43]

Recruiters and trainers also manipulate political grievances to motivate suicide bombers. The last will of the suicide bombers, whether videotaped or written personal statements, are readily available in FATA and invariably stress political grievances such as 'an Islamic country like Pakistan under high influence of anti-Islam forces'. Responsibility for most suicide attacks in Pakistan has been claimed by organizations that have clearly made a tactical decision to utilize suicide bombing against an unpopular government that is perceived as pro-US. Organizations such as TTP, Jamiatul Furqan and LeJ have been vocal in calling the Pakistani government an 'American puppet'. In July 2007 a group called Mujahideen-e-Islam published a pamphlet threatening more suicide attacks against Pakistani security forces if they failed to stop doing the bidding of the United States.[44] The pamphlet, entitled 'Till Islam Lives in Islamabad', urged Pakistani soldiers, 'Go to your homes and earn halal (pure) income for your families … instead of serving the Americans'.

Extreme poverty is another contributing factor to the rise of suicide terrorism in Pakistan. While suicide attackers elsewhere in the world tend not to be uneducated and of low economic status, most Pakistani suicide bombers are. According to Pakistani law enforcement officers, more than 95 per cent of suicide bombers in Pakistan come from very poor and less educated families. A majority come from southern Punjab, which is the traditional stronghold of Jaish-e-Muhammad.[45] Due to high levels of poverty in the region, parents prefer their children to receive religious education in madrasas instead of modern schools.[46] Terrorist outfits have been known to 'purchase' children for suicide missions from poor parents in Bahawalnagar, Bahawalpur and other districts of southern Punjab. Poverty also leads to some children as young as four years old being sold by their parents to human traffickers to be jockeys in the camel racing industry in the Gulf states. Therefore the possibility of some children being sold by their parents to terrorist outfits cannot be totally ruled out.

Motivations at the Group Level

Multiple terrorist and militant groups in Pakistan have used suicide bombing as a tactic to inflict massive damage on their foreign enemies, the Pakistan army, law enforcement and intelligence agencies as well as to obtain specific strategic goals.

It has been observed that whenever the government initiated military offensives against Al Qaeda elements in FATA, militants launched deadly suicide attacks targeting the Army and the law enforcement agencies in the settled (non-tribal) areas of Pakistan. These included attacks against the Special Services Group (SSG) commandos in Tarbela in September 2007, the Pakistan Air Force in Sargodha in November 2007, and the Pakistani police in Lahore in January 2008. These attacks were perpetrated at times when Pakistani security forces were engaged in heavy military offensives against the pro-Al Qaeda militants in FATA, and were clearly a tactic to divert the attention of the Pakistani military by extending the battleground to mainland Pakistan. After each suicide attack against security forces in major cities, the government had to halt military operations in FATA due to pressure from the public, civil societies and opposition political parties. Besides inflicting massive damage on security forces, these suicide bombings are intended to damage morale among the rank and file of the Pakistani armed forces. The militant outfits also seek to weaken the security forces that are fighting against the militancy and extremism in the country, and to compel them to question the rationale and vision of the Pakistani leadership regarding their alliance with the US in the war on terror.

Suicide bombers are perceived as strategic assets. In this respect, the intention is not only to inflict physical destruction more easily, but also to damage society's psyche and instill fear in opposing parties exposed to suicide terrorism.[47] In other words, the message they send out is that 'we are willing to die. Your lives mean nothing and you are insignificant to us.' This can produce an enormous amount of psychological stress for the targeted community, and cause a state of social paralysis brought about through sheer terror, resulting in the psychological cowering of a community.[48]

Suicide terrorism in Pakistan can also be described as a time-tested tactic used by the militants to target their political opponents. In the present landscape of violence, suicide bombers have targeted the former President Musharraf and his formal and informal political allies. Suicide bombers twice targeted the former Interior Minister of Pakistan, Aftab Ahmad Khan Sherpao, who spearheaded the government's campaign against Al Qaeda and its affiliated groups. In the first incident, 31 people were killed at a public meeting in the Station Koroona area of Charsadda on 27 April 2007. In the second attempt on his life during Eid-ul-Azha prayers, Sherpao again survived, but more than 60 villagers were killed and around 100 wounded.[49]

The Al Qaeda-Taliban nexus is also believed to be behind the brutal killing of Pakistan's popular leader Benazir Bhutto in December 2007.[50]

She invited the ire of foreign and local militants operating in Pakistan when she publicly came out against extremism and militancy in the country and supported the military operation against the Red Mosque. The terrorist outfit first made an attempt on Benazir Bhutto's life in October 2007 when she returned to Pakistan after eight years of self-exile in Dubai and London. Ms Bhutto landed in Karachi, where approximately 150,000 jubilant supporters were there to receive her at the airport. Two massive explosions targeted Ms Bhutto's vehicle as the procession approached the Karsaz Flyover. Although Ms Bhutto escaped unhurt, at least 150 people were killed and more than 550 were injured.[51] It was the deadliest terrorist suicide attack in the history of Pakistan. The attack bore the hallmarks of Al Qaeda and resembled the failed assassination attempts by Al Qaeda-linked terrorists on President General Pervez Musharraf and Prime Minister Shaukat Aziz. Intelligence reports also warned about the threats of suicide attacks against Ms Bhutto by militants linked to Al Qaeda, the Taliban and Baitullah Mehsud. The attack could have employed its affiliated local militant groups like Jamiatul Furqan, LeJ, SSP or Harkat-ul-Mujahideen.[52] These groups have remained active in Karachi since the 1990s. Terrorist attacks in the city in which they were involved include the kidnapping and eventual beheading of *Wall Street Journal* reporter Daniel Pearl (February 2002), the killing of eleven French naval technicians in a vehicle-borne suicide attack (May 2002), the vehicle-borne suicide attack on the US Consulate in Karachi (June 2002), the ambush attack on Corps Commander Karachi (June 2004), and suicide attacks on a Shi'a mosque (May 2005) and a US diplomat (March 2006). These groups allegedly received their instructions from an Al-Qaeda leader named Abu Faraj al-Libi, who was reportedly based in North Waziristan Agency. Claiming responsibility for Benazir Bhutto's assassination, Al Qaeda's commander and main spokesman said, 'We terminated the most precious American asset which vowed to defeat [the] *mujahedeen*'.[53]

Targeting high-profile individuals using the tactic of suicide bombing suggests that suicide terrorism is a tactical and strategic response from terrorist outfits to the uncertain conditions prevailing in Pakistan. However, the question arises: Does suicide bombing as a strategy succeed in achieving the terrorist's objectives? The answer is 'No'. Al-Qaeda and its associated groups were successful at eliminating their opponents – Pakistani security forces, foreigners, rival Shi'a sect and key political figures – and in destabilizing Pakistan. However, the considerable 'collateral damage' produced by suicide bombings resulted in an extensive strategic failure for Al Qaeda and its associates. Public sympathy for their cause declined dramatically in the aftermath of lethal suicide attacks that killed hundreds of civilians.

The assassination of the former Prime Minister, Benazir Bhutto, and 25 other people on 27 December 2007, for example, was a senseless high-profile killing that produced intense hatred against this kind of activity. Similarly, more than 150 innocent people were killed during the first attempt on her life in Karachi on 19 October 2007.

Another example is the killing of the police contingent at the GPO Chowk in Lahore on 10 January 2008. Despite the police's poor reputation, there was a public outpouring of grief for the young policemen who lost their lives in this senseless attack. People of all walks of life came to the blast site to lay wreaths in solidarity with the police and to condemn the attack.

The assassination of Lieutenant General Mushtaq Baig, the Sergeant General of the Pakistan Armed Forces, and seven others in Rawalpindi on 25 February 2008 was another tragic incident condemned by the people of Pakistan. General Baig was not just another army man to be eliminated. He was a very pious, professional, fine human being, whose loss in a brutal assassination was commented upon in the Daily Times:

&&There is a general unspoken rule that the terrorists are Islamists who kill liberals and secularists but leave the pious and the religious alone. Despite the fact that this 'rule' has been violated by the killers again and again, many among us unconsciously think ourselves safe if they carry enough markers of Islamic piety on themselves. General Mushtaq Baig was in many ways an exemplary officer. Brilliant in academics and outstanding in his military career as a professional, he was also a meticulously honest man. His goodness sprang from his faith in Islam. He said his prayers five times a day regularly, read his Qur'an and had learned it by heart. His photograph clearly shows him as a man who believed in suiting his appearance to his firmly held faith in Islam. Why was such a man killed by someone who seeks to enforce Islamic sharia in Pakistan and has vowed revenge for the destruction of Lal Masjid in 2007?[54]&&

Suicide attacks targeting public places also intensify public anger against terrorist groups. Initially, security forces were the main targets of suicide bombers and they were considered 'justified' by a large segment of Pakistani society. This is because the popular media and the masses view the Army and the other law enforcement agencies as mercenaries fighting the US war on Pakistani soil against their own people. Until the death squads of Islamist groups started targeting public places, funerals, public gatherings and mosques, public perception remained favourable towards the terrorist groups. The popular media outlets were reluctant to use the term 'terrorists' for suicide bombers. Rather, they were referred to as 'extremists'. However, suicide attacks at public places, funerals and mosques proved to be a huge strategic loss for the terrorist groups as they caused public perception to turn against them. Suicide bombers were termed as 'inhumane killers' instead of 'extremists' by the popular media.

Taliban militants in FATA and NWFP are also known to forcibly recruit children from local schools. A report published in April 2007 by the Urdu weekly *Nida-e-Millat* stated that on 21 March 2007 some Taliban militants entered the Government High School No. 1, in the Tank district of NWFP, assembled the students and delivered a lecture on Jihad and suicide attacks. At the end of the lecture, twenty-five students aged between ten and sixteen were forced to register their names for the suicide training. The school administration tried to interfere but the Taliban threatened to slaughter anyone who dared to stop them preaching about Jihad and forcibly recruiting students for the 'sacred mission'. On the same day, the Taliban visited the Government High School No. 3 and Junior Cadet School to recruit more suicide bombers: 30 young men were registered for suicide missions during the second recruitment drive.[55]

The use of children as suicide attackers increases the sense of barbarity. Statistical data illustrate that most suicide bombers were in their early youth. Terrorists reportedly strapped a suicide vest to an infant when they first attempted to kill Benazir Bhutto in October 2007.[56] The suicide bomber who assassinated Allama Hasan Turabi in Karachi was a sixteen-year-old Bengali boy.[57] The bomber who blew himself up at a Shi'a mosque on 17 January 2008 was a teenager. Similarly, a twelve-year-old boy was found with explosives strapped onto his body in the Mohmand Agency: he was later killed during what was reported to be an unsuccessful suicide attempt at a military checkpost on 15 January 2008.

Children who do not have access to modern education do not realize that the terrorists are using them for their nefarious designs in the name of Islam. In other words, rather than being the culprits, the new recruits are the hapless victims of insurgents.

Conclusion

Diverse elements contribute to shape the destructive trend of suicide terrorism that is posing a new security threat to the entire Pakistani society. The drivers and motivational factors behind suicide terrorism in Pakistan are multi-dimensional. A multi-dimensional phenomenon needs to be tackled by a multi-dimensional strategy involving political, social and economic reforms, along with use of force.

In order to counter suicide terrorism, the government must mobilize support from the general populace. Public awareness campaigns must be initiated against suicide terrorism. In the twenty-first century the electronic and print media in Pakistan has grown significantly. Pakistan, which had only one state-run television network in 2000, now has sixty private television channels and hundreds of newspapers. The increasing power of the print and electronic media in Pakistan could be used as a powerful tool to counter terrorist ideology. In the aftermath of deadly suicide attacks in Pakistan in 2007 and 2008, private media outlets produced very effective and appealing footage to challenge the use of suicide attacks on human, national and religious grounds. A survey released in July 2009 showed that 13 per cent of Pakistanis supported suicide bombers in 2002; by 2009 the support had dropped to 5 per cent.[58] Therefore, the government of Pakistan must engage the media in its drive against suicide terrorism.

Furthermore, operational measures must be taken to prevent suicide attacks. Collateral damage during military operations must be minimized. The consequences of air strikes and other operations generating high civilian casualties have been proved to have a negative effect on the government's overall counter-terrorism campaign. Many scholarly works demonstrate the importance of resisting 'over-reaction' to the threat of terrorism. Anti-government elements often count on the excessive use of retaliatory force, and the concomitant oppression of the community in which the militants are based in or from, in order to garner support because this generates and sustains support for them and their cause.[59] Data from the Palestinian case studies also emphasize the importance of humiliation and loss, both in the support for suicide attacks and in the actual supply of activists. Some scholars have found that desecration of sacred places and perceived humiliation – even more than death and destruction – move people to embrace violence.[60] In order to enhance the Pakistani army's counter-insurgency operations and to enable it to strike precisely, us and international assistance would be instrumental.

Intelligence is the key to precisely eliminating the physical infrastructure of suicide bombers. In the case of Israel, more than 80 per cent of suicide operations have been foiled through counter-intelligence operations.[61] Pakistani law enforcement agencies need to allocate more resources to enhance their human intelligence capabilities in conflict zones. Pakistani law enforcement agencies lack modern equipment to probe suicide attacks. Police forensic labs are not equipped with facilities for DNA testing and systems to check the identity of suspects. According to reports, investigators did not have a permanent mortuary where they could preserve body parts of suspected suicide bombers collected from the crime scene.[62] Investment would be required to equip Pakistani law enforcement agencies with modern technologies to probe suicide attacks, and enable security measures that could prevent the occurrence of potential suicide attacks.

However, it is far more difficult to prevent radicalization. Therefore, strategic measures must be created and enforced to discourage and de-radicalize the suicide bombers. It requires a change of suicide bombers' mindset through conditioning, training and brainwashing. Most militant organizations are adept at the task of distorting Islamic principles to convince new recruits. In doing so, terrorist operatives may attempt to make suicide bombing justifiable in defence of Islam. Most suicide bombers are unaware of the true teachings of Islam because they do not learn the Qur'an with translation and tafsir (commentary), and thus they easily fall into the trap of their 'leaders'. Therefore there is a dire need to divert sympathy for suicide bombers and delegitime suicide attacks.

Religious scholars in Pakistan must counter religious justifications of suicide attacks by terrorist groups theologically. The government must persuade these religious scholars to play a proactive role against suicide attacks. The clergy needs to publicize the fact that Islamic laws oppose such violent practices. For instance, the Holy Qur'an tells the Muslims 'do not kill yourselves' and warns that those who disobey will be 'cast on fire'. Prophet Muhammad (PBUH) is also reported to have said that a person who commits suicide cannot go to paradise. Islam prohibits the killing of innocent persons, non-combatants, women and children. Although efforts have been made in this regard, and Islamic scholars in Pakistan have issued fatwas (religious decrees) against suicide attacks, calling it un-Islamic, they have not been coordinated, publicized and propagated properly by the government in order to create a public response against suicide terrorism. The initial response from the clergy was not unanimous. While the Barelvis were vocal in condemning suicide bombings, calling it un-Islamic, the Deobandi scholars remained equivocal. The religious decrees issued by the Barelvis, however, had no impact as most of the terrorist outfits in Pakistan follow the Deobandi school of thought. It was only in October 2008 that religious scholars unanimously declared suicide bombings un-Islamic.[63] The conference during which the statement was issued was attended by all the important schools of clerical thought in the country: Jama'at Ahle Sunnat (Barelvi), Ahle Tashayyo (Shi'a), Ahle-Hadith, Jamaat-e-Islami, Jamiat Ulema-i-Islam (Deobandi), and the banned Sipah-e-Sahaba (Deobandi). The factions that endorsed the council call comprised all the jurisprudential brands of Islam known in Pakistan. This was meant to show that the fatwa was not being issued only by the 'moderate ulema' that are no longer in vogue, but by a Deobandi-Ahle Hadith consensus not known in the past to issue such religious verdicts.[64] The conference was held at Jamia Naeemia and presided over by its firebrand leader, Maulana Sarfaraz Naeemi. A joint religious decree by the leading religious scholars of Pakistan against suicide attacks irked the Pakistani Taliban and other terrorist outfits, who vowed to teach a lesson to those who dared oppose suicide attacks. On 12 June 2009 a suicide bomber dispatched by the Tehrik-e-Taliban Pakistan assassinated Maulana Sarfaraz Naeemi. The efforts undertaken by the clergy to challenge the religious justification of suicide missions faced a major blow. However, in the aftermath of the fatwa issued by the top religious scholars and the subsequent assassination of Maulana Naeemi, public opinion radically turned against the Taliban and their terrorist activities. As a result, a sharp decline in suicide attacks across Pakistan was witnessed.

Suicide bombers have a particular mindset that needs to be de-radicalized through proper learning and education. The onus lies on Islamic governments to allocate resources to spread literacy and a true understanding of Islam, especially in those areas where suicide bombers are produced.[65] Anti-terrorism literature should be included in the syllabus of primary classes to educate students, and the system of madrasas should have postings of educated Islamic scholars in religious places of learning and teaching.

The terrorist outfits in Pakistan maintain hundreds of suicide bombers on their beck and call. Considering the complexity of the issue, a long-term strategy is required to counter suicide terrorism in Pakistan on the operational and ideological level. Pakistan will remain vulnerable to the threat of suicide terrorism and it will take an ever-growing toll on the country. More suicide bombers will continue to emerge from the conflict zones of FATA, NWFP and the seminaries located across Pakistan.

7

Is Pakistan the Ground Zero of Terrorism?

How is it possible that the [Pakistani] system is based on Islamic foundations, yet this results in all this corruption, sabotage, and subordination to the West and the Americans? Yet it is the system that teaches the confusion which results in the creation of generations with a sentimental attachment to Islam, while in fact, practice, tradition, and general fascination [are sympathetic] to Western culture. Yet the Army – the uncrowned king in Pakistan – is subordinate to the Americans? Yet Pakistan has become the greatest ally of America in its crusader war against Islam?[1]

America is also providing substantial resources to support Pakistan's democracy and development. We are the largest international supporter for those Pakistanis displaced by the fighting. And going forward, the Pakistani people must know: America will remain a strong supporter of Pakistan's security and prosperity long after the guns have fallen silent, so that the great potential of its people can be unleashed.[2]

Contemporary Pakistan is fraught with challenges to its territorial integrity, economic viability, existing political system, socio-economic fabric and pursuit of foreign policy. After Pakistan's decision after 9/11 to side with the international community, the threat groups in the country pushed the country into mayhem. Jihadi groups, nurtured during the US-sponsored Afghan Jihad, together with a new generation of Jihadis born in the consequent environment after the international intervention in Afghanistan, are posing a threat to Pakistan's stability. US Defense Secretary Robert Gates conveyed his fear, in the aftermath of the Marriott attack, that militants pose an existential threat to Pakistan.[3] No other country seems to have suffered so much at the hands of terrorists and militants in recent years. Al Qaeda, Taliban and their allies in Pakistan, by becoming perpetrators of violence and terror, have targeted the government and the people of Pakistan.

Nevertheless, despite the mammoth human and economic cost, Pakistan has performed beyond its capacity in this global war against terrorism. Being a frontline ally in the international coalition's fight against Al Qaeda and its terror network, Pakistan has accepted its obligations with unparalleled responsibility. The coalition involved more than a hundred countries contributing in a variety of ways: militarily, politically, diplomatically, economically and financially. Nearly 65 nations, including Pakistan, actively supported the US-led global war on terrorism, with some 41 nations deploying nearly 16,000 troops to the US Central Command's region of responsibility. However, Pakistan's contributions towards this war surpass those of any other country, and remain unmatched by any standard.

As a consequence of the 9/11 attacks, Afghanistan became the battleground in the war on terror while Pakistan's western border areas became the principal launching pad for military operations in Afghanistan by the US-led coalition. Pakistan's proximity to Afghanistan, as well as its knowledge of the war-ravaged country, was crucial for the success of the anti-terrorism coalition. Prior to launching 'Operation Enduring Freedom' in Afghanistan, Pakistan was asked to:

- Close the Pakistan-Afghanistan border and to cut off all activities and transits of Osama bin Laden's Al Qaeda group members in and around Pakistan.
- Freeze the assets of Afghanistan's Taliban rulers in Pakistan.
- Halt the supply of fuel to the Taliban.
- Provide intelligence collected by Inter-Services Intelligence (ISI)

on Osama bin Laden, Al Qaeda and the Taliban.
- Allow the use of her air space for offensive military operations against Afghanistan.
- Permit the stationing of US forces in Pakistan in order to capture Osama bin Laden.
- Respond positively to further US requests for assistance.[4]

Pakistan chose to cooperate with the US in Afghanistan in intelligence, logistical support and border vigilance. Subsequently, it remained the only country that 'opened two-thirds of its airspace, diverted its commercial traffic, provided airbases and seaports for large amphibious operations and developed close cooperation with the Pentagon and the US intelligence community'. Apart from the 'vital' intelligence cooperation that Pakistan extended to the US to overthrow the repressive Taliban regime and dismantle the Al Qaeda network in Afghanistan, it was from Pakistan's two forward operational airbases at Jacobabad and at Dalbandin, located in Baluchistan on the Pak-Afghan border and so vital to US military operations in the region, that the US launched more than 57,000 military sorties against the Taliban-ruled Afghanistan. Pakistan spent a large portion of its logistical reserves to support the coalition. Pakistan also deployed troops in strength along the Afghanistan border,[5] despite a constant threat on the eastern border with her archrival India, especially during the direct confrontation with India after the December 2001 attack on the Indian Parliament. During that time of considerable tension with India, 80,000 Pakistani troops were deployed on the Pak-Afghan border in support of Operation Enduring Freedom to interdict and capture the fleeing Taliban and Al Qaeda remnants. Similarly, in the aftermath of the November 2008 terrorist attacks in Mumbai, when India mobilized thousands of troops on its border with Pakistan, 120,000 Pakistani troops remained committed on the western border in support of international efforts to stabilize and secure Afghanistan.

Pakistan's contributions to the war on terror were acknowledged by the US State Department:

1. Pakistan provided basing and over flight permission for all US and coalition forces.
2. Pakistan deployed a large number of troops along the Afghanistan border in support of Operation Enduring Freedom (OEF).
3. Pakistan spent a large portion of its logistical reserves to support the coalition, which was a very significant contribution, given Pakistan's economic difficulties and its own requirements for its

self-defense.

4. On March 14, 2002, a team of five Pakistani officials was attached with CENTCOM.

5. The Inter-Services Intelligence (ISI) helped in various phases of operations.[6]

According to a May 2006 study carried out by the Pakistan Institute for Peace Studies (PIPS), Pakistan 'arrested more than 1,000 Al Qaeda suspects between January 2002 and May 2006'. This included two-thirds of the top Al Qaeda leadership, which had fled to Pakistan following the overthrow of the Taliban regime and the setting up of a democratic government.[7] The prominent Al Qaeda leaders arrested or killed in Pakistan include Abu Zubaydah, Ramzi bin al-Shibh, Khalid Sheikh Mohamed, Abdullah al-Mohajir, Walid Mohammad bin Attash, Hafwan al-Hasham, Adil Al-Jazeeri, Haris bin Asim, Ahmed Khalfan Ghailani, Usaman bin Yousaf and Abu Faraj al-Libi. The fact that the largest number of Al Qaeda operatives around the globe were arrested or killed by Pakistan is proof enough of its commitment.

The study further discloses that Pakistani security forces during this period also killed 'more than 1,000 Al Qaeda fighters in operations in Pakistan', including Hamza Rabia (November 2005), who was Al Qaeda's chief of external operations, Abu Layth al-Libi (January 2008), Abu Khabab al-Masri (July 2008), who was Al Qaeda's top explosive expert, and Khalid Habib al-Masri (October 2008), who was fourth in Al Qaeda's chain of command. Such operations significantly hampered Al Qaeda's overall command and control capabilities, and severed its capabilities to strike regionally or globally. As a consequence, Al Qaeda declared the government of Pakistan as one of its chief enemies and called for its overthrow.[8]

One fact that is easily overlooked is that without Pakistan's aerial and land facilities, the US would not have been able to attack Afghanistan and provide weapons, food and other supplies to its troops in Afghanistan. Pakistan is the logistical hub for the supply of oil and material to US and NATO forces operating there. Every day 300 trucks carry more than three million gallons of fuel by road to the military forces. Plenty of other military goods are also transited via Karachi. In view of increasing attacks on NATO supplies in December 2008, the Western policy makers intensified their efforts to seek alternative routes through the Central Asian states of Kazakhstan, Uzbekistan and Tajikistan. While it is always wise to diversify supply lines, NATO should by no means view Tajikistan and Central Asia as a viable alternative to Pakistan. Many Central Asian states are being persuaded to provide alternative supply routes. Tajikistan will be the most significant of these: while other Central Asian states have only agreed to allow non-lethal goods, the Tajikistan route is envisioned to transport military items. The question arises as to whether alternative routes through the so-called 'stans' are viable. With the help of already existing networks of Islamist militants in Central Asia, the Taliban would not hesitate to target NATO's supply lines passing through volatile Central Asian states. Moreover, the vulnerability of the route would greatly increase due its length and passage through hostile areas well under the influence of warlords allied to Taliban.

The Central Asian region has been a home to various indigenous radical Islamist movements such as the Islamic Movement of Uzbekistan (IMU), East Turkistan Islamic Movement (ETIM), Islamic Jihad Union (IJU) and the Islamic Movement of Tajikistan (IMT). External groups such as Hizb-ut-Tahrir (HT) have also been able to consolidate their footholds in the region in recent years. These groups have maintained strong relationships with the Afghan Taliban and Al Qaeda; after bin Laden moved back to Afghanistan in May 1996, Al Qaeda has not only sent combat veterans to assist Islamist groups fighting in the region but also provided training facilities to their Central Asian comrades in Afghan camps.[9] It was only after 'Operation Enduring Freedom' that these groups were forced to leave Afghanistan and find new sanctuaries in FATA, where they established contact with a new brand of Pakistani Taliban.

Considering the expected escalation of the conflict, the Taliban and Al Qaeda could easily exploit their strong links with Central Asian militant groups to expand into that region. The most critical point of failure in the system would be Tajikistan, with its role in the shipment of military supplies into Afghanistan. An expected alliance of the battle-hardened militants of Al Qaeda, Taliban (both Afghan and Pakistani) and indigenous Tajik groups would easily outnumber the Tajik military, which consists of only around 8,800 troops.[10] Uzbekistan, which maintains a comparatively large army with approximately 53,000 active troops, would face a revival of the most lethal militant group in Central Asia, the IMU. It is worth mentioning here that the Central Asian militants were heavily involved in operations against the United States in 2001.[11] Chechen and Uzbek fighters, for example, fought in a stubborn and disciplined fashion against Northern Alliance forces in northern Afghanistan, and against US forces in the south and during 'Operation Anaconda'. In addition, Pakistan's army has suffered considerable casualties battling Chechens, Uzbeks and Uighurs since 2003 in its war against Al Qaeda and the Taliban forces in Waziristan.[12] How long the ill-equipped Central Asian militaries, with no experience of conventional or unconventional warfare, are likely to stand against battle-hardened, well-trained, well-organized and ideologically motivated Islamist militants is a question of critical importance. Despite the fact that the main supply route through Pakistan has been constantly threatened, Pakistani security forces have been successful at preventing a larger and strategically significant attack on NATO's supplies into Afghanistan. A US military spokesman was quoted as saying the losses were 'militarily insignificant' and would have only 'minimal effects on our operations'.[13] In the event of a spike in attacks on NATO supply lines, Central Asian militaries are unlikely to be able to provide a Pakistan-style response.

Similarly, if the unrepresentative governments of the Central Asian states agree to provide alternative routes for NATO's supply lines into Afghanistan, the Islamists would undoubtedly seek to capitalize on this move to bolster popular support. Once the governments approve NATO supply lines, the Islamist militants would exploit this decision and attempt to brand their regimes as 'anti-Muslim' and as ones who would play a role in the 'Western crusades against the Muslim brethren in Afghanistan'. Al Qaeda and the Taliban have frequently espoused this type of rhetoric in Afghanistan and Pakistan to forward their agenda and gain popular support.

Ultimately the battleground would be extended. In view of the global economic crisis, do NATO and the US possess enough military and monetary resources, and the will, to engage the Taliban, Al Qaeda and their allies beyond Afghanistan? Even if Western troops are deployed in the Central Asian states to safeguard shipments by road, will Russia allow NATO's operational extension in its backyard. In fact, the northern routes are not just longer, but are also expensive and still largely under Russian influence. This was observed in the expulsion of US forces from Kyrgyzstan in early 2009. As such, these routes can quickly develop acute vulnerabilities after becoming operational. Once the situation deteriorates in Central Asia, it would be difficult, if not impossible, to manage a conflict theatre that extends from FATA to Afghanistan and other Central Asian states.

Clearly, Pakistan remains the best option for the foreign forces' lifeline into Afghanistan. Though a trust deficit still exists between key NATO states and Pakistan, the latter is the only country in the region, apart from Afghanistan itself, that is willing or able to dedicate substantial resources from its security forces to protect NATO supply lines.

Pakistan, as can be seen, is engaged in a much deeper relationship with the United States on counterterrorism matters than has been publicly acknowledged. Pakistan tacitly approved US drone strikes inside Pakistani tribal areas to eliminate operational targets.[14] In early 2009 Dianne Feinstein, chairwoman of the Senate Intelligence Committee, disclosed that unmanned CIA Predator aircraft operating in Pakistan are flown from an airbase inside that country.[15] It was previously assumed that the aircraft were operated from US military installations in Afghanistan and remotely piloted from locations in the United States. Bruce Hoffman, a leading expert on terrorism, observed, 'If accurate, what this says is that Pakistani involvement, or at least acquiescence, [in the war on terror] has been much more extensive than has previously been known'.[16] Given the strong anti-US sentiment in the country, the government of Pakistan finds it difficult to let American forces carry out strikes openly, even those against high-value terrorist targets. A number of unpopular decisions have been taken by Pakistan, secretly or openly, as a frontline state in the fight against terror. Pakistan's tacit approval to allow the use of its soil and the willingness of the ISI to share intelligence with its American counterparts enabled the US to eliminate important terrorist targets in tribal Pakistan. American forces in Afghanistan began using unmanned aerial vehicles (UAVs) against Taliban and Al Qaeda targets within Pakistan with three reported strikes in 2005. This number remained mostly consistent throughout 2006 and 2007. However, in 2008 the number of such incidents increased to 40. Most were carried out in North and South Waziristan agencies, where many Taliban groups operate, some of whom are linked to Al Qaeda. It needs to be mentioned that the Haqqani network has a stronghold in North Waziristan, whereas attacks have not been as frequent in Bajaur or Mohmand, the regions where many believe Al Qaeda's senior leadership is residing. There have been some attempts to kill the Haqqani leadership but most of the Waziristan strikes are aimed at foreign militants and Pakistani Taliban working with them. As Al Qaeda targets tend to be more widespread, attempts to target them become more challenging. A significant number of foreigners were killed in 2008, specifically Arabs, Chechens, Central Asians and Africans. Pakistani Punjabis, who are not native to the FATA, have also been killed there. It cannot be denied that Pakistan suffered extensive collateral damage due to the drone attacks. However, the attacks have become increasingly precise, achieving greater success against high-value targets and less collateral damage.

The Price of Counter-Terrorism

In the regional and international context, Pakistan has been able to actively cooperate on anti-terrorism issues with many countries and organizations in the realm of intelligence sharing, military exercises and training. Being a signatory to eleven out of thirteen UN anti-terrorism conventions and an active member of the Counter-Terrorism Committee (CTC) of the UN, Pakistan has continually advocated broadening of its membership to promote inclusiveness, provide alternative perspectives and enhance transparency, and accountability in its work. Pakistan has helped many countries across the globe in averting deadly attacks by sharing timely intelligence based on various interrogation reports and analysis. Unfortunately, however, more often than not this cooperation goes unmentioned.

The fact that Pakistan has itself been a victim of terrorism ever since the invasion of Afghanistan by the former Soviet Union in December 1979 is another factor shaping Pakistan's policy and anti-terror efforts in collaboration with the international community. Jihad in Afghanistan resulted in the rise of the Kalashnikov culture, the spread of narcotics and other social evils. The mushrooming growth of religious militant organizations with strong external linkages in Pakistan was a corollary byproduct. It needs to be understood, however, that the anti-terrorism measures did not result merely as a response to the 9/11 attacks. Even before then Pakistan had been taking steps to fight terrorism in the country. In 2000 Pakistan sealed the Pak-Afghan border and prevented madrasa (religious seminary) students from crossing into Afghanistan without relevant documents. In February 2001 Pakistan promulgated the Anti-Weaponization Ordinance and launched a de-weaponization campaign. Some of the militant sectarian organizations were outlawed in August 2001, including LeJ and Sipah-e-Muhammad Pakistan (SMP), and some, like SSP and Tehrik-e-Jafria Pakistan (TJP), were placed under observation. Reforms were already underway when the 9/11 terrorist attack took place, reinvigorating Pakistan's resolve to join the international community in a global effort aimed at the eradication of terrorism.

However, Pakistan paid dearly for its commitment towards fighting terrorism, both domestically and internationally. In the war against terrorism, Pakistan became not only the front-line fighter, but also the front-line target of the terrorists.In 2003, causalities in terrorist violence numbered 189. In 2004, 2005, 2006, 2007 and 2008, casualties of terrorist violence stood at 863, 648, 2,450, 3,448 and 17,667, respectively. In 2006 there were 657 terrorist attacks in Pakistan,[17] but 2007 was even bloodier,as 1,306 suicide attacks and roadside bombings rocked four provinces as well as the federal capital, claiming 2,450 lives.[18] The dangerous trend of suicide hits specifically targeting armed forces personnel touched alarming heights in 2007, averaging more than one suicide attack a week. A tenfold increase in suicide bombing incidents in 2007 was also witnessed as compared to 2006, though many believe that the actual numbers of fatalities were considerably higher, given the understated official accounts and erratic reporting from various conflict zones. The year 2007 also topped in total casualities as 3,448 people were killed during various attacks and clashes: the highest number of casualties, 1,663, was reported from tribal areas, followed by the NWFP with 1,096 killings.[19] In 2008 a total of 2,148 terrorist attacks were reported.[20]

In terms of military fatalities, between 2001 and October 2008 the Pakistani security forces suffered a total of 1,368 casualties, while 3,348 personnel had been wounded.[21] Pakistan suffered more casualties than the coalition forces in Afghanistan, which lost a total of 986 troops in the same period.[22] Casualty rates for coalition troops in Afghanistan are far less than Pakistani casualties in FATA.

Pakistan's Inter Service Intelligence (ISI) has often been blamed by the Western media for covertly supporting the Taliban. If the statements were true why has it been a target of numerous deadly suicide attacks? As of June 2009, more than 50 officials of the ISI have been killed and 74 injured in multiple terrorists attacks by the Taliban. In 2009 three massive suicide hits specifically targeted the regional offices of ISI. Despite all the sacrifices rendered and contributions made by the Pakistan Army, ISI and other security services, the blatant propaganda against these institutions infuriates the Pakistani public. They feel more victimized by Al Qaeda and the Taliban than the West does, given the thousands of soldiers killed, and the fracturing of Pakistani society by dissent and suicide bombings. Such rhetoric also increases frustration within the Pakistan Army, which is regarded as one of the major players in eliminating terrorist networks from the region.

In this context, the suffering of the people of Pakistan due to suicide bombings caused by the situation in Afghanistan deserves attention. Iraq ranked first during 2007, experiencing more than 150 attacks carried out by human bombs; Afghanistan came second with more than 100 such attacks, and Pakistan third with 56 suicide hits. In 2008, however, Pakistan surpassed the insurgency-hit Afghanistan and Iraq in terms of casualties from suicide bombings. Between January and August 2008, a total of 28 suicide bombings were reported in Pakistan, claiming 471 lives and injuring 713 others.[23] Even though there were more suicide bombings in Afghanistan and Iraq, these claimed 463 and 436 lives respectively, and injured another 527 people in Iraq and 394 in Afghanistan. Of the eventual total of 967 people killed in suicide bombings across Pakistan in 2008, the number of civilian casualties was 513.[24] The number of policemen killed in these attacks stood at 133, followed by 321 personnel of the security forces who were targeted in the aftermath of the bloody Operation Silence carried out against the Lal Masjid in July 2007. The Pakistani security forces, especially the armed forces personnel, seem to be the main target of the human bombs.

The double attack that killed Benazir Bhutto, former prime minister and head of the Pakistan People's Party (PPP), in Rawalpindi on 27 December 2007 is believed to have been carried out by TTP. Similar attacks targeted former President Pervez Musharraf in December 2003 and July 2007, former Prime Minister Shaukat Aziz and other top civil and military officials in 2004, and the former Interior Minister, Aftab Khan Sherpao, in 2007. All the attacks on Pakistani leaders were orchestrated and planned by Al Qaeda but carried out by Al Qaeda-affiliated Pakistani terrorist groups. These attacks came after Al Qaeda leaders openly appealed for the overthrow of the Pakistani leadership in September 2003 and March 2004.[25]

The spillover effect of the Afghan conflict destabilized Pakistan's tribal areas. In early 2004 the Pakistani armed forces conducted military operations to purge Taliban and foreign terrorists from FATA, but by 2008 the military operation had still not delivered the desired results. In NWFP, at least 20 of the 24 districts witnessed low-intensity Taliban activity. At least 10,000 square kilometres of Pakistan's physical terrain between the Tochi River to the north and the Gomal River to the south was seriously affected by Taliban militancy. A map produced by the BBC Urdu Service in May 2009 suggested that only 38 per cent of the NWFP and the surrounding areas was under full government control.[26]

Economic Fallout

Terrorism not only destroys lives but has an equally devastating economic impact. In economic terms, Pakistan suffered tremendously due to the anti-terror war. According to CENTCOM data released in May 2003, Pakistan suffered losses of more than US$10 billion owing to the US operations in Afghanistan. A US report put it more aptly: 'Few nations suffered as much from terrorism in 2004 as Pakistan, and few did as much to combat it.'[27] The impact of the global air travel crisis was also felt acutely in Pakistan. With the country being recognized as a 'front-line' state in the war on terrorism, exports suffered because high-risk insurance rates had to be added to freight charges. Cargo capacity was also reduced as a result of most foreign airlines stopping flights to Pakistan.[28] All in all, costs of exports and imports rose tremendously for Pakistan. Worse still, US and other western importers not only cancelled existing orders, but also held up payments for previous shipments. President Musharraf expressed his concern over the issue in a press conference on 8 October 2001. Overall, the economic losses, initially calculated at Rs 1 billion, turned out to be Rs 3 billion by the first quarter of 2002, especially with direct foreign investment declining after 9/11. Total and fixed investment declined to 13.9 and 12.3 per cent, respectively, during 2001 and 2002.

Internal security threats that emerged after Pakistan's alliance with the international community to counter terrorism have hurt Pakistan significantly. The US Administration remained appreciative of the 'fine efforts' Pakistan has dedicated to this purpose and the country has repeatedly been described by the US as a 'key ally', an 'essential ally', and the 'most important partners in the war on terror'. The 9/11 Commission Report also recommended that the US Administrations 'retain a nuclear-armed Pakistan as an ally in the war on terrorism'. With regard to the post-9/11 economic benefits, the US removed the nuclear sanctions under which Pakistan had been placed. A major concession made on the multilateral front was the rescheduling of Pakistan's debt at low interest rates, saving the country US$1 billion between 2001 and 2004.[29] Earlier, debt rescheduling in 1999 and 2001 had been short term and at very high interest rates. The new debt rescheduling allowed Pakistan to maintain debt repayment sustainability. Similarly, relations with the IMF and the World Bank improved and Pakistan successfully concluded a three-year Poverty Reduction Growth Facility (PRGF) worth US$12.5 billion, becoming the fourth non-HIPC (Highly Indebted Poor Country) country having a PRGF facility. In addition, Pakistan successfully concluded a US$596 million standby arrangement with the IMF. According to the *Economic Survey 2001–02*, out of total commitments of US$3.9 billion, US$2.38 billion had been received.

Nevertheless, the economic benefits that have flowed to Pakistan after 9/11 have, at best, been of limited value as the main issue for the Pakistani economy is market access and foreign investment. The constant threat of terrorist strikes has inflicted a massive psychological blow to foreign investment. The terrorists successfully achieved their target of turning the country into a no-go area to do business.

Despite the economic fallout faced by Pakistan in the fight against global terror, the popular Western media and a segment of its intellectuals have always criticized Pakistan for not doing enough in the war on terror. Dr Stephen Cohen of Brookings Institute speculated during an interview with an Indian weekly that Pakistan had done nothing more than hand over ten Taliban members to the US for 10 billion dollars; this way, the US had to pay US$1 billion for each Taliban member.[30] In fact Pakistan received us$7 billion from the us (as of March 2008) in return for the use of Pakistani military and communications facilities.[31] The us is spending us$5.9 billion (per month) on Iraq and us$1 billion (per month) on Afghanistan,[32] but only us$1 billion per year on Pakistan.[33] What is seldom realized internationally, or by domestic audiences, is that the cost of war that Pakistan has borne and continues to bear is many times more than the aid it has received so far.[34] In its annual report, the Institute of Public Policy of Beacon House National University came up with a comprehensive study of the state of Pakistan's economy, in which the economic cost of the war on terror was estimated to have been us$31.4 billion since 2004/5, far in excess of the us$1.7 billion annual assistance. The indirect costs include a drop in investment, the inability to proceed with development work, loss of production time, increasing unemployment and the high cost of supporting displaced persons. As risk has increased, so has the cost of insurance and other overheads. Pakistan has suffered from capital flight, closure of businesses and industrial activity, and the stock market has taken a deep downturn.[35] Rather than what Cohen dismissed as an expensive trade, Pakistani intellectuals believe that the wisdom of hurling the whole country into the fire for just us$1 billion is highly questionable.

Conclusion

To summarize, Pakistan has been worst hit by the sweeping change in the global environment in the wake of the cataclysmic 9/11 attacks on the United States. There is at times an international perception that Pakistan is unwilling to counter the threat of terrorism even after having contributed beyond its capacity in the international war on terror. While there should be no reason to doubt Pakistan's willingness to fight against terror, it must be admitted that Pakistan's capability in this area may be lacking. The fact that Pakistan has become the primary victim, rather than a perpetrator of terrorism may not be apparent to many, giving rise to unwanted speculation and allegations. Pakistan will continue to suffer the unintended spillover effects of the Afghan war until Afghanistan is stable and the foreign forces are able to combat Al Qaeda and the Taliban. Pakistan's armed forces and intelligence agencies ought to be commended for their success in restricting the threat of the Islamist insurgency to the border areas of Pakistan, for apprehending more than one third of Al Qaeda's top leadership, for wiping out the top leadership of the Afghan Taliban,[36] and for sacrificing thousands of their personnel in the war against terror. Politically, economically and from the security point of view, the country is shaken to the core. The provinces of the NWFP and Baluchistan, as well as the entire belt extending towards Afghanistan, are living under the threat of extremism. NATO and US forces, with unlimited resources and the most advanced technology, have been struggling to deal with the Taliban since 2001, and still there is very little to be optimistic about. A report published in November 2007 revealed that the Taliban was then controlling half of Afghanistan.[37] To the dismay of the powerful and fiercely independent Pashtun tribes inhabiting the NWFP and FATA, Pakistan deployed 140,000 troops in tribal Pakistan.[38] Not only is the Pakistani regular army directly undertaking military operations in the restive areas of FATA, the Special Forces units of the Pakistani SSG are also directly engaged. Even if Pakistan remains the subject of criticism, it is still willing to risk its own security to support the war effort in Afghanistan, a commitment that Washington cannot expect from any of Afghanistan's neighbours. Since cross-border movement takes place from both sides of the Pakistan-Afghanistan border, it is equally the responsibility of ISAF-NATO forces to stop it. However, there is only a small presence of ISAF-NATO troops on the border opposite Pakistan's border checkpoints to halt cross-border infiltration. Pakistan maintains 1,000 checkpoints along the Afghan border, while only 100 have been established by the ISAF-NATO, US and Afghan forces on the Afghan side of the border.[39]

NATO must increase the number of its troops in the border regions where infiltration takes place more often. There is also a dire need to increase joint coordination between ISAF-NATO and Pakistan to reduce infiltration and fight terrorist sanctuaries on the border areas. Similarly, joint border patrolling should also be initiated to bring an end to the war of words that takes place between Pakistan, Afghanistan and international troops' concerning dereliction of their respective duties in fighting the Taliban insurgency in Afghanistan. The war against terrorism demands coordination between Pakistan, the US-NATO forces and other stakeholders. The blame game would only benefit the non-state actors who aim to jeopardize joint efforts to root out extremism and terrorism.

To fight the war till the end, the international community does not need to be 'overbearing and overwhelming', and can let Pakistan decide how to fight terrorism. It needs to understand that there is no quick-fix to the problem of militancy in Pakistan. Effective counter-insurgency operations require time and patience, especially when the insurgents are battle-hardened, well armed, well financed, enjoy the advantage of a friendly population, and have mastery over the terrain. The tribal areas of Pakistan, which are most affected by extremism and terrorism, might need five to ten years to be pacified through economic development, administrative reforms and military actions. Also, a significant investment by America and its allies in the economic uplifting of militancy-hit areas would help to bring down anti-American sentiments among the masses in general, and among tribesmen in particular. This is where maximum benefits may be accrued in the long run.

Instead of accusing Pakistan, despite all its commendable efforts in the war on terror, the international community needs to realize the complicated nature of the threat faced by Pakistan. The world ought to come forward to extend its all-out cooperation to this courageous and vital ally. If Pakistan is isolated internationally, terrorist groups will find it easy to paralyze the state and establish their authority in mainland Pakistan. An acknowledgement of Pakistan's contributions in the War on Terror by the international community would boost the morale of the Pakistani nation and the army. The most important battle in the war on terror is being fought in Pakistan. If the battle is lost, the ultimate winners will be the forces adverse to regional and global peace and security.

Appendices

Suicide Attacks in Pakistan (1995–2009)

The following tables illustrate the suicide terrorist attacks that have taken place in Pakistan since 1995. It starts with the first suicide terrorist attack carried out by Al Qaeda at the Egyptian Embassy in Islamabad, and goes on to show how the nature of suicide terrorism and the targets have changed over the years. The methods used have principally been vehicle-borne improvised explosive devices (VBIED) and the more recently categorized house-borne improvised explosive devices (HBIED). The table also illustrates that Pakistan's four provinces have been affected by suicide terrorism to varying degrees. Azad Kashmir is the only region saved from suicide attacks so far.

DATE	PLACE	TARGET
19 Nov 1995	Islamabad (Federal Capital)	Egyptian Embassy
14 June 2002	Karachi (Sindh)	American Consulate
4 July 2003	Quetta (Baluchistan)	Shi'a mosque
25 Dec 2003	Rawalpindi (Punjab)	President Musharraf
28 Feb 2004	Rawalpindi (Punjab)	Shi'a mosque
7 May 2004	Karachi (Sindh)	Shi'a mosque
30 July 2004	Fateh Jang (Punjab)	Prime Minister Shuakat Aziz
1 Oct 2004	Sialkot (Punjab)	Shi'a mosque
10 Oct 2004	Lahore (Punjab)	Shi'a mosque
27 May 2005	Rawalpindi (Punjab)	Shrine of Barri Imam, Shi'a procession
30 May 2005	Karachi (Sindh)	Shi'a mosque
9 Feb 2006	Hangu (NWFP)	Shi'a procession
2 March 2006	Karachi (Sindh)	US diplomat
11 April 2006	Karachi	Barelvi procession
26 June 2006	North Waziristan (FATA)	Security forces
14 July 2006	Karachi (Sindh)	Shi'a scholar, Allama Hasan Turabi
8 Nov 2006	Dargai (NWFP)	Security forces
22 Jan 2007	Khajuri (checkpoint) near Mir Ali, North Waziristan (FATA)	Army convoy moving from Bannu to Miranshah
25 Jan 2007	Patt Bazaar, Hangu (NWFP)	Civilians
26 Jan 2007	Marriott Hotel, Islamabad	Indian Republic Day function
27 Jan 2007	Kisakhawani Bazaar, Peshawar (NWFP)	Police and Muharram procession
29 Jan 2007	Liaqat Park, Dera Ismail Khan (NWFP)	Muharram procession
3 Feb 2007	Barakhel, Tank (NWFP)	Army convoy
17 Feb 2007	District courts, Quetta (Baluchistan)	Judge, lawyers and civilians
29 March 2007	Guliana Kharian (Punjab)	Army training camp
28 April 2007	Charsadda (NWFP)	Interior minister Aftab Ahmad Khan Sherpao
15 May 2007	Marhaba restaurant, Peshawar (NWFP)	Afghan civilians
28 May 2007	Boltonabad area, Tank (NWFP)	Frontier constabulary
4 July 2007	Gurbaz area, Bannu (NWFP)	Military convoy

CASUALTIES		ATTACK TACTIC
KILLED	INJURED	
14	–	VBIED
12	19	VBIED
47	63	HBIED
5	21	VBIED
1	3	HBIED
19	123	HBIED
7	44	HBIED
31	75	HBIED
5	6	HBIED
20	82	HBIED
6	19	HBIED
39	81	HBIED
4	54	VBIED
50	100	HBIED
7	14	VBIED
3	3	HBIED
43	46	HBIED
5 including 4 soldiers	23 including 20 soldiers	VBIED
1	5	VBIED
1 guard	5	HBIED
15 including police chief Malik Saad and DSP Raziq	40	HBIED
2	19	HBIED
2 soldiers	7 soldiers	VBIED
17 including a senior civil judge and 7 lawyers	35	HBIED
2 soldiers	7	HBIED
31	35	HBIED
27	31	HBIED
3 including officer	2 FC men	HBIED
10 including 6 soldiers	9	VBIED

DATE	PLACE	TARGET
12 July 2007	Miranshah, North Waziristan (FATA)	Political agent's office
12 July 2007	Mingora (two attacks), Swat (NWFP)	Policemen and military convoy
14 July 2007	Razmak town, Miranshah, North Waziristan (FATA)	FC convoy
15 July 2007	Dera Ismail Khan (NWFP)	Police recruitment centre
15 July 2007	Matta, Swat (NWFP) (two attacks)	Military convoy
17 July 2007	Mir Ali, North Waziristan (FATA)	Security checkpoint
17 July 2007	F/8 near district court, Islamabad	PPP reception at Chief Justice rally venue
19 July 2007	Garrison town, Kohat (NWFP)	Army mosque
19 July 2007	Hangu (NWFP)	Police training centre
19 July 2007	Hub (Baluchistan)	Chinese engineer's caravan
20 July 2007	Miranshah, North Waziristan (FATA)	Security checkpoint
27 July 2007	Aabpara market, Islamabad (Federal Capital)	Policemen
4 Aug 2007	Parachinar, Kurram Agency (FATA)	Civilians
17 Aug 2007	Tank (NWFP)	Security force convoy
18 Aug 2007	Bannu (NWFP)	Police and police checkpoint
18 Aug 2007	Mir Ali, North Waziristan (FATA)	Checkpoints
20 Aug 2007	Tall Hangu (NWFP)	Security forces checkpoint
24 Aug 2007	Mir Ali, North Waziristan (FATA)	Security forces convoy
24 Aug 2007	Asadkhel village, North Waziristan (FATA)	Security forces convoy
26 Aug 2007	Shangla district, Swat division (NWFP)	Police mobile
1 Sep 2007	Mamond, Bajaur Agency (FATA)	Bajaur scouts force
1 Sep 2007	Wana Jandola road, South Waziristan (FATA)	Security forces checkpoint

CASUALTIES		ATTACK TACTIC
KILLED	INJURED	
4	3	HBIED
3 policemen	–	VBIED
24	29	VBIED
29	56	HBIED
21 including 16 soldiers	40	VBIED
4 including 3 troops	2	HBIED
19	60	HBIED
19	22	HBIED
8	30	VBIED
31 including 8 security personnel	45	VBIED
4 including 1 soldier	5	VBIED
15 including 8 policemen	65	HBIED
10	42	VBIED
–	5 soldiers	VBIED
1 policeman	5	HBIED
4 soldiers	2	HBIED
6 including 4 soldiers	19	VBIED
5 soldiers	10	VBIED
2 soldiers	2	VBIED
4 policemen	1	VBIED
7 including 4 security personnel	9	VBIED
–	4	VBIED

DATE	PLACE	TARGET
4 Sep 2007	Qasim Market and RA Bazaar, Rawalpindi (Punjab) (two suicide attacks)	Defence services and civilians
11 Sep 2007	Dera Ismail Khan (NWFP)	Security personnel and civilians
13 Sep 2007	Tarbela Ghazi (NWFP)	SSG commandos
22 Sep 2007	Tank (NWFP)	Paramilitary convoy
1 Oct 2007	Bannu (NWFP)	Policemen and civilians
18 Oct 2007	Karsaz Chowk, Karachi (Sindh)	Benazir Bhutto welcome rally
25 Oct 2007	Police lines, Mingora, Swat (NWFP)	FC personnel convoy
30 Oct 2007	Near army house, Rawalpindi (Punjab)	High-security zone of presidency and army chief house
1 Nov 2007	Sargodha (Punjab)	PAF personnel
9 Nov 2007	Hayat Abad Peshawar (NWFP)	PML (Q) leader Amir Muqam's house
21 Nov 2007	Saidu Sharif airport, Swat (NWFP)	Security forces
24 Nov 2007	Hamza Camp and GHQ Rawalpindi (Punjab) (two suicide attacks)	Military personnel and installations
4 Dec 2007	Peshawar (NWFP)	Security forces checkpoint
9 Dec 2007	Ningwalai, Swat (NWFP)	Checkpoint
10 Dec 2007	Kamra Attock (NWFP)	Military vehicle carrying children of Pakistan Air Force employees
13 Dec 2007	Quetta (Baluchistan) (two suicide attacks)	Military checkpoint
15 Dec 2007	Nowshera Cantonment (NWFP)	Army Services Centre Colony
17 Dec 2007	Kohat (NWFP)	Army recruits
21 Dec 2007	Charsadda (NWFP)	Aftab Ahmad Khan Sherpao and others
23 Dec 2007	Mingora, Swat (NWFP)	Army convoy
27 Dec 2007	Liaqat Bagh Rawalpindi (Punjab)	Benazir Bhutto
7 Jan 2008	Swat (NWFP)	Security forces

CASUALTIES		ATTACK TACTIC
KILLED	INJURED	
30	68	HBIED / VBIED [double suicide attack]
18	18	HBIED
20	25	HBIED
–	1	VBIED
16 including 4 policemen	32	HBIED
145 including 20 police squad	350	HBIED
34 including 30 FC personnel	35	VBIED
8 including 4 policemen	30	HBIED
11 including 7 PAF officers	28	VBIED
4 including Pir Muhammad Khan, former minister, and 3 policemen	1	HBIED
–	3 security personnel	VBIED
18	40	VBIED / HBIED (double suicide attack)
–	–	HBIED
10 including 3 policemen	7	VBIED
–	21 including 18 children and 3 PAC employees	VBIED
5 soldiers	22 including 13 military personnel	HBIED (double suicide attack)
6 including 2 military personnel	20 including 8 soldiers	HBIED
12 army recruits	2	HBIED
60	120	HBIED
12 including 4 soldiers	29	VBIED
25 including Benazir Bhutto	48	HBIED
1	9	VBIED

DATE	PLACE	TARGET
10 Jan 2008	Lahore (Punjab)	Police
15 Jan 2008	Mohmand (NWFP)	Security forces
17 Jan 2008	Peshawar (NWFP)	Shi'a mosque
23 Jan 2008	Khyber (FATA)	Security forces
4 Feb 2008	Rawalpindi (Punjab)	Army bus
9 Feb 2008	Charsaddah (NWFP)	Political rally
13 Feb 2008	North Waziristan (FATA)	ANP office
17 Feb 2008	Kurram agency (FATA)	PPP rally
25 Feb 2008	Rawalpindi (Punjab)	Lt-General of Pakistan Army
29 Feb 2008	Dir (NWFP)	Funeral of police officer
1 March 2008	Bajaur (FATA)	Army convoy
2 March 2008	Darra Adam Khel (NWFP)	Tribal Jirga
4 March 2008	Lahore (Punjab)	Pak Naval War College
11 March 2008	Lahore (Punjab)	FIA Building
11 March 2008	Lahore (Punjab)	FIA investigation centre in Model Town
1 May 2008	Khyber Agency (FATA)	Pro-government Taliban commander
10 May 2008	Mingora (NWFP)	Security forces
18 May 2008	Mardan (NWFP)	Army training centre
20 May 2008	Kohat (NWFP)	Security forces
2 June 2008	Islamabad (Federal Capital)	Danish Embassy
13 July 2008	Dera Ismail Khan	Shi'a procession
19 Aug 2008	Dera Ismail Khan	Police and Shi'a procession
21 Aug 2008	Swat	Checkpoint
23 Aug 2008	Swat	Police station
6 Sep 2008	Peshawar	Police station
16 Sep 2008	Swat	Checkpoint
19 Sep 2008	Islamabad	Marriott Hotel
20 Sep 2008	North Waziristan	Military vehicle
22 Sep 2008	Swat	Checkpoint
2 Oct 2008	Charsadda	ANP President Asfand Yar Wali
6 Oct 2008	Bhakkar	Shi'a politician
9 Oct 2008	Khyber	NATO oil tankers
9 Oct 2008	Islamabad	Police line
10 Oct 2008	Orakzai Agency	Tribal Shi'a Jirga
16 Oct 2008	Swat	Police station
26 Oct 2008	Mohmand Agency	Checkpoint
29 Oct 2008	Bannu	Checkpoint

KILLED	INJURED	ATTACK TACTIC
CASUALTIES		
20	42	HBIED
1	—	HBIED
10	25	HBIED
2	2	HBIED
10	27	VBIED
25	35	HBIED
9	13	VBIED
47	109	HBIED
9	19	HBIED
49	40	HBIED
2	22	VBIED
45	52	HBIED
8	21	HBIED, VBIED
30	200	VBIED
3	7	HBIED
1	30	HBIED
1	3	VBIED
11	24	HBIED
1	9	HBIED
8	30	VBIED
4	—	HBIED
33	54	HBIED
11	—	VBIED
9	20	VBIED
39	80	—
5	12	VBIED
54	280	VBIED
12	20	—
12	3	VBIED
5	18	HBIED
26	62	HBIED
1	—	VBIED
1	9	VBIED
120	200	VBIED
4	29	VBIED
2	13	VBIED
1	14	HBIED

DATE	PLACE	TARGET
31 Oct 2008	Mardan	Senior police officer
2 Nov 2008	South Waziristan	Checkpoint
4 Nov 2008	Hangu	Checkpoint
6 Nov 2008	Swat	FC camp
6 Nov 2008	Bajaur	Tribal Jirga
11 Nov 2008	Peshawar	ANP's top leadership
12 Nov 2008	Charsadda	Army camp
17 Nov 2008	Swat	Checkpoint
20 Nov 2008	Bajaur	Tribal Jirga
28 Nov 2008	Bannu	Police van
1 Dec 2008	Swat	Checkpoint
3 Dec 2008	Charsadda	Security forces
4 Dec 2008	Swat	Checkpoint
5 Dec 2008	Orakzai	Checkpoint
9 Dec 2008	Buner	Eid congregation
28 Dec 2008	Buner	Police station
4 Jan 2009	Dera Ismail Khan	Policemen and government college
23 Jan 2009	Fizagat, Swat	Checkpoint
5 Feb 2009	Mingora, Swat	Police station
5 Feb 2009	D.G. Khan	Procession of Chehlum at Imambargah
6 Feb 2009	Jamrud, Khyber Agency	Nato supply trailers
9 Feb 2009	Bannu	Police and FC checkpoint
20 Feb 2009	Dera Ismail Khan	Funeral procession of the caretaker of an Imambargah
.23 Feb 2009	Bannu	DSP office
2 March 2009	Killi Karbala Pashin	JUI-F provincial leadership
11 March 2009	Peshawar	ANP minister Bashir Baloor
12 March 2009	Landi kotal, Khyber Agency	Charbagh Fort
16 March 2009	Pirwadhai Rawalpindi	Civilians
23 March 2009	Sitara Market Islamabad	Police station
26 March 2009	Jandola Tank	Peace community of Turkistan
27 March 2009	Jamrud, Khyber Agency	Mosque/Juma prayers and Khasadar force
30 March 2009	Bannu	Army convoy
4 April 2009	Miramshah, North Waziristan	Security forces convoy
4 April 2009	Margala road E-7, Islamabad	FC checkpoint
5 April 2009	Chakwal	Imambargah
15 April 2009	Harichand, Charsadda	Police checkpoint

CASUALTIES		ATTACK TACTIC
KILLED	INJURED	
10	24	–
11	5	VBIED
2	10	VBIED
6	16	VBIED
25	50	HBIED
4	9	HBIED
6	11	VBIED
4	7	VBIED
12	4	HBIED
9	16	–
11	68	VBIED
7	8	VBIED
1	–	HBIED
6	30	–
2	4	HBIED
44	19	HBIED
5 police, 6 civilians	12 police, 15 civilians	HBIED
3 FC	24 FC	HBIED
–	13 police	VBIED
40 civilians	60 civilians	HBIED
1 civilian, 1 paramilitary	6 civilians	VBIED
–	16 FC 2 police	VBIED
45 civilians	155 civilians	HBIED [1]
1 police	1 police	HBIED
6 civilians	15 civilians	HBIED
4 civilians	1 police, 4 civilians	HBIED
–	2 civilians, 1 FC	VBIED
15 civilians	28 civilians	VBIED
1 police	2 police, 2 civilians	HBIED
12 civilians	26 civilians	HBIED
64 civilians	173 civilians	HBIED
10 paramilitaries, 6 FC		
5 soldiers [2]	5 soldiers, 4 civilians	VBIED
13 civilians, 1 FC	4 FC, 26 civilians	HBIED
8 FC, 1 civilians	15 FC	HBIED [3]
30 civilians	140 civilians	HBIED
10 police, 8 civilians	10 civilians	VBIED [4]

DATE	PLACE	TARGET
18 April 2009	Doaba, Hangu	Army checkpoint and convoy
5 May 2009	Bara Qadeem, Peshawar	FC checkpoint
11 May 2009	Dara Adamkhel Kohat	FC checkpoint
21 May 2009	Jandola Tank	FC fort
27 May 2009	Lahore	Rescue-15, ISI
28 May 2009	Mattni, Peshawar	Police checkpoint
28 May 2009	Dera Ismail Khan	Security checkpoint
5 June 2009	Dir upper	Friday prayers in a mosque
6 June 2009	G-8/4, Islamabad	Rescue-15
9 June 2009	Peshawar	PC hotel
11 June 2009	Peshawar	Police
12 June 2009	Nowshehra	Military mosque
12 June 2009	Lahore	Dr Sarfaraz Naeemi[6]
22 June 2009	Battgram Mardan	Police checkpoint
26 June 2009	Muzaffarabad	Army barracks
30 June 2009	Qalat	Nato containers
2 July 2009	Choor Chowk, Rawalpindi	KRL employee bus
25 July 2009	Lakki Marwat	Police convoy
28 July 2009	Miramshah, NWA	Khasadar checkpoint
15 Aug 2009	Khawazkhela, Swat	Checkpoint
18 Aug 2009	Miramshah, NWA	Security checkpoint
22 Aug 2009	Kanjo, Swat	Security forces
23 Aug 2009	Momin Town, Peshawar	Ansar-ul-Islam leaders' house
27 Aug 2009	Torkham, Khyber Agency	Khasadar security post
30 Aug 2009	Mingora, Swat	Police training centre
12 Sep 2009	Doaba, Hangu	Police station
18 Sep 2009	Usterzai Kohat	Shi'a community
19 Sep 2009	Darah Adam Khel, Kohat	Security checkpoint
26 Sep 2009	Saddar, Peshawar	Askari Bank
26 Sep 2009	Bannu	Police station
28 Sep 2009	Bannu	Leader of Peace Committee
5 Oct 2009	F-7 Islamabad	UNWFP office
9 Oct 2009	Khyber Bazar, Peshawar	Civilian
12 Oct 2009	Shangla	Army convoy
15 Oct 2009	Kohat	Police station
16 Oct 2009	Peshawar	CIA office
20 Oct 2009	H-10 Islamabad (two attacks)	International Islamic University
23 Oct 2009	Kamra Attock	PA complex
24 Oct 2009	Lillah Kalarkahar, Rawalpindi	Motorway police

CASUALTIES		ATTACK TACTIC
KILLED	INJURED	
26 soldiers, 2 civilians	28 civilians, 17 soldiers, 7 police	VBIED
6 civilians, 1 FC	13 FC, 4 police, 21 civilians	VBIED
9 civilians, 3 FC	14 FC, 13 civilians	VBIED
5 FC, 4 civilians	35 civilians	VBIED
14 police, 16 civilians	328 civilians	HBIED
3 police, 1 civilians	3 police, 3 civilians	VBIED
3 police, 2 civilians	6 police, 5 civilians	HBIED
49 civilians	30 civilians	HBIED
2 police	5 police	HBIED
18 civilians	54 civilians	VBIED
2 police,[5] 1 civilian	7 police, 6 civilians	HBIED
8 soldiers, 4 civilians	101 civilians	VBIED
5 civilians	7 civilians	HBIED
2 police	7 police	VBIED
2 soldiers	6 soldiers	HBIED
4 civilians	11 civilians	VBIED
–	29 civilians	VBIED
1 civilian[7]	5 police, 3 civilians	VBIED
2 paramilitaries	5 paramilitaries	VBIED
3 soldiers, 2 civilians	5 soldiers	VBIED
3 civilians, 4 FC	5 FC	VBIED
3 soldiers	3 soldiers	VBIED
3 civilians	17 civilians	HBIED
22 paramilitaries	27 paramilitaries	HBIED
17 police	7 police	HBIED
–	2 police, 2 civilians	HBIED
40 civilians	70 civilians	VBIED
2 soldiers	1 civilian	HBIED
13 civilians	190 civilians	VBIED
10 police, 5 civilians	28 police, 27 civilians	VBIED
5 civilians	1 civilian	HBIED
5 civilians[8]	8 civilians	HBIED
52 civilians	147 civilians, 1 police	VBIED
41 civilians, 6 soldiers	58 civilians, 4 soldiers	VBIED
8 civilians, 3 police	22 civilians, 4 police	VBIED[9]
3 polic,e 12 civilians	3 police, 21 civilians	HBIED
9 civilians[10]	36 civilians	HBIED
2 soldiers, 6 civilians	17 civilians	HBIED
1 police	–	VBIED

DATE	PLACE	TARGET
28 Oct 2009	Pepal mandi, Peshawar	Civilian
2 Nov 2009	Maal road, Saddar, Rawalpindi	Intelligence agency officer
2 Nov 2009	Babu sabu interchange motorway, Lahore	Checkpoint
3 Nov 2009	Lachi, Kohat	PF firing range building
8 Nov 2009	Cattle market, Adezai Area, Peshawar	Civilian
9 Nov 2009	Ring Road, Peshawar	Police
10 Nov 2009	Farooqi-Azam Chock,[13] Charssada	Civilian
13 Nov 2009	Khyber Road, Peshawar	ISI's regional headquarters
13 Nov 2009	Bakkakhel, Bannu	Police station
14 Nov 2009	Pishtakhara intersection, Peshawar	Police checkpoint
16 Nov 2009	Badbhabera, Peshawar	Police station
19 Nov 2009	Judicial complex, Peshawar	Judicial complex
1 Dec 2009	Kabal, Swat	ANP provincial assembly
2 Dec 2009	E-8 Sector, Islamabad	Pakistan Naval Complex
4 Dec 2009	Parade Lane, Choor Chowk, Rawalpindi	Army mosque
7 Dec 2009	Peshawar	Session court
7 Dec 2009	Moon Market, Iqbal Town, Lahore (two attacks)	Civilian
8 Dec 2009	Bela Qasim cantonment area, Multan	ISI building
15 Dec 2009	Khosa market, D.G. Khan	Senior adviser to the Punjab chief minister house
17 Dec 2009	Isakhel village, Lakki Marwat	District Nazim Hujra
18 Dec 2009	Timergara, Lower Dir	Police lines Mosque
22 Dec 2009	Peshawar	Press club
24 Dec 2009	Arbab road, Saddar, Peshawar	Police checkpoint
24 Dec 2009	Shakrial, Islamabad	Qasr-i-Sakina, Imambargh
27 Dec 2009	Muzaffarabad	Muharram procession

CASUALTIES		ATTACK TACTIC
KILLED	INJURED	
118 civilians	250 civilians	VBIED[11]
38 civilians[12]	60 civilians	HBIED
1 police	10 police, 10 civilians	HBIED
–	–	HBIED
21 civilians	42 civilians	–
1 police, 2 civilians	5 civilians	VBIED
41 civilians	100 civilians	–
7 soldiers, 10 civilians	180 civilians	VBIED
7 police, 1 civilian	29 civilians	VBIED
12 civilians, 1 police	30 civilians	VBIED
3 civilians	47 civilians, 1 police	VBIED
5 police, 15 civilians	50 civilians	
1 civilian	11 civilians	HBIED
2 soldiers, 1 civilians	6 soldiers, 6 civilians	HBIED
30 civilians, 10 soldiers	40 civilians, 40 soldiers	HBIED
11 civilians, 2 police	39 civilians	–
70 civilians	150 civilians	HBIED
2 soldiers, 12 civilians	61 civilians	VBIED
33 civilians	60 civilians	VBIED
–	–	HBIED
13 police, 3 police, 10 civilians	8 police, 27 civilians	–
1 police, 2 civilians	14 civilians, 3 police	HBIED
1 police, 4 civilians	4 police, 21 civilians	–
1 civilian	1 police, 1 civilian	HBIED
4 police, 6 civilians	81 civilians	HBIED

DATE	LOCATION	CASUALTIES KILLED
22 Feb 2005	Khawaezai and Bayeezai, Mohmand	–
14 May 2005	Mir Ali, NWA	2
4 Dec 2005	NWA	–
14 Jan 2006	Damadola, Bajaur	30
30 Oct 2006	Khar, Bajaur	80
16 June 2007	Salamat Ghundi, NWA	34
3 Nov 2007	Miramshah, NWA	10
31 Jan 2008	Mir Ali, NWA	13
12 March 2008	Lwara Mundi, NWA	–
14 May 2008	Damadola, Bajaur,	15
16 March 2008	Wana, SWA	20
15 June 2008	Makeen, SWA	1
30 June 2008	Bara, Khyber	9
28 July 2008	Azam Warsak, SWA	6
13 Aug 2008	Wana, SWA	25
20 Aug 2008	Wana, SWA	
29 Aug 2008	Ganghikhel, SWA	–
30 Aug 2008	Korzai, SWA	5
31 Aug 2008	Tapi, NWA	6
1 Sep 2008	Tapi, NWA	6
3 Sep 2008	Jalal Khel, SWA	2
5 Sep 2008	Miramshah, NWA	5
8 Sep 2008	Miramshah, NWA	3
12 Sep 2008	Tol Khel, NWA	12
17 Sep 2008	Baghar Cheena, SWA	7
22 Sep 2008	Lwara Mundi, NWA	–
30 Sep 2008	Miramshah, NWA	5
1 Oct 2008	Miramshah, NWA	9
9 Oct 2008	Ghundai, NWA	9
11 Oct 2008	Miramshah, NWA	4
16 Oct 2008	Wana, SWA	4
22 Oct 2008	Miramshah, NWA	8

CASUALTIES INJURED	TARGETS
–	US drones spotted but no attack
–	Car carrying Al Qaeda operative Haitham al-Yemeni
–	Al Qaeda house, unknown casualties but high-ranking Hamza Rabia killed
6	Al Qaeda camp
–	Madrasa, many wounded
27	Taliban/Al Qaeda compound, possible joint US-Pak operation
–	Haqqani camp
–	Al Qaeda house, Abu Layth al-Libi killed
–	Haqqani Network
–	Al Qaeda compound, senior Algerian Al Qaeda operative killed
–	Pro-Taliban tribesman compound
–	Al Qaeda house, Algerian Al Qaeda operative killed
–	HQ of Tanzeem Amar Bil Maarouf Wa Nahi Munkar (Organization for the Promotion of Virtue and Prevention of Vice)
–	Baitullah Mehsud compound, Al Qaeda fighters killed
–	Taliban training camp, several Arabs and Turkmen dea
	Possible Al Qaeda compound, several deaths, including foreigners
–	Tribesman house, possible civilian injuries
2	Al Qaeda house, Canadian Arabs killed and Punjabis injured
8	Possible house of Al Qaeda facilitator Raees Khan, foreign militants dead
8	Al Qaeda house, Arabs and Uzbeks killed
–	Al Qaeda houses, possible Al Qaeda militants killed
–	Al Qaeda house, possible foreign casualties
20	Haqqani madrasa
14	Al-Badr house
3	Taliban camp
–	Pakistani troops fire at US drone
–	Unspecified house
–	House of local Taliban commander
–	Possible Al Qaeda house, 3 foreigners killed
–	Possible Al Qaeda compound, possible foreigners killed
–	Taliban house, Al Qaeda operatives killed
6	Haqqani madrasa, possible Al Qaeda casualties

DATE	LOCATION	CASUALTIES KILLED
27 Oct 2008	Shakai, SWA	20
31 Oct 2008	Mir Ali, NWA	–
31 Oct 2008	Wana, SWA	32
8 Nov 2008	Karikot and Shin Warsak, SWA	–
14 Nov 2008	Tapi, NWA	12
18 Nov 2008	Bannu, NWFP	6
22 Nov 2008	Mir Ali, NWA	3
7 Dec 2008	Bannu, NWFP	13
11 Dec 2008	Wana, SWA	7
21 Dec 2008	Karikot and Shin Warsak, SWA	2
22 Dec 2008	Wana, SWA	7
27 Dec 2008	Mandatta, SWA	20
1 Jan 2009	Karikot area of Wana, SWA	3 foreign militants, 2 local Taliban
2 Jan 2009	Ladha, SWA	3 local Taliban
14 Feb 2009	Ladha, SWA	2 Al Qaeda, 26 local, Uzbek and Afghan militants
12 Mar 2009	Kurram Agency	15 militants
01 April 2009	Orakzai Agency	12 militants
04 April 2009	Ditta Khel, NWA	13 militants and collaborators
08 April 2009	Wana, SWA	3 militants
19 April 2009	Wana, SWA	3 militants
29 April 2009	Ladha, SWA	6 (not confirmed)
9 May 2009	Sararogha, SWA	25 militants
16 May 2009	Mir Ali, NWA	21 local Taliban, 4 foreigners
14 Jun 2009	Ladha, SWA	3 militants
18 June 2009	Wana, SWA	12 militants
23 Jun 2009	Ladha, SWA	12 militants, 42 civilians
3 Jul 2009	Sarwakai, SWA	12 militants
7 Jul 2009	Ladha, SWA	14 militants

CASUALTIES INJURED	TARGETS
–	Taliban house, two key Taliban commanders, Eida Khan and Waheed Ullah, killed
–	Al Qaeda camps, Al Qaeda facilitator killed
–	Al Qaeda camps, Al Qaeda facilitator killed
–	Armed vehicles
–	Al Qaeda compound, Arabs and Uzbeks dead
–	Al Qaeda house, Al Qaeda commander Abdullah Azam al-Saudi killed
–	Militant hideout
–	TTP house
–	Madrasa complex
–	Taliban armed vehicles
–	Taliban weaponized vehicles
–	Taliban compound, Soviet-era Taliban commander Mohammad Omar killed
–	Foreign and local militants
–	Muqami and Punjabi Taliban
–	Al Qaeda hideout
50	Taliban training camp
15 militants	Training facility of Baitullah-led Taliban
–	Hideout of Al Qaeda terrorists
3 militants	Punjabi Taliban
5 militants	Taliban
4	Moving vehicle
–	Baitullah-led Taliban
–	Seminary, where Taliban were residing
–	Vehicle carrying militants
10 militants	Wazir Taliban training camp
7 militants	TTP camp and the subsequent attack on the funeral of Taliban killed in earlier attack
–	House of Mufti Noor Wali, a close aid of Baitullah Mehsud
–	Compound of TTP

DATE	LOCATION	CASUALTIES KILLED
5 Aug 2009	Ladha, SWA	5 militants including Baitullah Mehsud
21 Aug 2009	NWA	16 militants, 6 civilians
27 Aug 2009	Kaniguram, SWA	10 militants
7 Sep 2009	Mir Ali, NWA	7 militants including Ilyas Kashmiri and Mustafa Algaziri
8 Sep 2009	Miramshah, NWA	5 militants, 5 civilians
14 Sep 2009	Mir Ali, NWA	5 militants
29 Sep 2009	Sarrar rugha, SWA	5 militants
30 Sep 2009	Mir Ali, Naurak area, NWA	9 militants, including 5 foreigners (3 Uzbeks, 1 Arab and 1 Chechen)
15 Oct 2009	Danday Derpakhel, NWA	10 militants
24 Oct 2009	Damadola, Bajaur Agency	33 militants, including foreigners
5 Nov 2009	Norak village, NWA	4 militants
18 Nov 2009	Damadola area, Bajaur Agency	16
21 Nov 2009	Machikhel Azizkhel, NWA	8 militants, including 3 Afghans
8 Dec 2009	Spalga village, Miranshah, NWA	3 militants, including 2 Arabs
10 Dec 2009	Laddah, SWA	10 militants
17 Dec 2009	Degan Amber Shaga area, Miramshah, NWA (two attacks)	17 militants
18 Dec 2009	Dattakhel tehsil, NWA	7 militants, including 3 foreigners
26 Dec 2009	Saidgai area, Ghulam Khan tehsil, NWA	14 militants, including 3 foreigners
31 Dec 2009	NWA	5 militants
1 Jan 2010	Hakimkhel village, Mir Ali, NWA	2 militants

CASUALTIES INJURED	TARGETS
–	Baitullah Mehsud, head of the TTP
–	Siraj-u-Din Haqqani
6 militants	Militants Hideout
	Compound of Al Qaeda, Punjabi Taliban and HUJI
	House of Muhammad Ismail in Darga Mandai
3 militants	Al Qaeda terrorists, dead included Nazimuddin alias Yahyo, an important Uzbek comrade of Osama bin Laden
6 militants	Hideout of local Taliban named Irfan Shamankhel targeted, casualties included foreigners and Uzbeks
4 militants	Hideout of militant commander Gull
9 militants	Militants' hideouts
15 militants	Local militants
3 militants	Compounds of local tribesman
–	House of Taliban leader Moulvi Faqeer, some foreign nationals killed
2 militants	Militants
3 militants	Haqqani Network, Al Qaeda
8 militants	Three foreigners were among them. US claimed that Al Qaeda no.3 Abu Yahya al-Libi was killed but it was not confirmed. Later they said Saleh al-Somali was killed and not Al-Libi
11 militants	Foreign militants among them, including Al-Qaeda leader Zhoaib Alzahabi
8 militants	Haqqani Network
7 militants	TTP dead included Abdur Rehman alias Gud (Lam) a close aide of Gul Bahadar
2 militants	TTP
4 militants	Dead included an important militant commander named Haji Umar

DATE	LOCATION	CASUALTIES KILLED
3 Jan 2010	Mosakai village, Mir Ali tehsil, NWA	5 militants
6 Jan 2010	Sanzalai village, NWA (two attacks)	17 militants
8 Jan 2010	Tappai village, NWA	5 militants
9 Jan 2010	Ismail Khel villege, NWA	4 militants
14 Jan 2010	Shaktoi area, SWA	12 militants
15 Jan 2010	Zanani villege, Mirkhani area, Mir Ali tehsil, NWA (two attacks)	11 militants
17 Jan 2010	Ladha tehsil, Shaktoi, SWA	22 militants
19 Jan 2010	Degan area, NWA	6 militants
29 Jan 2010	Dattakhel area, NWA	15 militants
2 Feb 2010	Dattakhel village, NWA Miramshah, NWA	31 militants
14 Feb 2010	Mir Ali, NWA	7 militants
15 Feb 2010	Tappi village, Mir Ali, NWA	4 militants
17 Feb 2010	Tabbi Tolkhel, NWA	3 militants
18 Feb 2010	Danday Darpakhel, NWA	4 militants
19 Feb 2010	Toll Khel, NWA	1 militants
24 Feb 2010	Danday Darpakhel, NWA	9 militants
8 March 2010	Miramshah, NWA	5 militants
10 March 2010	Datakhel, NWA (two attacks)	14 militants
16 March 2010	Tehsil Datakhel, NWA	10 militants
17 March 2010	Hamzoni, Mezar villages, NWA	10 militants
21 March 2010	Lowari Mandi, NWA (two attacks)	8 militants
23 March 2010	Miramshah, NWA	6 militants
27 March 2010	Mir Ali, NWA	4 militants
30 March 2010	Tapi village, NWA	6 militants
11 April 2010	Miramshah, NWA	5 militants
13 April 2010	NWA	5 militants
16 April 2010	Tolkhel, NWA	6

CASUALTIES INJURED	TARGETS
2 militants	Dead included three Arab militants
7 militants	Militants
1 militants	
2 militants	
8 militants	Reports suggest that militant commanders named Qari Hussain, Asmatullah Mavia and Commander Khuwaja Muhammad Mehsud were among killed. Qari Hussain was mastermind of suicide bombing and involved in beheading of security forces (*Daily Aaj*, 16 January 2010)
3 militants	TTP
–	Killed included 4 Arabs, 2 Uzbeks and 9 other local Taliban militants were among them.
4 militants	
4 militants	Arab militants
10 militants	TTP, Al Qaeda
4 militants	4 Uzbek and 3 local militants also among those killed
1 militants	
–	Militants
2 militants	Dead included Muhammad Haqqani, son of Jalaluddin Haqqani[14]
–	Al-Qaeda leader, Sheikh Mansoor al-Masir was killed
6 militants	Qari Zafar, head of the Lashkar-i-Jhangvi reportedly killed in the attack.[15]
–	Militants
3 militants	Militants
1 militant	Killed including three foreigners
2 militants	Foreign militants, especially Arabs reportedly targeted
–	Compound owned by militants
3 militants	Militants
5 militants	Militants
–	Compound owned by a local militant
10 militants	Vehicle carrying Tehrik-e-Taliban Pakistan (TTP) militants
2 militants	Compound owned by militants
–	Militant vehicle and compound

References

INTRODUCTION

1 US Embassy, Islamabad, cable, 'Afghanistan: Tensions Reportedly Mount within Taliban as Ties with Saudi Arabia Deteriorate over Bin Ladin', 28 September 1998, Secret, 8 pp.
2 US Department of State, cable, 'Pakistan Support for Taliban', 26 September 2000, Secret, 4pp.
3 George W. Bush, The White House, 20 September 2001.
4 "Jundullah Responsible for Saravan Bombing", *Tehran Times*, 30 December 2008 and "Iran: Militants claim responsibility for suicide attack", Tehran, *AKI*, 29 December 2008.
5 Pak Institute for Peace Studies Database on terrorism.
6 'Colin Powell on Why Pak is a Key US Ally', *The Rediff*, 19 March 2004, www.rediff.com/news/2004/mar/19inter.htm, accessed 4 January 2009.
7 Richard A. Boucher, 'US Foreign Assistance to Pakistan', Senate Committee on Foreign Relations Subcommittee on International Development, Foreign Economic Affairs and International Environmental Protection, Washington, DC, 6 December 2007 and David Rogers, 'US Annual War Spending Grows', *Wall Street Journal*, 8 March 2006, http://online.wsj.com/public/article/SB114178357697392103-TjKUdWN4qoenDbAFbOI8Ywp2O_M_20070308.html?mod=blogs, accessed 24 September 2008.
8 www.nationalpriorities.org/costofwar_home, accessed 4 January 2009.
9 www.iraqbodycount.org, accessed 4 January 2009.
10 http://icasualties.org/oif, accessed 4 January 2009.
11 Salam Faraj, 'Arab World Hails Shoe Attack as Bush's Farewell Gift', Agence France-Presse, 15 December 2008; 'Iraqi Throws Shoes at Bush during Press Conference', *Huffington Post*, 14 December 2008.
12 George J. Church, 'Let's Change the Subject', *Time*, 18 April 2005.
13 Rüdiger Schöch, 'Afghan Refugees in Pakistan during the 1980s: Cold War Politics and Registration practice', www.unhcr.org/publ/RESEARCH/4868daad2.pdf, accessed 4 January 2009.
14 Many references have been made to this but only a few cases have been proven, and no extensive study has been conducted to verify the claim to date.
15 Ahmed Rashid, 'Descent into Chaos: The United States and the Failure of Nation Building in Pakistan, Afghanistan and Central Asia' (New York, 2008) p. 111.
16 The killings of Afghan Shi'as were witnessed in Persian-speaking regions during armed encounters between the Taliban and Northern Alliance, which was actively supported and financed by Russia, India and Iran.
17 See 'US "threatened to bomb" Pakistan', BBC South Asia, http://news.bbc.co.uk/2/hi/south_asia/5369198.stm, last updated 22 September 2006.

18 ICPVTR Database, Global Pathfinder 2, South Asia, Pakistan, Central Asia, Afghanistan; accessed 3 January 2009.
19 Ground zero is the starting point or centre of rapid and intense development of threat.

I TRIBAL PAKISTAN: THE EPICENTRE OF GLOBAL TERRORISM

1 Assistant Secretary of State for Intelligence and Research Carl W. Ford, Jr. to Secretary of State Colin Powell, 'Pakistan – Poll Shows Strong and Growing Public Support for Taleban', 7 November 2001, Unclassified, 3pp.
2 Assistant Secretary of State for South Asian Affairs Karl F. Inderfurth to Secretary of State Madeleine Albright, 'Pushing for Peace in Afghanistan', c. 25 March 1999, Secret, 6pp.
3 Barack Obama, USA Today, 3 August 2007.
4 http://english.aljazeera.net/news/asia-pacific/2007/06/2008525143040777971.html, accessed 15 April 2009.
5 Article 246(1) of the 1973 Constitution of Pakistan states, 'Federally Administered Tribal Areas include (i) Tribal Areas, adjoining Peshawar District; (ii) Tribal Areas, adjoining Kohat District; (iii) Tribal areas, adjoining Bannu district; (iv) Tribal Areas, adjoining Dera Ismail Khan district; (v) Bajur Agency; (v-a) Orakzai Agency; (vi) Mohamd Agency; (vii) Khyber Agency; (viii) Kurram Agency; (ix) North Waziristan Agency; and (x) South Waziristan Agency.'
6 Thomas H. Johnson and M. Chris Mason, 'No Sign until the Burst of Fire: Understanding the Pakistan-Afghanistan Frontier', International Security, XXXII/4 (Spring 2008), p. 41.
7 www.fata.gov.pk/subpages/climate.php, accessed 11 January 2010.
8 'History of FATA', http://fata.gov.pk/subpages/history.php, accessed 27 November 2009.
9 Ziad Haider, 'Desperate for Reform', Daily Times [Lahore], 27 August 2008.
10 Daniel Markey, 'Securing Pakistan's Tribal Belt', Council Special Report No. 36, Council on Foreign Relations Center for Preventive Action (August 2008), p. 6.
11 'Pakistan's Tribal Areas: Appeasing The Militants', Asia Report, no. 124 (11 December 2006), p. 9.
12 Fazal-ur-Rehman Marwat, 'The Genesis of Change and Modernization in Federally Administered Tribal Areas (FATA) of Pakistan', IPRI Journal, VII/2 (Summer 2007), p. 73.
13 Ashok K. Behuria, 'The Rise of Pakistani Taliban and the Response of the State', Strategic Analysis, XXXI/5 (2000), pp. 694–724.
14 Haider Zaman, 'Problems of Education, Health and Infrastructure in FATA', in Tribal Areas of Pakistan: Challenges and Responses, ed. Pervez Iqbal Cheema and Maqud-ul Hasan Nuri (Islamabad, 2005), p. 156.
15 Khalid Aziz, 'Causes of Rebellion in Waziristan', Criterion Magazine (April–June 2007).
16 www.fata.gov.pk/subpages/land.php, accessed 10 January 2008.
17 Daniel Markey, 'Securing Pakistan's Tribal Belt', Council Special Report No. 36, New York: Council on Foreign Relations Center for Preventive Action (August 2008), p. 7.
18 Article 247(2) of the 1973 Constitution, 'The President may, from time to time, give such directions to the Governor of a Province relating to the whole or any part of a Tribal Area within the Province as he may deem necessary, and the Governor shall, in the exercise of his functions under this Article, comply with such directions.'
19 Robert G Wirsing, 'Introduction: Emerging Trends and Developments in Pakistan's FATA- Implications for the United States', National Bureau of Asian Research, XIX/3 (August 2008), p. 12.
20 Khasadars are irregular forces under the control of a PA established to protect roads and other government installations and perform guard duties.
21 A malik is a respected tribal elder or influential personality of a local tribe. Political agents appoint a malik from different tribes on male inheritance (with the Governor's consent) and they are responsible for governing the behaviour of their respective tribes.

22 *Lungi* is also an official privilege and recognition granted by the political administration, although of a lower status than that of a *malik*.

23 'Building Judicial Independence in Pakistan', *Asia Report*, no. 86 (10 November 2004), p. i.

24 'Pakistan's Tribal Areas: Appeasing the Militants', *Asia Report*, no. 124 (11 December 2006), p. 6.

25 *Jirga* is a Pushto term for a decision-making assembly of male elders that handles criminal cases under FCR 1901.

26 'Pakistan's Tribal Areas: Appeasing the Militants', p. 6.

27 FCR (1901), sections 21–24.

28 'Bajaur Mission Fulfilled: Army: Chance to Net Zawahiri "Missed", Says Govt', *Dawn* [Karachi], 2 September 2008.

29 Interview, Pakistani Intelligence officer, Peshawar, May 2010, www.zmong-afghanistan.com/profiles/zwahiri.asp, accessed 14 February 2009; and Akram Gizabi, 'Bajaur: Tribe and Custom Continue to Protect al-Qaeda', *Terrorism Focus*, III/2 (18 January 2006).

30 Mushtaq Yusufzai, 'Maulana Faqir, Govt May Ink Peace Deal after Eid', *The News* [Pakistan], 22 October 2006.

31 Jayshree Bajoria, 'Pakistan's New Generation of Terrorists', Council on Foreign Relations, Backgrounder, 6 February 2008.

32 Justin Huggler, 'Eighty Die as Pakistan Bombs Madrassa Linked to Militants', *The Independent*, 31 October 2006.

33 Global Pathfinder II, The Database of the International Center for Political Violence and Terrorism Research, S. Rajaratnam School of International Studies, Nanyang Technological University, Singapore; accessed 14 February 2009.

34 Zulf Khan Afridi and Azka Jameel, 'Operation in Wana: Wanted al-Qaeda Ally Killed', *Pakistan Times*, 19 June 2004.

35 Ibid.

36 Pervez Musharraf, *In the Line of Fire* (London, 2006), pp. 265–70.

37 'Rashid Rauf among Five Killed in North Waziristan Drone Strike', *Daily Times*, 23 November 2008, www.dailytimes.com.pk/default.asp?page=2008\11\23\story_23-11-2008_pg1_9.

38 'Interview with Sheikh Ayman al-Zawahiri', IntelCenter, al-Qaeda Videos, no. 74, 5 May 2007 and ICPVTR research on al Sahab Sahab Institute for Media Production.

39 Musharraf, *In the Line of Fire*, p. 268.

40 The London Bombings, Briefing by the Secret Intelligence Service (SIS), UK, July 2006.

41 Ibid.

42 Sami Yousafzai and Ron Moreau, 'Terror Broker: Bin Laden needed a role in the Iraqi insurgency, and Zarqawi needed outside support. How a deadly deal was made', *Newsweek*, 11 April 2006. When Al Qaeda negotiated with leaders of other groups, Osama chose Al Qaeda personalities similar to them. Like Abu Musab, Abdal Hadi was very direct and candid: this made Abdal Hadi the natural choice. Interview, Anders Nielsen, Research Fellow, International Centre for Political Violence and Terrorism Research, Singapore, December 2007.

43 Ibid.

44 Office of the Director of National Intelligence, 'Profile on Abu Faraj al-Libi', September 2006.

45 Verbatim Transcript of Open Session Combatant Status Review Tribunal Hearing for ISN 10017, Guantanamo Bay, 9 March 2007.

46 'Accounts after 2005 London Bombing Point to Al Qaeda Role from Pakistan', *New York Times*, 13 August 2006.

47 Yousafzai and Moreau, 'Terror Broker'.

48 Dipesh Gadher, 'Al-Qaeda "planning big British attack"', *Sunday Times*, 22 April 2007.

49 Ian Cobain and Richard Norton-Taylor, 'The Phone Call that Asked: How Do You Make a Bomb?', *The Guardian*, 1 May 2007.

50 Peter Bergen and Paul Cruickshank, 'Al Qaeda on Thames', *Washington Post*, 30 April 2007.

51 Ibid.

52 Mohammad Siddique Khan also knew Khyam and his associate Mohomed Junaid Babar from the US. Owing to a security failure, however, the UK authorities did not monitor him or his deputy Sheezad Tanvir.

53 Bergen and Cruickshank, 'Al Qaeda on Thames'.

54 '7/7 "Mastermind" is Seized in Iraq' *The Times*, 28 April 2007.

55 'Accounts after 2005 London Bombing Point to Al Qaeda Role from Pakistan', *New York Times*, 13 August 2006.

56 Terrorist Threat in FATA/NWFP, Briefing by Intelligence Bureau, Pakistan, January 2009.

57 Ibid.

58 Ibid.

2 UNDERSTANDING THE PAKISTANI TALIBAN

1 Mushtaq Yusufzai, '3 Prominent Waziristan Militants: Commanders Resolve Differences', *The News* [Karachi], 21 February 2008.

2 Arif Yousafzai, 'Over 100 Soldiers "Stranded"', *The Post* [Lahore], 1 September 2007.

3 Dr Hasan-Askari Rizvi, 'Understanding the Insurgency' *Daily Times* [Lahore], 5 October 2008.

4 Claudio Franco, 'The Tehrik-e-Taliban Pakistan: The Bajaur Case', NEFA Foundation, July 2009, www.nefafoundation.org/miscellaneous/FeaturedDocs/nefa_ttp0709part1.pdf, accessed 13 July 2010. .

5 Zahid Hussain, 'Are We Losing the War against Militancy?', *Newsline* [Lahore] (July 2008).

6 Rohan Gunaratna and Syed Adnan Ali Shah Bukhari, 'Militant Organisations and their Driving Forces', Pakistan–Consequences of Deteriorating Security in Afghanistan, Swedish Defence Research Agency, January 2009.

7 Zahid Hussain, July 2008.

8 Interview with Syed Adnan Ali Shah, International Centre for Political Violence and Terrorism Research (ICPVTR), Singapore, 15 January 2009.

9 Group Profile 'Tehrik-e-Taliban Pakistan', ICPVTR Database, Global Pathfinder 2, South Asia, Pakistan, Central Asia, Afghanistan, accessed 3 January 2009.

10 Interview, senior intelligence officer, Peshawar, May 2010.

11 Ibid.

12 'Second Editorial: Tribal Areas under Centralised Command', *Daily Times* [Lahore], 16 December 2007.

13 Misbah Abdul-Baqi, 'Pakistani Taliban Disclosed; Emergence, Objectives, and Leadership', *Islam Online*, www.islamonline.net/servlet/Satellite?c=Article_C&cid=1203757776285& pagename=Zone-English-Muslim_Affairs%2FMAELayout, accessed 13 July 2010.

14 Hassan Abbas, 'Profile of Tehrik-e-Taliban Pakistan', *CTS Sentinel*, 1/2 (January 2008).

15 Faraz Khan, 'Taliban Capable of Taking Over Karachi: TTP', *Daily Times* [Lahore], 10 August 2008.

16 The Taliban also dislikes Altaf Hussain for his Shi'a background.

17 Faraz Khan, 'Taliban Capable of Taking Over Karachi: TTP'.

18 Interview with Syed Adnan Ali Shah Bukhari, ICPVTR, RSIS.

19 'Talibanization', as a generic term, has been used to define a combination of the Pakistani Taliban's ideological and political ambitions.

20 Faraz Khan, 'Baitullah Mehsud, LJ Join Hands in Karachi', *Daily Times* [Lahore], 4 September 2008.

21 Ibid.

22 Ibid.

23 'TTP Claims Responsibility for Nangarhar Bombing', *Daily Times* [Lahore], 15 June 2008.

24 Baitullah Mehsud's first TV interview with Al Jazeera, http://pakistanpolicy.com/2008/01/

29/baitullah-mehsuds-first-interview/, accessed 10 November 2008.

25 Rahimullah Yusufzai, 'Power-Sharing Formula to Maintain TTP Unity', *The News* [Lahore], 26 August 2009.

26 Hassan Abbas, 'A Profile of Tehrik-e-Taliban Pakistan', *CTS Sentinel*, 1/2 (January 2008).

27 Interview with Mansoor Khan Mehsud, Researcher at Pak Institute for Peace Studies (PIPS), Islamabad, July 2008.

28 Ramazan alias Salahuddin. Rohan Gunaratna, interviewer. 'The Surviving Suicide Bomber of the Serena Hotel in Kabul', Kabul, Afghanistan.

29 *Urdu Daily Waqt* [Lahore], 26 August 2008.

30 Ibid.

31 'Baitullah Mehsud Dies', *News Desk* [Karachi], 1 October 2008.

32 'Baitullah Mehsud is Alive: TTP', *The News* [Karachi], 1 October 2008.

33 Interview with Mansoor Khan Mehsud.

34 Bill Roggio, 'Pakistani Taliban Unites under Baitullah Mehsud', *The Long War Journal*, 15 December 2008, www.longwarjournal.org/archives/2007/12/pakistani_taliban_un.php, accessed 9 November 2008.

35 Mushtaq Yusufzai, 'Baitullah's Death Finally Confirmed by Taliban', *The News* [26 August 2009].

36 Rahimullah Yusufzai, "Poor Health, Insecurity Prompts Baitullah to Nominate Deputies', *The News* [Karachi], 25 August 2008.

37 'Hakimullah Mehsud New Chief: Faqir', *Dawn* [Karachi], 22 August 2009.

38 Syed Shoaib Hasan, 'Profile: Hakimullah Mehsud', *BBC South Asia*, 25 August 2009, http://news.bbc.co.uk/2/hi/south_asia/8219223.stm, accessed 14 July 2010.

39 Ibid.

40 Amir Mir, 'A Young Turk Takes over TTP, Ringing Alarm Bells', *The News* [Karachi], 28 August 2009.

41 Ibid.

42 George Friedman and Scott Stewart, 'The Khost Attack and the Intelligence War Challenge', www.stratfor.com/weekly/20100111_khost_attack_and_intelligence_war_challenge?utm_source=GWeekly&utm_medium=email&utm_campaign=100111&utm_content=readmore, 11 January 2010

43 Mushtaq Yusufzai, 'Hakimullah Dies of Wounds in Multan?', *The News* [Lahore], 10 February 2010.

44 Ibid.

45 Rahimullah Yusufzai, 'Power-Sharing Formula to Maintain TTP Unity', *The News* [Lahore], 26 August 2009.

46 'Pakistan Taliban Commander Vows Afghan Fight', *Dawn* [Karachi], 24 August 2009.

47 Interview with Mansoor Khan Mehsud, Pak Institute for Peace Studies, Islambad, July 2008.

48 Mazhar Tufail, 'TTP Infighting Led to Beheading of Polish Engineer", *The News* [Karachi], 12 February 2009.

49 Ibid.

50 Sohail Abdul Nasir, 'Al-Zawahiri's Pakistani Ally: Profile of Maulana Faqir Mohammed', *Terrorism Monitor*, IV/3 (9 February 2006), www.jamestown.org/terrorism/news/article.php?articleid=2369893, accessed 8 November 2008.

51 Ibid.

52 Hassan Abbas, 'A Profile of Tehrik-e-Taliban Pakistan'.

53 Interview with Syed Adnan Bukhari, Associate Research Fellow, International Centre for Political Violence and Terrorism Research (ICPVTR).

54 Sohail Abdul Nasir, 'Al-Zawahiri's Pakistani Ally: Profile of Maulana Faqir Mohammed', *Terrorism Monitor*, IV/3 (9 February 2006).

55 Ibid.

56 Ibid.

57 Iqbal Khattak, 'Mohmand Agency now under Taliban's Control', *Daily Times* [Lahore], 24 July 2008.

58 Ibid.

59 Ibid.

60 Sadia Sulaiman and Syed Adnan Ali Shah Bukhari, 'Hafiz Gul Bahadur: A Profile of the Leader of the North Waziristan Taliban', *Terrorism Monitor*, vii/9 (10 April 2009).

61 'Taliban Spokesman Maulvi Omar Captured', *The News* [Karachi], 19 August 2009, www. thenews.com.pk/top_story_detail.asp?Id=23945, accessed 2009.

62 Zahir Shah, 'Hostage to Jihad', *The Herald* [Karachi], October 2008.

63 Ibid.

64 Interview, Mazhar Mashwany, Superintendent of Police, cid, Karachi, June 2008.

65 'Jundullah Suspect Makes Startling Disclosures' *The News* [Karachi], 2 February 2008.

66 Interview, Mazhar Mashwany.

67 Interview, senior intelligence officer, Peshawar, May 2010.

68 Salis bin Perwaiz, 'ttp Financiers Held in Karachi', *The News* [Karachi], 25 August 2008.

69 Ibid.

70 *Daily Dawn*, 20 September 2009.

71 Ibid.

72 Ibid.

73 Ibid.

74 Ibid.

75 Ibid.

76 Ibid.

77 M.A.K. Lodhi, 'Arrested Militants Name raw, Afghan Agency for Funding,' *The News* [Karachi], 22 October 2008.

78 Ibid.

79 Ibid.

80 Ibid.

81 'Qaeda May Be Financing Baitullah Mehsud', *The Post* [Lahore], 28 January 2008.

82 Ibid.

83 'ttp is an Extension of Al Qaeda: Rehman', *Daily Times* [Lahore], 2 September 2008.

84 Bill Roggio, 'Pakistani Taliban Unites under Baitullah Mehsud', The Long War Journal, www. longwarjournal.org/archives/2007/12/pakistani_taliban_un.php, accessed 7 November 2008.

85 'Exclusive New Interview with Maulana Faquir Mohammed', nefa Foundation, http:// www1.nefafoundation.org/multimedia-intvu.html#faqirmuhammad1022, accessed 5 November 2008.

86 'Rising Terror Chief Worries u.s. Officials', www.cbsnews.com/stories/2008/03/17/evening news/main3946322.shtml, accessed 8 November 2008.

87 Video interview with Maulvi Omar, 29 August 2008, www.nefafoundation.org/multi media-intvu.html, accessed 8 November 2008.

88 Safdar Sial and Aqeel Yusafzai, 'Swat: A Symptom of a Deeper, Older Malady', Pak Institute for Peace Studies, 24 November 2007, www.san-pips.com/index.php?action=san& id=10, accessed 12 January 2008.

89 Maqbool Malik, 'Qari Zia Group Suspected in Wali Bagh Suicide Attack', *The Nation* [Lahore], 4 October 2008.

90 'Taliban Crossing Pak-Afghan Border to Fight in Bajaur', *Daily Times* [Lahore], 30 September 2008.

91 Video interview with Maulana Faqir Muhammad, October 2008, nefa Foundation, www. nefafoundation.org/multimedia-intvu.html, accessed 10 November 2008.

92 Bureau Report, 'Baitullah is on his Own, Say Afghan Taliban', *Dawn* [Karachi], 29 January 2008, www.dawn.com/2008/01/29/top18.htm, accessed 8 November 2008.

93 *Asia Times Online* claimed in January 2008 that the Taliban supreme leader Mullah

Muhammad Omar had removed Baitullah from the leadership of the Taliban movement for fighting in Pakistan at the expense of 'Jihad' in Afghanistan.

94 Saifullah Khalid, *Ummat* [Karachi], 8 September 2008.

95 'Deadliest Attack on a Military Installation, at Least 70 Killed', *Daily Times* [Lahore], 22 August 2008.

96 Urdu Daily *Express* [Lahore], 22 August 2008.

97 'Taliban Kill Rival Group Leaders', *Daily Times* [Lahore], 20 July 2008.

98 Javed Afridi, 'Anti-Taliban Militant Outfit's Head Shot Dead', *The News* [Karachi], 14 August 2008.

99 Interview, senior intelligence officer, Peshawar, May 2010.

100 Saifullah Khalid, Urdu daily *Ummat*.

101 Shakeel Anjum, 'Three Militant Outfits Join Hands with al-Qaeda', *The News* [Karachi], 27 August 2007.

102 Interview with an office bearer of Jamaat-al-Daawa (former Lashkar-e-Taiba), Islamabad, August 2008.

103 'Militant Killed over Madrassa Occupation', *Daily Times* [Lahore], 17 July 2008.

104 Mushtaq Yusufzai, '50 Killed as Two Militant Groups Clash in Mohmand', *The News* [Karachi], 19 July 2008.

105 Interview with an office bearer of Jamaat-al-Daawa, Islamabad, August 2008.

106 Hasbanullah Khan, 'Taliban Split into Two Factions in Bajaur Agency', *Daily Times* [Lahore], 29 July 2008.

107 Interview, Major General Michael Flynn, us Deputy Chief of Staff for Intelligence, Afghanistan, May 2010.

108 The fighters of Mullah Nazir started fighting against the Uzbeks under the banner of 'Mujahideen-e-Haq'.

109 A term used for the Taliban government of Afghanistan.

110 The letter was obtained from the tribal areas of Pakistan.

111 Mushtaq Yousafzai, 'Top Militant Commanders Resolve Rift', *The News* [Lahore], 21 February 2009.

112 Ibid.

113 Ibid.

114 Abdul Hai Kakar, 'Zainuddin: Qari se Commander banney tak', BBC Urdu, 23 June 2009, www.bbc.co.uk/urdu/pakistan/2009/06/090623_qarizain_profile_sen.shtml?s, accessed 25 July 2009.

115 Hamid Mir, 'Why Does Zainuddin Want to Kill Baitullah?', *The News* [Lahore], 21 June 2009.

116 Ismail Khan, 'Mehsuds Hedge their Bets as Game on to Isolate Baitullah', *Dawn* [Karachi], 16 June 2009.

117 Abdul Hai Kakar, 'Zainuddin'.

118 'Baitullah is us Agent, Claims Former Close Aide', *The News* [Lahore], 18 June 2009.

119 Ibid.

120 Iqbal Khattak, 'Qari Zainuddin Killed, Baitullah Accused', *Daily Times* [Lahore], 24 June 2009.

121 'Bhittani', www.nps.edu/programs/ccs/Docs/Pakistan/Tribes/Bhittani.pdf, accessed 20 July 2010.

122 Ibid.

123 'Pakistani Taliban Chief Wants Volunteers for Afghan Jihad', *Daily Times* [Lahore], 22 April 2006.

124 Caroline Wadhams and Colin Cookman, 'Faces of Pakistan's Militant Leaders', Centre for American Progress, 22 July 2009.

125 'Tribesmen Foil Militants' Bid to Blow Up Bridge in Jandola', *The News* [Lahore], 6 October 2007

126 Interview with Mansur Khan, Research Analyst with the Pakistan Institute of Peace Stud-

ies (pips), Islamabad, 29 August 2008.

127 'Militants Pull Back from Jandola', *Dawn* [Karachi], 25 June 2008.

128 'Clashes in Tank Leave Ten Dead', *Dawn* [Karachi], 8 August 2009.

129 *The News* [Lahore], 28 June 2009.

130 Caroline Wadhams and Colin Cookman, 'Faces of Pakistan's Militant Leaders',

131 'us Drone Strike Said to Kill 60 in Pakistan', *New York Times*, 24 June 2009.

132 Omer Farooq Khan, 'Another Militant Dares Mehsud', *Times of India*, 26 June 2009.

133 www.longwarjournal.org/archives/2009/08/good_pakistani_talib.php#ixzz0ObxGaENQ, accessed 18 August 2009.

134 Daily Times, 22 April 2006.

135 Mushtaq Yusufzai and Sailab Mahsud, 'Militants Link Soldiers' Release to Pullout', *The News* [Lahore], 3 September 2007.

136 Sadia Sulaiman, 'Empowering "Soft" Taliban over "Hard" Taliban: Pakistan's Counter-Terrorism Strategy', *Terrorism Monitor*, vi/15 (25 July 2008).

137 Mushtaq Yusufzai and Sailab Mahsud, 'Militants Link Soldiers' Release to Pullout'.

138 Interview of Maulvi Omar with Muzzamil Suharwardi.

139 Misbah Abdul-Baqi, 'Pakistani Taliban Disclosed; Emergence, Objectives, and Leadership'.

140 Ibid.

141 Interview of Maulvi Omar with Muzzamil Suharwardi.

142 'Terrorists Receiving Weapons from Afghanistan', *Daily Times* [Lahore], 12 October 2008.

143 Interview of Maulvi Omar with Muzzamil Suharwardi.

144 'Baitullah Mehsud's First Television Interview',,http://pakistanpolicy.com/2008/01/29/baitullah-mehsuds-first-interview/, accessed 5 November 2008.

145 Iqbal Khattak, 'Six Key Militant Outfits Operating in Darra', *Daily Times* [Lahore], 29 January 2008.

146 "ttp claims responsibility", *Daily Times*, Lahore, 04 September 2008.

147 'Taliban Claim Abduction of Foreign Engineers', *The Post* [Lahore], 1 October 2008.

148 'Taliban Claim Kidnapping of Chinese', *Daily Times* [Lahore], 3 September 2008.

149 Interview, senior intelligence officer, Peshawar, May 2010.

150 Javed Afridi, 'Anti-Taliban Militant Outfit's Head Shot Dead'. *The News* [Karachi], 14 August 2008.

151 Akhtar Shehzad, 'ttp Claims Responsibility, Tells Govt to Stay Away', *The News* [Karachi], 26 June 2008.

152 Yousuf Ali, 'Tribal Lashkars Need Govt. Support', South Asia Net, 10 November 2008, www.san-pips.com/PIPS-R&D-%20Files/Reports/R&D-Report-Article33/R&D-Report-A33-D.asp, last visited 12 November 2008.

153 Ibid.

154 Ibid.

155 According to the Inter Service Public Relations (ispr) of the Pakistan Army on 18 November 2009; 'Waziristan Myth Busted, Says ispr', *Daily Times* [Lahore], 19 November 2009.

156 Zafar Hilaly, 'What Lies in Waziristan', *The News* [Lahore], 31 August 2009.

157 Akhtar Amin, 'Militants Destroyed 125 Girls' Schools in 10 Months', *Daily Times* [Lahore], 21 August 2008.

158 tv interview with Maulvi Omar by Muzamal Suherwardy, a senior correspondent and talk-show host for the Khabrain media group's Urdu tv channel 5.

159 Interview with a suicide bomber, for geo tv's current affairs programme 'Jirga', 2nd July 2009.

160 Hasbanullah Khan, 'Taliban Split into Two Factions in Bajaur Agency', *Daily Times* [Lahore], 29 July 2008.

161 Hamid Mir, 'Baitullah Losing Control after New Peace Deals', *The News* [Karachi], 18 October 2008.

162 'Mehsud Offers Unconditional Surrender', *The Post* [Lahore], 2 November 2008.

163 'Sufi Muhammad Says Democracy, Communism, Socialism, Fascism are un-Islamic Sys-

tems of Governance', *Daily Times* [Lahore], 4 May 2009.

164 Zia-Ur-Rehman, 'The Role of TNSM in Talibanising the Malakand: a Journey into History up to the Present Times', *The News on Sunday*, 1 July 2007.

165 Ibid.

166 Amir Mir, 'Peace Deal to Legitimize TNSM', *The News* [Lahore], 18 February 2009.

167 Ibid.

168 GEO TV interview with Sufi Muhammad, 3 May 2009. The interview was also cited by the Urdu daily *Waqt* [Lahore], 4 May 2009, www.dailywaqt.com/default.asp, accessed 14 May 2009.

169 Ibid.

170 Ibid.

171 Ibid.

172 Jane Perlez and Pir Zubair Shah, 'Taliban Exploit Class Rifts in Pakistan', *New York Times*, 16 April 2009, www.nytimes.com/2009/04/17/world/asia/17pstan.html, accessed 16 May 2009.

173 Hamid Mir, 'Secret Details of Swat Peace Accord', *The News* [Lahore], 11 April 2009.

174 Ibid.

175 Javed Aziz Khan, 'Soldier who Led Operation against TNSM Passes Away', *The News* [Lahore], 20 April 2009.

176 GEO TV interview with Sufi Muhammad, 3 May 2009.

177 Umer Farooq, 'Profile: Maulana Sufi Muhammad', 1 May 2009, www.asharq-e.com/news.asp?section=3&id=16588, accessed 17 May 2009.

178 Interview, senior intelligence officer, Peshawar, May 2010.

179 Zia-Ur-Rehman, 'The Role of TNSM in Talibanising the Malakand'.

180 Ibid.

181 Muhammad Amir Rana, 'Backgrounder: Shariah Movement in Malakand', South Asia Net, Pak Institute for Peace Studies, 29 April 2008

182 Zia-Ur-Rehman, 'The Role of TNSM in Talibanising the Malakand'

183 Although a senior intelligence officer has disputed that the TNSM ever took a leading role in the humanitarian effort during the earthquake, interview, Peshawar, May 2010.

184 Ibid.

185 '80 Die in Air Attack on Bajaur Seminary', *The News* [Lahore], 31 October 2006, www.thenews.com.pk/print3.asp?id=3945, accessed 19 May 2009.

186 Amir Mir, 'Peace Deal to Legitimize TNSM'.

187 *The News* [Lahore], 18 June 2007

188 Interview, senior intelligence officer, Peshawar, May 2010.

189 Delawar Jan, 'Sufi Flays Terrorist Activities of Fazlullah', *The News* [Lahore], 31 March 2008.

190 Ibid.

191 Gulam Farooq, 'Sufi Says Disarm, TTP Says Enforce Sharia First', *Daily Times* [Lahore], 15 April 2009.

192 'Swat: Aarzi Bandobast, Taliban ki Tanzeem-e-no', BBC Urdu, 9 April 2009, www.bbc.co.uk/urdu/lg/pakistan/2009/05/090505_taliban_swat_rh.shtml?s, accessed 14 April 2009.

193 Ibid.

194 Haji Muhammad Adeel, the central vice president of the Awami National Party (ANP) and a witness to the Swat Peace Agreement, made this disclosure in a speech he delivered at Express Forum. Extracts of his speech were reported in *Urdu Daily Express* [Lahore], 12 May 2009.

195 Hasbanullah Khan, 'Taliban-TNSM Clash Leaves 2 Dead in Bajaur', *Daily Times* [Lahore], 20 April 2009.

196 'TTP Says Osama Welcome in Swat: Taliban Reject Peace Accord', *Daily Times* [Lahore], 22 April 2009.

197 Hardtalk, Interview with Sufi Muhammad, *Daily Times* [Lahore], 19 March 2009.

198 Hamid Mir, 'Secret Details of Swat Peace Accord', *The News* [Lahore], 11 April 2009.

199 'President Signs Nizam-e-Adl after NA Nod', *Daily Times* [Lahore], 14 April 2009.

200 'Two Taliban Groups Unite to Fight NATO', *Dawn* [Karachi], 1 July 2008.

201 Mushtaq Yousafzai, 'Fighting Feared as Pro-Govt Tribals Join Hands in Waziristan', *The News* [Karachi], 13 July 2008.

202 Nek Muhammad was the first pro-Taliban militant leader who rose to prominence through resisting the Pakistani security forces. Belonging to the most powerful clan, Yargul Khel, of the biggest sub-tribe, Zilli Khel of Ahmadzai Wazir tribe, Nek Muhammad centralized authority in his hands. Nek signed the Shakai Peace Agreement with Pakistan in April 2004, but the agreement broke down with both sides accusing the other of non-compliance. Fighting broke out again in June 2004. Nek Muhammad was killed in a Predator drone strike in June 2004 and was succeeded by Muhammad Omar Yargul Khel, followed by Mullah Nazir from the Kaka Khel clan.

203 Syed Saleem Shahzad, 'Taliban Wield the Ax Ahead of New Battle', *Asia Times Online*, 24 January 2008

204 Mushtaq Yusufzai and Malik Mumtaz Khan, 'NWA Militants Scrap Peace Deal', *The News* [Karachi], 30 June 2009.

205 Rahimullah Yusufzai, 'Army Facing Tough Choice after NWA Ambush', *The News* [Karachi], 30 June 2009.

206 Urdu daily *Waqt* [Lahore], 29 June 2009

207 Mushtaq Yusufzai and Malik Mumtaz Khan, 'Airplanes Pound Militant Positions in NWA', *The News* [Karachi], 30 June 2009

208 Ibid.

209 'Pakistan Tribal Elders Shot Dead', BBC, 7 January 2008.

210 'Gunmen Shoot Dead Pro-Pakistan Militant Commander', *Dawn* [Karachi], 1 June 2008.

211 Sadia Sulaiman, 'Empowering "Soft" Taliban Over "Hard" Taliban: Pakistan's Counter-Terrorism Strategy', Jamestown Foundation, VI/15, 25 July 2008.

212 Also see 'Mahsud Challenged by New Militant Bloc', *Daily Times* [Lahore], 2 July 2008.

213 'Wazir Tribes Ratify New Militant Bloc', *Daily Times* [Lahore], 8 July 2008.

214 'Mahsud Challenged by New Militant Bloc', *Daily Times* [Lahore], 2 July 2008.

215 Syed Saleem Shahzad, 'Dadullah's Death Hits Taliban Hard', *Asia Times Online*, 15 May 2007, www.atimes.com/atimes/South_Asia/IE15Df01.html.

216 'Taliban Slap Taxes in Miranshah', *Dawn* [Karachi], 23 October 2006.

217 Syed Adnan Ali Shah Bukhari.

218 Aamir Latif, 'Punjabi Taliban Rise in Waziristan', *Islam Online*, 22 April 2007, www.islam-online.net/servlet/Satellite?c=Article_C&cid=1177155819817&pagename=Zone-English-News%2FNWELayout, accessed 2 May 2009

219 'Deadly Tehreek-e-Taliban Punjab', *Daily Times* [Lahore], 26 August 2009.

220 'Rashid Rauf among Five Killed in North Waziristan Drone Strike', *Daily Times*, 23 November 2008, www.dailytimes.com.pk/default.asp?page=2008\11\23\story_23-11-2008_pg1_9, accessed 23 July 2010.

221 Al-Badr is the site of the first battle of Islam near Medina. 'US Forces Strike inside Pakistan Territory Again; 12 Killed', *Rediff News*, 12 September 2008, www.rediff.com/news/2008/sep/12uspak.htm, accessed 23 July 2010.

222 Syed Saleem Shahzad, 'Rise of the Neo-Taliban', *Asia Times Online*, 14 November 2007, www.atimes.com/atimes/South_Asia/IK14Df05.html, accessed 30 September 2009.

223 '50 Killed as Two Militant Groups Clash in Mohmand', *The News* [Karachi], 19 July 2008, www.thenews.com.pk/top_story_detail.asp?Id=16072, accessed 23 July 2010.

224 Interview with Qari Aleemullah Sabir (a pseudonym), former member of Sipah-e-Sahaba Pakistan (SSP) and currently working with Harkat-ul-Jihad-e-Islami. Dera Ghazi Khan, South Punjab, 18 July 2009.

225 Urdu daily *Khabrain* [Lahore], 18 April 2008.

226 Imtiaz Gul, 'Talibanisation of Khyber Agency', www.weeklypulse.org/pulse/article/2101, 3

July 2008.

227 Imtiaz Gul, 'Talibanisation of Khyber Agency', www.weeklypulse.org/pulse/article/2101, 3 July 2008.

228 Nasrullah Afridi, 'Mangal Bagh Resigns as LI Chief', *The News* [Karachi], 26 November 2008.

229 'NEFA Exclusive: An Interview with Mangal Bagh', 1 May 2008, www.nefafoundation.org/miscellaneous/nefamangalbagh0608.pdf, accessed 22 November 2008.

230 Rahimullah Yusufzai, 'The Man from Bara', *The News on Sunday* [Karachi], 11 May 2008

231 Ibid.

232 'Pakistan-Based Militant Group Lashkar-e-Islam Vows "to Spread Islam across the World"', http://memri.org/bin/latestnews.cgi?ID=SD190608, accessed 15 November 2008.

233 Rahimullah Yusufzai, 'The Man from Bara'.

234 Ibid.

235 Ibid.

236 Nasrullah Afridi, 'Mangal Bagh Resigns as LI Chief'.

237 Profile of Mangal Bagh, www.pakspectator.com/profile-of-mangal-bagh/, 17 April 2008.

238 M. Waqar Bhatti, 'An Encounter with the Taliban', *The News* [Karachi], 21 July 2008.

239 Interview, senior intelligence officer, Peshawar, May 2010.

240 Rahimullah Yusufzai, 'The Man from Bara'.

241 Imtiaz Gul, 'Talibanisation of Khyber Agency'.

242 Rahimullah Yusufzai, 'The Man from Bara'.

243 M. Waqar Bhatti, 'An Encounter with the Taliban', *The News* [Karachi], 21 July 2008.

244 'Pakistan-Based Militant Group Lashkar-e-Islam Vows "to Spread Islam across the World"'.

245 *The News* [Lahore], 16 March 2007.

246 Urdu daily *Khabrain* [Lahore], 18 April 2008.

247 Rahimullah Yusufzai, 'The Man from Bara'.

248 'Mangal Bagh Claims He Refused to Join Taliban', *The News* [Karachi], 21 April 2008.

249 Javed Afridi, 'Anti-Taliban Militant Outfit's Head Shot Dead', *The News* [Karachi], 14 August 2008.

250 Rahimullah Yusufzai, 'The Man from Bara'.

251 Yousaf Ali, 'JUI-F Grand Jirga to Soothe Tirah Clashes', *The News* [Karachi], 7 July 2008.

252 'Bid to Assassinate Mangal Bagh Foiled', *The News* [Karachi], 23 July 2008.

253 Interview, senior intelligence officer, Peshawar, May 2010.

254 'Govt Suspends Bara Operation', *Daily Times* [Lahore], 5 July 2008.

255 'Govt Strikes Peace Deal with LI', *Statesman* [Peshawar], 10 July 2008.

256 'Mangal Bagh Reappears in Bara', *The News* [Karachi], 28 July 2008.

257 Tanzeem Ansar-ul-Islam, www.khyber.org/articles/2007/TanzeemAnsar-alIslam.shtml, accessed 25 November 2008.

258 Ibid.

259 Rahimullah Yusufzai, 'Talibanization Became a Cult in FATA', *The News on Sunday*.

260 Syed Saleem Shahzad, 'Smoke and Mirrors in the Khyber Valley', *Asia Times Online*, 1 July 2008, www.atimes.com/atimes/South_Asia/JG01Df01.html, accessed 6 December 2008.

261 Khadija Abdul Qahaar, 'About Amar Bil Maarouf Wa Nahi Munkar', Jihad Unspun, 12 September 2008, www.jihadunspun.com/indexside_internal.php?article=1002817&list=/index.php&, accessed 8 December 2008.

262 Ibid

263 Syed Saleem Shahzad, "Taliban bitten by a snake in the grass" *Asia Times Online*, www.atimes.com/atimes/South_Asia/JD26Df01.html, 26 April 2008

264 Syed Saleem Shahzad, "Smoke and mirrors in the Khyber Valley"

265 Ibid

266 Qazi Rauf, "Hakimullah Group claims responsibility for madrassa attack", *Daily Times*, Lahore, 03 May 2008

267 Nasrullah Afridi, "Seven activists of Bara-based group killed in Afghanistan", *The News*, Karachi, 10 November 2008

268 NEFA Exclusive: An Interview with Haji Namdar, 2 May 2008, www.nefafoundation.org/miscellaneous/FeaturedDocs/nefanamdar0808.pdf

3 TERRORISM AND KARACHI

1 Al Qaeda member. Syed Saleem Shahzad, 'New al-Qaeda Focus on NATO Supplies', *Asia Times*, 12 August 2008.

2 Ibid.

3 Interview, Dr Sohaib Suddle, Inspector General of Police, Sindh Province, and former Director General Intelligence Bureau (IB), June 2008.

4 Sohrab K. H. Katrak, *Karachi, that Was the Capital of Sindh* (Lahore, 1963).

5 *Pakistan 2008 Crime and Safety Report: Karachi*, OSAC, 20 February 1988.

6 More than 50 per cent of the foreign and Pakistani bank assets in Pakistan are concentrated in Karachi.

7 Syed Saleem Shahzad, 'New al-Qaeda Focus on NATO Supplies'.

8 Interview, Dr Sohaib Suddle.

9 Interview, Dost Ali, Police Headquarters, Karachi, June 2008.

10 Ibid.

11 Ibid.

12 Interview, Tariq Jamil, Additional Inspector General Sindh, previously Chief of Police of Karachi, June 2008.

13 Ibid.

14 Ibid.

15 Interview, Dost Ali.

16 Laurent Gayer, 'A Divided City: "Ethnic" and "Religious" Conflicts in Karachi, Pakistan', May 2003, www.ceri-sciencespo.com/archive/mai03/artlg.pdf., p. 3.

17 Tai Yong Tan and Gyanesh Kudaisya, *The Aftermath of Partition of South Asia* (London, 2000), p. 185, and Laurent Gayer, 'A Divided City', p. 3.

18 Laurent Gayer, "A Divided City', p. 3.

19 Ibid.

20 Ibid., p. 7.

21 Interview, Babar Khattack, Capitol City Police Officer (CCPO), with the rank of Additional Inspector General of Police. He was previously the head of the Special Branch for Sindh Province.

22 Laurent Gayer, "A Divided City', p. 4.

23 H. Meyerink, 'Karachi's Growth in Historical Perspective', *Between Basti Dwellers and Bureaucrats: Lessons in Squatter Settlement Upgrading Karachi*, ed. J. W. Schoorl, J. J. van der Linden and K. S. Yap (Oxford, 1983), p. 8.

24 Syed Shoaib Hasan, 'Crime and Punishment', *The Herald*, December 2001, p. 28.

25 Amir Farooqi, Senior Superintendent of Police, Central Police Office, Karachi, Pakistan, 1 June 2008.

26 Personal observation, Karachi, Pakistan, 1 June 2008.

27 Faraz Khan, 'Law Enforcers Afraid of Govt's Blurred Policy', *Daily Times* [Karachi], 25 August 2008. and Salis bin Perwaiz, "TTP Financiers Held in Karachi', *Daily Times* [Lahore], 25 August 2008.

28 Interview, Mirza Saud, Deputy Inspector General, CID, Provincial Police of Sindh, Karachi, May 2008. Mirza Saud is the most senior counter-terrorism officer in the Province of Sindh.

29 In 1969 a Jamaat-e-Islami member rammed a vehicle into an entourage when the Polish and Pakistani heads of state were at Karachi airport, killing the Polish Foreign Minster

and members of Pakistan's intelligence community.

30 ISI alleged that Jaye Sindh was supported by India's foreign intelligence service, the Research and Analysis Wing (RAW). In retaliation for ISI support for Sikh militancy in Punjab, RAW wanted to destabilize Karachi by supporting both Jaye Sindh and MQM.

31 Interview, Babar Khattack.

32 Ibid.

33 Ibid.

34 http://hazara.net/persecution/leaflet/leaflet.html.

35 Imtiaz Ali, 'The Father of the Afghan Taliban: An Interview with Maulana Sami-ul-Haq', *Global Terrorism Analysis*, IV/2 (23 May 2007).

36 Report on Terrorism in Sindh, CID Karachi, April 2008.

37 Interview, Babar Khattack.

38 Interview, Babar Khattack

39 Report on Terrorism in Sindh, CID Karachi, April 2008

40 Ibid.

41 Interview, Fayyaz Khan, Senior Suprintendent of Police, CID, Karachi, June 2008. Khan arrested the HUMA leadership.

42 Interview, Mirza Saud.

43 Yosri Fouda and Nick Fielding, *Masterminds of Terror: The Truth behind the Most Devastating Attack the World Has Ever Seen* (London, 2004). Fouda met and interviewed the Al Qaeda operational leadership in Karachi,.

44 Peter Bergen, *The Osama bin Laden I Know: An Oral History of the Al Qaeda Leader* (New York, 2006) and Peter Bergen, *Holy War, Inc.: Inside the Secret World of Bin Laden* (New York, 2001). Bergen provides numerous references to the Al Qaeda network in Karachi.

45 Interrogation, senior Al Qaeda operative, CIA, undisclosed location, 22 August 2003.

46 Interview, Ali Soufan, former Supervisor Agent, FBI, New York, July 2008.

47 Interrogation, senior Al Qaeda operative.

48 Interview, Ali Soufan, former Supervisor Agent, FBI, New York, July 2008.

49 Interrogation, senior Al Qaeda operative.

50 Ibid.

51 Ibid.

52 David Rohde, 'Threats and Responses: The Terror Network; Al Qaeda Uses Teeming Karachi as New Base, Pakistanis Say', *New York Times*, 1 November 2002.

53 'US: al-Qaeda Hit Hard by Arrests', *AP*, 1 May 2003

54 Walid bin Attash, US Director of National Intelligence, High Value Detainee Biographies, 6 September 2006 and 'US Alert on Karachi Consulate', BBC, 2 May 2003.

55 Massoud Ansari, 'Al-Qa'eda Bombers "Planned Attack" on Karachi US Consulate', 4 May 2003.

56 Ibid.

57 Syed Shoaib Hasan, BBC News, Islamabad, 6 August 2008.

58 Ali Abd al-Aziz Ali, US Director of National Intelligence, High Value Detainee Biographies, 6 September 2006.

59 Majid Khan, US Director of National Intelligence, High Value Detainee Biographies, 6 September 2006.

60 Eric Schmitt, 'Pakistani Suspected of Al Qaeda Ties is Held', *New York Times*, 5 August 2008.

61 Ahmed Khalfan Ghailani, US Director of National Intelligence, High Value Detainee Biographies, 6 September 2006.

62 Steve Butcher, 'Muslim Convert Charged over Alleged Links with Al Qaeda', *Sydney Morning Herald*, 19 November 2004.

63 www.miamiherald.com/multimedia/news/padilla/.

64 Sidney Jones, 'Still a Real Threat', *Tempo*, iv/6 (14–20 October 2003) [*Bali Bombing: One Year On*], and Karl Malakunas, 'JI Arrests Have "Dismantled" Cell: Minister', *The Age*, 18

December 2003.

65 'Some Still Roam Free', *Tempo*, iv/6 (14–20 October 2003) [*Bali Bombing: One Year On*]

66 Ibid.

67 Ibid.

68 Interview.

69 Salis bin Perwaiz, 'TTP Financiers Held in Karachi', *Daily Times* [Lahore], 25 August 2008.

70 Report on Terrorism in Sindh, CID Karachi, April 2008

71 Soon after the incident a case FIR No. 183/2007 u/s 302/324/427/34 3/4 Expl: 7-ATA, dated 19 October 2007, was registered by the SHO, PS Bahadurabad, Karachi, on behalf of the State.

72 Report on Terrorism in Sindh, CID Karachi, April 2008.

73 Ibid.

74 Interview, Fayyaz Khan, Senior Superintendent of Police, CID, Karachi Police, April 2008.

75 Report on Terrorism in Sindh, CID Karachi, April 2008.

76 Interview, Mirza Saud, DIG, CID, Karachi, May 2008. According to Saud, Akhtar had transformed into a man of peace under the influence of a cleric.

77 Report on Terrorism in Sindh, CID Karachi, April 2008.

78 Ibid.

79 Punjabi Taliban is the term used to identify them by the Pakistani Taliban. However, the constituent groups of Punjabi Taliban called themselves mujahideen. Interview, Syed Adnan Ali, Pakistan specialist, ICPVTR, Pakistan Desk, Rajaratnam School of International Studies, Singapore, 16 August 2008.

80 Report on Terrorism in Sindh, CID Karachi, April 2008.

81 Interview, counter-terrorism specialist, CID, Karachi, June 2001.

82 Interview, counter terrorism specialist, CID, Karachi, June 2001.

83 Ibid.

84 Ibid.

85 Interview, Dr Sohaib Suddle.

86 Interview, Mirza Saud.

87 Report on Terrorism in Sindh, CID Karachi, April 2008.

88 Ibid.

89 Ibid.

90 Interview, Mirza Saud

91 Report on Terrorism in Sindh, CID Karachi, April 2008.

92 Ibid.

93 Interviews, police officers, CID Karachi, April 2008.

94 Report on Terrorism in Sindh, CID Karachi, April 2008.

95 Interview, Dr Sohaib Suddle.

96 Interview, Amir Rana, Pakistan Institute of Peace Studies, Lahore, August 2008.

97 Interview, Tariq Jamil, Additional Inspector General Sindh, previously Chief of Police of Karachi, April 2008.

98 'Indian Madrassa Issues Fatwa against Terrorism', *Daily Times* [Karachi], 2 June 2008. p. A4.

99 Report on Terrorism in Sindh, CID Karachi, April 2008.

100 Interview, Dr Sohaib Suddle.

101 Ibid

102 Ibid

103 Interview, Babar Khattack, Police Chief of Karachi, April 2008.

104 Tufail Ahmad, 'The Role of Pakistan's Madrassas', Urdu-Pashtu Media Project, MEMRI, no. 462 (21 August 2008)

105 Ibid.

106 Interview, Dr Sohaib Suddle.

107 Interview with Arshad Ali, a leading investigative journalist, Regent Plaza Hotel, Karachi, by Khuram Iqbal, Research Analyst, ICPVTR, 7 August 2008.

108 Ibid.

109 Interview, Dr Sohaib Suddle.

110 Ibid.

111 A CD shop owner in Karachi said that FBI and Pakistani FIA generally ask questions about the international D-Company network, who is transferring the money and how many bank accounts they have. They are more interested in the foreign currency accounts in Pakistan and abroad, rather than what is actually earned through piracy and alternative financial resources. Interview, Amir Rana, Pakistan Institute of Peace Studies, Lahore, August 2008.

112 Interview, counter-terrorism specialist, CID, Karachi, June 2001.

113 While providing support for fear of harm is implicit coercion, providing support under a clear threat is explicit coercion.

114 There is widespread evidence of MQM presence in the Shi'a areas. Side by side with Shi'a flags, Khomeni posters, mosques and minarets of classic Iranian style, and Shi'as dressed in black, MQM flags and MQM colours painted on buildings were prominent. Personal observation, Karachi, 1 June 2008.

115 Amir Farooqi, Senior Superintendent of Police, Central Police Office, Karachi, 1 June 2008.

116 The student wing of PMLN also doubles up as its militia wing.

117 Interview, Dost Ali, Superintendent of Police, Police Headquarters, Karachi, April 2008.

118 Interview, Babar Khattack.

119 Interview, Dr Sohaib Suddle.

4 MAINLAND PAKISTAN TERRORIST GROUPS

1 Jamiat Ahle Hadith, Rantburg, Organizations, www.rantburg.com/dOrg.asp?ID=106 .

2 'Lashkar Moves to Give Struggle a "Pure Kashmir Colour"', *The Hindu*, 27 December 2001.

3 'In the Spotlight: Lashkar-i-Taiba ("Army of the Pure")', CDI Terrorism Project, 12 August 2002, www.cdi.org/terrorism/lt-pr.cfm, accessed 5 August 2010.

4 'General History of the Dispute: The Truth about Kashmir', www.armyinkashmir.org/history/history4.html.

5 Government of India, 'Pakistan's Involvement in Terrorism against India', p. 57.

6 Ibid.

7 'Brutal Terrorist Group Active in Kashmir: Lashkar-e-Toiba ('Army of the Pure')', www.hvk.org/hvk/articles/0701/6.html.

8 Saeed's address to the Lahore Press Club on 18 February 1996.

9 'Pakistani Terrorists Threaten to Unfurl Flag at Red Fort', *The Sword of Truth*, 14 December 1999, www.swordoftruth.com/swordoftruth/archives/newswatch/199951/news7.html. India celebrates its Independence Day every year on 15 August at the Red Fort in New Delhi.

10 'Who Are the Kashmir Militants?', BBC News, 19 February 2003, http://news.bbc.co.uk/1/hi/world/south_asia/1719612.stm, accessed 3 November 2009.

11 Seema Mustafa, 'The Asian Age', 8 February 1999, www.jammu-kashmir.com/archives/archives1999/99february8.htm.

12 One of the LET's leaders, Abdul Rehman Makki, claimed in a rally organized in Islamabad in February 2000 that the organization had a network in Hyderabad, which would become active in the next six months, and that they would be making a declaration of separation (from India). See 'Militant Chiefs Warn Musharraf', *The Hindu*, 6 February 2000, www.hinduonnet.com/2000/02/06/stories/03060003.htm

13 'Profile: Lashkar-e-Toiba', BBC News, 26 August 2003, http://news.bbc.co.uk/1/hi/world/south_asia/3181925.stm, accessed 4 November 2008.

14 'Lashkar-e-Toiba Bases near Mumbai?', hinduworld.tripod.com, 16 August 2001, http://hinduworld.tripod.com/views/letbases.html.

15 'City a Vital Base for LET's Covert Plans', *The Hindu*, 24 Nov 2002.

16 'Lashkar-e-Toiba Bases near Mumbai?'.

17 'Lashkar Moves to Give Struggle a "Pure Kashmir Colour"', *The Hindu*, 25 December 2001, www.jammu-kashmir.com/archives/archives2001/kashmir20011225a.html.

18 'Lashkar-e-Toiba Shifts Shop', Tehelka.com, 27 December 2001, www.tehelka.com/ channels/ currentaffairs/2001/dec/27/printable/ca122701lashpr.htm.

19 'Lashkar Operating under Four Names', *The Tribune*, 25 July 2002.

20 'Patterns of Global Terrorism 2002', US Department of State, 30 April 2003.

21 'Lashkar-e-Toiba', Kashmir Herald on the Web, 1/8 (January 2002), www.kashmirherald.com/profiles/lashkaretoiba.html.

22 B. Raman, 'Banning the Banned: Counter-Terrorism a la Musharraf', South Asia Analysis Group, Paper no. 842 (20 November 2003), www.saag.org/papers9/paper842.html.

23 '60 Offices, Seminaries Sealed in Punjab: Crackdown Launched in Peshawar', *The Dawn*, 17 November 2003.

24 *Daily Times* [Lahore], 19 November 2003.

25 Mohammad Shehzad, 'Banned LET Collects Millions in Charity, Hides', www.pakistan-facts.com/ article.php?story=20030324114000592.

26 'Patterns of Global Terrorism 2002'.

27 B. Raman, 'LET: Al Qaeda's Clone', South Asia Analysis Group, Paper no. 729, 7 July 2003, www.saag.org/papers8/paper729.htm.

28 'Patterns of Global Terrorism 2002'.

29 Seema Mustafa, 'The Asian Age'.

30 'Patterns of Global Terrorism 2002'.

31 'Pakistan: Madrasas, Extremism and the Military', ICG Asia Report, no. 36, 29 July 2002, p. 16, www.911investigations.net/IMG/pdf/doc-957.pdf?PHPSESSID=b92a12c5d30b8d5bb28 c7fccd4b651fb.

32 Kaushik Kapisthalam, 'Pakistan Faces its Jihadi Demons in Iraq', *Asia Times Online*, 14 July 2004, www.atimes.com/atimes/South_Asia/FG14Df04.htm.

33 'Hafiz Mohammed Saeed: Pakistan's Heart of Terror', *Kashmir Herald*, II/2, July 2002, www.kashmirherald.com/profiles/HafizMohammedSaeed.html.

34 'Allah's Army', www.sabrang.com/cc/comold/march98/neighbor.htm.

35 Since the early 1990s, Pakistan has observed 5 February as an official holiday known as 'Kashmir Day'.

36 Mohammad Shehzad, 'The Apocalyptic Vision of Hafiz Saeed', SikhSpectrum.com, no. 10, March 2003, www.sikhspectrum.com/032003/hafiz.htm.

37 'Young Terrorists Signing Up by Thousands', OneWorld.net, www.fourwinds10.com/news/ 05-government/H-war/03-terrorism-war/2003/05H3-08-08-03-young-terrorists-sign-up-by-thousands.html.

38 'Invitation to a New Markaz', *The News on Sunday*, 26 October 2003, www.jang.com.pk/ thenews/oct2003-weekly/nos-26-10-2003/dia.htm#1.

39 Mohammad Shehzad, 'The Apocalyptic Vision of Hafiz Saeed'.

40 Kaushik Kapisthalam, 'Lashkar-e-Musharraf', Observer Research Foundation, www.observerindia.com/analysis/A057.htm.

41 Urdu daily *Nawa-e-Waqt*, 18 March 2006.

42 'Sorry: Your Extremism is Showing', *Daily Times*, 11 May 2006.

43 'Hafiz Mohammed Saeed: Pakistan's Heart of Terror'.

44 'Pakistan Freezes Militant Fund', BBC News, 24 December 2001.

45 'Pak Arrests Lashkar, Jaish Chiefs', *Indian Express*, 31 December 2001.

46 *People's Daily*, 2 April 2002, http://fpeng.peopledaily.com.cn/200204/02/eng20020402_ 93306.shtml.

47 'ISI Toys with Sept 11-Type Terror', Independent Media Centre, 4 February 2002, http:// india.indymedia.org/en/2003/02/3100.shtml.

48 ISI Toys with Sept 11-Type Terror', Independent Media Centre, 4 February 2002, http://

india.indymedia.org/en/2003/02/3100.shtml.

49 S1 Toys with Sept 11-Type Terror', Independent Media Centre, 4 February 2002, http://
india.indymedia.org/en/2003/02/3100.shtml.

50 'Brutal Terrorist Group Active in Kashmir: Lashkar-e-Toiba – "Army of the Pure"',
www.hvk.org/hvk/articles/0701/6.html.

51 Nearly 300,000 Kashmiri Pandits, the original Hindu inhabitants of Kashmir valley, have
been driven out of their ancestral homeland because of terrorist activities; www.kashmir-
information.com/Terrorism/machine.html.

52 'Lashkar-e-Toiba: Army of the Pure', Institute for Conflict Management, www.ict.org.il/
inter_ter/orgdet.cfm?orgid=81.

53 'Allah's Army', www.sabrang.com/cc/comold/march98/neighbor.htm.

54 'Profile: Lashkar-e-Toiba', BBC News, 26 August 2003, http://news.bbc.co.uk/1/hi/
world/south_asia/3181925.stm.

55 'Allah's Army'.

56 B. Raman, 'Lashkar-e-Toiba: Its Past, Present and Future', www.saag.org/papers2/
paper175.htm.

57 'Terror in the Hands of a Teenager', www.atimes.com/atimes/South_Asia/DI17Df05.html.

58 Praveen Swami, 'Lethal Remittance', Front Line, xxi/1 (3–16 January 2004), www.flonnet.
com/fl2101/stories/20040116003202600.htm.

59 Ibid.

60 'Negotiating Peace in Kashmir', 18 June 2000, www.chowk.com/show_article.cgi?aid=
00000826&channel=civic%20center.

61 Mohammad Shehzad, 'The Apocalyptic Vision of Hafiz Saeed'.

62 'Professor Terror', op. cit.

63 Ibid.

64 B. Raman, 'Time to Be on our Toes', The Week, 17 July 2005, www.the-week.com/25jul17/
currentevents_article10.htm.

65 'Jamaat Al Dawa', Rantburg: The Organizations, www.rantburg.com/thugburg/dOrg.asp?
ID=77.

66 'Lashkar-e-Toiba is New Al Qaida Face' , Observer Research Foundation, 15 June 2003,
www.observerindia.com/analysis/A002.htm.

67 'Group Profile: Lashkar-e-Taiba (LET)', www.start.umd.edu/start/data/tops/terrorist_
organization_profile.asp?id=66, addressed 17 August 2010.

68 'Terrorist Group Profiles: Lashkar-e-Tayyiba', http://library.nps.navy.mil/home/tgp/lt.htm.

69 'US Pakistani Extremists Aid Terrorists', Seattle Post-Intelligencer, 14 September, 2005.

70 'Jihad Recruitment is on the Rise', July 29, 2003, www.pakistan-facts.com/article.php?
story=20030729154610902.

71 Ibid.

72 John Wilson, 'Time to Decapitate Lashkar', www.observerindia.com/analysis/A467.htm.

73 'Allah's Army', reproduced in People's Review, 7–14 January 1999.

74 'Terror in the Hands of a Teenager'.

75 Ibid.

76 'Jihad Recruitment is on the Rise'.

77 Ibid.

78 Ibid.

79 National Herald, Annual Issue, 1999, reproduced in People's Review, 7–14 January 1999,

80 www.expressindia.com/kashmir/kashmirlive/lashkar.html.

81 B. Raman, 'Markaz Dawa al Irshad: Talibanisation of Nuclear Pakistan', www.saag.org/
papers/paper6.html.

82 'JEM, LET among 5 Banned Outfits Back in Business', Daily Excelsior, 11 September 2003.

83 B. Raman, 'Banning the Banned: Counter-Terrorism à la Musharraf', South Asia Analysis
Group, Paper no. 842 (20 November 2003).

84 'Invitation to a New Markaz', The News on Sunday, 26 October 2003, www.jang.com.pk/

thenews/oct2003-weekly/nos-26-10-2003/dia.htm#1.

85 Ibid.

86 'Young Terrorists Signing Up by Thousands'.

87 'Guns Won't Be Muzzled as Jihadis Feel Musharraf Has Betrayed Them', *South Asia Tribune*, www.satribune.com/archives/jan11_17_04/opinion_amirmir.htm.

88 'Professor Terror', op. cit.

89 'Musharraf Blocking Jihad against US: Hafiz Saeed', op. cit.

90 'India's Most Wanted', *Frontline*, XIX/2 (19 Jan – 1 Feb 2002).

91 'General's Manoeuvre', *Frontline,* XIX/2 (19 Jan – 1 Feb 2002), www.frontlineonnet.com/fl1902/19020040.htm.

92 Reports vary with regard to the arrest of militants belonging to the five militant organizations that the Pakistani government declared as terrorist outfits. The Associated Press reported on 15 January 2002 that 'nearly 1,500 extremists' were detained. Susan Milligan of the *Boston Globe* reported '1,957 people [taken] into custody' and 'the closing of 615 offices . . . affiliated with any of the five militant groups' (17 January 2002). These latter numbers are close to those reported by *Dawn* (16 January 2002). The *Los Angeles Times* reported on 29 January 2002 that 'police have rounded up 2,500 people'.

93 See *Dawn*, 16 January 2002.

94 "LET Leader among 15 Held in AJK Raid", *The News* [Karachi], 9 December 2008.

95 Janghvi is derived from Jhang, a region in Punjab, http://canadagazette.gc.ca/partII/2003/20030619-x/html/extra-e.html.

96 'Public Safety and Emergency Preparedness Canada', www.psepc-sppcc.gc.ca/national_security/counter-terrorism/Entities_e.asp, accessed 31 March 2005.

97 Naziha Syed Ali, 'End of Manhunt', *Newsline* [Lahore] (June 2002).

98 Interview, senior intelligence officer, Peshawar, May 2010.

99 'Lashkar e Jhangvi', www.satp.org/satporgtp/countries/pakistan/terroristoutfits/Lej.htm, accessed 31 March 2005.

100 Feature report, Urdu daily *Ummat* [Karachi], 17 July 2002

101 ARY TV, 16 March 2008.

102 Naziha Syed Ali, 'End of Manhunt', *Newsline* [Karachi], June 2002.

103 'In Death, as in Life', *Newsline* [Lahore] (October 2003).

104 Ibid.

105 Amir Mir, "The True face of Jihadis", Mashal Books, Lahore, 2004, p. 179

106 Interview, senior intelligence officer, Peshawar, May 2010.

107 Shahzad Malik, "LJ forming new militant cells" *Daily Times*, Lahore, 2 October 2006

108 Mohammad Amir Rana has reviewed these points in Jan 2005 at IDSS, NTU, Singapore during a research visit.

109 Naziha Syed Ali, "End of Manhunt", *Newsline*, Lahore, June 2002

110 Amir Rana, 'LJ Forms Squad to Avenge Azam Tariq Murder', *Daily Times* [Lahore], 29 January 2008.

111 Shahzad Malik, 'LJ Forming New Militant Cells', *Daily Times* [Lahore], 2 October 2006.

112 Ibid.

113 Amir Rana, *A to Z of Jehadi Organizations in Pakistan* (Lahore, 2006), p. 206.

114 Ibid.

115 'Lashkar e Jhangvi', www.satp.org/satporgtp/countries/pakistan/terroristoutfits/Lej.htm, accessed 31 March 2005.

116 Ibid.

117 Ibid.

118 Ibid.

119 Amir Rana, *A to Z of Jehadi Organizations in Pakistan*, p. 208.

120 Conversation with Mohammad Amir Rana, IDSS, NTU, January 2005

121 'Terrorist Group Profile: Lashkar-e-Jhangvi', MIPT Terrorism Knowledge Base, www.start.umd.edu/start/data/tops/terrorist_organization_profile.asp?id=65, accessed 17 August

2010.

122 Shahzad Malik, '17 Banned Groups Warned against Collecting Hides', *Daily Times* [Lahore], 28 December 2006.

123 Aayan Ali, 'Extremist Militants or Kidnappers?', *Daily Times* [Lahore], 22 January 2006.

124 Massoud Ansari, 'A Profile in Terror: The Story of a Sectarian Terrorist's Life by the Gun', *Newsline* (August 2003).

125 Massoud Ansari, 'The Enemy Within', *Newsline* [Karachi] (June 2004).

126 Maqbool Arshad, Urdu monthly *Fact* [Lahore], xiii (November 2004).

127 Riaz Suhail, BBC Urdu.

128 Animesh Roul, 'Lashkar-e-Jhangvi: Sectarian Violence in Pakistan and Ties to International Terrorism', *Terrorism Monitor*, iii/11 (2 June 2005), www.jamestown.org/single/?no_cache=1&tx_ttnews[tt_news]=497, accessed 9 August 2010.

129 '"Lashkar e Jhangvi", www.satp.org/satporgtp/countries/pakistan/terroristoutfits/Lej.htm, accessed 31 March 2005.

130 'Lashkar-e-Janghvi', *Kashmir Herald*, ii/9 (February 2003), www.kashmirherald.com/profiles/Lashkar-e-Jhangvi.html, accessed 31 March 2005.

131 Afzal Khan, 'The War on Terror and the Politics of Violence in Pakistan', *Terrorism Monitor*, ii/13 (1 July 2004), p. 7.

132 US State Department, *Patterns of Global Terrorism 2003* (April 2004), www.state.gov/documents/organization/31912.pdf, accessed 1 April 2005.

133 'Lashkar-e-Jhangvi', South Asia Terrorism Portal, www.satp.org/satporgtp/countries/pakistan/terroristoutfits/Lej.htm, accessed 31 March 2005.

134 Amir Mir, 'Plot to Kill Musharraf Unearthed', *The News*, 18 December 2008, http://thenews.com.pk/arc_default.asp.

135 'In Death, as in Life', *Newsline* [Lahore] (October 2003).

136 C. Christine Fair, *Urban Battle Fields of South Asia: Lessons Learned from Sri Lanka, India and Pakistan* (Santa Monica, CA, 2004), p. 110.

137 US Department of State, *Patterns of Global Terrorism 2003*, p. 127.

138 Christine Fair, *Urban Battle Fields of South Asia*, p. 110.

139 Ibid.

140 Ibid.

141 Ibid, p. 111.

142 Ibid.

143 Amir Rana, *A to Z of Jehadi Organizations in Pakistan*, p. 263.

144 'Significance of Qari Saifullah Akhtar's arrest', *Daily Times* [Lahore], 9 August 2004.

145 Ibid.

146 Amir Rana, *A to Z of Jehadi Organizations in Pakistan*, p. 269.

147 Urdu monthly *Fact* (September 2004), www.fact.com.pk/archives/sept/facturdu/qari.htm, accessed 29 February 2008.

148 'Qari Saifullah's Arrest Shows No One Being Spared', *Daily Times* [Lahore], 9 August 2004

149 Amir Rana, *A to Z of Jehadi Organizations in Pakistan*, p. 265

150 Urdu monthly *Fact* [Lahore] (September 2004).

151 'Significance of Qari Saifullah Akhtar's Arrest'.

152 Interview with Mohammad Amir Rana, IDSS, January 2005.

153 P. G. Rajamohan, 'Harkat-ul-Jihad-al-Islami Bangladesh (HUJI-BD)', Institute for Conflict Management (ICM), accessed 11 March 2005 from ICM's portal.

154 Amir Rana, *A to Z of Jehadi Organizations in Pakistan*, p. 266.

155 These insights were provided by Mohammad Amir Rana in his discussions with ICPVTR research analysts, IDSS, NTU, December 2004.

156 Arif Jamal, 'Fighter Yes, Thinker No', www.pakistanlink.com/Letters/2004/Aug04/27/02.html, accessed 29 February 2008.

157 Amir Rana, *A to Z of Jehadi Organizations in Pakistan*, p. 267.

158 Ibid., p. 268.

159 Amir Rana, *Jihad* (Lahore, 2004).
160 'Significance of Qari Saifullah Akhtar's Arrest'.
161 Amir Rana, *A to Z of Jehadi Organizations in Pakistan*, p. 267.
162 Urdu weekly *Akhbar-e-Jehan* [Karachi] (28 Feb–6 March 2005).
163 'UN List of Affiliates of al-Qaeda and the Taliban', www.un.org/sc/committees/1267/consoltablelist.shtml, accessed 17 October 2007.
164 'Significance of Qari Saifullah Akhtar's Arrest'.
165 Ibid.
166 Urdu daily *Khabrein* [Lahore] (4 August 2004).
167 'Significance of Qari Saifullah Akhtar's Arrest'.
168 Urdu monthly *Fact* [Lahore] (September 2004).
169 Maqbool Arshad, *Jehadis* (Lahore, 2006).
170 Amir Rana, *A to Z of Jehadi Organizations in Pakistan*, p. 269.
171 Arif Jamal, 'Fighter Yes, Thinker No'.
172 Urdu daily *Khabrein* [Lahore], 12 January 2002.
173 'Qari Saifullah in Custody', *Daily Times*, 9 August 2004.
174 'Militant Linked to BB's Murder Arrested', *The Post* [Lahore], 27 February 2008.
175 'The Karachi Raid', *The Post* [Lahore], 31 January 2008.
176 Ibid.
177 Urdu weekly *Nida-e-Millat* [Lahore] (24–30 June 2004).
178 Pakistan 2008 Crime and Safety Report: Karachi, OSAC, 20 February 1988.
179 Interview, counter-terrorism specialist, CID, Karachi, June 2008.
180 Ibid.
181 Ibid.
182 'Jundullah Claims 600 Suicide Bombers Present in Karachi', *Daily Times* [Lahore], 4 February 2008.
183 Ibid.
184 'A Rapist Turned Militant', *Dawn* [Karachi], 2 February 2008.
185 'Qasim Toori Captured, not Killed: Minister', *The Post* [Lahore], 31 January 2008.
186 Editorial: The trail of Jandullah, *Daily Times*, Lahore, 31 January 2008
187 Ibid.
188 'Jundullah Claims 600 Suicide Bombers Present in Karachi'.
189 'Jundullah Suspect Makes Startling Disclosures', *The News*, Karachi, 02 February 2008
190 'A Rapist Turned Militant'.
191 Interview, counter-terrorism specialist, CID, Karachi, June 2008.
192 'Jundullah Claims 600 Suicide Bombers Present in Karachi'.
193 'Gunbattle in Karachi: 7 Militants, 2 Cops Killed', *The Post* [Lahore], 30 January 2008.
194 Urdu weekly *Nida-e-Millat* [Lahore] (24–30 June 2004).
195 Ibid.
196 Interview, counter-terrorism specialist, CID, Karachi, June 2008.
197 Ibid.
198 Interview, Khuram Iqbal, CID Sindh officer, Karachi,6 August 2008.
199 Interview, Fayyaz Khan, CID, Karachi Police, April 2008.
200 Ibid.
201 Abbas Naqvi, 'They Were Targeting Karachi and its Leaders', *Daily Times* [Lahore], 18 February 2007.
202 Interview by Khuram Iqbal of CID Sindh officer in Karachi.
203 Abbas Naqvi, 'They Were Targeting Karachi and its Leaders'.
204 Ibid.
205 Ibid.
206 Qari Shahzad, who was wanted by the authorities with a reward of Rs 500,000, was killed in Wana while making a bomb.
207 Abbas Naqvi, 'They Were Targeting Karachi and its Leaders'.

208 Ibid.

209 Interview by Khuram Iqbal of CID Sindh officer in Karachi.

210 Ibid.

211 Ibid.

212 Abbas Naqvi, 'They Were Targeting Karachi and its Leaders'.

213 Ibid. The police officers they planned to target were Raja Umar Khatab, Farooq Awan, Fayyaz Khan and Manzur Mughal.

214 Interview, Fayyaz Khan, CID, Karachi Police, April 2008.

215 'New Emerging Jihadi Militant Groups: Tehrik-e-Islami Lashkar-e-Muhammadi (TILM)', CID, Karachi, April 2008.

216 Ibid.

217 Others arrested were Muhammad Kashif Ehsan alias Sohail, Muhammad Bin Ahmad, Muhammad Arshad alias Asad, Muhammad Zeeshan alias Mastan Baloch, Waseem Ahmad alias Waseem. Urdu daily *Ummat* [Karachi], 27 February 2008.

218 Ibid.

219 New Emerging Jihadi Militant Groups: Tehrik-e-Islami Lashkar-e-Muhammadi (TILM)'.

220 Interview by Khuram Iqbal of CID Sindh officer, Karachi, 6 August 2008.

221 Interview, Saud Mirza, DIG, CID, April 2008.

222 'New Emerging Jihadi Militant Groups: Tehrik-e-Islami Lashkar-e-Muhammadi (TILM)'.

223 Ibid.

224 Weekly *Takbir* [Karachi] (5–11 March 2008).

225 Interview by Khuram Iqbal of CID Sindh officer, Karachi, 6 August 2008.

226 'New Emerging Jihadi Militant Groups: Tehrik-e-Islami Lashkar-e-Muhammadi (TILM)'.

227 Ibid.

228 Faraz Khan, '7 Rimpa Plaza NGO Workers' Killers Held after Six Years', *Daily Times* [Lahore], 27 February 2008

229 'New Emerging Jihadi Militant Groups: Tehrik-e-Islami Lashkar-e-Muhammadi (TILM)'.

230 'Three "Killers" of Christian Charity Workers Held', *Daily Times* [Lahore], 15 April 2008.

231 Urdu daily *Ummat* [Karachi], 27 February 2008.

232 Amir Mir, 'Shi'a-Sunni Conflict in Pakistan', http://lrrp.wordpress.com/2004/11/10/shia-sunni-conflict-in-pakistan-by-amir-mir, accessed 21 August 2008.

233 Amir Rana, *A to Z of Jehadi Organizations in Pakistan*, p. 414.

234 South Asia Terrorism Portal (SATP), 'Sipah-e-Mohammed Pakistan, Terrorist Group of Pakistan', www.satp.org/satporgtp/countries/pakistan/terroristoutfits/SMP.htm.

235 B. Raman, 'Musharaf's Ban: An Analysis', South Asia Analysis Group, Paper no. 395, 18 January 2002, www.hvk.org/hvk/articles/0102/71.html.31990.

236 South Asia Terrorism Portal (SATP), 'Tehreek-e-Jaferia Pakistan, Terrorist Group of Pakistan'.

237 Amir Rana, *A to Z of Jehadi Organizations in Pakistan*, p. 414.

238 'Bail Plea Of Raza Naqvi Put Off', *The Nation* [Lahore], 23 October 2003.

239 South Asia Terrorism Portal (SATP), 'Tehreek-e-Jaferia Pakistan, Terrorist Group of Pakistan'.

240 B. Raman, 'The Karachi Attack: The Kashmir Link', 26 February 2003, www.rediff.com/news/2003/feb/26raman.htm.

241 Ibid.

242 Amir Rana, *A to Z of Jehadi Organizations in Pakistan*, p. 416.

243 Ibid.

244 www.satp.org/satporgtp/countries/pakistan/terroristoutfits/SMP.htm.

245 B. Raman, 'Pakistan: The Shia Anger', South Asia Analysis Group, Paper no. 810, 7 October 2003, www.saag.org/papers9/paper810.html.

246 South Asia Terrorism Portal (SATP), 'Sipah-e-Mohammed Pakistan, Terrorist Group of Pakistan'.

247 Ibid.

248 http://satp.org/satporgtp/countries/pakistan/terroristoutfits/HuMA.htm, accessed 28 August 2008.

249 'Life for 3 for Bid to Kill Pakistan's Musharraf', www.reuters.com/article/featuredCrisis/idUSISL106678, accessed 27 August 2008.

250 Interview, counter-terrorism specialist, CID, Karachi, June 2008.

251 Ibid.

252 Amir Rana, 'The Dos and Don'ts of Terrorism', *Daily Times* [Lahore], 5 June 2004.

253 Comment by Major-General Salahuddin, head of the Rangers, at a press conference on 8 July 2002, see http://findarticles.com/p/articles/mi_qn4158/is_20020709/ai_n12629153, accessed 28 August 2008.

254 Interview, counter-terrorism specialist, CID, Karachi, June 2008.

255 Amir Rana, 'The Dos and Don'ts of Terrorism'.

256 Amir Rana, *Jihad* (Lahore, 2004).

257 Interview, counter-terrorism specialist, CID, Karachi, June 2008.

258 The bombs went off between four and ten minutes apart.

259 *Daily Times* [Lahore], 5 April 2006.

260 'Indian Home Minister L. K. Advani's Statement on the Identity of the Hijackers', SAPRA India, www.subcontinent.com/sapra/terrorism/tr_2000_01_06_001.html.

261 B. Raman, 'Jaish-e-Mohammad Rebaptised?', South Asia Analysis Group, Paper no. 337, 12 October 2001, www.southasiaanalysis.org/papers4/paper337.html, accessed 11 August 2010..

262 'The Terrorist Threat: Proscribed Terrorist Groups', UK Home Office, http://tna.euro parchive.org/20100419081706/http://security.homeoffice.gov.uk/terrorist-threat/proscribed-terrorist-orgs/proscribed-terrorist-groups/

263 Interview with Amir Rana, IDSS, NTU, January 2005.

264 Government of India, 'Pakistan's Involvement in Terrorism against India', pp. 16–17.

265 Niraj Kumar, Joint Commissioner of Police, New Delhi, cited in 'India Claims to Avert Spectacular Attack', Associated Press, 31 August 2003.

266 Al-Rasheed, 'From a Welfare Trust to a Terrorist Empire', http://meadev.nic.in/news/clippings/20010927/ht1.htm.

267 'Banned Terror Outfits Resurface in Pakistan', *Hindu International*, 11 September 2003, www.hindu.com/thehindu/2003/09/11/stories/2003091112071200.htm, accessed 6 May 2005.

268 Ibid.

269 'Jaish e Mohammad', www.fas.org/irp/world/para/jem.htm, accessed 6 May 2005.

270 B. Raman, 'Jaish-e-Mohammad Rebaptised?'

271 'Profile: Maulana Masood Azhar', BBC News: South Asia, 16 December 2002, http://news.bbc.co.uk/1/hi/world/south_asia/578369.stm, accessed 5 May 2005.

272 Ibid.

273 UN Press Release GA/L/3007, 3 October 1996, http://66.102.7.104/search?q=cache:WGLpW1MQjs8J:www.fas.org/nuke/control/nt/docs/ga-l-3007.htm+Hans+Christian+Ostro+&hl=en, accessed 5 May 2005.

274 'All Western Hostages Killed, Claims Harkat Militant', SAPRA India

275 'Information on Hijacked Indian Airlines Flight IC 814', Embassy of India, Washington, DC, www.indianembassy.org/archive/IC_814.htm#Background%20Information, accessed 6 May 2005.

276 Ibid.

277 Interview with Amir Rana, Director Pak Institute for Peace Studies, Islamabad, at IDSS, NTU, Singapore, January 2005.

278 Ibid.

279 Jason Burke, *Al-Qaeda: Casting a Shadow of Terror* (London, 2003), p. 81.

280 Ibid, p. 82.

281 Ibid.

282 Paul Thompson, 'Sept 11's Smoking Gun: The Many Faces of Saeed Sheikh', updated 25 Feb 2003, www.cooperativeresearch.org/timeline/main/essaysaeed.html, accessed 14

December 2004.

283 The camp, located 15 km southwest of Kabul, was run by Harakat-ul-Mujahideen and Arabs loyal to Osama bin Laden. 'Afghanistan: Militia Activities', www.globalsecurity. org/military/world/afghanistan/militia-fac.htm, accessed 6 May 2005. Officially Al Qaeda did not established any training camps, but supported training for HUM and HUJI. Interview with Amir Rana, IDSS, NTU, January 2005.

284 Government of India, 'Pakistan's Involvement in Terrorism against India', p. 41.

285 www.fas.org/irp/world/para/jem.htm.

286 B. Raman, 'Musharraf and Terrorism', www.sarg.org.

287 Government of India, 'Pakistan's Involvement in Terrorism against India'.

288 www.hindustantimes.com/news/5797_00290008,75500.htm, 21 October 2002.

289 Interview with Mohammad Amir Rana, IDSS, NTU, January 2005.

290 K. Santhanam, Sreedhar, Sudhir Saxena and Manish, *Jihadis in Jammu and Kashmir: A Portrait Gallery* (New Delhi, 2003), p. 200.

291 'Banned Pak Terror Groups Back in Action', *Daily Excelsior*, 11 September 2003, www.hvk. org/articles/0903/132.html, accessed 16 August 2010.

292 'India Claims to Avert Spectacular Attack', Associated Press, 31 August 2003.

293 Government of India, 'Pakistan's Involvement in Terrorism against India', p. 31.

294 *Indian Express*, 31 December 2001, www.indiaexpress.com/news/world/20011231-0.html.

295 *The Tribune*, 4 October 2002.

296 '60 Offices, Seminaries Sealed in Punjab: Crackdown Launched in Peshawar', *Dawn* [Karachi], 17 November 2003.

297 'Jamali Defends Action against Banned Outfits', *Dawn* [Karachi], 17 November 2003.

298 B. Raman, 'Banning the Banned: Counter-Terrorism à la Musharraf', South Asia Analysis Group, Paper no. 842 (20 November 2003).

299 Associated Press, 16 September 2003.

300 Urdu Monthly *Fact*, May 2006, www.fact.com.pk

301 'The War Within?', *Newsline*, June 2001, www.newsline.com.pk/NewsJune2001/coverstory4.htmn.

302 It is important to understand that there are two major sects in Islam: Sunni (Ahle-e-Sunnat) and Shi'a (Ahle-e-Tashi). Barelvi and Deobandi are known as the different subsects within the Sunni school of thought

303 Official ST handout obtained from an ST activist during a field interview, Karachi, September 2006.

304 Hasan Mansoor, 'From Sectarian to Mainstream Politics: ST Remains at a Crossroads', *Daily Times* [Lahore], 13 April 2006.

305 asan Mansoor, 'From Sectarian to Mainstream Politics: ST Remains at a Crossroads', *Daily Times* [Lahore], 13 April 2006.

306 Ibid.

307 Amir Rana, *A to Z of Jehadi Organizations in Pakistan* (Lahore, 2006), p. 377.

308 www.sunnirazvi.org/library/booklets/deoband.htm#Beliefs%20of%20deobandi,%20 tablighi%20&%20wahabi%20groups.

309 ttp://www.sunnirazvi.org/library/booklets/deoband.htm#Beliefs%20of%20deobandi, %20tablighi%20&%20wahabi%20groups.

310 'ST Announces 71 Candidates for 2008 Election', *Daily Times* [Lahore], 4 December 2007/

311 Interview with ST activist, Karachi, September 2006.

312 Amir Rana, *A to Z of Jehadi Organizations in Pakistan*, p. 377.

313 'Sunni Tehreek Takes a Hit', *Daily Times* [Lahore], 13 April 2006.

314 '1m Sacrifices but Lower Hide Collection', *Daily Times* [Lahore], 4 December 2007.

315 'Dawat-e-Islami Beats KKF in Zakat Collection', *Daily Times* [Lahore], 30 October 2006.

316 Amir Rana, *A to Z of Jehadi Organizations in Pakistan*, p. 374.

317 Ibid.

318 Hasan Mansoor, 'From Sectarian to Mainstream Politics: ST Remains at a Crossroads'.

319 The MQM manifesto can be assessed at www.mqminternational.org/site/manifesto2008. aspx.

320 Ibid.

321 Dr Haider K. Nizamani, 'MQM on Slippery Slope', *Daily Times* [Lahore], 29 May 2007.

322 MQM Factsheet, published by Fedration of American Scientists, www.insaf.pk/Forum/tabid/53/forumid/1/tpage/1/view/topic/postid/2730/Default.aspx#2730, accessed 18 August 2008.

323 Report by Fareed Farooqui, *Daily Times* [Lahore], 3 May 2008.

324 Interview with Muhammad Ali, ex-member of MQM, Karachi.

325 Munir Ahmad, *Altaf Hussain* (Lahore, 1996), p. 268.

326 Ibid.

327 www.mqminternational.org.

328 MQM manifesto.

329 'Terrorist Organization Profile: Muttahida Qami Movement (MQM)', www.start.umd.edu/start/data/tops/terrorist_organization_profile.asp?id=73, accessed 17 August 2010.

330 Dr Haider K. Nizamani, 'MQM on Slippery Slope'.

331 MQM Factsheet.

332 www.insaf.pk/Forum/tabid/53/forumid/1/tpage/1/view/topic/postid/2730/Default.aspx#2730, accessed 28 August 2008.

333 Ibid.

334 *The Herald* [Karachi], June 1994, pp. 35–6.

335 Azhar Abbas, *The Herald* [Karachi], September 1998.

336 Ibid.

337 Ibid.

338 www.atimes.com/atimes/South_Asia/EG09Df09.html.

339 'Tehrik-e-Islami Won't Leave MMA', *Daily Times* [Lahore], 2 August 2003.

340 'Naqvi Claims TJP now Functional', *Daily Times* [Lahore], 11 July 2005.

341 www.satp.org/satporgtp/countries/pakistan/terroristoutfits/TJP.htm, accessed 15 September 2008.

342 Azhar Abbas, *The Herald* [Karachi], September 1998.

343 *Washington Post*, 28 November 1998.

344 www.cisrirb.gc.ca/en/research/publications/index_e.htm?docid=153&cid=170&sec=CH03, accessed 16 September 2008.

345 In an interview with *Newsline* [Karachi], Qari Shafiq-u-Rehman, SSP's Information Secretary, Sindh, accused Allama Sajid Naqvi of killing Maulana Azam Tariq. See www.newsline.com.pk/newsOct2003/stopoct3.htm.

5 INSTABILITY IN THE REGION: THE WIDER EFFECT OF MILITANCY IN PAKISTAN

1 Barack Obama, CNN, 31 October 2008.

2 Karl F. Inderfurth, Assistant Secretary of State for South Asian Affairs, to Madeleine Albright, Secretary of State, 'Pushing for Peace in Afghanistan', 25 March 1999, Secret, 6pp.

3 'India Has Largest Number of Domestic Terror Groups', *Times of India*, 24 June 2009, http://timesofindia.indiatimes.com/NEWS/India/India-has-largest-number-of-domestic-terror-groups/articleshow/4694618.cms, accessed 7 September 2009.

4 Ryan Clarke, 'The Rising Wave of Domestic Terrorism: Time for New Delhi to Face Reality', South Asia Net, www.san-pips.com/PIPS-SAN-Files/SAN-SouthAsia/SAN-South Asia-Article49/San-SA-A49-D.asp, accessed 6 February 2009.

5 Khuram Iqbal, 'Mumbai Terror: Blaming External Connection will Mislead Indian Counter-terrorism Discourse', South Asia Net, 1 December 2008, www.san-pips.com/index.php?action=san&id=98, accessed 10 September 2009.

6 Mohammad Zainal Abedin, 'Indian Intelligence Involvement In Chittagong Hill Tracts

of Bangladesh', Global Politician, 9 May 2006, www.globalpolitician.com/22108-india-bangladesh, accessed 11 September 2009.

7 Binalaksmi Nepram, *South Asia's Fractured Frontier* (New Delhi, 2002), pp. 153.

8 Pak Tribune Discussion Forum, www.paktribune.com/pforums/posts.php?t=440&start=1, accessed 11 September 2009.

9 Ibid.

10 'Delhi HR group suspects RAW Involvement in Madhesh Turmoil', *Telegraph Nepal*, 1 September 2009, www.telegraphnepal.com/news_det.php?news_id=6193, accessed 11 September 2009.

11 PRMI official statement, http://noiri.blogspot.com/2007/02/peoples-resistance-move ment-of-iran.html, accessed 12 December 2007.

12 Shahzada Zulfiqar, 'Interview with Abdul Malik Reiki, Chief of Iran's Jundallah Group', *Herald* [Karachi], September 2008.

13 *The Nation* [Lahore], 23 December 2007.

14 www.roozonline.com, accessed 22 August 2008.

15 *Asia Times Online*, 8 June 2006.

16 http://gedrosia.blogspot.com/2006/08/political-parties-or-groups-of.htmlJondollah.

17 Shahzada Zulfiqar, 'Interview with Abdul Malik Reiki, Chief of Iran's Jundallah Group'.

18 Ibid.

19 'Iran Arrests Terrorist Ringleader Abdolmalek Rigi', *Tehran Times*, 24 February 2010, www.tehrantimes.com/index_View.asp?code=214785, accessed 2 March 2010.

20 Islamabad's ambassador to Tehran, Mohammad Abbasi, disclosed this in the aftermath of Reiki's arrest. See 'Islamabad Helped in Regi's Arrest: Envoy', *The News* [Lahore], 25 February 2010.

21 'People's Resistance Movement of Iran Rejects Allegations of Al Qaeda Ties', http://intelli briefs.blogspot.com/2007/02/peoples-resistance-movement-of-iran.html, accessed 11 December 2007.

22 'US "Supporting Terrorists": Iran', *Al Jazeera English*, 5 April 2007.

23 'Brother of Jundullah Leader Makes New Revelations', Tehran Times Political Desk, 21 January 2009, www.tehrantimes.com/Index_view.asp?code=199206, accessed 2 March 2010.

24 Ibid.

25 Statement attributed to a former CIA officer in a news report by ABC News, 'The Secret War Against Iran', 3 April 2007, http://blogs.abcnews.com/theblotter/2007/04/abc_news_exclus.html, accessed 26 March 2009.

26 'Brother of Jundullah Leader Makes New Revelations'.

27 Shahzada Zulfiqar, 'Interview with Abdul Malik Reiki, Chief of Iran's Jundallah Group'.

28 Nasim Zehra, 'Beyond the Jundullah Attacks', *The News* [Lahore], 2 November 2009.

29 Ibid.

30 Shahzada Zulfiqar, 'Interview with Abdul Malik Reiki, Chief of Iran's Jundallah Group'.

31 Ibid.

32 'People's Resistance Movement of Iran', Anti-Mullah, http://noiri.blogspot.com/2007/02/peoples-resistance-movement-of-iran.html, accessed 18 August 2010.

33 'The Secret War Against Iran', ABC News Exclusive, 3 April 2007, http://blogs.abcnews.com/theblotter/2007/04/abc_news_exclus.html, accessed 26 March 2009.

34 'Iran Arrests 90 Members of Jundullah', *Daily Times* [Lahore], 13 April 2007.

35 Shahzada Zulfiqar, 'Interview with Abdul Malik Reiki, Chief of Iran's Jundallah Group'.

36 Editorial, 'Pakistan's Jundullah and the Plaint from Iran' *Daily Times* [Lahore], 21 March 2009.

6 THE SUICIDE TERRORIST THREAT IN PAKISTAN

1 Muhammad Iqbal (1877–1938), the ideological founder of the Islamic state of Pakistan, Roznama Jasarat, Pakistan, 22 November 2009.
2 Dr Ayman al-Zawahiri, Principal Strategist, Al Qaeda, after the Pakistani raid on the Lal Masjid, 11 July 2007.
3 Syed Salahuddin, the Hizbul Mujahideen chief, Jamaat-e-Islami meeting, Swat District, NWFP, September 2009.
4 Suicide terrorism is defined as a mode of operation that requires the death of its perpetrator to ensure its success.
5 Khuram Iqbal, 'Drivers of Suicide Terrorism in Pakistan', RSIS Commentaries, 27 February 2008, www.pvtr.org/pdf/commentaries/RSIS0212008.pdf, accessed 24 December 2008.
6 'Pakistan Security Report 2007', Pak Institute for Peace Studies, January 2008, Islamabad.
7 Raza Hamdani, BBC Urdu, 23 March 2008, www.bbc.co.uk/urdu/pakistan/story/2008/03/080323_suicide_attacks_sen.shtml, accessed 25 March 2008.
8 UNAMA report on suicide attacks in Afghanistan, September 2007, www.unama-afg.org/docs/_UN-Docs/UNAMA%20-%20SUICIDE%20ATTACKS%20STUDY%20-%20SEPT%209th%202007.pdf , accessed 28 December 2008.
9 Scott McConnell interview with Robert Pape, 'The Logic of Suicide Terrorism: It's the Occupation, not the Fundamentalism', American Conservative, 18 July 2005.
10 Paul Wolf, 'The Assassination of Ahmad Shah Massoud', 14 September 2003, www.ratical.org/ratville/CAH/ASMassoud.html, accessed 6 September 2008.
11 Tim McGirk, 'Bomb Kills 14 at Egypt's Embassy', The Independent, 20 November 1995.
12 Steve Macko, 'Terrorist Bomb Attack on Egyptian Embassy in Pakistan', www.emergency.com/egyptbom.htm, accessed 29 June 2008.
13 '"Context of November 19, 1995: Islamic Jihad Attacks Egyptian Embassy in Pakistan', www.cooperativeresearch.org/context.jsp?item=a111995embassybombing#a111995embassybombing accessed 28 June 2008.
14 'Al-Qaeda Family: A Family Divided', CBC News Online, 3 March 2004, www.cbc.ca/news/background/khadr/alqaedafamily2.html, accessed 12 June 2008.
15 Amir Mir, 'Abu Faraj Al-Libbi's Arrest a Decisive Blow to Al Qaeda', Cobra Post, www.cobrapost.com/documents/Abufaraj.htm, accessed 6 April 2009.
16 Tariq Butt, 'Suicide Bombers, Handlers & Financiers are All Pakistani: Malik", The News, 9 September 2008.
17 'Danish Embassy Bomber "from Mecca" – al Qaeda Leader', Reuters, 22 July 2008. www.reuters.com/article/latestCrisis/idUSSP66665, accessed 14 September 2009.
18 Interview with an official of Intelligence Bureau (IB), Islamabad, 6 January 2008.
19 Feature report, Urdu daily Ummat [Karachi], 17 July 2002.
20 Saifullah Khalid, Urdu daily Ummat [Karachi], 4 February 2008.
21 Ibid.
22 Maqbool Arshad, Urdu monthly Fact [Lahore], no. 13 (November 2004).
23 'Charsadda and the Cult of Suicide-Bombing', Editorial Daily Times [Lahore], 25 December 2007.
24 Abdul Hai Kakar, BBC Urdu, 10 January 2008, www.bbc.co.uk/urdu/story/2008/01/printable/080110_bombers_suicide_rza, accessed 26 February 2008.
25 UNAMA report on suicide attacks in Afghanistan, September 2007.
26 'If You Carry Out a Suicide Attack, You Will not Die', Daily Times [Lahore], 28 May 2008.
27 Amir Mir, 'Surge in Suicide Bombings', The Post [Lahore], 25 January 2008.
28 'Pakistan Security Report 2008', Pak Institute for Peace Studies, Islamabad, January 2009.
29 Azaz Syed, 'Suicide Bomber in Sargodha Blast Identified', Daily Times [Lahore], 25 January 2008.
30 'Suicide Bomber Presented before Media', Daily Times [Lahore], 4 November 2008.
31 Sabz Ali Tareen, 'Would-be Bomber Held in Charsadda', The News [Lahore], 18 March

2009.

32 Interview with a member of the TTP, Lahore, July 2008..

33 'Curses & Revenge Spells', 27 June 2007, http://easterncampaign.wordpress.com/2007/06/27/pashtuns-must-have-their-revenge-sometimes/, accessed 5 April 2009.

34 Interview with Aftab Ahmad Khan, a native Pashtun of Charsadda district, MWFP, 5 April 2009.

35 'Pashtuns', www.globalsecurity.org/military/world/pakistan/pashtun.htm, accessed 5 April 2009.

36 Conversation with Senior Intelligence Bureau (IB) officer who investigated numbers of arrested suicide bombers in Pakistan, Islambad, December 2008.

37 Interview with Aqeel Yousafzai, journalist associated with *Frontier Post*, Peshawar, July 2008.

38 'Jundullah Claims 600 Suicide Bombers Present in Karachi', *Daily Times* [Lahore], 4 February 2008.

39 Dilawar Khan Wazir, 'Fidayeen Muslamano ka aitmi plant hein', BBC Urdu, 22 March 2009, www.bbc.co.uk/urdu/pakistan/2009/03/090322_taliban_video_na.shtml?s, accessed 5 April 2009.

40 'Held Would-be Bomber Reveals Target', *The News* [Karachi], 13 September 2008.

41 Shumaila Arif, Urdu monthly *Fact* [Lahore], no. 37 (May 2007).

42 Interview with Aqeel Yousafzai.

43 Dilawar Khan Wazir, 'Fidayeen Muslamano ka aitmi plant hein'.

44 'Militants Vow "Gift of Death"', *The Post* [Lahore], 24 July 2007.

45 Urdu Daily *Jang* [Karachi], 15 September 2007.

46 Most of the madrasas in Pakistan offer free religious education along with free boarding to the children enrolled.

47 Aqab Malik, 'The Suicide Dream', *Dawn*, 6 May 2009.

48 Ibid.

49 Usman Manzoor, 'Major Suicide Attacks in Pakistan since 9/11', *The News*, 30 March 2009, www.thenews.com.pk/daily_detail.asp?id=169849, accessed 12 April 2009.

50 Bill Roggio, 'Al Qaeda Takes Credit for Bhutto Assassination', 27 December 2007, www.longwarjournal.org/archives/2007/12/al_qaeda_takes_credi.php, accessed 13 January 2008.

51 Geo TV.

52 Syed Adnan Ali Shah Bukhari, 'Democracy under Threat?', RSIS *Commentary*, 25 October 2007, www.rsis.edu.sg/publications/Perspective/RSIS1112007.pdf, accessed 15 April 2009.

53 Syed Saleem Shahzad, 'Pakistan: Al-Qaeda Claims Bhutto's Death', Adnkronos International, 27 December 2008, www.adnkronos.com/AKI/English/Security/?id=1.0.1710322437, accessed 5 April 2009..

54 'Another Targeted Terrorist Attack', Editorial, *Daily Times* [Lahore], 27 February 2008.

55 Waseem Shiekh, Urdu Monthly *Fact* [Lahore], April 2007.

56 Judi McLeod, 'Benazir Bhutto Can Identify Jihadist Carry Bomb-Strapped Child?', Canada Free Press, 23 November 2007, www.canadafreepress.com/index.php/article/757, accessed 28 June 2008.

57 Maqbool Arshad, Urdu monthly *Fact* [Lahore], no. 28 (August 2006).

58 Anwar Iqbal, 'Decline in Support for Suicide Attacks in Pakistan', *Dawn*, 24 June 2009.

59 'Suicide Attacks in Afghanistan (2001–2007)', United Nations Assistance Mission in Afghanistan, 9 September 2007.

60 Scott Atran, 'The Moral Logic and Growth of Suicide Terrorism', *Washington Quarterly*, XXIX/2 (Spring 2006), pp. 127–47.

61 Sara De Silva, 'Preventing Suicide Terrorism', Terrorism Risk Briefing, June 2009, www.pvtr.org/pdf/commentaries/PreventingSuicideTerrorism.pdf, accessed 15 September 2009.

62 Imran Asghar, 'Bottom Line : Police Lack Modern Equipment to Probe Suicide Attacks', *Daily Times* [Lahore], 20 April 2009.

63 'Suicide Bombing un-Islamic, only State Can Declare Jihad: Fatwa", *Daily Times* [Lahore],

15 October 2008.

64 'Fatwa against Suicide Bombings', Editorial, *Daily Times* [Lahore], 16 October 2008.

65 Nazia Nazar, 'The Menace of Suicide Bombing', *The Post*, 10 June 2009.

7 IS PAKISTAN THE GROUND ZERO OF TERRORISM?

1 Ayman al-Zawahiri, *The Morning and the Lamp* [Al Qaeda publication] (March 2010).

2 Barack Obama, on the way forward in Afghanistan and Pakistan, US Military Academy, West Point, 1 December 2009.

3 David Morgan, 'Gates Says Militants Pose "Existential Threat" to Pakistan', 24 September 2008, www.boston.com/news/nation/washington/articles/2008/09/24/gates_says_militants_pose_existential_threat_to_pakistan/, accessed 9 February 2009.

4 Tariq Rauf, 'US Seeks Pakistan's Assistance', Center for Non-Proliferation Studies, Monterey Institute for International Studies, http://cns.miis.edu/research/ wtc01/pak.htm

5 '10,000 More Pakistani Troops to Guard Afghan Border', 28 June 2006, www.indiadefence.com/reports-2156, accessed 5 February 2009.

6 US State Department, Fact Sheet, International Information Program, 23 May 2002, http://usinfo.state.gov/topical/pol/terror/02052312.htm.

7 Muhammad Amir Rana, '1,000 Al-Qaeda Suspects Arrested From Pakistan', 26 May 2006, www.san-pips.com/PIPS-R&D-%20Files/Reports/R&D-Report-Article9/R&D-Report-A9-D.asp, accessed 2 October 2008.

8 '"Al Qaeda Tape" Urges Pakistan Revolt', BBC News, 25 March 2004, http://news.bbc.co.uk/2/hi/south_asia/3570091.stm, accessed 21 August 2010.

9 Michael Scheuer, 'Central Asia in Al-Qaeda's Vision of the Anti-American Jihad, 1979–2006', *China and Eurasia Forum Quarterly*, IV/2 (2006), p. 7.

10 International Institute of International Studies, *The Military Balance 2009* (London, 2009).

11 Michael Scheuer, 'Central Asia in Al-Qaeda's Vision of the Anti-American Jihad, 1979–2006'.

12 Ibid.

13 'US Calls Attacks on NATO Military Depots in Pakistan "Insignificant"', 9 December 2008, www.thaindian.com/newsportal/india-news/us-calls-attacks-on-nato-military-depots-in-pakistan-insignificant_100128722.html, accessed 21 August 2010.

14 Karen DeYoung and Joby Warrick, 'Pakistan and US Have Tacit Deal on Airstrikes', *Washington Post*, 16 November 2008.

15 Greg Miller, 'Predator Drones Flown from Base in Pakistan, US Lawmaker Says', *Chicago Tribune*, 12 February 2009.

16 Ibid.

17 'Pakistan Security Report 2006 and 2007', Pak Institute for Peace Studies, Islamabad.

18 'PIPS Security Report 2007', Pak Institute for Peace Studies, www.san-pips.com/PIPS-R&D-%20Files/Reports/R&D-Report-Article1/R&D-Report-A1-D.asp, accessed 28 September 2008.

19 Ibid.

20 'Pakistan Security Report 2008', Pak Institute for Peace Studies, Islamabad.

21 Report by Abdul Hai Kakar, BBC Urdu, www.bbc.co.uk/pakistan/story/2008/10/printable/081002_pak_army_figures.shtml, accesssed 3 October 2008.

22 www.icasualties.org/oef/, accessed 5 October 2008.

23 Amir Mir, 'Pakistan Tops Iraq, Afghanistan in Suicide Bombing Deaths', *The News* [Karachi], 15 September 2008.

24 'Pakistan Security Report 2008'.

25 '"Al Qaeda Tape" Urges Pakistan Revolt', BBC News.

26 Pakistan conflict map, BBC, 13 May 2009, http://news.bbc.co.uk/2/hi/south_asia/8046577.stm, accessed 22 June 2009.

27 'No Match for Pakistan in Terror War: US' *Daily Times* [Lahore], 28 April 2005.

28 Shireen M. Mazari, 'Pakistan in the Post-9/11 Milieu', *Strategic Studies*, xxii/3 (2002), http://issi.org.pk/journal/2002_files/no_3/comment/1c.htm, accessed 25 September 2008.

29 Ibid.

30 Nayyar Zaidi, 'Global War on Terror: Who is Paying a Hard Price?', *Akhbar-e-Jehan* [Karachi], 10–16 March 2008.

31 Ibid.

32 David Rogers, 'US Annual War Spending Grows', *Wall Street Journal*, 8 March 2006, http://online.wsj.com/public/article/SB114178357697392103-TjKUdWN4qoenDbAFbOI8Y wp2O_M_20070308.html?mod=blogs, accessed 24 September 2008.

33 In an interview with a British newspaper in August 2008, Pakistan's president Asif Ali Zardari said that the US has been providing Pakistan with an US$1 billion annually to support the war on terror. Extracts from this interview were reprinted in *The Nation* [Lahore], 10 August 2008.

34 Talat Masood, 'The Cost of War', *The News* [Lahore], 15 June 2009.

35 Ibid.

36 In early 2010 Pakistani law enforcement agencies dismantled the command and control structure of the Afghan Taliban by arresting nine of Mullah Omar's eighteen key close aides within two months.

37 'Taliban Control Half of Afghanistan, Says Report', *Daily Telegraph*, 22 November 2007, www.telegraph.co.uk/news/worldnews/1570232/Taliban-control-half-of-Afghanistan-says-report.html, accessed 11 April 2009.

38 Interview, senior intelligence officer, Peshawar, May 2010.

39 Pakistan's former Foreign Minister, Khursheed Mehmud Kasuri, mentioned the statistics during his meeting with then British Foreign Secretary Margaret Beckett in early 2007. He was quoted by the International Institute for Strategic Studies, www.iiss.org/whats-new/iiss-in-the-press/press-coverage-2007/february-2007/cheney-visit-turns-up-heat-on-pakistan/?vAction=fntUp, accessed 28 January 2009.

APPENDICES

1 Gunmen had killed the caretaker, Sher Zaman, on Thursday. Two more people were killed in riots that broke out after the attack. Police and eyewitnesses said the bomber, aged between 20 and 22 and sporting a short beard, ran into the mourning procession and blew himself up in the middle of the crowd. Angered by the attack, a large mob of protesters took over the streets, firing into the air, pelting vehicles with stones, ransacking shops and torching buses. They also erected roadblocks by burning tyres and fired on police.

2 Two civilians were killed and four injured when the Army returned fire.

3 The TTP claimed responsibility and said that their group would carry out two suicide attacks per week (*The News*, 6 June 2009)

4 Two vehicles laden with explosives were used in the attack.

5 One policeman died eight days later (*Daily Aaj*, 20 June 2009).

6 A renowned religious scholar and head of Jamia Naeemia.

7 One of the injured later died on 29 July (*Daily Mashraq*, 30 July 2009).

8 Four Pakistan and an Iraqi were killed. The suicide bomber was dressed in a military uniform.

9 TTP spokesman Usman said that the attack was revenge for the killing of two of their activists. He warned that Taliban planned to attack three sensitive installations in Kohat.

10 One girl student died of her injuries on 6 December 2009 (*Daily Jang*, 7 December 2009)

11 Sources claimed that more than 150kg of explosives were used.

12 Most of the dead were military employees and elderly civilians.

13 A powerful suicide car bomb exploded in a crowded intersection in Charsadda bazaar.

14 'Jalaluddin Haqqani's Son Killed in Drone Attack', *Dawn*, 20 February 2010.
15 'Punjabi Taliban Leader Qari Zafar Killed', *Dawn*, 26 February 2010.

Bibliography

The 9/11 Commission Report: Final Report of the National Commission on Terrorist Attacks upon the United States (New York, 2004)

Abbas, Sohail, *Probing the Jihadi Mindset* (Islamabad, 2007)

Atran, Scott, 'Mishandling Suicide Terrorism', *Washington Quarterly*, xxvii/3 (2004), pp. 67–90

——, 'The Moral Logic and Growth of Suicide Terrorism', *Washington Quarterly*, xxix/2 (2006), pp. 127–47

Conflict and Peace Studies [research journal of the Pak Institute for Peace Studies]

Government of Pakistan, 'Report of the Parlimentary Committee on Balochistan', Report no. 7 (2005)

Gunaratna, Rohan, *Inside Al Qaeda: Global Network of Terror* (New York, 2002)

Iqbal, Khuram, 'Counter-Insurgency in Balochistan: Pakistan's Strategy, Outcomes and Future Implications', Pak Institute for Peace Studies (15 July 2008)

Moghadam, Assaf, 'The Roots of Suicide Terrorism: A Multi-Causal Approach', in *Suicide Terrorism: Root Causes of a Dulture of Death*, ed. Ami Pedazhur (London, 2006), pp. 81–107

Pape, Robert, *Dying to Win: The Strategic Logic of Suicide Terrorism* (Chicago, 2005)

Peace and Security Review [research journal of the Bangladesh Institute of Peace and Security Studies]

Rana, Muhammad Amir, *A to Z of Jehadi Organizations in Pakistan* (Lahore, 2006)

Rashid, Ahmed, *Descent into Chaos: The United States and the Failure of Nation Building in Pakistan, Afghanistan, and Central Asia* (New York, 2008)

Sareen, S., *The Jihad Factory: Pakistan's Islamic Revolution in the Making* (New Delhi, 2005)

Schweitzer, Yoram, 'Suicide Bombings: The Ultimate Weapon?', International Institute for Counter-Terrorism (2001), http://www.ict.org.il/Articles/tabid/66/Articlsid/68/currentpage/26/Default.aspx, accessed 22 August 2010

South Asia Net, Pak Institute for Peace Studies, Islamabad

News Resources

Editions of the following newspapers have been consulted:

Daily Times, Lahore
The News, Lahore
Dawn, Karachi
The Post, Lahore
Ummat, Karachi [Urdu daily]
Jang, Karachi [Urdi daily]
Fact, Lahore [Urdu monthly]
Friday Times
Herald
Newsline
The Hindu
The Times of India
New York Times
The Guardian
International Herald Tribune
The Times
Washington Post

Websites

S. Rajaratnam School of International Studies (RSIS): www.rsis.edu.sg
Pakistan Institute for Peace Studies (PIPS): www.san-pips.com
Bangladesh Institute of Peace and Security Studies (BIPSS): www.bipss.org.bd
NEFA Foundation: www.nefafoundation.org
Government of Pakistan: www.pakistan.gov.pk
Federally Administered Tribal Areas (FATA) Secretariat: www.fata.gov.pk
Balochvoice: www.balochvoice.com
Balochwarna: www.balochwarna.com
Hizb ut Tahrir: www.hizbuttahrir.org
Muttahida Quami Movement (MQM): www.mqminternational.org
Hindu Vivek Kendra: www.hvk.org
Yeh Hum Naheem Foundation: www.yehhumnaheen.org
Iraq Coalition Casualty Count: www.icasualties.org
SITE Intelligence Group: www.siteintelgroup.org
The Middle East Media Research Institute (MEMRI): www.memri.org